Alastair
Sawday's

Special Places to Stay

Fifth edition
Copyright © 2008 Alastair Sawday
Publishing Co. Ltd

Published in March 2008

Alastair Sawday Publishing Co. Ltd,
The Old Farmyard, Yanley Lane,
Long Ashton, Bristol BS41 9LR, UK
Tel: +44 (0)1275 395430
Fax: +44 (0)1275 393388
Email: info@sawdays.co.uk
Web: www.sawdays.co.uk

The Globe Pequot Press,
P. O. Box 480, Guilford,
Connecticut 06437, USA
Tel: +1 203 458 4500
Fax: +1 203 458 4601
Email: info@globepequot.com
Web: www.globepequot.com

Design concept: Company X, Bristol
Maps: Maidenhead Cartographic Services
Printing: Butler & Tanner, Frome
UK distribution: Penguin UK, London

ISBN-13: 978-1-901970-95-1

Responsible business: we are committed to being a green and socially responsible
business. Here are a few things we already do: our pool cars run on recycled cooking oil
and low-emission LPG; our award-winning eco-offices are equipped with solar-heated
water, wood-pellet heating, and rainwater-fed loos and showers; and we were the world's
first carbon-neutral publishing company. Find out more at www.sawdays.co.uk

Paper and print: we have sought the lowest possible ecological 'footprint' from the
production of this book. Whenever possible, we use paper that is either recycled (with
a high proportion of post-consumer waste) or FSC-certified, and give preference to
local companies in order to foster our local economy and reduce our carbon footprint.
Our printer is ISO 14001-registered.

Hôtel du château – Baynal et cazeral.
Chateau de Monrecour : 18 muns

Alastair
Sawday's

Special Places
to Stay

French Hotels
& Châteaux

4 Contents

6   Index by département

We are a small company, born in 1994 and growing slowly but surely every year – in 2007 we sold our millionth book. We have always published beautiful and immensely useful guide books, and we now also have a very successful website.

There are about 35 of us in the Company, producing the website, about 20 guide books and a growing series of environmental books under the Fragile Earth imprint. We think a lot about how we do it, how we behave, what our 'culture' is, and we are trying to be a little more than 'just a publishing company'.

Environmental & ethical policies

We have always had strong environmental policies. Our books are printed by a British company that is ISO14001 accredited, on recycled and/or FSC-certified paper, and we have been offsetting our carbon emissions since 2001. We now do so through an Indian NGO, which means that our money goes a long way. However, we are under no illusions about carbon-offsetting: it is part of a strong package of green measures including running company cars on gas or recycled cooking oil; composting or recycling waste; encouraging cycling and car-sharing; only buying organic or local food; not accepting web links with companies we consider unethical; and banking with the ethical Triodos Bank.

In 2005 we won a Business Commitment to the Environment Award and in 2006 a Queen's Award for Enterprise in the Sustainable Development category. All this has boosted our resolve to promote our green policies.

Eco offices

In January 2006 we moved into our new eco offices. With super-insulation, under-floor heating, a wood-pellet boiler, solar panels and a rainwater tank, we have a working environment kind to ourselves and to the environment. Lighting is low-energy, dark corners are lit by sun-pipes, materials are natural and one building is of green oak. Carpet tiles are from Herdwick sheep in the Lake District. The building is a delight to work in.

Ethics

We think that our role as a company is not much different from our role as the individuals within it: to play our part in the community, to reduce our ecological footprint, to be a benign influence, to foster good human relationships and to make a positive difference to the world around us.

Another phrase for the simple intentions above is Corporate Responsibility. It is a much-used buzz-phrase, but many of those adopting it as a policy are getting serious. A world-wide report by the think-tank Tomorrow's Company has revealed quite how convinced the world's major companies are that if they do not take on full responsibility for their impact, social and environmental, they will not survive.

The books – and a dilemma

So, we have created popular books and a handsome website that do good work. They promote authenticity, individuality and good local and organic food – a far cry from corporate culture. Rural economies, pubs, small farms, villages and hamlets all benefit. However, people use fossil fuel to get there. Should we aim to get our readers to offset their own carbon emissions, and the B&B and hotel owners too?

We are gradually introducing green ideas into the books: the Fine Breakfast Scheme that highlights British and Irish B&B owners who use local and organic food; celebrating those who make an extra environmental effort; gently encouraging the use of public transport, cycling and walking. We now give green and 'social' awards to pubs in our pub guide.

In 2006 we published the very successful *Green Places to Stay*, focusing on responsible travel and eco-properties around the globe. Bit by bit we will do more, and welcome ideas from all quarters. Our aim is to be a pioneering green publisher, and to be known as one. We hope one day to offer energy audits to our owners, to provide real help to those who want to 'go green'. And we will continue to champion the small-scale. We will also continue to oppose policies that encourage the growth of air traffic – however contradictory that might seem.

Our Fragile Earth series

The 'hard' side of our environmental publishing is the Fragile Earth series: *The Little Earth Book*, *The Little Food Book* and *The Little Money Book*. They consist of bite-sized essays, polemical, hard-hitting and well researched. They are a 'must have' for anyone who seeks clarity about some of the key issues of our time. We have also published *One Planet Living* with WWF.

A flagship project is the *The Big Earth Book*; it is packed with information and a stimulating and provocative read. It is being promoted, with remarkable generosity, by Yeo Valley Organic.

Lastly – what is special?

The notion of 'special' is at the heart of what we do, and highly subjective. We discuss this in the introduction to every book. We take huge pleasure in finding people and places that do their own thing – brilliantly; places that are unusual and follow no trends; places of peace and beauty; people who are kind and interesting – and genuine.

We seem to have touched a nerve with hundreds of thousands of readers; they obviously long for the independence that our books provide, for the warm human contact of Special Places, and to be able to avoid the banality and ugliness of so many other places.

A night in a Special Place can be a transforming experience.

Alastair Sawday

Susan Herrick Luraschi has created this book. She has done so in the teeth of the winds of change, the sort of change that has your computer refusing to cooperate, then going slow, then defying you openly. The final emergence of this beautiful book represents a triumph of the human spirit, particularly Susan's. She has succeeded in teasing out of the French system a remarkable collection of hotels. They are the best of France. They say more about her than any number of newspaper articles. They are lovable, admirable, handsome, and of brilliant value.

In support of Susan have been: Russell Wilkinson, her technical doctor; Becci Stevens, her *administratrice*; Ann Cooke-Yarborough, without whom many of our books would be impossible; Jackie King, constant with her advice; Jo Boissevain editing, and Nicola Crosse, Kate Shepherd, Florence Oldfield and Melanie Harrison all providing rich support of one kind or another. As usual, there is a 'creator' and a 'team' — mutually dependent. I am grateful to them all.

Alastair Sawday

Series Editor Alastair Sawday
Editor Susan Herrick Luraschi
Editorial Director Annie Shillito
Writing Jo Boissevain, Viv Cripps,
Nicola Crosse, Susan Herrick Luraschi,
Matthew Hilton Dennis, Abigail Hole,
Helen Pickles, Aideen Reid
Inspections Katie Anderson,
Richard & Linda Armspach,
Andrew Bamford, Helen Barr,
Miranda Bell, Ann Cooke-Yarborough,
Meredith Dickinson, Sue Edrich,
Janet Edsforth-Stone,
John & Jane Edwards, Valerie Foix,
Georgina Gabriel, Diana Sawday Harris,
Annette Parker, Elizabeth Yates,
Susan & Barney Lenheim
*Thanks to those people who did a few
inspections or had a go at a write-up!*
Accounts Bridget Bishop,
Rebecca Bebbington, Christine Buxton,
Sandra Hasell, Amy Lancastle,
Sally Ranahan
Editorial Sue Bourner,
Kate Ball, Jo Boissevain, Nicola Crosse,
Roxy Dumble, Melanie Harrison,
Jackie King, Wendy Ogden, Florence
Oldfield, Kate Shepherd, Becci Stevens,
Rebecca Thomas, Danielle Williams
Production Julia Richardson,
Tom Germain, Anny Mortada
Sales & Marketing & PR
Rob Richardson,
Thomas Caldwell, Sarah Bolton
Web & IT Russell Wilkinson,
Chris Banks, Isabelle Deakin,
Joe Green, Brian Kimberling

The debate rages: Can Sarkozy succeed in taking the 'belle' out of 'la belle France'? He seems determined to re-boot France in the direction of the Anglo-Saxon model. For most French men and women it is an appalling prospect, a denial of everything that makes France what it is. The world needs France just as she is, not – for Heavens' sake – just as she might become. Can you imagine the French, en route to the office, drinking coffee in take-away cups on the hoof, eating Pot Noodles at their desks for lunch, flying abroad for a quick weekend boozing in Prague, filling town centres with half-naked crowds hell-bent on self-destruction? How much fun would it be to go to France then?

But a moment's reflection gives hope. How on earth can Sarkozy succeed where others have failed? If he tackles the farmers they will barbecue sheep on the Champs Elysées, block motorways and bring the country to a halt in other imaginative ways. If he threatens the 35-hour week there will be another revolution. The biggest threat comes from the global economy and the insidious ways in which it undermines obstacles. Let us hope that the French remain alert to the dangers.

For those of us who travel in France, the survival of the French hotel is just as important as the survival of the baguette. We love the endearing eccentricities of French hotels, the

unpredictable characters of their owners, their occasional irascibility and imaginative gestures, their personal styles and the brilliance of their aesthetic. Long may we range between chateau and farm, villa and cottage, valley manoir and mountain chalet. Long may they be very French, invulnerable to the predatory instincts of soulless hotel chains.

This book is full of just the sort of hotels you have come to love in France. Please use them generously, and tell them to stay as they are.

Alastair Sawday

Photo: Tom Germain

Here you have the fifth — and richest ever — edition of a guide that grew out of our *French Bed & Breakfast* guide and a desire to celebrate the personality and non-conformity of what can loosely be described as small hotels. Ranging from the small and intimate to the grand and gracious they include guest houses, châteaux, maisons and chambres d'hôtes.

As a company we believe that eco-awareness and sustainability generally should be central to what we do — we only have one planet to live on, but we consume the earth's resources as if there were three. This is madness! So, to draw attention to what many owners who feel the same are doing we have chosen to highlight the green initiatives of four special places in this guide (their pages are tinted green). This is a small subjective selection to demonstrate a range of undertakings — many more folk are also taking action and some never stopped, eg farming organically, sourcing food locally, maintaining their buildings using natural materials and keeping their energy consumption and carbon footprint as low as possible.

France is blessed with great food and a richness of scenery and rural living that is hard to beat

Many of our owners are unhappy about rampant consumerism and have decided to adopt a more sustainable way of life. Composting and recycling are just the starting point for the owners of places with these special green entries. Flow reducers are used in loos and showers to help save water, along with roof-top containers to hold rainwater, and diversion systems to use grey water for the garden. Heating using thermal pipes, natural gas or solar panels saves on emissions, and one owner provides all his electricity from solar panels too. Animals live naturally and without too much interference, forests are planted,

Photo left: Hôtel Cuq en Terrasses, entry 250
Photo right: Le Hameau des Baux, entry 327

hedgerows looked after, food sourced locally and reclaimed materials used as much as possible. We applaud these owners, along with many others who are travelling the same road.

But please don't think we are losing sight of the other values that make a place special. No amount of greenery can make up for a lack of genuine hospitality and an owner's pride in and dedication to their guests having the best possible experience under their roof and in their region. For many of the owners in this book it's 'in the blood', as the business has succeeded from generation to generation. We celebrate these places, for their continuity, their history, their tenacity, and their good value. We hope they survive forever as they are part of the French landscape. Others are newer to the game and maybe to the area and come with fresh enthusiasms and sparkling ideas — we wish them all well in an increasingly demanding world where guests' expectations are ever higher.

All are part of that fantasy of being warmly welcomed after being caught in a storm, seeing a light in the distance and knocking at an unknown door.

Bon Voyage!

Susan Herrick Luraschi

Photo: Castelnau des Fieumarcon, entry 269

Special Places are just that – special. We select them for their fascination and character, but also for the people who run them. We like them small, we like them family-run, we like château-chic and truly trad and all those in between. We know you like them because you tell us so.

Passion is a word not normally associated with the world of hospitality, but passion – and commitment – is important to us. And flair? We see it in a carved door lovingly restored or a beautiful antique in just the right corner, in the taste of the freshest scallop or the tenderest veal medallion ... and we are very happy when we learn that the owner will serve breakfast until noon.

We like them small, we like them family-run, we like château-chic and truly trad and all those in between

France is blessed with great food and a richness of scenery and rural living that is hard to beat. Our owners have originality, energy and independence and give more than a passing nod to tradition and regional differences.

Inspections

We visit every property. Atmosphere, welcome and value for money are key:

Photo: Château de Massillan, entry 343

each place is judged on its own merit, not by comparison. But it is unfair to expect the same service and comfort from a small family-run hotel at €70-a-room as from a full-service hotel at €200. Friendly staff are more important to us than jacuzzis, a bowl of fresh flowers more important than a satellite TV. (And we are earnestly trying to let our owners know that a cup of (decent) tea at the right moment is an important goal to reach.)

Feedback

A huge 'thank you' to all of you who have taken the time and trouble to write to us about your experiences and to recommend new places. We always follow up on your comments, and will take people in to and out of the book in response to what you and our inspectors tell us, so please stay in touch

and let us know about your discoveries — use the form on our website at www.sawdays.co.uk, or later in this book.

Subscriptions

Owners pay to appear in this guide. Their fee goes towards the cost of inspections (every single entry has been inspected by a member of our team before being selected), of producing an all-colour book and maintaining our website. We only include places and owners that we find positively special. It is not possible for anyone to buy their way into our guides.

Disclaimer

We make no claims to pure objectivity in choosing our Special Places to Stay. They are here because we like them. Our opinions and tastes are ours alone and this book is a statement of them; we hope that you will share them.

We have done our utmost to get our facts right but apologise unreservedly for any mistakes that may have crept in. Feedback from you is invaluable and we always act upon comments. With your help and our own inspections we can maintain our reputation for dependability.

You should know that we do not check such things as fire alarms, swimming pool security or any other regulation with which owners of properties receiving paying guests should comply. This is the responsibility of the owners.

Photo right: Château des Briottières, entry 145
Photo left: Hôtel Relais Sainte Anne, entry 262

Finding the right place for you

The guest houses and chambres d'hôtes range from the small and intimate to the grand and gracious. Officially they are limited in size from 5 to 7 rooms. Those which are small and owner-run or in historical buildings, as are the châteaux, often don't have lifts or porters, so do call ahead and book that ground-floor room if you foresee a problem. Expect to feel a privileged guest in your chosen house and to gain a fascinating glimpse of a French way of life.

For the hotels we have ignored the 'star' system. This is because it uses criteria different from ours. A hotel that we think the world of may be near the bottom of the official 'star' list simply because it has no lift. Other owners, unwilling to be swept into a bureaucratic system or to partition an 18th-century bedroom to create a bigger bathroom, refuse to apply for a star rating. The system is technical and incapable of accounting for character, style or warmth of welcome, the very things that we rate most highly.

Do keep in mind that food takes priority in some restaurants with rooms. At inns or auberges rooms are secondary, but they are comfortable and clean. Kitchen gardens have popped up all over the place and *le terroir* – seasonal, fresh and local food – is de rigueur. Be sure to book as the typical auberge can feed more people that it can sleep. Remember, too, that dinner is not served before 7.30pm and, outside the larger towns, last orders may be taken no later than 9pm.

Traditional hôtellerie is thriving with its intricate wall-coverings, Régence, Louis XIV and XV furniture in harmony with the buildings themselves, classic cuisine in the kitchens. This is the image of France that many travellers have in mind – and it's hugely popular. One reader called such a place "a minimalist's nightmare": he absolutely loved it, in all its glory.

By contrast there is a growing number of boutique hotels who keep things bare, fresh and light, using colour schemes of white, cream and grey. There may be one or two pieces of exquisite furniture and the odd splash of colour, but nothing that jars the eye, just space and serenity. These places may have variations of nouvelle cuisine with a sprinkling of foreign spice. A meat-and-potatoes personality would not feel at home here.

Read the descriptions carefully and pick out the places where you will be comfortable. If 'antique beds' sound seductively authentic, remember they are

Photo: Auberge à la Bonne Idée, entry 12

liable to be antique sizes too (190cm long, doubles 140cm wide). If in doubt, ask, or book a twin room (usually larger). A problem well-defined is halfway solved: do discuss any problem with your hosts – they can usually do something about it on the spot. If you find anything we say misleading (things and people do change in the lifetime of a guide), or you think we miss the point, please let us know.

Do plan, if possible, to stay more than one night on your travels; some of our hoteliers feel that 'zapping' has now entered their world and they miss the complicity (and serenity) of longer visits.

Maps
The general map of France is marked with the numbers of the detailed maps, as are the individual entries. The entry numbers on the detailed maps show roughly where the hotels are. Our maps should be used in conjunction with a large-scale road map.

Symbols
Below each entry in the book you will see some symbols based on information owners give us. At the very back of the book is a short table explaining what each symbol means, but below is a slightly fuller explanation of two of them. Use the symbols as a guide, not as a statement of fact – owners occasionally bend their own rules, so it's worth asking.

Pets – Even though a place may be listed as accepting animals, some will only take small dogs; others will limit the number

of animals staying at the same time. Do check ahead. There is always a supplement to pay.

Smoking – Non-smoking means no smoking is allowed anywhere in the building.

Quick reference indices
At the back of the book we list places that are suitable for wheelchair users, accessible by public transport, offering a double room for €100 or less, and with secure parking ... do take a look.

Green entries
We have chosen, very subjectively, four places which are making a particular effort to be eco-friendly and have given them a double-page spread and extra photos to illustrate what they're up to. This doesn't mean other places in the guide are not taking extra green iniatives – many are – but we have highlighted just a few examples.

Extra beds and cots for children, at extra cost, can often be provided; ask when booking.

Bathrooms

Assume all bedrooms are 'en suite', either with bath or shower. We say if a bedroom has either a separate or a shared bathroom. For simplicity we refer to 'bath'. This doesn't necessarily mean it has no shower; it could mean a shower only.

Expect to feel a privileged guest in your chosen house and to gain a fascinating glimpse of a French way of life

Bedrooms

Bedrooms are described as follows:
• double — one double bed
• twin — two single beds
• triple — three single beds
• family room — mix of beds (sometimes sofabeds) for three or more people; a family room will always have a double bed
• duplex — a room on two floors with a staircase
• suite — either one large room with a sitting area or two or more interconnecting rooms, plus one or more bathrooms
• apartment — similar to a suite but sometimes with an independent entrance and possibly a small kitchen; if it comes after the '+' in the rooms description, it is categorised as 'self-catering' and has a kitchen.

Photo left: Auberge Le Chalet des Troncs, entry 308
Photo right: The Five Hotel, entry 67

Meals

The number and type of courses you will be offered for lunch and dinner varies. Some places have set menus at fixed prices. Most places serving lunch will have a good value menu during the week, changing the menu and the prices on the weekend.

Many places offer a table d'hôtes dinner to overnight guests. This means the same food for all and absolutely must be booked ahead, but may not be available every night. (We have indicated the distance to the nearest restaurant when this is the case.) You may be dining at

your own table, but often the meal is shared with other guests at a communal table. These are sometimes hosted by Monsieur or Madame (or both) and are usually a wonderful opportunity to get to know your hosts and to make new friends among the other guests.

If a late arrival is unavoidable, some hosts will prepare a cold meal if given advance notice. Remember these are not all hotels with full staff.

Prices

The first price range is for two people sharing a room: the lower price indicates the least expensive room in low season; the higher price, the most expensive room in high season. If breakfast is not included, we say so and give the price. Prices are given for 2008–2009 but are not guaranteed so please check when you book. If there are no single rooms, there will generally be a reduction for single occupancy of a double.

Do look into attractive half-board terms and special prices for children. Half-board (demi-pension) includes breakfast and dinner. Full-board (pension complète) includes all three meals. Prices given are generally per person ('p.p.'). Ask about reduced rates when booking longer stays and out of season visits.

Taxe de séjour is a small tax that local councils can levy on all visitors; you may find your bill increased by €0.50-€2 per person per day to cover this.

Do plan, if possible, to stay more than one night on your travels; some of our hoteliers feel that 'zapping' has now entered their world and they miss the complicity (and serenity) of longer visits

Booking

It is essential to book well ahead for July and August and wise for other months. All places now have websites and email addresses. However, please remember that technology may be put aside at busy times and a small place may just not have the time or the personnel to respond quickly to email requests.

Some places require a deposit to confirm a booking. If you cancel you are likely to lose part or all of it so check the exact terms when you book. A credit card number is the standard way to place a deposit.

Payment

MasterCard and Visa are generally welcome; American Express is often accepted in the upper range hotels. The few places that don't accept credit cards are indicated at the end of their description. Drawing cash is easy as virtually all ATMs in France take Visa and MasterCard.

Tipping

Almost all restaurants include tax and a 15% service charge (service compris) in their prices.

If a meal or service has been particularly good, leaving another €1.50 (or 2%-3%) is customary, as is leaving the waiter the small change from your bill if you pay in cash. If service is not included (service non compris), a 15% tip is appropriate.

In hotels tip porters €1.50 for each bag and chambermaids €1.50 a day. Taxi drivers should receive 10%-15% of the metered fare. Small tips of about €1 are reasonable for cloakroom attendants, ushers and museum tour guides.

Closed

When given in months, this means for the whole of both months named. So, 'Closed: November-March' means closed from 1 November to 31 March.

Electricity

You will need an adaptor plug for the 220-volt 50-cycle AC current. Americans also need a voltage transformer (heavy and expensive).

Photo: Just 2 Suites, entry 273

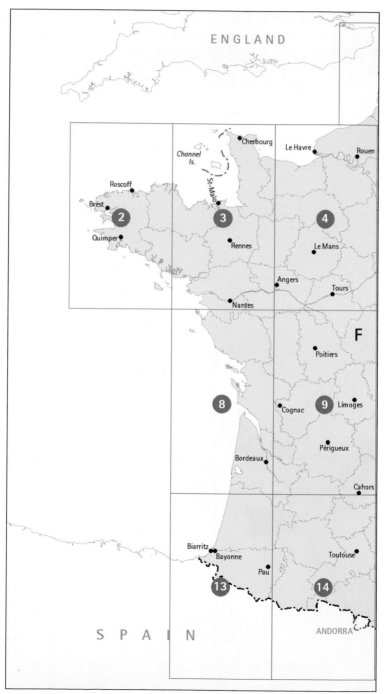

Medical & emergency procedures

If you are an EC citizen, it's a good idea to have a European Health Insurance Card with you in case you need any medical treatment. It may not cover all the costs so you may want to take out private insurance as well.

To contact the emergency services dial 112: this is an EU-wide number and you can be confident that the person who answers the phone will speak English as well as French, and can connect you to the police, ambulance and fire/rescue services.

Other insurance

If you are driving, it is probably wise to insure the contents of your car.

Roads & driving

Current speed limits are: motorways 130 kph (80 mph), RN national trunk roads 110 kph (68 mph), other open roads 90 kph (56 mph), in towns 50 kph (30 mph). The road police are very active and can demand on-the-spot payment of fines.

Directions in towns

The French drive towards a destination and use road numbers far less than we do. Thus, to find your way à la française, know the general direction you want to go, ie the towns your route goes through, and when you see *Autres Directions* or *Toutes Directions* in a town, forget road numbers, just continue towards the place name you're heading for or through.

Photo: istock.com

Map 1

27

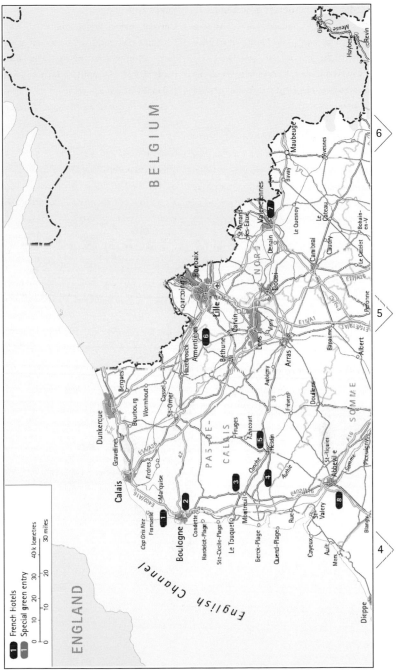

©Maidenhead Cartographic, 2008

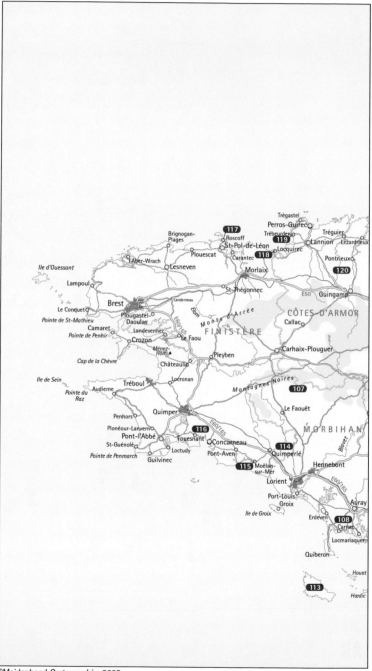

Map 3   29

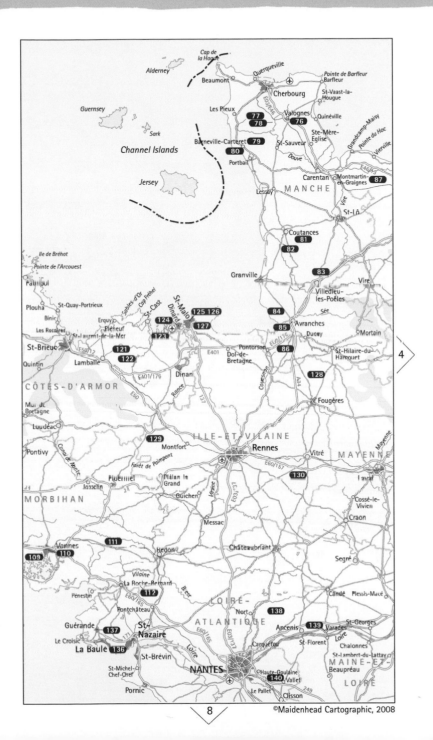

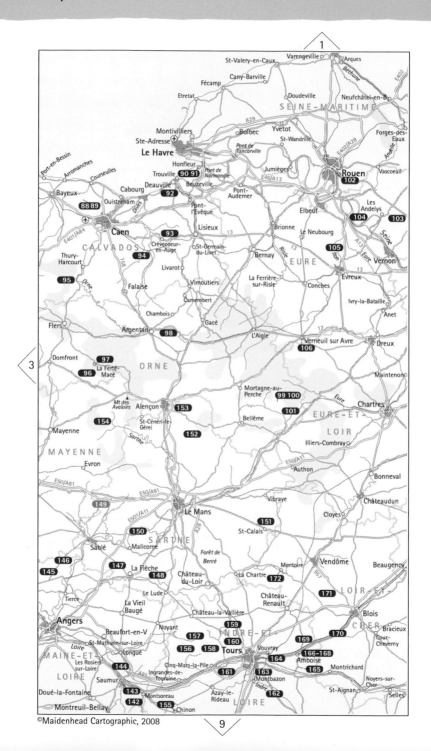

Map 5   31

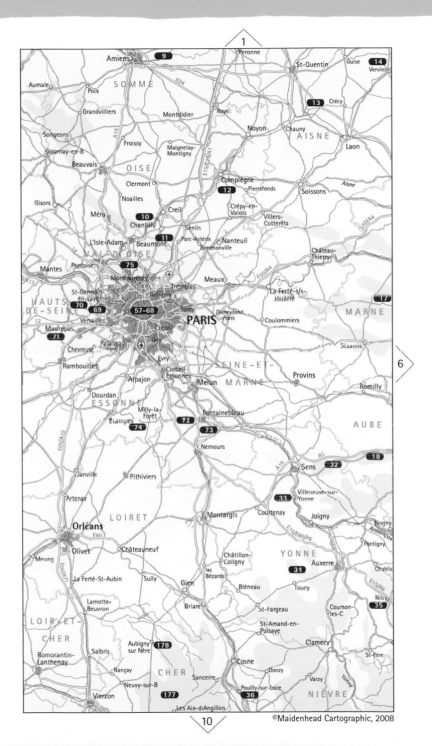

©Maidenhead Cartographic, 2008

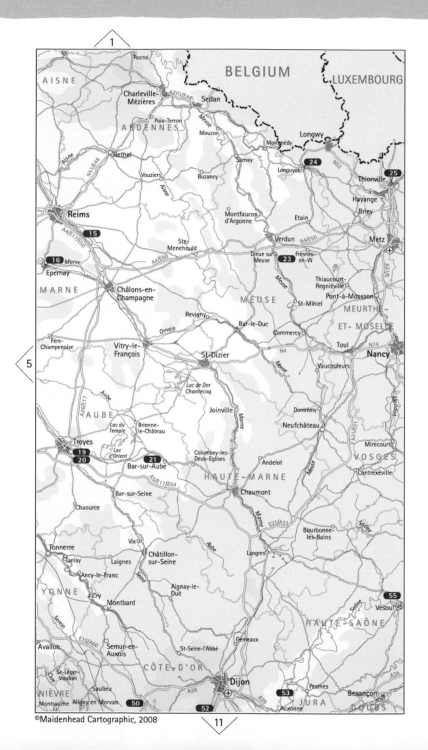

©Maidenhead Cartographic, 2008

Map 7   33

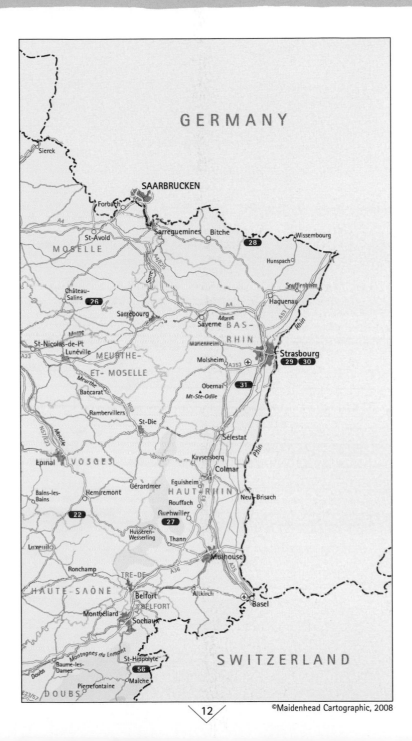

©Maidenhead Cartographic, 2008

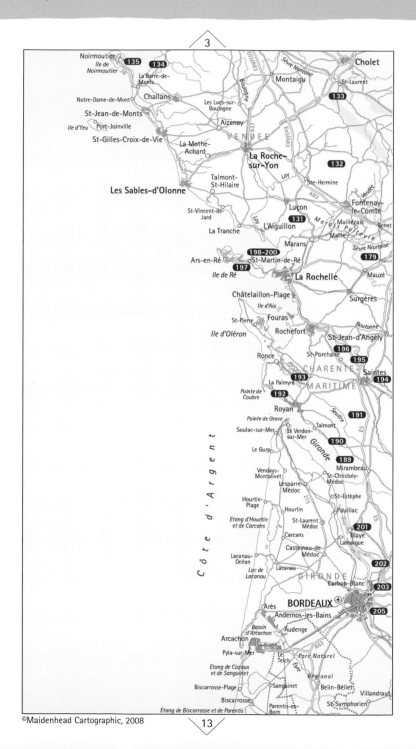

Map 9   35

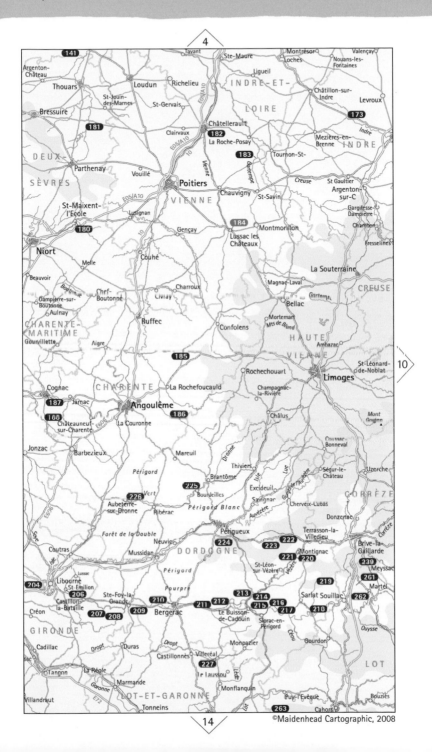

©Maidenhead Cartographic, 2008

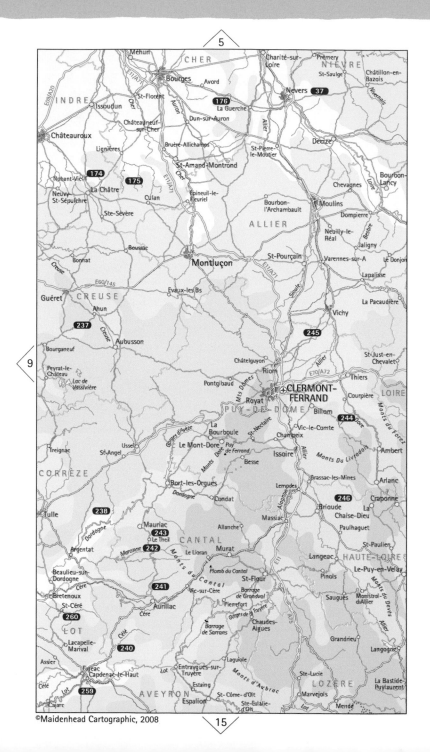

Map 11   37

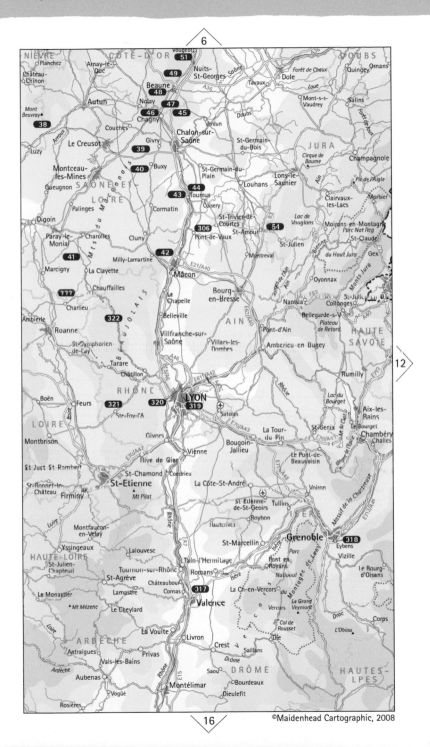

Map 13   39

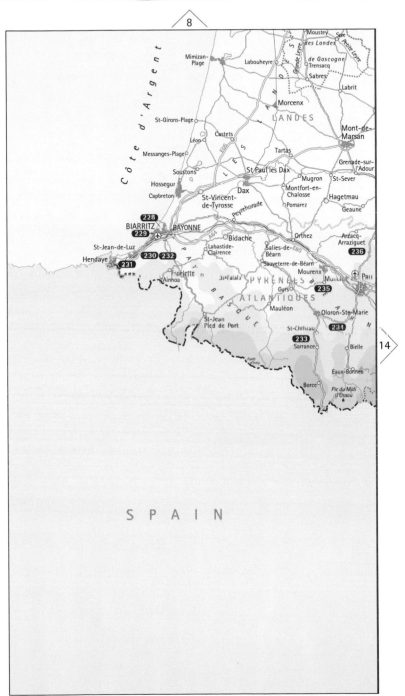

©Maidenhead Cartographic, 2008

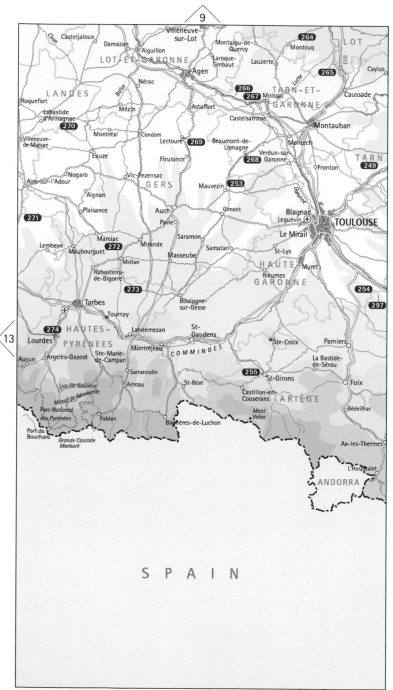

Map 15   41

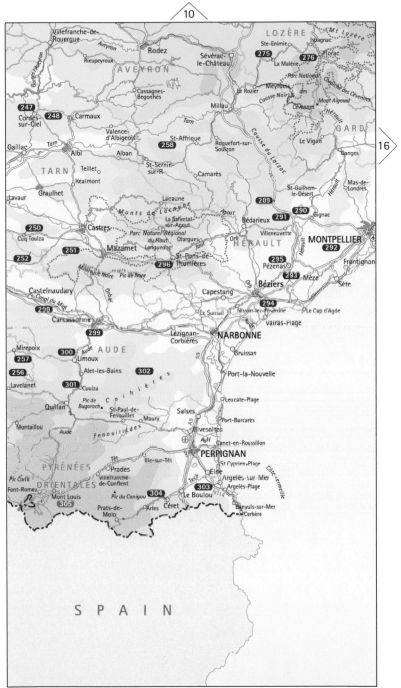

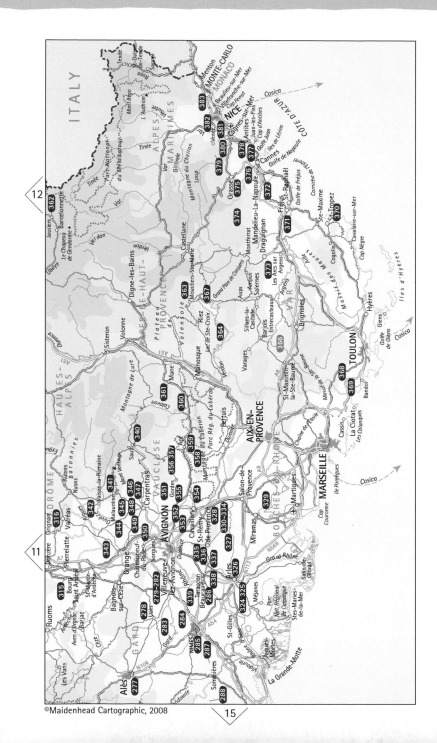

The North • Picardy • Champagne – Ardenne

Hôtel Saint Jean

Here is a pleasing little hotel a short sprint from the sea, its newly painted cream and white façade embellished with natty red awnings for each window – a hint of things to come. Step into a pristine reception lobby off which lie three refreshingly colourful public areas: a lounge dressed in classic French style, with glossy books and soft lights for browsing, a snazzy bar in rich purple and a light, bright, wicker-furnished breakfast room for the morning after, at whose tables continental breakfasts are temptingly spread. A lift delivers you to three compact floors of super-comfortable, wall-to-wall carpeted bedrooms with views – rooftops at the back, church and river at the front – sporting two-tone colour themes (brown and sandstone; dark green and cherry; crimson and flame-red). Walls, furniture and bathrooms are white, hand basins are round and modern, towels fluffy and new. Outside, sailing boats, cliff top walks and candy-coloured Victorian villas (worthy of a guided walk or two) await your attention. Unless, of course, you are off to the ferry. *24-hour room service.*

Price	€80. Family rooms €95-€105.
Rooms	24: 8 twins, 11 doubles, 5 family rooms for 3-4.
Meals	Breakfast €10.
Closed	30 December-15 January.
Directions	A16 Calais-Boulogne, exit 33 Wimereux Nord onto route de la Trésorerie (D242); 1.5 km, left onto D237 into Wimereux; follow Quai de Wimille to junction & bridge. Hotel on right at stop sign.

Juliette Delattre
1 rue Georges Romain,
62930 Wimereux, Pas-de-Calais

Tel	+33 (0)3 21 83 57 40
Email	contact@hotel-saint-jean.fr
Web	www.hotel-saint-jean.fr

L'Enclos de l'Evêché

Up gracious steps you enter the 1850 mansion that almost rubs shoulders with Boulogne's basilica. All is polished parquet and hotel-like perfection, with the personal touch we so like. The charming young owners usher you up to bedrooms either on the first floor of the main house (preferable) or above the restaurant. Each one is airy, uncluttered and large, themed according to its name: 'Desvres' (a porcelain town), pretty and serene, all white painted furniture and blue toile de Jouy; 'Godefroy de Bouillon' (an 11th-century knight from Boulogne), rustic, with sand-blasted rafters and impeccable limewashed walls. Bathrooms are stocked with toiletries and towels, some have jacuzzis. Their restaurant, with a capacity for 40, now serves lunch and dinner – food takes priority here. Pascaline and Thierry serve in the evening, so another crew awaits you at breakfast, perhaps in the salon with the immense 19th-century sideboards. There's a suntrapped courtyard, a day room for TV and a choice of tables for breakfast – be as convivial or as peaceful as you like. *No credit cards. Payment requested upon arrival.*

Price	€70-€135.
Rooms	5: 2 doubles, 1 twin, 1 single, 1 family room for 4.
Meals	Breakfast included. Lunch & dinner €19.50, except Sat/Sun. Closed Sun eve & Monday. Book ahead.
Closed	Rarely.
Directions	Follow signs to 'Vieille Ville' & to car park 'Enclos de l'Evêché'. House next to car park & cathedral.

Pascaline & Thierry Humez
6 rue de Pressy, 62200 Boulogne sur Mer, Pas-de-Calais

Tel	+33 (0)3 91 90 05 90
Fax	+33 (0)3 91 90 05 94
Email	contact@enclosdeleveche.com
Web	www.enclosdeleveche.com

Auberge d'Inxent

And, the lucky winner is… some people who collect bottle caps do win prizes. A sommelier in a restaurant in Lille, Jean-Marc won a Perrier contest on the luck of a draw. Off he tripped with his young wife and two children to a most emerald green valley and claimed a whitewashed, geranium-boxed, 18th-century country inn. Order a trout on their vine-covered terrace and back comes a live one in a bucket from their superb trout farm across the road by the river Course. Needless to say Jean-Marc's exceptional, reasonably priced wine list and creative use of local produce should lead to a prolonged stay, and the nearby ramparts of Montreuil Sur Mer are well worth a visit. Inside all is wonky wooden beams, low ceilings, a battery of copper pans behind the original zinc countertop, red-checked tablecloths and the warmth and cosiness of a modest country kitchen with open fires on chilly days. The beamed-ceiling bedrooms have been recently furnished with cherrywood copies of antiques and the walls papered to look ragged. Some of the best people win the best prizes.

Price	€65–€72.
Rooms	5: 3 doubles, 2 twins (1 with terrace).
Meals	Breakfast €9. Lunch & dinner €15–€38. Restaurant closed same dates as hotel.
Closed	Tuesday and Wednesday; Tuesday only in July & August; 20 December-20 January; 1 week in July.
Directions	From Boulogne N1 for Samer. After Samer at 5km head for Bernieulles, Beussent, Inxent.

Laurence & Jean-Marc Six
La Vallée de la Course, 62170 Inxent, Pas-de-Calais

Tel	+33 (0)3 21 90 71 19
Fax	+33 (0)3 21 86 31 67
Email	auberge.inxent@wanadoo.fr

Le Manoir

Wrought-iron gates, a gravel drive, a spreading lime and afternoon tea on the terrace – gracious country living. Jennifer (English) and Helmut (German) – former Sawday hosts from Romney Bay House in Kent – run the 18th-century manor house with friendly professionalism and exacting attention to detail. So much space – three reception rooms, large bedrooms, 12 hectares of parkland... you can be as private or as gregarious as you like. The salon and sitting room are elegant with deep sofas and creamy walls; breakfasting under the chandelier in the dining room, all polished tables and rich reds, makes you feel truly pampered. The three carpeted bedrooms are civilised spaces of soft lighting, well-chosen antiques and pretty porcelain; you could be staying with a country-house friend. Throw open the windows in the morning: the views across manicured lawns, formal garden and orchard to countryside will put a big smile on your face. No evening meals but lots of excellent dining in Montreuil, and beaches, riverside walks and birdwatching in abundance.

Price	€140.
Rooms	3: 2 doubles, 1 twin.
Meals	Breakfast €10. Restaurants in Montreuil & Gouy Saint André.
Closed	2 weeks in June; Christmas.
Directions	From A16 exit 25 for N39 Arras & Hesdin. Exit for Campagne les Hesdin. Look for Gouy St André; right at main crossroad; 1st iron gate on left.

Jennifer & Helmut Gorlich
34 rue Maresquel, 62870 Gouy St André,
Pas-de-Calais

Tel	+33 (0)3 21 90 47 22
Fax	+33 (0)3 21 86 70 98
Email	helmut.gorlich@wanadoo.fr
Web	www.lemanoir-france.com

Les Trois Fontaines

Here is a long, low, plain Scandinavian style building dressed up to look like a typical French inn – and succeeding. It fits into the little market town (wonderful market on Thursday mornings) as if it had always been there. Arnaud Descamps is friendly and anxious to please. He took over in 1999 and concentrates on the quality of the food – only fresh produce – served in his panelled, chequer-floored dining room: the short menu changes every day and there's a special one for children. Bedrooms are in separate buildings overlooking the fine garden: six are brand new and are no-frills minimalist; ten are traditional French with quiet wallpapers and candlewick bedcovers. In the new wing, twin rooms are very comfortable, simply and decently clad with good quality pine, dark blue carpet, good lighting, pristine bed linen. All are sparkling clean and each room has its own table and chairs for summer breakfasts facing the garden. It is, indeed, a very typical small French hotel; it is quiet, good value and well placed for cross-channel visitors as well as the great beaches of Le Touquet and Berck.

Price	€56-€71.
Rooms	16 doubles.
Meals	Breakfast €7. Lunch & dinner €18-€34.
Closed	20 December-5 January.
Directions	From Calais for Arras. After Montreuil, N39 for Hesdin. Follow signs to Marconne centre. Opposite the Mairie.

Arnaud Descamps
16 rue d'Abbeville,
62140 Marconne Hesdin, Pas-de-Calais

Tel	+33 (0)3 21 86 81 65
Fax	+33 (0)3 21 86 33 34
Email	hotel.3fontaines@wanadoo.fr
Web	www.hotel-les3fontaines.com

Station Bac Saint-Maur

All aboard! Vincent, Chef de Gare, and his young crew of conductors man the bistro: an imaginatively converted, 1921 red-bricked railway station filled with vintage suitcases and trunks spewing old tourist brochures. There are miniature tin trains, a wind-up wooden telephone, hand-held lanterns, sepia etchings on the walls, old station wall clocks and a paraphernalia of reminders of the golden era of train travel. You dine in the station, then retire to your rooms in the carriage of an authentic 'PLM' that travelled the Paris, Lyon, Mediterranean lines. Book in advance and you will be served in the elegant restaurant compartment with its warm mahogany walls inlaid with mother-of-pearl. Retire to your first-class couchettes (authentic, so narrow) to dreams of the Orient Express. As if on cue, a real train passes by every now and again adding its clanking to the authenticity. A full playground just outside, a children's menu and antique highchairs make this a super place for kids. Groups can take a tour along the La Lys aboard a barge; the lock is 400m from the station.

Price	€35–€65.
Rooms	6 Pullman compartments each with 2 singles, all sharing 2 showers.
Meals	Breakfast €6.50. Lunch & dinner in station €8.50–€24; on board €28–€70. Child meal €6.50.
Closed	23 December–5 January.
Directions	From A25 exit 9 for Erquinghem to Sailly. At Bac St Maur, 2nd left immediately after Havet factory.

Vincent Laruelle
La Gare des Années Folles, 77 rue de la Gare,
62840 Sailly sur la Lys, Pas-de-Calais

Tel	+33 (0)3 21 02 68 20
Fax	+33 (0)3 21 02 74 37
Email	chefdegare@wanadoo.fr
Web	www.stationbacsaintmaur.com

Auberge du Bon Fermier

Forget your high heels, for the cobblestones in the flowered courtyard penetrate into the bar, reception and restaurant of this 16th-century auberge. It is a maze of passageways, burnished beams and tiny staircases. A bright copper-bellied washbasin greets you at the top of the stairs leading to the rooms. Looking down from a glassed-in corridor, you can almost hear the clatter of hooves arriving in the courtyard, now a quiet terrace for afternoon tea and snacks. The rooms are all different, one with tapestried curtains and walls, another with red bricks and wooden struts, all with baths and bathrobes. There are also two larger, lighter ground-floor rooms with post-modern lamps and tables. Downstairs, a suit of armour guards a wooden reception dais and comes to life in the evenings when the main restaurant is lit only by candles. The passengers jostling between Paris and Brussels were probably delighted to have been delayed in this cosy staging inn. Monsieur Beine takes enormous trouble to create new menus with his chef and most diners would raise a glass and make a toast in his direction.

Price	€110-€130. Singles €85-€105.
Rooms	16: 14 doubles, 2 singles.
Meals	Breakfast €9.50
	Lunch & dinner €26-€47.
Closed	Rarely.
Directions	From Cambrai A2 for Brussels, exit Valenciennes centre. Do not get off autoroute before. Continue for Valenciennes centre. Signed.

Monsieur Beine
64 rue de Famars,
59300 Valenciennes, Nord

Tel	+33 (0)3 27 46 68 25
Fax	+33 (0)3 27 33 75 01
Email	beinethierry@hotmail.com
Web	www.bonfermier.com

Château de Béhen

Horsey people and families will be in clover. There are donkeys to stroke, bicycles to hire and horses to ride. Surrounded by wooded parkland, the red-brick building with limestone trim started life as a summer residence, later its ground floor was extended. In the 1950s the Cuveliers moved in, adding paddocks and a pond for swans. Today there are six large and lovely bedrooms for guests. Classically French, in sympathy with the style of the place, they have solid oak floors with rugs, bedspreads plain or toile de Jouy and warm colours. Original panelling graces the first-floor rooms while those above have sloping ceilings and a beam or two. Bathrooms are hotel-perfect with double basins of mottled marble. Norbert-André, who managed stud pacers in Australia for ten years, has come home to cook, and he does a grand job. Four-course table d'hôtes, at single tables if preferred, may include salt-marsh lamb or fish in cream sauce. Cheeses are local, vegetables are fresh-picked, banquets can be arranged. An equestrian address, and a magnificent one.

Price	€110-150. Suites & family room €144-€204.
Rooms	6: 2 doubles, 1 twin, 1 suite for 2, 1 suite for 4, 1 family room for 4.
Meals	Breakfast included. Dinner with wine, from €39; book 2 days ahead.
Closed	Rarely.
Directions	Calais A16 to Abbeville exit 23; A28 to Rouen. Exit 3 Monts Caubert to D928; 800m, right to Behen. Behind church, then 200m beyond, on right.

Cuvelier Family
8 rue du Château,
80870 Béhen, Somme

Tel	+33 (0)3 22 31 58 30
Fax	+33 (0)3 22 31 58 39
Email	norbert-andre@cuvelier.com
Web	www.chateau-de-behen.com

Le Macassar

Le Macassar is named after the rare ebony used in the drawing room panelling – one exquisite example of many intricacies here. This gem of an 19th-century townhouse was restyled in the Twenties and Thirties to please a pretty young wife – but it's more 'femme fatale' than blushing belle. The master suite is the epitome of Art Deco glamour, ash and bird's-eye maple furniture set off by turquoise velvet walls, a carved stone fireplace and fine contemporary art. The 'colonial' suite is more muted in white and cream, while the Louis XV style rooms have oriental carpets and painted panelling. All have CD players, feather duvets, extravagant bathrooms and masses of space. Downstairs are several luxurious corners in which to lounge rakishly: pluck a book from the Art Nouveau study and admire its collection of glass, savour the textures and tones of the Moroccan room, play a round of billiards in the old library. Outside, an Italianate courtyard, a splashing fountain and a haze of lavender. In spite of the gorgeousness, it's easy to feel at home. The hosts are charming, the town small and historic.

Price	€160–€240.
Rooms	6: 1 double, 1 twin, 4 suites.
Meals	Breakfast included. Hosted dinner with wine €40 (Sunday only). Groups on request.
Closed	Rarely.
Directions	A16 exit 20 Amiens Nord; after tollgate, right at r'bout onto ring road (Rocade). Exit 36a Corbie; follow signs into Corbie, then centre ville. On main square.

Miguel de Lemos
8 place de la Republique,
80800 Corbie, Somme

Tel	+33 (0)3 22 48 40 04
Email	info@lemacassar.com
Web	www.lemacassar.com

Ferme de La Canardière

Forty kilometres north of Paris sits a long house of classic 18th-century stamp. Sabine, smiling and generous, is a professional cook and has just opened this immaculate guest house, its French windows gazing down the valley. Gleaming polished limestone floors lead to a light, airy sitting room with squashy leather sofas and huge stone fireplace. Tucked privately in one corner, light bouncing from creamy walls, are two big bright bedrooms that lead directly onto a terrace, narrow lawn and pool. A traditional draped bedhead in pretty putty and white ciel-de-lit is partnered by splendid horsy curtains and posters echoing equestrian glories. The twin   rich blue bedcovers, antique cherrywood tables   feels elegantly restrained and formal. Bathrooms tiled from top to bottom in blue and white are sybaritic. In the cook's kitchen, where Sabine produces her wonderful homemade breakfasts (ingredients from the family's cereal farm), you may also book into a cookery master class. This is deep in the heart of French racing country: who knows, you may get an insider tip for the French Derby. *No credit cards.*

Price	€150. Singles €130. Extra bed €25.
Rooms	2: 1 double, 1 twin.
Meals	Breakfast included.
	Hosted dinner, 4 courses with wine, €30.
	Restaurants 10 minute walk.
Closed	Never.
Directions	From Chantilly, N16 towards Creil.
	On leaving Chantilly, cross bridge; first
	left opposite 'arc of triomphe' onto
	Rue Guilleminot to viaduct; straight
	ahead; house on right up above road.

Sabine Choain
20 rue du Viaduc,
60500 Gouvieux-Chantilly, Oise
Tel   +33 (0)3 44 62 00 96
Fax   +33 (0)3 44 55 94 93
Email   contact@fermecanardiere.com
Web   www.fermecanardiere.com

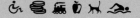

Relais d'Aumale

In a little village, the forest of Chantilly on its doorstep, this multi-faceted hunting lodge has character and a dazzling collection of armagnac on the carved stone mantelpiece. The lounge is deliciously tempting in its rich red garb with beams above and more bottles on the side. In contrast, the 1990s dining room is all glass, airiness and light, opening onto the terrace for long summer dinners. Even if you do not opt for the champagne dinner there is an amazingly extensive wine list to choose from to complement your foie gras and roasted pigeon. Breakfast is usually in the cosy, panelled room next to the bar. There's a garden, too. Bedrooms are comfortable without being exciting: a good size, with excellent custom-made furniture and the occasional antique; warm, soft colours and fabrics; good bathrooms and double glazing. The two big suites in the 'Little House' by the road are light, pale and very smart. And of course, the Noble Horse, star of Chantilly, is everywhere, arranged on walls, cabinets and shelves by the relaxed and naturally friendly Hofheinz couple and their daughter.

Price	€130-€156. Suites €190-€260.
Rooms	24: 22 twins/doubles. Petite Maison: 2 suites for 4.
Meals	Breakfast €14. Lunch €28-€36. Dinner from €44.
Closed	Christmas & New Year.
Directions	From Paris A1 for Lille, exit 7 onto N17 to Chantilly for 4km; left after La Chapelle en Serval onto D924a towards Montgrésin; signed in village.

Monsieur & Madame Hofheinz
37 place des Fêtes Montgrésin,
60560 Orry La Ville, Oise

Tel   +33 (0)3 44 54 61 31
Fax   +33 (0)3 44 54 69 15
Email   relaisd.aumale@wanadoo.fr
Web   www.relais-aumale.fr

Auberge à la Bonne Idée

Deep in the forest, the walled village is worth a visit and the Bonne Idée is where Parisiens and Belgians come to escape the excitement, knowing they will find a sound welcome, country peace and superb food. The inn, once a woodcutters' dive, still has masses of old timber and tiling in what could be called romantic-rustic style. Start with a drink by the fire in the bar, move to an elegant table in the dining room where bread warms by the great fire, and delve into a fine, gourmet meal. The emphasis is on food here – and in summer there's a terrace and space for children to play. Bedrooms, four in the main house, the rest in the converted stables, some still in their brown 70s garb, are gradually being renovated by the new owners in a bright, stylish contemporary fashion, nicely adapted to the fabulous hulk of the building. A favourite would be the ochre-orange room with its mushroom, beige and white contrasting bedding and fine brick-coloured bathroom. Some rooms and apartments have terraces. Ideal for walking, cycling, riding and relaxing; Compiègne and the great castle of Pierrefonds are close.

Price	€75–€90. Apartments €105–€150.
Rooms	23: 20 doubles, 3 apartments for 2–4 (without kitchen).
Meals	Breakfast €9. Lunch €30–€65. Dinner €45–€85. Restaurant closed Sun evenings & Mondays in winter.
Closed	January.
Directions	A1 exit 9 for Verberie & Compiègne. Through Verberie, left on D332 for Compiègne for 5km, right on D85 for St Jean aux Bois.

Yves Giustiniani
3 rue des Meuniers,
60350 Saint Jean aux Bois, Oise

Tel	+33 (0)3 44 42 84 09
Fax	+33 (0)3 44 42 80 45
Email	a-la-bonne-idee.auberge@wanadoo.fr
Web	www.a-la-bonne-idee.fr

Entry 12 Map 5

Domaine Le Parc

Down a sweeping horse-chestnut lined drive between tailored lawns you approach this 18th-century mansion built on castle foundations. The river Oise slides gently by. There are ten lawned and tree'd acres here, and at the back, a brick-walled belvedere terrace with soaring views over woodland, untamed countryside and river. Inside, wander at will – between a gracefully decorated dining room, breakfast room and library and a sitting room with gorgeous soft sofas. Up the spiral oak staircase are the bedrooms and suites, classically and elegantly decorated, some with more of those views. Strong colours with floral fabrics stand out against striped or patterned fabric walls, luxurious bathrooms have Balneo baths; clusters of antique bottles on the window ledges and an antique hobby horse add whimsical touches to a formal décor. Dutch Jos has previously won stars for his cooking, Anne is a former maître d'hotel, both are consummate, multi-lingual hosts, and you dine on the terrace in summer. The local town is no picture but beyond are fortified churches and great Gothic cathedrals. *No credit cards.*

Price	€65–€85.
Rooms	5: 3 doubles, 2 twins.
Meals	Breakfast included. Dinner €35.
Closed	20 December–5 January.
Directions	Between Saint-Quentin and Laon; A26 exit 12; in Dainzy 2nd right.

Jos & Anne Bergman
Rue de Quesny,
02800 Danizy, Aisne

Tel   +33 (0)3 23 56 55 23
Email   leparc.bergman@wanadoo.fr,
        contact@domaineleparc.fr
Web   www.domaineleparc.com

La Tour du Roy

Madame, with references from all over the world, wears the chef's hat here: food is centre-stage, and resoundingly applauded. Monsieur, a delightful character, is wedded to his hotel, which he bought roofless 31 years ago and has renovated and re-renovated beautifully. You arrive in the attractive courtyard with its flowerbeds and stone fountain. The building has nooks, crannies and corners, swathes of original brickwork and restored stone details. The dining room is, of course, seriously inviting, dressed in wood and marble, pretty antiques and unusual windows and alcoves. The turrets, all that remain of the 11th-century town fortifications where the original building stood, have amazing semi-circular bedrooms, stained-glass windows, hand-painted basins, tapestries. Beds are old carved pieces and every room contains a framed menu from a different restaurant – the corridors are lined with framed menus, too! A place to spoil yourself with days of luxurious living and eating. They can arrange canal trips and champagne tastings, château visits and steam-train journeys. Not for minimalists.

Price	Doubles & apartments €110–€185. Suites €185–€250.
Rooms	22: 12 doubles (main building), 2 (tower), 5 (separate building). 3 apartments for 4 (ramparts).
Meals	Breakfast €15. Picnic €15. Lunch & dinner €40–€70. Restaurant closed Tuesday lunch & Monday.
Closed	Rarely.
Directions	A26 exit 13 to Vervins on N2. Follow Centre Ville signs. Hotel directly on right.

Monsieur & Madame Desvignes
Lieu dit La Tour du Roy,
02140 Vervins, Aisne

Tel	+33 (0)3 23 98 00 11
Fax	+33 (0)3 23 98 00 72
Email	latourduroy@wanadoo.fr
Web	www.latourduroy.com

Hôtel le Cheval Blanc

In a sweet village of 500 souls, off the village square, a modest, relaxing, family-run hotel in roaming riverside grounds. White plastic furniture sits under dainty parasols and Virginia creeper adds character to a plain façade. This is a scattered and surprising property, comprising a converted barn, cottages, outbuildings and a watermill. Bedrooms flaunt a variety of colours, sizes and styles, from floral-traditional to floral-modern… several glass-top tables, coordinating country cottons, satin chintz, glossy bathrooms; many have extremely nice garden views. Young Madame is fifth generation owner of this venerable business, her husband is chef de cuisine and the restaurant seating 100 has had a tasty reputation ever since Napoleon III's military camp passed by. Now, billowing curtains, fancy table linen and floral porcelain are a fitting accompaniment to the classic French gourmet menus, of which there are three; food takes top billing here. The wine list is extensive – this is Champagne! Ask about special packages: cellar tours, mountain bike rides, boat trips and more.

Price	€63–€119. Suites & apartment €159.
Rooms	24: 10 doubles, 9 twins/doubles, 4 suites, 1 apartment for 4 (no kitchen).
Meals	Breakfast €12. Lunch & dinner €25–€59.
Closed	February.
Directions	Exit 26 Reims. N44 toward Chalons en Champagne for 24km. Left onto D37 at Les Petites Loges to Sept Saulx.

	Armelle & Fabien Abdalalim rue du Moulin, 51400 Sept Saulx, Marne
Tel	+33 (0)3 26 03 90 27
Fax	+33 (0)3 26 03 97 09
Email	cheval.blanc-sept-saulx@wanadoo.fr
Web	www.chevalblanc-sept-saulx.com

Le Clos Raymi

What more seductive combination than champagne and culture? Easy to get to from both Reims Cathedral and the champagne vineyards, this enticing home has the added attraction of Madame Woda herself. Ever attentive to the comfort of her guests, she purrs with pride in her renovation of the Chandon (the other half of Moët) family house. The intricate, pale blue mosaic covering the entrance hall and the hardwood staircase were left alone but her artistic touch is everywhere: shades of cream, beige and extra pale grey; good beds dressed in vintage linens; attractive bathrooms with scented lotions; fresh flowers in every room; etchings and paintings from the 1930s; books of poetry on a shelf. Take a peek at the downstairs bathroom with its Cubist paintings and an interesting replacement for the usual sink. A champagne aperitif can be organised in a splendid little sitting room and, if weather permits, the buffet breakfast can be taken in the parasoled garden behind the house. Madame Woda will help organise champagne tastings and has her favourite people to recommend. Gracious living here.

Price	€100–€160.
Rooms	7 doubles.
Meals	Breakfast €14. Restaurant 500m.
Closed	Rarely.
Directions	From Paris A4 exit Château Thierry; N3 to Epernay.

Madame Woda
3 rue Joseph de Venoge,
51200 Epernay, Marne

Tel	+33 (0)3 26 51 00 58
Fax	+33 (0)3 26 51 18 98
Email	closraymi@wanadoo.fr
Web	www.closraymi-hotel.com

Château d'Etoges

Louis XIV himself was impressed by the beauty of the garden, fountains and ponds at Etoges, used as a stopover by various kings of France on journeys east. This moated château was built early in the 17th century and restored as a hotel in 1991 by the family who has lived here for over a century. If you enjoy waking up in beautiful sheets, this is for you. Rooms are all different and two have intriguing little mezzanine bedrooms over the bathroom – presumably originally for servants, now great fun for children. Many rooms have four-posters; all are furnished with antiques and are extremely French. If you fancy breakfast in bed, it will appear on a lace-covered table, with bread, croissants and a bowl of fruit. If you prefer to wander downstairs, choose from a buffet and sit on the terrace if it's warm. This could be a luxurious base for champagne tastings or simply a very pleasant break, convenient if you're heading for eastern France, like Louis XIV or, more likely, meandering south through Reims. It's easy country for cycling or you can try punting if you feel this is more in tune with the surroundings.

Price	€95–€200. Suites €200.
Rooms	28: 26 twins/doubles, 2 suites.
Meals	Breakfast €14.
	Lunch & dinner €32–€72.
	Children's meals €15.
Closed	22 January–13 February.
Directions	From Paris A4 exit 18 at Ferté sous Jouarre, follow signs for Chalons en Champagne. In centre of Etoges.

Madame Filliette-Neuville
4 rue Richebourg,
51270 Etoges, Marne

Tel	+33 (0)3 26 59 30 08
Fax	+33 (0)3 26 59 35 57
Email	contact@etoges.com
Web	www.etoges.com

Domaine du Moulin d'Eguebaude

The secluded old buildings house two owner-families, a restaurant, several guest rooms and 15 tons of live fish. Fishing folk gather on Sundays to catch trout in the spring water that feeds the ponds; groups come for speciality lunches. Four-course meals may include watercress soup, steamed trout with cider, a selection of local cheeses and cinnamon custard. For breakfast around the large table there are brioches, baguettes, croissants, yogurt, cottage cheese, fruit salad, cereals, apple juice and their own jams and honey. Created from an old mill 40 years ago, the compact bedrooms under the caves are small-windowed, simply furnished and prettily decorated in rustic or 'grandmother' style. Further rooms in the cottage across the driveway have been newly built in the regional half timbered style. At one end of their shop – packed with cottage-industry goodies (charcuterie, honey, jams, wine and champagnes) is a wide floor of thick glass under which immense fish can be seen swimming to and fro between the water tanks. Wonderful service and good English spoken. *No credit cards.*

Price	€49–€72.
Rooms	6: 2 doubles, 1 twin, 1 triple, 2 family rooms.
Meals	Breakfast included. Dinner with wine €21, book ahead.
Closed	Rarely.
Directions	From Paris A5 exit 19 on N60 to Estissac; right on to Rue Pierre Brossolette; mill at end of lane (1km).

Alexandre & Sandrine Mesley
36 rue Pierre Brossdette,
10190 Estissac, Aube
Tel   +33 (0)3 25 40 42 18
Fax   +33 (0)3 25 40 40 92
Email   eguebaude@aol.com

Hôtel Champ des Oiseaux

Only the Museum of Modern Art stands between the cathedral and this amazingly pure group of 15th-century houses in the centre of lovely, unsung Troyes. One is dazzled by the astonishing timbers, beams and rafters, inside and out, seduced by the simplicity of the beautifully jointed stone paving, the wooden floors, the softly luminous natural materials: the owners had their brilliant restoration done by craftsmen who knew the ancestral methods and made it look 'as good as 1460 new'. Corridors twist around the creeper-climbed courtyard and the little internal garden, staircases change their minds, the place is alive with its centuries. Each bedroom has a personality, some soberly sandy and brown, others frivolously floral; they vary in size and status but all are warmly discreet in their luxury and good furniture. And, of course, bathrooms are perfect modern boudoirs. The unexpected salon, a long, white barrel vault of ancient stones, the original stonemason's craft lovingly revealed, was once a cellar. The Boisseau family can be justifiably proud of their contribution to medieval Troyes. Perfection.

Price	€120–€170. Suites €200–€220.
Rooms	12: 9 twins/doubles, 3 suites for 2-3.
Meals	Breakfast €15.
	Great restaurants nearby.
Closed	Never.
Directions	In centre of Troyes, very close to the Cathedral.

Madame Boisseau
20 rue Linard-Gonthier,
10000 Troyes, Aube

Tel	+33 (0)3 25 80 58 50
Fax	+33 (0)3 25 80 98 34
Email	message@champdesoiseaux.com
Web	www.champdesoiseaux.com

La Maison de Rhodes

An exceptional find, a 16th-century timber-framed mansion that once belonged to the Templars. Monsieur Thierry's breathtaking renovation has brought a clean contemporary style to ancient bricks and mortar. Highlights include an interior courtyard of cobble and grass and heavy wooden doors under the coachman's porch that give onto the street. The house sits plumb in the old quarter of Troyes, on the doorstep of the cathedral. Bedrooms are bona fide jaw-droppers – expect the best in minimalist luxury. Huge beds are dressed in white linen, ancient beams straddle the ceilings. Walls are either exposed rough stone, or smooth limestone, or a clever mix. Bathrooms, too, are outstanding; most are enormous and have terracotta floors, big bath tubs, fluffy robes. Views are to the cathedral spires, the courtyard or the formal gardens of the Museum of Modern Art, directly opposite. A perfect blend of old and new, an exhilarating architectural landscape. Troyes is full of wonders, though the bibulous may be tempted to venture beyond the city walls. The region is quite well-known for its local tipple – champagne

Price	€143-€187. Suites €225-€250.
Rooms	11: 8 doubles, 3 suites for 2-4.
Meals	Breakfast €17. Dinner €30-€50. Restaurant closed Sundays.
Closed	Never.
Directions	In centre of Troyes, at the foot of the cathedral.

Thierry Carcassin
18 rue Linard-Gonthier,
10000 Troyes, Aube

Tel	+33 (0)3 25 43 11 11
Fax	+33 (0)3 25 43 10 43
Email	message@maisonderhodes.com
Web	www.maisonderhodes.com

Le Moulin du Landion

Time stands still at this weathered, beautiful, half-timbered mill on the river in the southern Champagne region, close to the Foret d'Orient. Come for a romantic weekend of champagne and roses, explore famous vineyards and talk wine with knowledgeable merchants in medieval Troyes. Families head to Nigloland's leisure park, walkers ramble through peaceful villages of half-timbered old buildings with limestone trim, and energetic people cycle county lanes in pastoral landscapes dotted with mature oaks and vineyards. In this small, modestly priced and good value hotel, where neat, traditionally furnished, comfortable bedrooms in converted stone buildings overlook garden and stream, the emphasis is on the kitchen. On the geranium-bright terrace with its dramatic river views or in the rustic dining rooms tucked around the retired paddle wheel – a spectacular sight – escargots and saucissons vie for attention with gourmet offerings. After an escapist dinner à deux, ignore the scales, drift off to the sound of the river and wake to French breakfast in bed.

Price	€77-€88.
Rooms	16 twins/doubles.
Meals	Breakfast €10.
	Lunch & dinner €23-€56.
Closed	17-27 December.
Directions	A5 exit 22 & 23. Route 19 between Troyes & Chaumont N19; follow signs to Nigloland.

Aubertin-Heckmann Family
5 rue St Léger,
10200 Dolancourt en Champagne, Aube

Tel	+33 (0)3 25 27 92 17
Fax	+33 (0)3 25 27 94 44
Email	contact@moulindulandion.com
Web	www.moulindulandion.com

Lorraine • Alsace

Auberge de la Vigotte

Young and enthusastic, Michel and Jocelyne have done up this 18th-century farmhouse overlooking valleys and conifer coated mountainsides. Michel is a passionate cook and Jocelyne teaches English in a local school. Rooms have carved or painted beds and all look out onto fantastic views. With tennis, volleyball and a children's play area, this is a perfect place for families. You can also ride, or swim in a lake in the grounds, while in the winter you can go cross-country skiing. Meals are a mix of very traditional and more contemporary: ranging from pigs' trotters to beef cheeks to tomatoes with cardamom. An hour from Mulhouse, 700m up, on the gentle slopes of the Vosges, the auberge is set in densely wooded countryside: total peace and quiet. In winter you will find a roaring fire and a warm welcome, in the summer you can swim in a private lake and round off your day with dinner out on the terrace. Although somewhat off the beaten track for English holidaymakers, this would make a good stopover, and could also be a great choice for an out-of-doors holiday.

Price	€65–€100. Singles €55. Half-board option €55 p.p. (min. 3 nights).
Rooms	17: 7 twins/doubles, 7 singles, 1 suite for 2, 2 family rooms for 3-4.
Meals	Breakfast €7. Lunch & dinner €18–€38, book ahead. Child €8. Restaurant closed Tues & Wed.
Closed	25 October-20 December.
Directions	From Remiremont D23 then D57. Follow white signs to Auberge.

Michel & Jocelyne Bouguerne-Arnould
1 La Vigotte,
88340 Girmont Val d'Ajol, Meuse

Tel	+33 (0)3 29 61 06 32
Fax	+33 (0)3 29 61 07 88
Email	courrier@lavigotte.com
Web	www.lavigotte.com

Hostellerie du Château des Monthairons

If you fancy peace and quiet in beautiful grounds, or a spot of fishing, this would be a fine choice. Monthairons served as an American military hospital in the First World War but was a base for German troops in the Second. It is now run by three couples of the Thouvenin family, who bought it 20 years ago. One couple looks after the restaurant and food, the others run the hotel and grounds. Because of the personal touch, you'll feel at home here in spite of the size. Bedrooms are smart, classic French and come in all sizes, with some duplex suites which would be perfect for families. Those who love exploring, swimming and canoeing would be in their element here; the Meuse meanders through the huge grounds. Apparently a former owner diverted the river especially and the nearby meadow is now known as the 'old river'. The restaurant is elegant and full of flowers – more for a special dinner than a quick bite with the children. Unusual activities? Choose between an introduction to fly-fishing, a leisurely ride in a horse-driven carriage or dive into the new spa for a steam bath.

Price	€95–€180. Duplexes & suites €160–€180. Apartments €230–€320.
Rooms	25: 6 twins, 8 doubles, 1 twin/double, 4 duplexes for 2-4, 4 suites for 2-4, 3 apartments (without kitchens)
Meals	Breakfast €13–€14.50. Lunch weekdays €25. Dinner €34–€82.
Closed	January–10 February.
Directions	From Paris A4 exit 30, Voie Sacrée. Follow direction for St Mihiel until Lemmes. At the end of Lemmes, last road on left. Continue to Ancemont, at last crossroad right to the Château.

Madame Pierrat
55320 Dieue sur Meuse,
Meuse

Tel	+33 (0)3 29 87 78 55
Fax	+33 (0)3 29 87 73 49
Email	accueil@chateaudesmonthairons.fr
Web	www.chateaudesmonthairons.fr

Lorraine

Restaurant with rooms

Le Mas & La Lorraine

A proud building, solidly French, with flowers cascading from every window. The hotel is a nostalgic reminder of a lost era – the great days of steam trains. It stands across the square from the station and was built in 1925 to cater for the travellers the railway brought; the Italian Express stopped here. These days it is more of a restaurant-with-rooms, the emphasis clearly on the ambrosial food. Monsieur Gérard took over from his parents 37 years ago, yet still cooks with unwavering exuberance and flair; his *grandes soirées dégustation* are not to be missed. Course after course flies at you: coquilles Saint Jacques, foie gras, fillet de veau, gratin d'ananas à la crème de coco. Meals are taken in a big rustic restaurant, a convivial room where an open fire roars in winter. Every now and then live music nights are held and you dine to the accompaniment of classical guitar or jazz piano. Downstairs: off-white armchairs and huge bay windows in the airy sitting room; upstairs, simply furnished bedrooms that are clean, functional and reasonably priced. Belgium and Luxembourg are within easy reach.

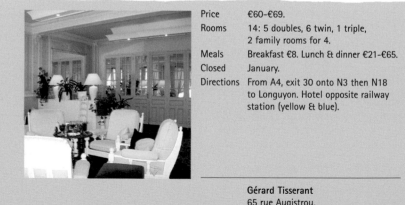

Price	€60–€69.
Rooms	14: 5 doubles, 6 twin, 1 triple, 2 family rooms for 4.
Meals	Breakfast €8. Lunch & dinner €21–€65.
Closed	January.
Directions	From A4, exit 30 onto N3 then N18 to Longuyon. Hotel opposite railway station (yellow & blue).

Gérard Tisserant
65 rue Augistrou,
54260 Longuyon, Meurthe-et-Moselle

Tel	+33 (0)3 82 26 50 07
Fax	+33 (0)3 82 39 26 09
Email	mas.lorraine@wanadoo.fr
Web	www.lorraineetmas.com

L'Horizon

The house is only 50 years old but its arcading anchors it and Virginia has crept all over it, clothing its façade in lively warm character. Here is comfortable living in graceful surroundings, as in an elegant private house. A huge terrace envelops the ground floor – from here and from the smart restaurant you have plunging views over Thionville with an astounding, glittering cityscape at night. Some first-floor rooms give onto a balcony over the same view. Despite the surprising hall with its marbled flooring and glamorous tented ceiling, the bedrooms are classic French chic (though carpets may be a little worn here and there and some rooms are smaller than others) and bathrooms border on the luxurious. But above all, you will warm to your utterly charming hosts. Monsieur Speck is passionate about Second World War history: the Maginot Line is all around, Thionville is on the Liberty Road that is marked every kilometre from Cherbourg in Normandy to Bastogne in Lorraine. He is fascinating on the subject.

Price	€98–€145.
Rooms	12 doubles.
Meals	Breakfast €11. Lunch & dinner €39–€53. Restaurant closed Saturdays & Monday lunchtimes.
Closed	January.
Directions	From A31 exit 40 to Thionville. Follow signs for Bel Air Hospital north of town. At hospital bear left up hill leaving town. Hotel 400m on left.

Jean-Pascal & Anne-Marie Speck
50 route du Crève-Cœur,
57100 Thionville, Moselle

Tel	+33 (0)3 82 88 53 65
Fax	+33 (0)3 82 34 55 84
Email	hotel@lhorizon.fr
Web	www.lhorizon.fr

Château d'Alteville

A house with more than a whiff of history. The château was built for one of Napoleon's generals, and the two paintings that hang in the Louis XVI salon were gifts from the Emperor. Monsieur's family has farmed here for five generations; he now welcomes guests with kindness and much attention. Bedrooms are solidly traditional with carved armoires, Voltaire armchairs and draped bedheads; parkland views float in through the windows; bathrooms are functional but adequate. Downstairs is more stylish: a library/billiard room, a multi-fenestrated sitting room and a dining room where splendid dinners are eaten by candlelight in the company of your lively, intelligent hosts. Bigger parties are entertained in the trophy-lined *salle de chasse*. Recline on the sound-proofed terrace at the back and gaze on the château-esque grounds, or pull on your hiking boots and follow your nose though woodland, circumnavigating the odd lake. Madame, soul of the house, cooks with skill and fills the place with flowers.

Price	€68–€91.
Rooms	5: 4 doubles, 1 twin.
Meals	Breakfast included. Hosted dinner €31–€38.50, book ahead. Wine €10.
Closed	15 October–15 April.
Directions	From Nancy N74 for Sarreguemines & Château Salins. At Burthecourt x-roads D38 to Dieuze; D999 south 5km; left on D199F; right D199G to château.

David Barthélémy
Tarquimpol,
57260 Dieuze, Moselle

Tel	+33 (0)3 87 05 46 63
Fax	+33 (0)3 87 05 46 64
Email	chateau.alteville@caramail.com

Hostellerie Saint Barnabé

It feels good here. The young owners of this angular, 100-year-old, flower-decked hotel are spontaneously smiley, chatty and attentive. He is the chef – trained with France's best and chef at Château d'Isenbourg for some years, so food is important here, and good. She is the perfect adviser on what to do between the Vosges hills and the Alsace plain: there are typical villages and wine-growers to visit, bike rides and good fishing places (they also have mini-golf on the spot). The ferny woods are full of paths and burbling brooks and there's skiing in season. There are two sorts of guest rooms: in the main house they are big, decorated with care and individuality (the yellow and white room has an iron-frame canopied bed, the red and white one twin head cushions and super-soft quilts), with smashing bathrooms and the odd balcony; in the separate building behind, they are smaller and more old-fashioned (and cheaper!) but are gradually being renovated. Here, bedroom doors all have typically Alsatian hand-painted, floral decoration. A great place for nature lovers and gourmets. Good value.

Price	€76–€103.
Rooms	27 twins/doubles.
Meals	Breakfast €12. Lunch (Mon-Sat) €13. Dinner €19.50–€65. Picnic on request
Closed	3 days at Christmas; 3 weeks in Jan.
Directions	From N83 (betwen Belfort & Colmar) D430 for Guebwiller & Lautenbach. D429 for Buhl then Murbach. On left.

Clémence & Eric Orban
53 rue de Murbach,
68530 Murbach, Haut-Rhin

Tel   +33 (0)3 89 62 14 14
Fax   +33 (0)3 89 62 14 15
Email   hostellerie.st.barnabe@wanadoo.fr
Web   www.hostellerie-st-barnabe.com

Hôtel Anthon

Smaller than mountains, grander than hills, the lushly wooded slopes are pure Vosges forest, the clear Steinbach snakes its way through pastures, red rocky outcrops emerge in forbidding contrast to such bucolic enchantment. This little restaurant with rooms, in the same deep pinky-orange colour as the rocks, is in typical Vosges style. Inside, warm wood, including a fine carved staircase, echoes the living forest. It is sweetly simple – not basic in any way, just pretty and uncluttered, with carved wardrobes and Vosges dining chairs, peachy-beige or muted turquoise-green paintwork and coir floors. Bedrooms are not big but, again, prettily done with gingham duvets, starched cloths on round tables, windows onto the quiet night. The first-floor breakfast room is delightful – immaculate white cloths and regional pottery – but the restaurant, definitely in a different class, is the heart of this place. In the big, embracing room with its refined table settings and service, delicious dishes await you – and Madame's collection of soup tureens is dazzling.

Price	€60. Suite €98.
Rooms	8: 3 doubles, 4 twins, 1 suite.
Meals	Breakfast €10. Lunch & dinner €24–€45; gourmet dinner €61. Restaurant closed Tuesdays & Wednesdays.
Closed	January.
Directions	From Haguenau D3 & D27 through Woerth to Lembach (25km); left to Niedersteinbach & Obersteinbach. Hotel in village centre.

Danielle Flaig
67510 Obersteinbach,
Bas-Rhin

Tel	+33 (0)3 88 09 55 01
Fax	+33 (0)3 88 09 50 52
Email	info@restaurant-anthon.fr
Web	www.restaurant-anthon.fr

Hôtel Cardinal de Rohan

The atmosphere here is a rare combination: stylish and polite yet utterly friendly, plushly comfortable but not overwhelming. Standing in the historic centre, the solid building round its central courtyard in traditional 17th-century Strasbourg layout has been virtually rebuilt, with proper respect for its tall narrow neighbours, three rows of roof windows and tangles of geraniums down the façade. An 18th-century Gobelins tapestry graces the elegant sitting room; the breakfast room, pale and restful, feels like a country-house dining room· high-backed cane chairs, ivory cloths, antique chest of drawers. Top floor rooms have pine-clad sloping ceilings and dormer windows, lower rooms are sober, masculine dark and pale blue or rich, warm ginger and cream or spring-fresh green. They come in 'rustic' or 'period' décor, have good velvet or thick contemporary fabrics, clean lines and rich French swag effects. There are gilt-framed mirrors, the occasional antique armoire and smart marble-and-tile bathrooms. Superb comfort, friendliness and attention to detail are the hallmarks here.

Price	€73–€145.
	Triples & family rooms €145–€155.
	Child under 12 in parents' room, free.
Rooms	36: 28 twins/doubles, 4 triples,
	4 family rooms for 2–3.
Meals	Breakfast €12. Restaurants nearby.
Closed	Rarely.
Directions	From ring road, exit Place de l'Etoile for
	Centre Ville & Cathédrale to
	underground car park (Place Gutenberg).
	Book ahead for private car park.

Claude Hufajen
17–19 rue du Maroquin,
67000 Strasbourg, Bas-Rhin

Tel	+33 (0)3 88 32 85 11
Fax	+33 (0)3 88 75 65 37
Email	info@hotel-rohan.com
Web	www.hotel-rohan.com

Hôtel du Dragon

In old Strasbourg's hub, looking over river and cathedral, the Dragon is grandly, solidly 17th century on the outside, sleekly, refreshingly 20th century within. Built as a private mansion – Louis XIV stayed on his way to visit Marie-Antoinette in Austria – it became a hotel 15 years ago. The little courtyard received a classically pedimented porch and potted shrubs: a pretty place for an evening drink. Inside, they took a deeply contemporary approach and it is sober, infinitely stylish and extraordinarily restful. Variegated grey and white are the basics: mushroom curtains on white walls, superb grey pinstripe carpeting, an arresting pattern of grey and white tiles in the bathrooms, muted mauve bedcovers for a dash of colour. And some good abstract paintings and sculptures here and there, displayed to great advantage. Some have river views and others see the cathedral's lovely spire. After 20 years as a mountain guide, Monsieur Zimmer returned to his native Strasbourg and has made the Dragon as welcoming as it is elegant. He is quiet and gentle and has a predilection for English-speaking guests.

Price	€79–€121. Apartments €153.
Rooms	32: 30 twins/doubles, 2 apartments for 3 (without kitchen).
Meals	Breakfast €11.
Closed	Open all year.
Directions	Across the river from Petite France, off Quai St Nicolas.

Jean Zimmer
2 rue de l'Ecarlate,
67000 Strasbourg, Bas-Rhin

Tel	+33 (0)3 88 35 79 80
Fax	+33 (0)3 88 25 78 95
Email	hotel@dragon.fr
Web	www.dragon.fr

Hôtel à la Ferme – L'Aigle d'Or

In a simple, colourful Alsatian village lies a superbly converted old farm, encircled by shrubs, roses, manicured hedges and a pretty bricked terrace. Bedrooms are splendid, a good size and comfortable, with polished floorboards, oriental rugs and fine beds, one carved in Alsatian style. The suites are in the outbuilding next door. In summer, choose a suite with an all-wood veranda; in winter, a cosy, part-panelled room in the main house: worth it for the scent of the baking. Delicious brioches and pastries are served in the wainscotted breakfast room warmed by an immense ceramic stove. Jean-Philippe's father mans the bar, his mother and grandmother help in the kitchen, Brigitte does front of house, Jean-Philippe is master chef and the food is outstanding. Chalked up on the board are escargots, foie gras, asparagus in season, choucroute, tarte flambé, apfelstrudel. One dining room is filled with ancient beams and antique cupboards, the other, elegantly contemporary, has old-gold velvet curtains and a fine inlaid wooden ceiling. A superb place run by a family that is professional, enthusiastic, endearing.

Price	€83–€135. Suites €114–€118.
Rooms	7: 3 doubles. Annexe: 4 suites for 2–4.
Meals	Breakfast €14. Lunch & dinner €32–€69. (Not Monday eve or Tuesday).
Closed	Rarely.
Directions	From Strasbourg A35 south, exit N83 dir. Colmar; 14km then exit Erstein. Immediately right; 2km; right onto D288 for Osthouse. Signed in village.

Jean-Philippe & Brigitte Hellmann
10 rue du Château,
67150 Osthouse, Bas-Rhin

Tel	+33 (0)3 90 29 92 50
Fax	+33 (0)3 90 29 92 51
Email	info@hotelalaferme.com
Web	www.hotelalaferme.com

Burgundy • Franche Comté

Photo: istock.com

Auberge des Vieux Moulins Banaux

Take a 16th-century mill straddling a rushing stream (and five minutes from a motorway), add a quartet of young, international, energetic talent, stir vigourously... and you have a recipe for success for a little auberge in Burgundy. Guillaume and his team started with the dining room and kitchen and completed a renovation in only a few years. The man in the kitchen serves great food: a saffron-sauced brochette of scallops with caramelised endives; slender panna cotta strawberry tarte accompanied by a sorbet of roses and strawberries. There are Sabien and Lukas (German), Tony (French) who alternate between dining room and reception; Guillaume (Franco-Dutch) pitches in everywhere. There is still carpeting on the corridor walls and, in some of the bedrooms, a 50s feel, but it is the food that is the priority here, and it is fabulous. Join a leisurely feast on the great dining terrace overlooking the large park and river, then try your hand at boules – or walk off lunch on the trail nearby. You are 45 minutes from the chablis vineyards – the position is perfect. The best rooms are on the first floor.

Price	€42–€52.
Rooms	15: 13 doubles, 2 triples
Meals	Breakfast €7.50 Lunch & dinner €22.50–€28.50. Restaurant closed Monday lunchtimes.
Closed	26 May–1 June 2008; 27 October–7 November 2008.
Directions	A5 exit 19 Villeneuve l'Archevêque. Signed.

Guillaume Hamel
18 route des Moulins Banaux,
89190 Villeneuve l'Archevêque, Yonne

Tel	+33 (0)3 86 86 72 55
Fax	+33 (0)3 86 86 78 94
Email	contact@bourgognehotels.fr
Web	www.bourgognehotels.fr

Auberge La Lucarne aux Chouettes

Perhaps it's an unfair advantage to be owned by a legend of French cinema. This 17th-century wharf warehouse on the majestic river Yonne, converted by Leslie Caron 14 years ago, is locally cherished for its great food, comfort and charm. Behind, the medieval town rises through narrow streets to the cathedral; under the gaze of graceful bedrooms, barges and pleasure boats ply their trade; down below, the flower bedecked terraces, star-gazers gaze and sip a glass. Navigate steep stairs to those lofty beamed rooms with canopied beds and polished terracotta floors. Or head to the romantically attired, big top-floor loft with its pretty bed covers, river views and open-plan bathroom, demurely hidden behind striped and swagged blinds. In the kitchen, a renowned Japanese chef works his magic. On tree shaded terraces and under the beautifully raftered ceiling of the dining room, rustically clad waiters ferry sophisticated food and local wines with proper deference to well-dressed tables. Winter fires and soft chandeliers make for warm intimate evenings, even in this great dining hall.

Price	€99. Suite €150. Loft & duplex €170.
Rooms	4: 1 double, 1 suite for 2, 1 loft for 2 or 3, 1 duplex for 2 or 3.
Meals	Breakfast €10. Lunch €25–€46. Dinner €46. Restaurant closed Sunday evening & Monday.
Closed	January, Sunday evening & Monday.
Directions	From A6, exit 18 onto D943 for Joigny. Left onto N6 to Villeneuve sur Yonne. Auberge on river quayside; signed. Parking possible in front of Auberge.

Leslie Caron
Quai Bretoche,
89500 Villeneuve sur Yonne, Yonne

Tel	+33 (0)3 86 87 18 26
Fax	+33 (0)3 86 87 22 63
Email	lesliecaron-auberge@wanadoo.fr
Web	www.lesliecaron-auberge.com

Petit Manoir des Bruyères

A rococo place unlike anything you've seen. Behind the creeper-clad façade with only the Burgundian roof as a clue is eye-boggling glamour: a vast beamed living room, an endless polished dining table, rows of tapestried chairs, many shiny ornaments. Upstairs, stagger out of the loo – once you've found the door in the trompe l'œil walls – to cupids, carvings, gildings, satyrs, velvet walls and clouds on the ceilings. There's a many-mirrored bathroom reflecting multiple magical images of you, marble pillars and gold-cushioned bath; a Louis XIV room with red/gold bathroom with gold/ivory taps; an antique wooden throne with bell-chime flush. 'Madame de Maintenon' has a coronet canopy, a long thin bull's eye window and a shower that whooshes between basin and loo. The 'biscuit' is taken by the deeply, heavily pink suite with its carved fireplace, painted ceilings and corner columns – wild! But such is the enthusiasm of the owners, the peace of house and garden, the quality of comfort, food and wine, that we feel it's perfect for lovers of French extravaganza. Theatrical, delightful and joyous.

Price	€140–€220.
Rooms	5: 3 doubles, 1 suite for 2, 1 suite for 2–3.
Meals	Breakfast included. Hosted dinner at communal table or separate tables, €40. Book ahead.
Closed	Never.
Directions	From Auxerre D965 to Villefargeau; right on C3 to Bruyères.

Pierre & Monique Joullié
89240 Villefargeau, Yonne

Tel	+33 (0)3 86 41 32 82
Fax	+33 (0)3 86 41 28 57
Email	jchambord@aol.com
Web	www.petit-manoir-bruyeres.com

Hôtel de la Beursaudière

Monsieur Lenoble's attention to detail is staggering. Not content with creating a buzzing, cheerful restaurant he has lovingly transformed a priory and farm buildings – stables, dovecotes, stone structures on varied levels, wooden verandas topped with red-patterned burgundian roof tiles – into a very seductive hotel. Each bedroom has a trade for a theme: a typewriter and old books for the 'writer'; antique irons for the 'laundress'; horse and ox collars for the 'ploughman'; vine-decorated wooden panels for the 'wine-grower'. The walls have been lightly skimmed in plaster in natural shades of ochre, pigeon-egg grey or light yellow. Floors are terracotta or flagstone, stone walls are painted, rafters exposed and windows round or cottage square with curtains of vintage linens and lace. Beds are king-size, mattresses are excellent and TVs are hidden in antique cabinets. Most bathrooms are open plan so as not to detract from the beams and volumes. There is even a sheltered sun lounge on the terrace only overlooked by sparrows. A nice place to sit and sample your chilled choice picked up in Chablis.

Price	€75-€115.
Rooms	11: 5 twins, 6 doubles.
Meals	Breakfast €10.
	Lunch & dinner €19-€46.
Closed	Last 3 weeks of January.
Directions	A6 exit 21 Nitry; right to Nitry for 500m. Left at church toward Vermenton for 200m. Signed.

	M & Mme Lenoble
	5-7 rue Hyacinthe Gautherin,
	89310 Nitry, Yonne
Tel	+33 (0)3 86 33 69 70
Fax	+33 (0)3 86 33 69 60
Email	message@beursaudiere.com
Web	www.beursaudiere.com

Le Relais Fleuri/Le Coq Hardi

Anyone who loves France and what it stands for will coq-a-doodle-do. This small, modest hotel was built in the 30s to cater to the ever-increasing motor trade – from Paris to the south of France. It experienced its heyday in the late 50s and 60s when the rich and famous would stop over for a night or two to wine and dine before heading down to St Tropez. Unfortunately this all ceased when these people became the 'jet set'. These hotels and restaurants are now seeing a revival; often near motorways yet set away from the speed lanes and traffic jams, they are a reminder of a more civilised era when the pace of life was slower and food a priority. Meals are served on a lime tree covered terrace overlooking the Loire. Judging by the smiles of the customers staggering away at 4pm it is worth staying here for the food alone. Some of the hotel's original rooms upstairs have terraces over the garden; the newly decorated rooms are pleasantly done in blue or yellow. Philippe has added a small new bistro where those who are just beginning their vacation and have not yet slowed down may be served a quicker meal.

Price	€60-€90.
Rooms	9: 8 doubles, 1 suite.
Meals	Breakfast €11 Lunch & dinner €25-€60. Bistro meals €19. Restaurant closed Tues & Wed October-end April.
Closed	Mid-December-mid-January.
Directions	From A77, exit 25 & on through Pouilly sur Loire. Hotel opp. Cave Cooperative.

Philippe & Dominique Martin
42 avenue du la Tuilerie,
58150 Pouilly sur Loire, Nièvre

Tel	+33 (0)3 86 39 12 99
Fax	+33 (0)3 86 39 14 15
Email	le-relais-fleuri-sarl@wanadoo.fr
Web	www.lerelaisfleuri.fr

Château de Prye

The Queen of Poland, Marie-Casimire, lived here at the tail end of the 17th century – in this château extraordinaire, this architectural curiosity. The rooms are vast, the marble stables are palatial and the corridors heave with antlers and stag heads from previous ancestors; the history is intriguing. The young Marquis and Marquise, recently installed, have joyfully taken up the challenge of running both château and estate (they breed Charolais cattle) and host their national and international guests with grace and ease. Each cavernous bedroom is furnished with antiques – a triple-mirrored wardrobe from the Thirties, a Breton carved bedstead, a vintage oil-fuelled heater; bathrooms are en suite. Take a peek at the château kitchen with its wonderful old range and copper saucepans... from here breakfast is dispatched to a boudoir-like room with pretty white wainscotting. This turreted, neo-Gothic château, its woodlands, gentle river and age-old trees of exotic and distant origins are contained within seven kilometres of walls... relish the fairy tale.

Price	€90–€147.
Rooms	4: 2 doubles, 2 suites for 2–4.
Meals	Breakfast included.
	Dinner €35, book ahead.
Closed	Mid-October–mid-April.
Directions	Nevers–Château-Chinon exit 36; at r'bouts, signs for Château Chinon & Sauvigny les Bois; D18 thro' Sauvigny les Bois. Gates between the two pavillons open manually.

Magdalena & Antoine-Emmanuel
du Bourg de Bozas
58160 La Fermeté, Nièvre
Tel   +33 (0)3 86 58 42 64
Fax   +33 (0)3 86 58 47 64
Email   info@chateaudeprye.com
Web   www.chateaudeprye.com

Château de Villette

Coen and Catherine – he Dutch, she Belgian – fell in love with this little château in 2002, did it up together, then had their wedding here. They've opened just four rooms to guests (forming two suites) so they can spoil you properly. And get to know you over dinner. (Though, should you prefer a romantic dinner for two, they'll understand.) Deep in the Parc de Morvan, the château was built in 1782 as a summer retreat. Bedrooms, charmingly decorated by Catherine, are large, light and airy, with warm colours and polished floors. They are dressed in château-style finery with canopied four-poster or draped bedheads (except for the twin sleigh bed in one of the family rooms). Bathrooms are as they should be – new claw foot baths carry exquisite antique taps – and views sail out of great windows to meadows and woodland beyond. Your five-course dinner is served in a candlelit dining room or outside – you choose. The grounds are perfect for duck and pheasant shoots, or fly-fishing in the crystal clear waters. Families would love it here; Beaune and the vineyards lie temptingly close. *Cash or cheque only.*

Price	€150–€210. Suites €220–€350.
Rooms	4: 1 double, 1 twin, 2 family rooms for 3. Rooms interconnect to form 2 suites for 5.
Meals	Breakfast included. Dinner €45, book ahead. Call to choose menu.
Closed	Rarely.
Directions	From N6 exit Beaune for Autun. N81 for Moulins for 18km, right to Poil. Through village, 2nd left. Signed.

Catherine & Coen Stork
58170 Poil, Nièvre

Tel	+33 (0)3 86 30 09 13
Fax	+33 (0)3 86 30 26 03
Email	catherinestork@wanadoo.fr
Web	www.stork-chateau.com

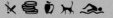

Le Monestier

We almost got lost here, but the valley is a pretty place to lose yourself. You enter a jewel of a village, then pass two fine horse-chestnuts flanking the high and handsome iron gate; a swimming pool is set in the grass. Margrit and Peter are Swiss and bought the *maison bourgeoise* in 1998; they occupy the ground floor. Peter can be seen walking round in an apron: he and Margrit are in charge of the cooking and you can expect some excellent meals. Rooms are extremely comfortable with romantic views over roofs of old village house, vine covered slopes and traditional agricultural fields. A favourite would be the room with the alcove-fitted bathroom, its claw-foot bath and draped shower hidden behind fine oak panelling. Passageways are clad with numerous richly coloured oriental rugs. One bedroom has its own loo and a bathroom down the corridor, but this is made up for by a private terrace on top of one of the towers. Tennis, fishing, riding and golf are all close at hand. More importantly for many, you can walk to the vineyards of Mercurey, Givry and Rully. Gentle living.

Price	€85–€95. Singles €70.
Rooms	5 twins (1 with separate bath across hall, wc in room).
Meals	Breakfast included. Dinner €24, book ahead. Restaurants nearby.
Closed	Closed occasionally mid-November–mid-March.
Directions	A6 exit Chalon Nord; right for Châtenoy le Royal, D978 for 9km for Autun. Left at r'bout for Givry. After 75m, D48 right for Vallée des Vaux, through Mellecey Bourg, continue on road. Signed.

Margrit & Peter Koller
Le Bourg, 71640 Saint Denis de Vaux,
Saône-et-Loire

Tel	+33 (0)3 85 44 50 68
Fax	+33 (0)3 85 44 58 34
Email	71640lemonestier@wanadoo.fr
Web	www.lemonestier.com

L'Orangerie

Ring the bell on the gate, then slip through the gardens. They are alive with colour and the sound of a bubbling brook. Light spills into the sitting room entrance through vine-clad arched windows, with cream walls and Indian rugs adding to the simple elegance of this gracious *maison de maître*. Antiques and travel are David's passion, his gentle Irish brogue enchanting; it's no surprise to hear he interviews European royalty for a 'prestigious' magazine. The grand staircase in the centre of the house could have come straight off a 1930s luxury cruise liner, interesting paintings and stylish oriental fabrics contribute to a mix of styles that somehow go well together. Bedrooms vary in size, with seersucker linen and antique prints; they are truly lovely and bathrooms are classically tasteful. Being in the heart of Burgundy vineyard country you are also immersed in silence. Terraced lawns lead down to the heated swimming pool, the trees and meadows. Sybaritic, but in the best possible taste, in one of the most beautiful areas of France. *Cash or euro cheque only. Minimum stay two nights.*

Price	€72–€102.
Rooms	5 twins/doubles.
Meals	Breakfast included.
	Hosted dinner with wine, €25–€40, on request.
Closed	Mid-November–mid-March.
Directions	From A6, exit Chalon Sud on N80 for Le Creusot; exit Moroges. Signed from village centre.

David Eades & Niels Lierow
Vingelles, 71390 Moroges,
Saône-et-Loire

Tel	+33 (0)3 85 47 91 94
Fax	+33 (0)3 85 47 98 49
Email	info@orangerie-moroges.com
Web	www.orangerie-moroges.com

Entry 40 Map 11

Château de Vaulx

It was described in 1886 as "well-proportioned and elegant in its simplicity." It is as lovely now and in the most beautiful position, high on a hill, with views that stretch to distant purple mountains. Marty, your host, and Viki and Nema (a Jack Russell and a Cane Corso) will greet and escort you to the west wing. Downstairs, a fully panelled drawing room with chandeliers, a huge dining room with fresh flowers. Two large bedrooms and two suites have been refurbished on the first floor. Sleep peacefully: not a hint of traffic rumble here. The gardens have been spruced up, the lawns manicured, the box balls tightly topiaried; stroll down the romantic avenues in dappled sunlight. Future plans include an orchard, the introduction of bees and a swimming pool. The views are glorious, the birds twitter, there's countryside all around and plenty of places to visit, including a 13th-century bell tower in the village. In La Clayette is Bernard Dufoux, one of the best chocolate makers in France (there are monthly tastings and lessons); in Sainte Christophe is a weekly cattle market. Burgundy lies at your feet.

Price	€100–€115. Suite €139.
Rooms	4: 2 doubles, 2 family suites for 4.
Meals	Breakfast included. Dinner €30, book ahead. Restaurant 3km.
Closed	Rarely.
Directions	From Charolles, D985 dir. Clayette. Straight ahead, cross Changy, Tourny, and railway crossing. After 1km, 2nd road signed Vaulx. Up to top of hill, right at crossing. Ring bell on large iron gate.

Marty Freriksen
71800 Saint Julien de Civry,
Saône-et-Loire

Tel	+33 (0)3 85 70 64 03
Fax	+33 (0)3 85 70 64 03
Email	marty@chateaudevaulx.com
Web	www.chateaudevaulx.com

Château des Poccards

It is all most comforting and welcoming, the Tuscan-style villa built in 1805 to woo a Tuscan beauty living in Burgundy. Now run by a husband and wife team ever on the go, the cream and ochre villa has become an exemplary guest house. After a day's sampling the great restaurants of Lyon, exploring the wine routes of Beaune or the shops of Geneva, what nicer than to return to a big retro tub in a bathroom that sparkles with uplighters and oozes warm towels? Bedrooms are all generously big and different, with pretty terracotta floors and pale-papered walls, cream beds, elegant furnishings and *tout confort*. Some have windows to all sides so you feel you're in the tree tops – bliss when the sun streams in. In the mature park, a serene pool with wooden loungers and vineyard views. Families would be happy here, as would romancers. Excellent breakfasts are supplied by your hosts at white-clothed tables in a gracious room; a piano in the corner, windows to a terrace, a sumptuous parquet floor. Good value for money. *No credit cards.*

Price	€100–€140.
Rooms	6 doubles. Some rooms connect.
Meals	Breakfast included.
	Restaurants 10-min drive.
Closed	January–February.
Directions	A6 exit 28 to Sennecé Les Maçon toward Laizé. Left to Laizé & Blagny. At stop, 1st left to Hurigny; 1st right up Rue de la Brasse; 100m on left.

Catherine & Ivan Fizaine
120 route des Poccards,
71870 Hurigny, Saône-et-Loire

Tel	+33 (0)3 85 32 08 27
Fax	+33 (0)3 85 32 08 19
Email	chateau.des.poccards@wanadoo.fr
Web	www.chateau-des-poccards.com

Château de Messey

An impressive bull keeps his eye on his harem and shares the buttercup meadows with this 16th-century château surrounded by duck-filled ponds and working vines. Monsieur is the cellar master, Madame manages the château with charming efficiency. Aperitifs in the cellar are part of the evening ritual and Monsieur may surprise you with an enormous bottle of cognac after a dinner of poulet de Bresse or Charolais beef with vegetables from the garden. Some of the guest bedrooms are in the beautifully rustic vine workers' cottages built with exposed stone in a U-shape around a grassed courtyard leafy with weeping willow and wall-creeping shrubs. They are right by the river which has formed a lake on its way through; a lovely place to sit out on the grass under the parasols. The pricier rooms in the château are decorated in period-style, graced with high ceilings and long vineyard views. A superior elegance reigns in the salon, overlooking the vines at the back and peonies and rose bushes at the front. A most welcoming if sometimes busy place.

Price	€77–€155. Cottages €210–€600 per week.
Rooms	4 + 4: 2 twins, 1 twin/double, 1 triple. 4 cottages for 2-6.
Meals	Breakfast included. Hosted dinner €30, wine included.
Closed	January.
Directions	From A6 exit to Tournus; in centre turn right on D14. Château on left of D14 between Ozenay & Martailly, 9km from Tournus.

Bernard & Marie-Laurence Fachon
71700 Ozenay,
Saône-et-Loire

Tel	+33 (0)3 85 51 16 11
Fax	+33 (0)3 85 51 33 82
Email	chateau@demessey.com
Web	www.demessey.com

Maison Nièpce

All the modern necessities, of course, but otherwise little has changed since the old inn was turned into a family mansion by the uncle of Joseph (Nicephore) Nièpce, inventor of photography. It's a bit like staying in a charming museum – a place of candlelight, atmosphere and 18th-century elegance, plus a dash of antique grime. The owners and their golden retriever live in one great wing and guests in the other, while two odoriferous cats roam freely. First-floor passageways run hither and thither to graceful rooms with good beds and bathrooms, fine antiques and oriental rugs. On the slopey-ceilinged second floor, La Chambre Nièpce can link up to form a three-room apartment with bathroom. A display of arms in one bedroom and an oven for baking bullets in another recall the Revolution; a third, less bellicose, has serried ranks of books. Plump for a room at the back, quieter than those on the street, and gaze down on the big and enchanting walled garden. Breakfast and dinner (usually table d'hôtes) are in the fascinating dining room, aglow with copper pans.

Price	€50–€110. Apartment €460 per week.
Rooms	5 + 1: 1 double, 4 twins. Apartment for 4.
Meals	Breakfast €8. Dinner €23, book ahead.
Closed	Rarely.
Directions	20km south of Chalon sur Saone, N6 dir. Macon; left on leaving village.

Huguette & Jehan Moreau de Melen
8 avenue du 4 Septembre, 7
1240 Sennecy le Grand, Saône-et-Loire

Tel	+33 (0)3 85 44 76 44
Fax	+33 (0)3 85 44 75 59
Email	moreau.jehan@wanadoo.fr
Web	www.maisonniepce.com

La Dominotte

On the edge of an old Burgundian village, a farmhouse where grapes were gathered, pressed and stored; you can still see the round traces of the barrels on the breakfast room wall. They are less visible in the evening with low lighting and candles when snacks are served from 4 to 6pm; a blackboard announces the daily specialities, maybe snails or a selection of local cheeses and wine. This simply stylish room leads onto the garden, recently landscaped with bushes to obscure the fence around the pool. Surrounding land is flat fields with mature trees in the distance. The Franssens are courageously launching a second career after teaching (she) and sales (he) in Holland. Multi-lingual and welcoming, they have been here since 1998 so are an excellent source for the plethora of cultural visits and gastronomy nearby. Rooms on the ground floor of the barn are more for sleeping than lounging about in; most have mellow exposed stone, some are beamed, all keep their original slit windows. The views over the garden and pool are best from the airy, spacious family room upstairs with its extra long beds.

Price	€90–€124. Family room €150.
Rooms	11: 10 doubles,
	1 family room for 4 (with kitchen).
Meals	Breakfast included.
	Late afternoon snacks.
	Hosted dinner €22–€25 twice weekly.
Closed	22 November–mid-March.
Directions	A6 Dijon & Beaune exit 24.1
	to Bligny les Beaune onto D113, t
	hen to Demigny D18; left at T-junc.
	after Casino & pharmacy; 3rd on left
	to end of village; last house on right.

Madame Franssen
Jasoupe le Bas,
71150 Demigny, Saône-et-Loire

Tel	+33 (0)3 85 49 43 56
Fax	+33 (0)3 85 49 91 35
Email	info@la-dominotte.com
Web	www.la-dominotte.com

Château de Chassagne-Montrachet

You are in top wine country. The driveway passes through a small vineyard to the business-like château – winery in the middle, chambres d'hôte to the right. The stark 19th-century exterior does not prepare you for the modernism within: the sweeping wooden stairway, the slate and pink-marble floor, the stunning leather furniture, the extraordinary billiard room with bamboo decoration and underfloor lighting. The refreshing irreverence continues upstairs; you might spot a Jacobsen 'egg' chair, relish the sumptuousness of purple walls and oak floor or enter a room of zen-like calm. Windows show the vineyards floating away to the hills of the Massive Central or the Saône valley; on a good day you can see the Alps. Bathrooms are amazing; most have tubs surrounded by wooden decking, one has a double sink of rough-cast bronze mounted on rock – half basin, half art. Breakfast at two large steel tables on sculpted chairs by a wonderful fireplace and floor-to-ceiling doors. The château restaurant is 300 metres away and there's excellent walking in the hills. *Wine tour included, by arrangement.*

Price	€250.
Rooms	6 doubles.
Meals	Breakfast included. Lunch €40-€50, with fine wines for tasting.
Closed	Never.
Directions	From Beaune, N74 exit Chassagne-Montrachet; château signed at village entrance.

Francine Picard
5 rue du Château,
21190 Chassagne Montrachet, Côte-d'Or

Tel	+33 (0)3 80 21 98 57
Fax	+33 (0)3 80 21 98 56
Email	contact@michelpicard.com
Web	www.michelpicard.com

Le Clos

Breakfast on the terrace overlooking the neat and pretty *jardin de curé*, then choose your suntrap in the garden – full of hidden corners. Or, under the shade of big trees, wander among the quaint agricultural machinery that sculpturally dots the lawns. The rustic white-shuttered farmhouse has been renovated with tender loving care to reveal exposed limestone walls and massive rafters. There's a charming country breakfast room and a light and lofty lounge, whose ancient tiles have been garnished with oriental rugs and sofas. Bedrooms are large, with matching floral bed linen and curtains, new carpets, substantial antiques, and the odd exotic touch. Bathrooms sparkle and there are no half measures: big bath tubs, walk-in showers, an abundance of towels and robes. No restaurant, but have a drink at the bar and and a chat with Alain – a professional hotelier with a dry sense of humour. The pretty residential village is deep in wine country – and when you've had your fill of burgundies and beaunes, there are mustards to try in a nearby village!

Price	€70–€110. Suites €140-€200.
Rooms	24: 19 twins/doubles, 5 duplex suites.
Meals	Breakfast €10. Restaurant 100m; many others in Beaune, 3km.
Closed	December–January.
Directions	From Lyon A6 exit 24.1 towards Beaune centre; 300m r'bout to Montagny Les Beaune on D113. Signed.

M & Mme Alain Oudot
22 rue Gravières,
21200 Montagny lès Beaune, Côte-d'Or

Tel	+33 (0)3 80 25 97 98
Fax	+33 (0)3 80 25 94 70
Email	hotelleclos@wanadoo.fr
Web	www.hotelleclos.com

La Terre d'Or

Jean-Louis can share his love for Burgundy with you in many ways: he can explain how those elegant vintages are produced, arrange cookery lessons with a local chef, or show you a vestige of Roman art. All this (and more) by bike, horseback, jeep or hot-air balloon. He and Christine have two houses, each surrounded by a large terraced garden and century-old trees. One is contemporary and multi-levelled, the cottage is stone-walled and traditional, perfect for an independent party with its sitting room, corner kitchen and everything you need. The big beautiful bedrooms, each with its own entrance, have magnificent views of the vineyards and the Beaune; some have terraces or patios. The Martins have used old beams, rosy tiles, polished wine-growers' tables and chairs. You might have one of your wine classes in the grotto under the house where a river used to run; the stalactites are still there. Jean-Louis can also be persuaded to host a barbecue by the pool. This is the kind of place where you book for two nights and end up staying a week. Heaven. *Group price for themed holidays: wines, cooking, culture.*

Price	€160–€205. Cottage €360.
Rooms	5 + 1: 1 doubles, 1 twin
	Cottage for 4–6
	(1 double, 1 duplex for 2–4).
Meals	Breakfast €15. Picnic available.
	Restaurant within walking distance.
Closed	Rarely.
Directions	From Beaune, D970 for Auxerre &
	Bouze Les Beaunes. After 2km right to
	La Montagne. Well signed.

Christine & Jean-Louis Martin
Rue Izembart La Montagne,
21200 Beaune, Côte-d'Or

Tel	+33 (0)3 80 25 90 90
Fax	+33 (0)3 80 25 90 99
Email	jlmartin@laterredor.com
Web	www.laterredor.com

Le Hameau de Barboron

The scents of beeswax, lavender and milled soap will soothe the weariest spirit; the handsome country antiques, the fine linen and the smooth flagstones will charm you. Once home to the agent of a vast domaine of moor, forest and wild boar, this intimate 16th-century hamlet, beautifully run by Odile (who also happens to produce grands crus) is tucked into a hillside in the heart of Burgundy. The pale stonework, covered in small terracotta tiles, has been faultlessly renovated. In a charming cobbled central courtyard, troughs of lavender partner weathered metal tables and chairs; all around, in a daisy chain of buildings, are the bedrooms, public rooms and boutique of this lovely little hotel. Heavily beamed rooms with plain stone walls, prettily softened by fabrics, are inviting. Gleaming wooden bedsteads, deep mattresses and white stitched quilts promise sound sleep. Wake to the joy of a powerful shower in a sparkling blue and white bathroom, then wander across the cobbles for a generous continental breakfast in the breakfast room, cheerful with pink, blue and yellow china.

Price	€100–€135. Triple €150. Suites €160–€200. Restaurant 3km.
Rooms	17: 12 doubles, 1 triple, 3 suites for 2, 1 suite for 2-4.
Meals	Breakfast €15. Brunch €28. Dinner on request.
Closed	Never.
Directions	From A6, exit Beaune, dir. Savigny lès Beaune. Signed from village.

Odile Nominé
21420 Savigny lès Beaune, Côte-d'Or

Tel	+33 (0)3 80 21 58 35
Fax	+33 (0)3 80 26 10 59
Email	lehameaudebarboron@wanadoo.fr
Web	www.hameau-barboron.com

Château de Créancey

Fiona and Bruno fell in love with Créancey on sight – a brave and passionate response to crumbling 17th-century walls and fallen beams. They have lavished a small fortune on a stylish restoration, lacing ancient bricks and mortar with contemporary luxuries: exposed oak beams scrubbed clean, lime-rendered walls to soak up the light, an infusion of antiques that mix with the odd minimalist piece. Sumptuous, uncluttered bedrooms have huge beds, old rugs, fresh flowers, plush armchairs. Bathrooms are equally faultless (Imagine the best of everything and you are halfway there). Even the taps burst with water, the rarest of French rarities. An exceptional breakfast with homemade jams is taken in the hall. In the sitting room, the enormous fireplace can burn whole trees (well, almost). There's a snug library, too, a dovecote in the garden and, 300m from the château, a line of trees flank the Canal de Bourgogne. Bring your bike and pedal on the footpath past the Charolais cattle that graze in the surrounding fields. On your doorstep, enough châteaux, cellars and monasteries to keep you busy for a month.

Price	€160–€230. House €560 €720.
Rooms	5 + 1: 2 doubles, 1 twin, 1 family room for 3, 1 suite for 4. House for 2–4.
Meals	Breakfast included. Dinner €50, only for groups occupying whole château.
Closed	Rarely.
Directions	From A6, exit at Pouilly en Auxois. At 1st roundabout to Créancey; D18 1km into village. Château on left; entrance at rear opposite the Mairie.

Fiona de Wulf
21320 Créancey, Côte-d'Or

Tel	+33 (0)3 80 90 57 50
Fax	+33 (0)3 80 90 57 51
Email	chateau@creancey.com
Web	www.creancey.com

Hôtel de Vougeot

Rows of vines sweep down an incline, surround the regal Château de Clos de Vougeot (shown above) in tones of pale yellow stone like a sepia photograph, and come to an abrupt halt at the back doorstep of this modest converted townhouse. For centuries Clos de Vougeot was considered the finest of all burgundies; the Cisterian monks planted some of the vines in the 12th century. Thirty hogsheads were sent to Rome in 1371 to celebrate the election of Pope Gregory XI; the gift-bearing abbot was soon made a cardinal. The cloister, cellar and enormous presses are among the most interesting examples of architecture in Burgundy. The best rooms here have views of both the château and the vines. You are on your own here with a key to come and go as you like. Everything has been kept simple and clean; the rough outlines of the dark timbers are a nice contrast to the white walls, light coloured bedspreads, new parquet floors and honey-pine furniture. Splash out on one of the huge rooms. A copious buffet breakfast served under the ground floor stone arches will be a perfect start to your day.

Price	€58–€108.
Rooms	16: 12 doubles, 1 triple, 2 quadruples, 1 room for 5.
Meals	Buffet breakfast €9. Cold plate €20.
Closed	23 December–23 January.
Directions	A31 exit Nuits St Georges, D974 towards Vougeot. Hotel in village.

Alain Senterre
18 rue du Vieux Château,
21640 Vougeot, Côte-d'Or

Tel	+33 (0)3 80 62 01 15
Fax	+33 (0)3 80 62 49 09
Email	contact@hotel-vougeot.com
Web	www.hotel-vougeot.com

Castel de Très Girard

Nuits Saint Georges, Gevrey Chambertin, Clos de Vougeot, Vosne Romanée – all tongue-twisters in the best sense of the word and all strewn in your path as you travel down the trunk road from Dijon. Why not stop here and be greeted by Sébastien and his young, friendly team who handle everything in the nicest manner? The warmth not only comes from the embers in the fireplace by the leather club chairs but from the general ambience of this recently renovated wine press and 18th-century Burgundian manor. There are confident touches of burgundy reds (naturally) or sun-yellows in the padded fabrics on the beds and just enough stone and beam have been exposed to give the large bedrooms character; small vestibules ensure ultimate peace. Even the big, gleaming white bathrooms have views over the rooftops or to the Côte de Nuits vineyards. The chef and his assistant *pâtissier* are poets with a magic touch transforming the freshest ingredients into pure delight. Sébastien picks out artists of the moment to be shown on the walls and best bottle of wine for your repast. Not to be missed.

Price	€115–€129. Triples & suites €147–€188.
Rooms	9: 2 doubles, 5 triples, 2 suites.
Meals	Buffet breakfast €14. Lunch €22.50–€80. Dinner €40–€80.
Closed	Rarely.
Directions	20km from Dijon. A31 exit Dijon Sud for Nuits St Georges on N74, then right to Morey St Denis. Signed.

Sébastien Pilat
7 rue Très Girard,
21220 Morey St Denis, Côte-d'Or

Tel	+33 (0)3 80 34 33 09
Fax	+33 (0)3 80 51 81 92
Email	info@castel-tres-girard.com
Web	www.castel-tres-girard.com

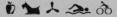

Château de Flammerans

All is fresh, luxurious, relaxing – and Guy has the perfect pinch of passion for Burgundian cuisine even though he hails from Cantal. Ask to see the 18th-century kitchen with its original painted ceiling where he teaches the secrets of jambon persillé or fricassée d'escargot. The billiard room and the library are just off the entrance hall with its superb 19th-century ceramic tiles and a handsome iron banister leads upstairs. You may breakfast on the large balcony overlooking the park, in the sitting room with its creamy walls, oriental rugs, green and gold upholstered easy chairs, or in the elegant dining room. Bedrooms are big and uncluttered with working fireplaces and mineral water on the side tables. You'll find robes in the gorgeous bathrooms along with weathered marbled floors from the south of France. If you are lucky, you'll catch one of the concerts – maybe baroque or jazz – that Guy and Catherine organise. Sit and dream on a bench in a shady glen, gaze at the magnificent red oaks, discover the glistening ponds (one was used to clean the carriage wheels). A pleasing place.

Price	€73-€135. Suites €145-€175.
Rooms	6: 3 doubles, 1 twin, 2 suites.
Meals	Breakfast included. Light lunches available. Hosted dinner with drinks, €45; book ahead.
Closed	Never.
Directions	A6/A39/N5. Auxonne D20 towards Flammerans. Signed in Auxonne.

Guy & Catherine Barrier
21130 Flammerans,
Côte-d'Or

Tel   +33 (0)3 80 27 05 70
Fax   +33 (0)3 80 31 12 12
Email   info@chateaudeflammerans.com
Web   www.chateaudeflammerans.com

Château Andelot

Winding narrow roads lead higher and higher, through woods and foothills, until you reach the top... where conical towers, a mighty keep and thick-walled ramparts spread themselves along a cliff top and the wooded valley falls away. Pass through the monumental entrance portal and the adventure begins: the 12th century castle is as dramatic inside as out. The bedrooms – main château or rampart buildings – are grand but uncluttered spaces of antiques, fine fabrics, cool tiles, rich rugs and lavish bed covers; bathrooms are as luxurious as those of a starry hotel. All have million-dollar views over plunging valleys to the Jura mountains and the Swiss border, and Mont Blanc on a good day. Why get up? Why, indeed. No need to make breakfast, or dinner; fruits and vegetables are grown on the grounds; the château comes with attentive staff. Eat in the vaulted dining room below the vast, beamed, tapestry-hung sitting room with plump sofas, soft carpeting and oils. Tennis court, swimming pool, formal garden and terrace... a special place for celebrations and reunions. *Booking essential.*

Price	€100–€200.
	Weekly & monthly rental possible.
Rooms	6 + 1: 4 doubles, 1 twin, 1 suite for 2-4.
	Apartment for 2-4.
Meals	Breakfast included. Dinner €40.
	Light supper €20.
	Children under 10 half price. Book ahead.
Closed	Rarely.
Directions	A39 exit 10 onto D56, then D3 to
	St Amour & Andelot. 2km after Thoissia,
	on left, small lane leading to gate.

Anne Drolet
Rue de l'Église,
39320 Andelot lès St Amour, Jura

Tel	+33 (0)3 84 85 41 49
Fax	+33 (0)3 84 85 46 74
Email	info@chateauandelot.com
Web	www.chateauandelot.com

Château d'Epenoux

Next to the dear little 18th-century château stands a tiny baroque chapel tenderly maintained by the ladies of the house. Suzanne and Eva have given both the facelift they deserved – windows sparkle and floorboards gleam. Your friendly, unassuming hosts have opened up five airy bedrooms on the first floor to guests. All are generously big and different: the suite, prettily papered in blue, its twin beds draped with soft white duvets, has long windows overlooking majestic trees, copses and lawns. The large double is panelled in French green; fresh, feminine Mona Lisa is all deep pink walls and a cream sofa. Sparkling white bathrooms come with lashings of hot water. Sink into the wildly floral armchairs in the blue-carpeted salon for a pre-dinner aperitif, then into the grand dining room with its huge glass chandelier for dinner: maybe slices of perfectly roasted duck with a well chosen wine. Wander round the park afterwards and admire the ancient trees, or take a short drive to charming Vesoul, notable for its lake and recreational park, and intriguing Gothic façades in the old quarter.

Price	€90–€100.
Rooms	5: 4 doubles, 1 suite.
Meals	Breakfast included. Dinner €24.
Closed	Rarely.
Directions	From Chaumont, N19 to Vesoul, D10 for approx. 4 km. Château on left at entrance to village of Epenoux.

Eva Holz & Susanne Hubbuch
70000 Pusy et Epenoux,
Haute-Saône

Tel	+33 (0)3 84 75 19 60
Fax	+33 (0)3 84 76 45 05
Email	chateau.epenoux@orange.fr
Web	www.chateau-epenoux.com

Hôtel Taillard

A family business indeed! In 1875 Jean-François' grandfather began serving meals in the farmhouse kitchen; later his son added a dining room, and guest bedrooms followed. Now Jean-François carries on the tradition and has a young son waiting in the wings. Perhaps Grandpère would raise eyebrows at the new jacuzzi, sauna, gym and outdoor pool... but the food has become more gourmet and very good it is too, served on a terrace with bewitching views. You're at the back of beyond, on a wooded mountainside above the village of Goumois, Switzerland is just across the river Doubs (come for the fly-fishing, take a guide) and the scenery is pure, perfect Heidi. The bedrooms, spread through two buildings, are a mixture of sizes and styles, mainly classic or contemporary chic but with a few mavericks for fun: one in Seventies style with a plum sofa, another with a fashionably metallic four-poster, another overblown rococo... Bathrooms vary, but all are good, clean and functional. The garden is neatly styled, with roses and clipped hedges, horse chestnuts for shade and just the right amount of colour.

Price	€82–€96. Family suites €125–€165.
Rooms	21: 16 doubles, 5 family suites.
Meals	Buffet breakfast €12. Lunch €23–€75. Dinner €33–€75. Restaurant closed Wednesdays Oct–Nov, lunchtimes April–June & September.
Closed	Mid-November–March.
Directions	From A36 exit 6 for Montbéliard Sud then D437 for Maîche/Bern. After St Hippolyte D437 left to Goumois. Hotel on right before town.

Monsieur Taillard
Route de la Corniche,
25470 Goumois, Doubs

Tel	+33 (0)3 81 44 20 75
Fax	+33 (0)3 81 44 26 15
Email	hotel.taillard@wanadoo.fr
Web	www.hoteltaillard.com

Paris – Île de France

Hôtel Saint Merry

If you love the old and quirky and are not afraid of a few stairs, this is for you. The hotel huddles against the late-Gothic church of St Merry whose clock tower cornice thrusts its way into the top-floor suite; in the first-floor reception you find an elaborate pew, linen-fold panels, a telephone in a confessional; in another room, a couple of buttresses provide the most original of low-flying bed canopies. From brocante and flea market came the wherewithal to make the old house worthy of its origins, neo-Gothic pieces were reworked to create this astounding environment, atmospheric paintings chosen to enhance it. The sober décor sets off the festival of carving: plain velvet or 'medieval-stripe' fabrics, great cast-iron light fittings, original beams and stonework – and some strangely colourful bathrooms (the new shower rooms are excellent). The big rooms are almost majestic, the cheaper ones are smaller and basic, the suite a masterpiece of style and adaptation (surely Paris's only Gothic salon). *No lift. Difficult access in pedestrian street.*

Price	€160–€230. Suite €335–€407.
Rooms	12: 6 doubles, 3 twins, 2 triples, 1 suite for 6.
Meals	Breakfast €11.
Closed	Never.
Directions	Metro: Hôtel de Ville (1, 11), Châtelet (1, 4, 7, 11, 14). RER: Châtelet-Les Halles. Buses: 38, 47, 75. Car park: St Martin.

Pierre Juin
78 rue de la Verrerie,
75004 Paris

Tel	+33 (0)1 42 78 14 15
Fax	+33 (0)1 40 29 06 82
Email	hotelstmerry@wanadoo.fr
Web	www.hotelmarais.com

Grand Hôtel des Balcons

Service produces tea on winter afternoons, a clothes line over the bath, and a feast of a breakfast (sumptuous cooked spread, fresh fruit salad...) that's free on your birthday! Owners and staff appear to work with lightness and pleasure. Having decorated her Art Nouveau hotel by taking inspiration from the floral 1890s staircase windows, Denise Corroyer now teaches ikebana and flowers the house – brilliantly – while her son Jeff and his wife manage – charmingly. Rooms are simple yet pleasing. The five big family rooms have smart décor and pretty modern lamps, parquet floors and two windows, good bathrooms (two basins, pretty tiles) and loads of space. Other rooms are not big but purpose-made table units use the space judiciously, amusing prints decorate the walls and front rooms have balconies with planted window boxes. At the back, you may be woken by the birds. An eagle eye is kept on maintenance, beds are firm, bathrooms good, colours and fabrics simple and bright. Good value, good people.

Price	€90–€210.
Rooms	50: 25 doubles, 14 twins, 6 singles, 5 family rooms for 4.
Meals	Breakfast €12.
Closed	Never.
Directions	Metro: Odéon (4, 10). RER: Luxembourg. Buses: 21, 27, 24, 58, 63, 86, 87, 96. Car Park: École de Médecine.

Denise & Pierre Corroyer & Jeff André
3 rue Casimir Delavigne,
75006 Paris

Tel	+33 (0)1 46 34 78 50
Fax	+33 (0)1 46 34 06 27
Email	grandhoteldesbalcons@orange.fr
Web	www.balcons.com

Hôtel Opéra Richepanse

At the centre of a throbbingly busy shopping and business district, the cool 1930s look and courteous welcome of the Richepanse promise rest and quiet in proper four-star fashion. The marquetry, the panelling, the smooth suede furniture and the stylish mouldings of the lobby/salon were custom-designed for the deep renovations. It feels clean-cut and rich. There's a minor concession to things more ancient in the atmospheric stone vault where the floor is blue, the panelling is oak and the sumptuous breakfast buffet calls. Bedrooms are a good size, some are enormous. They have carpeting in caramel, tobacco and chocolate or a soft coral in the superior rooms, clean limbed 1930s-style furniture and excellent thick-textured fabrics for curtains and bedcovers — no swags, no frills, no fuss. This gives space to appreciate the interesting reproductions that draw the eye and even, in the magnificent great suites, original paintings. Bathrooms are, of course, superb with the latest in basin design, triple mirrors and simple, smart tiling. Modern comforts, old-style attention and service.

Price	€240–€350. Suites €450 €590.
Rooms	38: 20 doubles, 15 twins, 3 suites.
Meals	Breakfast €12–€17.
Closed	Never
Directions	Metro: Madeleine (8, 12, 14). Concorde (1, 12). RER: Auber & Roissy bus-Opéra. Buses: 42, 52, 84, 94. Car Park: Madeleine.

Édith Vidalenc
14 rue du Chevalier de St George,
75001 Paris

Tel	+33 (0)1 42 60 36 00
Fax	+33 (0)1 42 60 13 03
Email	hotel@richepanse.com
Web	www.richepanse.com

Hôtel Gavarni

The neat little Gavarni astonishes still, heaving itself up into the miniature luxury class on ropes of rich draperies, interesting pictures, heavenly bathrooms and superb finishes. From its amazing ground floor of deep raspberry and yellow richness, tailor made murals and pretty breakfast room, you may expect more delights. The suites and doubles at the top are big and stunning with their jacuzzis, fine canopies and beautiful furniture – supremely French with Eiffel Tower views – yet never overdone. The first four floors are less luxurious but the quality is the same: thick lovely carpets, finely stitched quilts, heavily draped curtains and good little pieces of furniture. One tiny single is as tempting as toffee in pale mauve, cream and florality with the original white marble fireplace and its ornate mirror. The triumph is those cramped little shower rooms which have gained so much space with their utterly ingenious made-to-measure red 'granite' basin unit, shower and loo. Now with a patio for breakfast this is a superb combination of rich, strong modern style and pure traditional comfort.

Price	€99–€450. Singles €99–€150. Suites €290–€450.
Rooms	28: 13 doubles, 4 twins, 4 singles, 3 suites, 4 family rooms for 3.
Meals	Breakfast €13.
Closed	Never.
Directions	Metro: Passy (6), Trocadéro (6, 9). RER: Boulainvilliers. Buses: 22, 32. Car park: Garage Moderne, Rue de Passy.

Xavier Moraga
5 rue Gavarni,
75116 Paris

Tel	+33 (0)1 45 24 52 82
Fax	+33 (0)1 40 50 16 95
Email	reservation@gavarni.com
Web	www.gavarni.com

Hôtel du Jeu de Paume

The Île Saint Louis is the most exclusive 17th-century village in Paris and this renovated 'tennis court' – three storeys soar to the roof timbers – is one of its most exceptional sights. Add genuine care from mother and daughter, fresh flowers, time for everyone and super staff. Provençal in style, smallish rooms give onto quiet courtyards, have rich fabrics, pale walls, good bathrooms, old beams, stones, parquet. Duplexes have tiny staircases and cupboards below; some rooms show the building's beautiful beamy skeleton, some have little terraces; the new apartments over the street have tall windows, space and style. We love it – for its sense of history, eccentricities, aesthetic ironies, peaceful humour and feel of home; and for its unconventional attitudes and relaxed yet thoroughly efficient staff – so what matter that storage is limited? The lounge has chocolate brown sofas round a carved fireplace and Scoop the soft gold dog; breakfast is beneath the magnificent timbers by the surrealistic columns; work-out is in vaulted cellars. *Let Madame Prache know if your stay spans an anniversary.*

Price	€165-€335. Suites €545. Apartments €600-€900.
Rooms	30 + 2: 25 twins/doubles, 1 triple, 2 duplexes, 2 suites. 2 apartments for 4-6.
Meals	Breakfast €18. Room service on request.
Closed	Rarely.
Directions	Metro: Pont Marie (7), Cité (4), St Paul (1). RER: St Michel-Notre Dame. Buses: 67. Car Park: Pont Marie.

Elyane Prache & Nathalie Heckel
54 rue St Louis en l'Île,
75004 Paris

Tel	+33 (0)1 43 26 14 18
Fax	+33 (0)1 40 46 02 76
Email	info@jeudepaumehotel.com
Web	www.jeudepaumehotel.com

Hôtel Le Relais Saint Honoré

Unique, the rue Saint Honoré is a delight: once past the gardens of the Presidential Palace it becomes human-sized and unpasteurised, as it meanders along the Tuileries, crosses the Place Colette and then charges into an area of higgledy-piggledy streets and iconoclastic shops, some of which have been there forever. The Relais, once a brasserie frequented by Jean Cocteau, dates from 1650. After 17 months of careful renovation there are now 13 small but perfect rooms and two larger suites. No patching-over here: every detail has been overseen by Paul Bogaert, a knowledgeable and experienced hotelier. Some are invisible – the finest mattresses and softest fleece blankets enveloped in fine cotton – others less so. The beams, removed and stored for over a year, have been painted lapis lazuli blue, bamboo green or cranberry red to pick up nuances from exquisitely patterned fabrics on curtains and bedheads. The bathrooms have huge mirrors and heated towel rails; breakfast is classic French or with cereals. No ostentation, no frills, just pure comfort with a caring staff.

Price	€202. Suites €300–€340.
Rooms	15: 13 twins/double, 2 suites.
Meals	Breakfast €13.
Closed	Never.
Directions	Metro: Tuileries (1), Pyramides (7, 14). RER: Musée d'Orsay. Buses: 68, 72. Car park: Marché Saint Honoré.

Paul Bogaert
308 rue Saint Honoré,
75001 Paris

Tel	+33 (0)1 42 96 06 06
Fax	+33 (0)1 42 96 17 50
Email	relaissainthonore@wanadoo.fr
Web	www.relaissainthonore.com

Hôtel Relais Montmartre

There are good reasons why artists still live in this village, tucked in behind that giant marshmallow of a church, the Sacré Coeur. It could be the views over the rooftops of Paris, or the meandering little streets, or Montmartre's transformation at dusk as the day's façades become bistro, bar and club. It deserves much more than an afternoon visit so book into this new little jewel and the secrets of this 'rediscovered' neighbourhood will be revealed. Just up from *Amélie*'s celebrated café, tucked into a tiny side street, the entrance is discreet. Elegance and intimacy blend in the lobby with fireplace, antique desk and side table; the sofa, the large pouf, the period chairs and the curtains are an extraordinary mix of rich fabric; the small trellised patio set with sunny yellow garden furniture is the cherry on the cake. In the rooms, upholstered, deep-cushioned armchairs complement the quilted headboards and bedcovers in dreamy pastels or reds, pinks and greens, mixing and matching with care. The mattresses are dreamy, the staff are attentive; this is simple luxury at its best.

Price	€155–€195.
Rooms	26 doubles.
Meals	Breakfast €13.
Closed	Never.
Directions	Metro: Blanche (2), Place de Clichy (13, 2) Abbesses (12). RER: Gare du Nord. Buses: 30, 54, 80, 95. Car park: Private parking, enquire at hotel.

	Paul Bogaert
	6 rue Constance,
	75018 Paris
Tel	+33 (0)1 70 64 25 25
Fax	+33 (0)1 70 64 25 00
Email	contact@relaismontmartre.fr
Web	www.relaismontmartre.fr

HotelHome Paris 16

Ah, a flat in Paris – with a difference. Old style charm meets air conditioning and mod cons in this classic turn-of-the-century building. There's a family-like atmosphere, thanks to Laurence, alongside all the services you expect of a hotel; beds are made every day, linen and towels changed as you want, laundry machines are available and there's space to store your suitcase. The tiniest lift in Paris will get your bags up or down (and you follow) to the big rooms, each with a salon and a fabulous customised kitchenette. Charming are the marble fireplaces, antique ceramic radiators and moulded ceilings; modern are the ochre walls, bright carpets on parquet floors and armchairs in gay green and yellow plaid. Big family apartments on the top floor have two or three bedrooms; smaller ones on the ground floor have views on the garden. A glass roof runs across a narrow courtyard lush with ferns, green and black bamboo, acacia, jasmine and honeysuckle – perfect for leisurely breakfast or afternoon tea. Step out to genteel bustle and the shadow of the Eiffel Tower looming over you. A perfect Paris base.

Price	€175–€460.
Rooms	17 apartments: 5 for 2-3, 10 for 4, 2 for 6.
Meals	Breakfast €8. Baker next door.
Closed	Rarely.
Directions	Metro: Jasmin (9). RER Boulainvilliers. Bus: 22, 52. Car park: Some private parking, enquire at hotel.

Laurence Vivant
36 rue George Sand,
75116 Paris

Tel	+33 (0)1 45 20 61 38
Fax	+33 (0)1 40 50 90 77
Email	hotelhome@wanadoo.fr
Web	www.hotelhome.fr

Hôtel de Banville

Deliciously Parisian, as is the owner Marianne Moreau, the Banville has the elegance of inherited style and the punch of ultra-modern fittings (the sober stone corridors and cherry-red, brass-knobbed doors are fantastically numbered and lit from below ground). You feel welcomed into a private château where gilt-edged Old Masters supervise the gracious salon with its buffed grand piano (the owner sings on Tuesday nights). The designs are wondrous and fairy-lit. 'Marie', in subtle tones from palest eggshell to rich red loam, has a gauzily canopied bed, a delicious little terrace (Eiffel Tower view) and a brilliant bathroom with thick curtains for soft partitioning, 'Amélie' is sunnily feminine in pale yellow and soft ginger; the three 'Pastourelles' are freshly countrified in gingham and weathered blinds; 'Paul' above has a handsome slate bathroom. Other rooms, full of light, gentle colours and intimacy, have an airy touch, perfectly chosen modern and period furniture and fabulous bathrooms. Staff are delightful – hospitality could have been born here. *Chauffeur for airport pick-up & private tours.*

Price	€270–€310
Rooms	38: 37 twins/doubles, 1 suite.
Meals	Breakfast €18. Light meals €8–€20.
Closed	Never.
Directions	Metro: Porte de Champerret (3), Pereire (3). RER: Pereire. Buses: 92, 84, 93. Car Park: Rue de Courcelles.

Marianne Moreau
166 boulevard Berthier,
75017 Paris

Tel	+33 (0)1 42 67 70 16
Fax	+33 (0)1 44 40 42 77
Email	hotelbanville@wanadoo.fr
Web	www.hotelbanville.fr

Jardin de l'Odéon

When the cubists 'discovered' African art, revered were most things ethnic. Hence the marriage of tall ebony Egyptian scribes, an Ashanti statue and the reclining nude à la Picasso overlooking the clean lines of the Art Deco salon. The pleasant, airy lounge and breakfast area with its velvet striped chairs and bistro benches continue in the 30s feel. Just beyond, the tranquil sounds of a splashing fountain emerge from a jasmine planted terrace; bathed in morning sun, it will tempt you to prolong your breakfast moment. Renovations are recent: curtains and bedcovers mix and match handsome check and stripe fabric in reds, toffees and blues. Those at the back have views of the patio and birdsong, some have exquisite private terraces large enough for a table and chairs; those on the street glimpse the columns of the magically lit Odéon. Effervescent, smiley Sylvia places orchids in the salon and lights candles at night; she will see to it that you are well taken care of. All this on a quiet, tiny street leading down to the bustle of St Germain or up to the Jardins Luxembourg.

Price	€70–€225. Family €166–€450.
Rooms	41: 19 doubles, 17 twins, 1 single, 4 family rooms.
Meals	Breakfast €13.
Closed	Never.
Directions	Metro: Odeon (4,10) Luxembourg; RER: St Michel-Notre Dame. Buses: 21, 27, 38, 58, 63, 82, 84, 85, 86, 87, 89. Car park: École de Médecine.

Sylvia Harrault
7 rue Casimir Delavigne,
75006 Paris

Tel	+33 (0)1 53 10 28 50
Fax	+33 (0)1 43 25 28 12
Email	reservation@hoteljardinodeonparis.com
Web	www.hoteljardinodeonparis.com

The Five Hotel

Sensual, seductive and secret, the The Five Hotel has more than one ace up its sleeve. Holding a royal flush, Philippe Vaurs belongs to a new generation of adventurous hoteliers willing to go in new directions; a young international clientele will flip for this unpretentious yet hip homage to the five senses. The rooms are small, playful, more like love cocoons; reserve your choice of scent when booking! There are white duvets (de rigueur these days) on the best mattresses, a ribbon of colour draped across each; there may be splash of turquoise on a wall or a cornflower blue pattern on a sliding panel over a window. The low-key lacquered original art work is the inspiration, an integral part of the décor, not just an add-on. Pin-points of light (fibre optics) shower down from starry ceilings, delineate a glass table, or more surprisingly, shine like tiny diamonds embedded in tiled bathrooms. A fringed canopied bed in one room, a floating mattress in another and a suite with a jacuzzi on a terrace. Fun. A split of champagne is offered to our readers. *Five minutes from RER B: direct line CDG Airport.*

Price	€180–€320. Singles €150–€180. Suite €320–€420.
Rooms	19: 8 doubles, 5 twins, 5 singles, 1 suite for 1–4.
Meals	Breakfast €15. Lunch & dinner €20.
Closed	Never.
Directions	Metro: Les Gobelins, Censier Daubenton (7). RER: Port Royal. Buses: 21, 91. Car park: Marché des Patriaches

Monsieur Philippe Vaurs
3 rue Flatters,
75005 Paris

Tel	+33 (0)1 43 31 74 21
Fax	+33 (0)1 43 31 61 96
Email	contact@thefivehotel.com
Web	www.thefivehotel.com

Hôtel Relais Saint Sulpice

Almost on the back doorstep of the Saint Sulpice, tucked into one of those tiny magic streets untouched by the passage of time, this is the perfect hideaway for sleuthing around for clues for *The Da Vinci Code* or spotting the literati of Saint Germain des Près. You might almost miss the entrance if you are not careful; it's more an entryway into an aristocratic 18th-century home than a door to a hotel. The womb-like salon continues the lived-in feeling with screened mahogany bookcases, back-lit *objets* lining the top shelves, a pair of 1940s armchairs and a couple of large Chinese jars; a big gilt mirror sits in a corner to reflect light from the high windows. No reception desk to speak of here, just a friendly spirit behind a small desk to hand out the keys to your small but cosy room. The attention to detail is impressive – perhaps a fringe-like frieze along the top walls and door or an elegant wrought-iron bed and bistro table – while most bathrooms have little trompe l'oeil 'rugs' of colourful tiles under the basins. A glass roof and a bounty of greenery give a winter garden feel to breakfast.

Price	€175–€210. €245 for 3.
Rooms	26: 19 doubles, 7 twins. Extra beds.
Meals	Breakfast €12.
Closed	Never.
Directions	Metro: Odeon (4 and 10), Mabillon (10). RER: St Michel Notre-Dame, Luxembourg. Buses: 58, 70, 63, 86, 87, 96, 84. Car park: Place Saint Sulpice & Marché Saint-Germain.

Hélène Touber
3 rue Garancière,
75006 Paris

Tel	+33 (0)1 46 33 99 00
Fax	+33 (0)1 46 33 00 10
Email	relaisstsulpice@wanadoo.fr
Web	www.relais-saint-sulpice.com

Cazaudehore – La Forestière

The rose-strewn 'English' garden is like an island in the great forest of St Germain and it's hard to believe the buzzing metropolis is just a short train journey away. The first Cazaudehore built the restaurant in 1928, the second built the hotel in 1973, the third generation apply their imaginations to improving both and receiving their guests with elegant French charm. The buildings are camouflaged among the greenery, summer eating is deliciously shaded under rose-red parasols; hotel guests have the elegant, beamed dining room with its veranda to themselves (there are several seminar and reception rooms). Food and wine are the main focus – the wine tasting dinners are renowned and the chef's seasonal menus are a delight, skilfully mixing tradition and invention: you will eat supremely well here. Bedrooms have been well renovated in a refined but unostentatious style with good fabrics, original gentle colour schemes – saffron, blue and green, for example – period furniture and prints, and masses of character. The perfect treat for an occasion. *Winter jazz dinners.*

Price	€195-€210. Suites €250-€270.
Rooms	30; 13 doubles, 12 twins, 5 suites.
Meals	Breakfast €18.
	Lunch & dinner with wine, €55-€70.
	A la carte €85. Child €23.
	Restaurant closed Sun dinner & Mon,
	1 Nov-31 Mar.
Closed	Rarely.
Directions	A13 for Rouen exit 6 for St Germain
	en Laye on N186. N184 for Pontoise.
	Hotel on left 2.5km after château.

Philippe Cazaudehore
1 avenue Kennedy,
78100 Saint Germain en Laye, Yvelines

Tel	+33 (0)1 39 10 38 38
Fax	+33 (0)1 39 73 73 88
Email	cazaudehore@relaischateaux.com
Web	www.cazaudehore.fr

Pavillon Henri IV

The historic and artistic credentials are impeccable. Dumas, Offenbach and Georges Sand stayed here; the Sun King was born in a room off the entrance hall. There's a fascinating mix of styles, too – Renaissance domed roof, Art Nouveau porch – and materials – ivory limestone, rosy brick. As for the views, the panorama sweeps across the valley of the Seine to Paris and La Défense. Relish them from the rooms, the restaurant, the terrace: feel on top of the world. Since the hotel changed ownership some years ago the bedrooms have been undergoing a gradual and welcome transformation, from classic sobriety to luxurious charm, while reception rooms are big and beautiful – white walls, shining parquet and mellow rugs, gilded antiques, moulded cornices and marble busts, sumptuous chandeliers and striking flowers. The dining is unquestionably lavish, and should you wish to walk off your indulgence afterwards, a wrought-iron gateway allows you into the vast walled and terraced gardens of Château de St Germain en Laye next door. Supremely enjoyable, wonderfully French.

Price	€125–€210. Suites €280–€550.
Rooms	42: 30 twins/doubles, 12 singles.
Meals	Breakfast €15. Lunch €45 (not July/Aug). Dinner à la carte about €90. (Closed Sat lunch & Sun eve; also August & Christmas.)
Closed	Never.
Directions	A13 Paris-Rouen; exit St Germain en Laye on N186 to St Gerain 'centre' via Ave Général Leclerc. At r'bout, over to Ave Gambetta; right at end onto Rue Thiers. On left.

Charles Eric Hoffmann
19-21 rue Thiers,
78100 Saint Germain en Laye, Yvelines

Tel	+33 (0)1 39 10 15 15
Fax	+33 (0)1 39 73 93 73
Email	reservation@pavillonhenri4.fr
Web	www.pavillonhenri4.fr

Saint Laurent

Slow-paced medieval Monfort L'Amaury, 45 minutes from Paris, is home to some remarkable Renaissance stained-glass windows in the town church, 16th-century cobblestone paving, a Ravel festival in October and this superb private home built under Henry IV at the beginning of the 17th century. The renovation is recent and thorough – a lift, excellent soundproofing and in good taste: old rafters reign in some bedrooms, the exposed beamed ceiling in the breakfast room is splendid and skilful carpentry is evident in the light oak used in the panelling, headboards and cupboards that warm the pure white walls and simple elegant bedspreads. Ground floor rooms have private terraces looking out on the lawn where Madame Delabarre puts out fine summer chairs for relaxing under the huge linden trees. Each room bears the name of a tree or plant in the nearby Rambouillet forest, and a framed ode to the fern, beech or rhododendron has been created by an artist. There is a big accent on a full breakfast here which includes ham, eggs and cheese. A nice stop before heading for Paris or the airports.

Price	€88–€158. Suites €178
Rooms	18: 12 doubles, 3 twins, 3 suites.
Meals	Breakfast €11; €8 on weekends. Restaurants within walking distance.
Closed	1-22 August.
Directions	From Paris, A13, A12, N12 towards Dreux then Monfort L'Amaury. In Monfort, through gates for car park.

Madame Christiane Delabarre
2 place Lebreton,
78490 Monfort L'Amaury, Yvelines

Tel	+33 (0)1 34 57 06 66
Fax	+33 (0)1 34 86 12 27
Email	reception@hotelsaint-laurent.com
Web	www.hotelsaint-laurent.com

Hôtel de Londres

Gaze on the Château de Fontainebleau, one of France's loveliest buildings, from your room in this 18th-century hostelry that stands opposite. The hotel has been in the family for three generations; Monsieur Philippe runs it quietly and considerately, with occasional help from his brother. The sitting room has an 18th-century classical look; also rich colours, comfy armchairs, plump cushions, fine displays of flowers. The breakfast room has the feel of a small brasserie, and both rooms have views to Fontainebleau. Bedrooms, on the upper floors, are similarly classical in style – smart, spotless, traditional; colours are bold, fabrics floral. A sense of timelessness pervades this peaceful place, and you could hardly be better placed for exploring the Forest of Fontainebleau, the hunting grounds of kings. As for the château, it was built around the keep of a smaller medieval building, completed in 1550 and has been added to over the years; the gallery of François I is considered one of the finest in Europe. You can visit free on Sundays and it's magnificently floodlit at night.

Price	€110–€160. Suites €150–€180.
Rooms	15: 5 doubles, 1 single, 2 triples, 7 suites.
Meals	Breakfast €10.
Closed	23 December–9 January; 12–18 August.
Directions	A6 exit Fontainebleau for Château. Hotel opposite Château.

Philippe Colombier
1 place du Général de Gaulle,
77300 Fontainebleau, Seine-et-Marne

Tel	+33 (0)1 64 22 20 21
Fax	+33 (0)1 60 72 39 16
Email	hdelondres1850@aol.com
Web	www.hoteldelondres.com

Château de Bourron

Surrounded by perfectly clipped yew and box topinières, the early 17th-century château built on fortress foundations is hugely warm and inviting. Louis XV and his in-laws once met here; now it is owned by a charming young family. Inside is a feast of original Versailles parquet, oriental rugs and period pieces, exquisite fabrics and elegant tapestries. (Public rooms are reserved for receptions.) Pass the gold antique sedan chair, sentinel-like on the landing, and drift off to the east wing and guests' quarters. Rooms, in deep reds and golds, display pale marble bathrooms, gilt mirrors and Pierre Frey interiors: five-star stylishness in a château setting. On the first floor are a day room and a library, with panelled walls and shelves laden with leather-covered volumes. Outside, more treasures to uncover. The 80 acres of walled gardens and woodland are extraordinary... statues of Ceres and St Joseph, a chapel in one of two small pavilions, and the St Sévère spring supplying moat, canal and village wash house. Beyond lies the pretty village.

Price	€160–€300.
Rooms	4 twins/doubles.
Meals	Breakfast €15. Catering for receptions.
Closed	Rarely.
Directions	Paris-Lyon A6 exit Fontainebleau. At 'obelisk' r'bout for Nemours-Montargis on N7; 8km. Right for Villiers-sous-Grez, follow Bourron Marlotte Centre. Ring interphone at wooden gates in 2nd courtyard.

Comte & Comtesse Guy de Cordon
14 bis, rue du Maréchal Foch,
77780 Bourron Marlotte, Seine-et-Marne

Tel	+33 (0)1 64 78 39 39
Fax	+33 (0)1 64 78 35 35
Email	bourron@bourron.fr
Web	www.bourron.fr

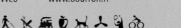

Château de Buno

The swathe of iron and limestone staircase is stunning, inviting you up to a suave and spacious sitting room on the landing – white leather sofa, black cushions, ethnic rug. Off here, remarkable bedrooms lie. There has always been a château on this romantic, riverside site – today's edifice has a rough-stone, medieval finish, plentiful shutters and a neo-Renaissance tower – but the inside could hardly present a more extreme contrast to the husk. The lines and curves come to us from the 1950s and the furnishings have been daringly re-dressed. Corinne, eager to please, fascinated by art and design, masterminds it all: the original lighting installations, the glowing vintage pieces, the immaculate and immaculately preserved bathrooms. All but one of the rooms is large, luminous and exudes class: a sweep of parquet topped by a vibrant Art Deco rug, a majestic Third Empire bed, a boudoir in the tower. Pastries and fresh fruits grace the breakfast trays, transported outside in summer, candlelit dinners are delivered to your suite, and the swans and the fish-stocked river float serenely by. *No credit cards.*

Price	€240-€270.
Rooms	5: 1 double, 4 suites.
Meals	Breakfast €15. Dinner, 4 courses, €40 (served in your room).
Closed	Rarely.
Directions	A6 Lyon, exit 13 onto D948. Milly la Foret 6.5km; D837 to Maisse; D449 at church to Gironville; 200m, left (in Petit-Gironville) to Buno Bonnevaux. On left, 400m after level crossing.

Corinne & Olivier Merciecca
Le Petit Gironville,
91720 Gironville sur Essonne, Essonne

Tel	+33 (0)1 64 99 35 25
Fax	+33 (0)1 64 99 35 25
Email	chateaudebuno@hotmail.com
Web	www.chateaudebuno.fr

Hostellerie du Prieuré

An immaculate, small French hotel in a beautiful medieval village, with bedrooms that are really quite something. Decorated with a flourish and a theme, from boudoir chic to Eastern exotica, all have have Middle Eastern carpets, gorgeous textiles, crisp sheets. There's purple-walled 'Aladdin' with an octagonal Syrian table and a silver hand basin and mirror in the bathroom, and lovely 'Coloniale' with a bamboo four-poster, Indochine prints and magnificent long views – down the village street all the way to Paris (25 kilometres) Bathrooms are worth a wallow, thanks to scented oils and fine soaps. Yves and Frédérique are a warmly professional couple and breakfast is worth getting up for, served in the creamy-walled Café de la Côte with its long velvet banquette and 1900s-style bar. The restaurant is a couple of houses away, exuberantly decorated and specialising in gourmet dishes (try the ravioli of double prawns with ginger butter). The wine list is as long as your arm and you have a choice of nine champagnes. All this luxury on the edge of fine forest; take the bikes and explore.

Price	€110–€180.
Rooms	8: 2 doubles, 1 twin, 4 suites, 1 family room.
Meals	Breakfast €12. Lunch €28–€42 (not Mondays). Dinner €28–€42 (not Sundays).
Closed	Never.
Directions	From Paris A15 for Cergy Pontoise, exit 115 dir. Taverny; exit St Leu La Forêt, St Prix on D139; 2nd street on right at r'bout; St Prix Village D144; left at light dir. Chauvry D193.

Frédérique & Yves Farouze
74 rue Auguste Rey,
95390 Saint Prix, Val-d'Oise

Tel	+33 (0)1 34 27 51 51
Fax	+33 (0)1 39 59 21 12
Email	contact@hostelduprieure.com
Web	www.hostelduprieure.com

Normandy

Le Manoir de Savigny

Walk around the grounds and you might catch deer nibbling on acorns or a coypu by the lily-covered lake. At the end of a poplar lined avenue, surrounded by meadows, it's hard to believe this handsome manor house is ten minutes from busy Valognes. Dating from the 16th century, it's part of an attractive group of farm buildings including an old cider press. The Bonnifets have kept original features – floor tiles, beamed ceilings, spiral stone staircase – blending them with strong colours and *objets* from their travels in Indonesia and Morocco. The result is a warm, relaxed, faintly exotic feel. Bedrooms are large and light-filled, with seagrass or rugs on stripped wood floors, pale plaster walls, striking beds – maybe brass or pretty wrought-iron – lacy bedcovers and a carefully chosen antique or two. Bathrooms are richly tiled, strikingly coloured, perhaps with a roll top or corner bath. Breakfast, in the sunny dining room with its vast fireplace, carved chairs and dark beams, is a generous spread. Well-placed for Cotentin's beaches, Bayeux, Cherbourg – or borrow bicycles and pack a picnic. *No credit cards.*

Price	€60–€100. Suite €135.
Rooms	5: 4 doubles, 1 suite for 5.
Meals	Breakfast included.
	Restaurants 1.5–3km.
Closed	Rarely.
Directions	From Cherbourg N13 exit Valognes to St Sauveur le Vicomte on D2. Then D24 for Le Gibet. 50m first left towards Savigny. 1km.

Corrine & Éric Bonnifet
50700 Valognes,
Manche

Tel	+33 (0)2 33 08 37 75
Email	reservation@manoir-de-savigny.com
Web	www.manoir-de-savigny.com

Château de Pont Rilly

The Roucherays' passion, talent, attention to detail and good dose of patience have wrought a miracle of beauty and harmony. They have only been here 25 years (ten of which were spent with workers in their midst) but when a cubic metre of archives from the 18th century turned up giving itemized details on colour, paintwork, fabric… there was only one choice. It helps to be a restorer like Jean-Jacques who mixes his own paints, and a decorator like Annick who creates the bedspreads, curtains and cushions. Breakfast is served in the old kitchen with its monumental fireplace and original spit mechanism. The beds in the rooms above sit on rare Marie Antoinette parquet, tall windows are draped in white voile; one overlooks the front moat, paddocks and long drive, and a stone staircase leads up to the suite. Bath tubs are panelled, basins are set in stone surrounds. There are trout and eel in the stream, donkeys, sheep and goats in the paddocks and Léonne, a friendly peacock, shows up for the welcome. *Minimum stay three days November-March.*

Price	€150. Cottages €650-€1,500 per week.
Rooms	4 + 2: 3 doubles, 1 suite for 3. 2 cottages, 1 for 4, 1 for 6-8.
Meals	Breakfast included. Restaurants 3km.
Closed	Rarely.
Directions	From Cherbourg RN13 south. At approach to Valonges exit 'Zone d'Armanville'. D62 towards Sottevast. 5km to château entrance on right.

Annick & Jean-Jacques Roucheray
50260 Négreville,
Manche

Tel	+33 (0)2 33 40 47 50
Email	chateau-pont-rilly@wanadoo.fr
Web	www.chateau-pont-rilly.com

Château de Saint Blaise

You will be staying in the coach house, not the château. Everything will be perfect, right down to the bathroom flowers. When Ernst bought the coach house a few years back nothing remained of the building but the walls. He rescued two staircases, one stone, one spiral, and a balustrade from another place; you would never know the old building had lapsed from grace. The Grande Suite is a rich shade of dark blue, with a Napoleon III bed and draped curtains; one tall window overlooks the courtyard, with its pond of pink lilies and fish, the other looks onto fields. The Petite Suite is in blue and beige, with the same views and a narrow but elegant bed. You are served breakfast in a small, pretty room, with flowers on the table. It can be as late as you like and the staff will be delighted to light the fire in winter. There is fresh orange juice, coffee or tea and the eggs just as you like them. Guests are welcome in the large grounds, the wonderful walled garden and the deep blue and burgundy salon with gleaming leather chesterfield and chairs. Such attention to detail, such peaceful luxury.

Price	€220-€250.
Rooms	Coach House: 2 suites.
Meals	Breakfast included, Restaurant 3km.
Closed	November-March.
Directions	N13 Cherbourg-Valognes, exit Bricquebec. D902 for 10km then right on route Les Gromonts. Château entrance 100m on left.

M Ernst Roost
50260 Bricquebec,
Manche

Tel	+33 (0)2 33 87 52 60
Fax	+33 (0)2 33 87 52 61
Email	info@chateaudesaintblaise.com
Web	www.chateaudesaintblaise.com

Hôtel des Ormes

A great little seaside hotel, facing the marina. The swoop up the gravel drive, past formal box hedges in tall terracotta pots, deposits you outside a pretty ivy-covered stone house with fabric awnings over the upstairs windows – very French, very traditional. Don't be fooled; the interiors are light, bright and dressed up in contemporary, natural hues; taupes, beiges and greys, with splashes of colour from striped and floral cushions or fresh flowers in a vase. The sitting room is perfect for chillier days, so bring a book, play a board game; coir matting is cosy and the sofas are deep. In summer, the garden is the perfect place to be, preferably on a ruby-red lounger overlooking the harbour and listening to the murmer of the sea. Food is taken seriously and you look out over its source; oysters, lobster, gambas – or order the plateau de mer and try everything. Puddings are divine, so you'll need a siesta in a quiet, creamy room with a gentle sea breeze. Special sea bass fishing weekends can be organised, or a day trip to Jersey with a salty old sea dog to guide you and a champagne picnic lunch stowed away.

Price	€73-€155.
Rooms	12: 10 doubles, 1 twin, 1 triple.
Meals	Breakfast €11. Lunch/dinner €35-€45. Dinner à la carte €11-€110. Half- & full-board options. Oct-May: restaurant closed Sun eve, Mon & Tues.
Closed	3 January-4 February.
Directions	From Cherbourg D900 towards Carteret, then D904 and D650 for 37km. Right on D130 for Ave de la Mer, right on Bd Martime for Promenade Barbey d'Aurevilly.

Flavia & José de Mello
Promenade Barbey d'Aurevilly,
50270 Barneville Carteret, Manche

Tel	+33 (0)2 33 52 23 50
Fax	+33 (0)2 33 52 91 65
Email	hoteldesormes@wanadoo.fr
Web	www.hoteldesormes.com

Hôtel Restaurant des Isles

Book early for José's fishing weekends when the tides run high, all equipment provided. Or take a half-day excursion in a horse-drawn cart along the coast to the market at Portbail to try the oysters; the horse will find the way home. Reserve a day trip to Jersey or Guernsey, a quad bike or a course in land yachting – the owners can organise special weekends in five languages. Flavia, who is Portugese, and José, who is Brazilian, are an international pair, full of ideas for a honeymoon couple or a group of friends. The whole hotel, facing due west and looking out to sea, has been completely refurbished and is squeaky clean, light and modern. There are seven rooms along one side of the property which have access to a long balcony overlooking a splendid outdoor heated pool and jacuzzi; each has a balcony, a table, two chairs and a parasol. Everything is white including the lime-washed parquet floors; interesting colours are added in a bed throw, a cushion, a lamp. Friendly staff and good value, from the generous breakfast to the choice of menus for lunch and dinner, ensure this a busy place.

Price	€69–€119.
Rooms	30: 21 doubles, 4 twins, 1 triple, 4 family rooms.
Meals	Breakfast €10. Half- & full-board options. Dinner €16–€35.
Closed	Rarely.
Directions	From Cherbourg D900 towards Carteret, then D904 and D650 for 37km. Right on D130 for Ave de la Mer, right on Blvd Martime.

Flavia & José de Mello
9 Boulevard Maritime,
50270 Barneville Carteret, Manche

Tel	+33 (0)2 33 04 90 76
Fax	+33 (0)2 33 94 53 83
Email	hotel-des-isles@wanadoo.fr
Web	www.hoteldesisles.com

Le Castel

A classical Napoleon III château– deep in Normandy countryside, large but not palatial, grand but not ornate. The Parisian socialite, who built this 19th-century mansion for his lover, chose well. Tucked in two hectares of park and garden with views of rolling meadows, it's private but not isolated – 15 minutes to Mont Martin, beaches and Coutances, an hour to Mont Saint Michel and the Bayeux Tapestry. Nick and Jon create a house-party atmosphere which you can join or not as you choose. There's plenty of space: two salons are scattered with French and oriental furniture, while a white baby grand creates a striking note. French windows open to the terrace and garden. Eat here or with other guests amongst cut-glass and candlesticks in the dining room. The menu might include roast duck with raspberries, pears in red wine and local cheeses. Bedrooms are classic country house: striped or silk wallpaper, polished French beds, perhaps an escritoire or a marble washstand. Treat as a relaxing stopover near channel ports, or stay and chat to the new pet llamas.

Price	€110-€150.
Rooms	6 + 1: 4 doubles, 1 twin, 1 family suite for 3-4. Cottage for 2.
Meals	Breakfast included. Hosted dinner €38. Book ahead.
Closed	Never.
Directions	From Montpinchon, D102 to Pavage. Right at junction, immediately left onto D252. Le Castel 2 minutes on left; entry at the second white gate.

Nicholas Hobbs & Jon Barnsley
50210 Montpinchon,
Manche

Tel   +33 (0)2 33 17 00 45
Email   enquiries@le-castel-normandy.com
Web   www.le-castel-normandy.com

La Verte Campagne

Profoundly rural, surrounded by pastures and orchards, fronted by roses and clematis, is this very old (1702) auberge. From time to time, celebrities and politicians would escape here to relish the food and the deep peace. André is maître d'hôtel, while Lynne is an excellent chef, responsible for the restaurant and fresh-from-the-oven pastries for breakfast. En suite bedrooms are comfortable and there are a clutch of 1960s collectors-item bathrooms that are all of a colour: one blue, one pink; the rest are plain white. The sitting room is cosy, with tapestry wall hangings, pictures from the area and a monumental stone fireplace with a wood-burning stove, off here, a tartan walled, low-ceilinged bar and a tempting selection of fine whiskies. Oriental rugs add a stylish touch. The restaurant is romantic with another great stone fireplace and a log fire; specialities include preserved duck with honey, fresh fish from Granville and lamb from nearby Mont St Michel. Most come to eat well, make merry and tuck into bed! A real country auberge.

Price	€50–€78. Half-board €58–€65 p.p.
Rooms	7; 4 doubles, 1 twin, 1 triple, 1 single.
Meals	Breakfast €7. Lunch €13.50–€45. Dinner €24–€45. Picnic lunches €0.50. Restaurant closed Wednesday.
Closed	1–15 December.
Directions	From Caen, A84 dir. Rennes, exit 37, 6km to Gavray. A7 junc. right, dir. Coutances on D7 for 9km, D49 dir. Montmartin sur Mer to Trelly, signed from village.

	André & Lynne Tamba
	Le Hameau Chevalier,
	50660 Trelly, Manche
Tel	+33 (0)2 33 47 65 33
Fax	+33 (0)2 33 47 38 03
Email	lavertecampagne@wanadoo.fr
Web	www.lavertecampagne.com

Le Manoir de l'Acherie

A very short way from the motorway this hotel, deep in the Norman countryside, is a lovely, ever-so-French discovery: an old granite house with immaculately tended gardens and an ancient granite cider press sunk into the lawn brimming over with red roses. At one side is a chapel, now bedrooms; on the other is an extension providing a sort of *cour d'honneur* entrance. Some of the furniture is authentically old though most is solid quality repro in the 'rustic' Norman style; rooms are carpeted, bed covers are patterned, curtains are frilly. Mother and daughter Cécile handle the hotel and restaurant service, father and son run the kitchen – they have won several prizes for their culinary efforts. The tables are dressed in prim, cream tablecloths. Dark wooden beams, well worn floor tiles and a giant stone fireplace create a pleasant, cosy feel. The small number of people running this establishment and the quiet unstressed, unhurried but efficient way they do so, is admirable. The only concession one must make is to arrive before 7pm; last orders in the restaurant are at 8.30pm.

Price	€50–€110. Singles €42. Half-board €65–€95 p.p.
Rooms	19: 9 doubles, 4 twins, 2 singles, 4 suites.
Meals	Breakfast €8. Lunch & dinner €17–€40. Children's meals €10. Restaurant closed Mon, Sept–June; Sun eve mid-Oct to week before Easter.
Closed	Two weeks in November & February.
Directions	A84 exit 38 Brecey-Villedieu for Vire. Over 2nd r'bout for 2km; over main road with Président dairy opp.

Stéfhane & Cécile Poignarant
Sainte Cecile,
50800 Villedieu les Poêles, Manche

Tel +33 (0)2 33 51 13 87
Fax +33 (0)2 33 51 33 69
Email manoir@manoir-acherie.fr
Web www.manoir-acherie.fr

Les Hauts

General Eisenhower slept here and took the bed with him! It was returned, however, as you will return to this informal house, with its ornate Art Deco reception rooms and unusual interior design. Everyone is taken with the spot: perched in a beautiful garden of three hectares above the sea, with exceptional views to Mont Saint Michel. Madame Leroy is warm, bubbly, as theatrical as her house. The bedrooms range from a canopied four-poster and Art Deco frieze to a delicately pretty pale pink double with blue-green paintwork, or the new Napoleon suite in fuchsia pinks and purple. Bathrooms have their original 19th-century porcelain fittings. The beach, 100m away, is pebbled but others are just a short drive. Breakfast might keep you going until supper: a buffet of proper French food, it includes charcuterie, cheese, five different breads, 12 different jams and homemade cake. Outside, find a steep terrace exuberant with magnolias, rhododendrons, azaleas, camellias, canna lilies and those misty views. Travel across the bay at low tide – to Mont Saint Michel – by foot, on horseback, or with a guide.

Price	€95–€180.
Rooms	8: 5 doubles, 2 twins, 1 suite for 4.
Meals	Breakfast included.
	Dinner €38 with wine, book ahead.
	Restaurants 5 minute walk.
Closed	Rarely.
Directions	From Cherbourg, N13 to Valognes; D2 to Coutances; D971 to Granville; D911 (along coast) to Jullouville; on to Carolles & St Jean Le Thomas (6.5km from Jullouville).

André & Suzanne Leroy
7 avenue de la Libération,
50530 Manche

Tel   +33 (0)2 33 60 10 02
Email   contact@chateau-les-hauts.com
Web   www.chateau-les-hauts.com

La Ramade

La Ramade, half a century old, was built in golden granite by a livestock merchant who made his fortune. Véronique took it on in 2001 and transformed it from B&B into charming hotel, fulfilling a long-held dream. Her individual interiors are a pleasing mix of modern and brocante finds – with Veronique's own Breton cradle sweetly displayed on the second floor. Bedrooms feel feminine and are named after flowers. Blue-carpeted Laurier has white-painted furniture and steps to a bathroom with a sunken bath, Coquelicot has a poppy theme and matching yellow curtains and towels. Pretty Eglantine has a canopied bed and afternoon sun streaming through large windows, Amaryllis – tailor-made for wheelchairs – a superb hydromassage shower. The grounds are filled with mature trees that give privacy from the road, and you are near Mont St Michel and the sea – a great spot for children who will love the guided tour across the great bay at low tide. Véronique now has added a lovely glassed-in veranda for breakfast or dining and a bar for samplings of the local pommeau – or a calvados before tucking into bed.

Price	€68-€115.
Rooms	11: 4 doubles, 3 twins, 1 suite, 3 family rooms for 3-4.
Meals	Breakfast €10. Light supper €15 off-season, book ahead. Crêperie within walking distance; many restaurants in Avranches.
Closed	January-6 February; 20-30 November.
Directions	From Avranches D973 for Granville; over river, then left on D911 for Jullouville; immediately on right.

Véronique Morvan Gilbert
2 rue de la Côte, Marcey les Grèves,
50300 Avranches, Manche

Tel	+33 (0)2 33 58 27 40
Fax	+33 (0)2 33 58 29 30
Email	hotel@laramade.fr
Web	www.laramade.fr

Château de Boucéel

The embroidered linen sheets enfold you in a smooth embrace that is a metaphor for the Boucéel experience. The Count's family have lived in the listed château since it was built in 1763 but he and the Countess have worked in Paris and Chicago and theirs is an elegant, unstuffy lifestyle which you are welcome to join. He, a quietly simple aristocrat, will recount fascinating details from his family history while she, energetic and communicative, prepares a succulent apple cake for your breakfast. The delightful bedrooms, named and portraited for the uncles and grandmothers who slept there, are beautifully done in just the right dusty yellows and misty greys for the original panelling, and have superb parquet floors, antiques and personal touches. And if you meet the kindly lady ghost, be properly polite to her, she's a marquise. Breakfast, on fine china, is in the soft green, round, panelled and mirrored dining room with French windows to the lush park, which comes complete with grazing geese, lake and ancient chapel. It's a treat to stay in this gently grand and gracious château.

Price	€135–€165.
Rooms	5: 2 doubles, 3 suites.
Meals	Breakfast included. Restaurant 6km.
Closed	January.
Directions	From Avranches for Mont St Michel exit 34; N175 exit D40 St Michel/Antrain; left for Antrain, 6km on D40; left D308 for St Senier de Beuvron: château entrance 800m.

Comte & Comtesse Régis
de Roquefeuil-Cahuzac
50240 Vergoncey, Manche

Tel	+33 (0)2 33 48 34 61
Fax	+33 (0)2 33 48 16 26
Email	chateaudebouceel@wanadoo.fr
Web	www.chateaudebouceel.com

Château de Colombières

When the marshes were tidal, the château was an island fortress. Towers, turrets, 2.8m-thick walls, arrow slits, arches, moat: history jumps out at you. A long curving drive, a breathtaking first view, a bridge to a courtyard and there is Monsieur — charming, witty, dapper. The château has been in his wife's family for 300 years and he knows every inch by heart. Enter the grand 18th-century dining room, where breakfasts are served at a table under the gaze of an ancestress, rescuer of Colombières after the Revolution. The suites are three centuries older. One is reached via a rare circular elm-tread stair; its salon, vast, carpeted and inviting, has a monumental stone fireplace and a red and cream striped sofa; duck through the stone archway to the bedroom in the tower with the floral balaquined bed. The Louis XVI room is as lofty, as sumptuous, its fabrics pink, bold and coordinated, its bathroom with new green tiles and medieval tomettes. Garden arbours are equipped with chairs… wander at will, fish in the moat. It is a privilege to stay here — with Monsieur *tout compris*!

Price	€130–€180.
Rooms	3: 1 double, 1 suite for 2, 1 suite for 4.
Meals	Breakfast €10. Child breakfast €5. Restaurant 10km.
Closed	15 November–15 March.
Directions	From Bayeux D5 to Colombières, right on D29, left on D29A. Signed.

Etienne de Maupeou d'Ableiges
14710 Colombières, Calvados

Tel	+33 (0)2 31 22 51 65
Fax	+33 (0)2 31 92 24 92
Email	colombieresaccueil@tiscali.fr
Web	www.chateaudecolombieres.com

Manoir de Mathan

A perfect size is this elegant manor house, introduced by a lovely crunching sound on the gravelled driveway and a 17th-century baroque arch. Finding this sober elegance in a typical Bessin farm, with its large courtyard and outbuildings, makes you wonder if all the farmers around here weren't aristocrats. Stay awhile and relax in the lounging chairs on the lawned grounds under the branches of mature trees. It's evident that the renovation was done with much loving thought and care; revealed and enhanced are the lovely beams and timbers, exposed stone walls, original fireplaces and spiral staircase. The large bedrooms were given proper space and light, bathrooms well integrated; it is classy but never overdone. The beds are big, the furniture regional but light and well-chosen, the windows large with over-the-field views. Some suites have canopied beds; some rooms are on the ground floor for easy access. Meals are a ten-minute stroll to the sister hotel up the road (La Rançonnière). Perfectly placed for Bayeux *and* near the landing beaches: you'll need two or three days to enjoy it all.

Price	€120–€160. Suites €165–€190.
Rooms	20: 13 doubles, 7 suites.
Meals	Breakfast €11. Lunch & dinner at Ferme de la Rançonnière, €9–€43.
Closed	Rarely.
Directions	From Caen exit 7 to Creully on D22 for 19km. Right at church for Arromanches on D65. 1st on right.

Vereecke & Sileghem families
14480 Crépon, Calvados
Tel   +33 (0)2 31 22 21 73
Fax   +33 (0)2 31 22 98 39
Email   ranconniere@wanadoo.fr
Web   www.ranconniere.com

Ferme de la Rançonnière

A drive through the narrow crenellated archway into the vast grassy courtyard and history leaps out and grabs you. It was originally a fortified seigneurie – the tower dates from the 13th century – to protect against English reprisal sorties after William the Conqueror arrived in England. Inside are exposed timbers and stone walls. One amazing family suite has stone steps which lead down into a double bedroom then up a spiral staircase to a children's bedroom in a tower with tiny glazed windows. Rustic is the look; a butter churn in the corridor, large carved armoires and a well-worn kneading trough in a large family room remind you that this was a working farm. Off the main restaurant is a large, vaulted, stone-flagged sitting area with a log fire at one end making a perfect spot for after-dinner coffee. The bright breakfast room and terrace face south to catch the morning light. Young, efficient Isabelle Sileghem and her husband, with help from a devoted staff, keep this place humming. Book ahead for the best rooms. Entirely wonderful.

Price	€55–€150. Suites €160–€180.
Rooms	47: 37 twins/doubles/triples. Manoir: 10 suites.
Meals	Breakfast €11. Lunch €22. Dinner €48. Restaurant closed 3-25 January.
Closed	Rarely.
Directions	From Caen exit 7 to Creully on D22 for 19km. There, right at church for Arromanches on D65. In Crépon, hotel 1st on right.

Vereecke & Sileghem Families
Route d'Arromanches,
14480 Crépon, Calvados

Tel	+33 (0)2 31 22 21 73
Fax	+33 (0)2 31 22 98 39
Email	ranconniere@wanadoo.fr
Web	www.ranconniere.com

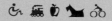

La Petite Folie

Fabulously situated for exploring Honfleur, these two townhouses double as havens from the artistic bustle. Most likely built for a sea captain in the 1830s, the commanding main one displays a façade heavily shuttered with grand mansarde windows. Its more modest but older neighbour is a gorgeous 14th-century home, containing two apartments (with kitchenettes) that extend beneath a canopy of beams from street to garden side. American born Penny married Frenchman Thierry and they set out tailoring bedrooms lavishly and beautifully, each an enchanting mix of handsome bedsteads, plump duvets, lacquered armchairs, mahogany chests of drawers and whirls of different tones, even a touch of theatrical black-lace print wallpaper in one. The ground-floor sitting room, as wide as the house, offers red suede sofas at one end and a leather chesterfield at the other. The garden is a compact, neatly planted square of charm, its focal point a summerhouse with a Byzantine flourish and belvedere views out to sea. All this, and a delightful hostess. *No credit cards.*

Price	€130–€155. Apartments €160.
Rooms	5 + 2 : 4 doubles, 1 twin (extra bed available). 2 apartments: 1 for 2, 1 for 2–4
Meals	Breakfast included. Book breakfast ahead for apartments. Restaurants within walking distance.
Closed	January.
Directions	A13 exit Beuzeville; A29 exit Honfleur. Signs for 'centre' & 'jardin public'. Rue Haute parallel to Blvd Charles V.

Penny & Thierry Vincent
44 rue Haute,
14600 Honfleur, Calvados

Tel	+33 (0)6 74 39 46 46 (mobile)
Email	info@lapetitefolie-honfleur.com
Web	www.lapetitefolie-honfleur.com

Hôtel Maison de Lucie

Named after Lucie Delarue Mardrus, the romantic novelist and poet who was born here, the 1850 house in the heart of Honfleur is shielded by a high wall. Sunshine illuminates panelled walls and leather sofas, the parquet'd salon has an Edwardian air, and bedrooms, elegantly colour-themed, now expand into an adjoining house, those on the second floor overlooking the estuary. Furnishings are immaculate – plum taffeta, burgundy velvet – new beds are big and reading lamps won't ruin your eyes. Bathrooms are awash with potions and lotions, there are fresh orchids and vivid rugs, roll top baths and antique chests of drawers. And wide views over rooftops and away to the sea. Our favourite room rests under the eaves, but all are lovely. In the courtyard, the old caretaker's house is now a suite, its ground-floor sitting area furnished in a deliciously decadent 1930s manner; another room has a small new terraced courtyard area. Soak away your cares in the brick-walled jacuzzi and take your time over a breakfast of bacon, eggs and cheese – either in bed or in the sun. A charming couple, a warm welcome.

Price	€150–€220. Suites €315.
Rooms	12: 10 doubles, 2 suites.
Meals	Breakfast €18. Restaurants accessible by foot, 120m.
Closed	25 November-20 December, 7-18 January.
Directions	Five minutes from A13, signed from Église Sainte Cathérine.

Nadim Haddad & Muriel Daridon
44 rue Capucins,
14600 Honfleur, Calvados

Tel	+33 (0)2 31 14 40 40
Fax	+33 (0)2 31 14 40 41
Email	info@lamaisondelucie.com
Web	www.lamaisondelucie.com

Hostellerie de Tourgéville

There were real stars in the 70s, when film director Claude Lelouch built his glorified 'Norman quadrangle' as a club for friends; now there are just giant photographs. But his adorable private cinema is still here, as are pool, gym and sauna. Timbers and stones are genuinely old; the all glass ground floor is thoroughly modern. Open plan sitting and dining areas are in blond oak, soft cushions and warm colours. Most rooms are soberly decorated with high-quality fabrics, matt satin curtains, beige carpet, the odd antique and those ubiquitous film stars. Ground-floor rooms and triplexes (effectively up ended suites with the bathroom on a balcony between salon and bedroom) have small private terraces. Triplexes also have fine double-height fireplaces on their stone-flagged floors, plus two deep sofas. A dream of a mini Tudor manoir hides away in the forest, perfect for a honeymoon couple, and the chef has an excellent reputation. A very special place to stay: in Lelouch's words, "a hotel for people who don't like hotels".
Minimum stay two nights May–August.

Price	€125–€175. Duplex €190–€240. Triplex €270–€330. Cottage €280–€340.
Rooms	26: 6 doubles, 13 duplex & 6 triplex apartments, 1 cottage for 2–4 (without kitchen)
Meals	Breakfast €16. Dinner €39–€56.
Closed	17 February–11 March.
Directions	A13 exit for Deauville N177; left at r'bout D27; 1st left; 1st left D278.

Wilhelm Stoppacher
Chemin de l'Orgueil,
14800 Tourgéville Deauville, Calvados

Tel	+33 (0)2 31 14 48 68
Fax	+33 (0)2 31 14 48 69
Email	reservation@hostellerie-de-tourgeville.fr
Web	www.hostellerie-de-tourgeville.com

Château Les Bruyères

Marcel Proust was indulged here when he visited the spa in Cabourg; he'd be pampered still. Through the imposing gates, down the beech and chestnut avenue, past the manicured lawns... expectations rise as you approach and are met on arrival. Monsieur is chef de cuisine, madame keeps thoroughbreds, their daughter spoils you with massages and essential oils and the family has an obvious predeliction for beautiful things. Château les Bruyèrres is a houseful of treasures and chinoiserie. Orchids on the dining table, modern art on the walls, plush red-carpeted corridors and fine repro furniture; it is very civilised. In the salon are big rugs on black and white tiles, a flurry of small armchairs and settees, a large open fire and glazed cabinets full of fine china. Ten tickety-boo bedrooms await in the 19th-century château and a further four in the 18th-century slate-hung manor that adjoins it; all ooze luxury and calm. Outside are several acres of parkland in which hides a turquoise pool. *Gastronomic & pampering weekends.*

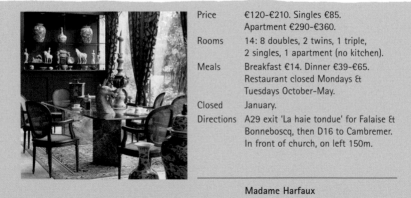

Price	€120–€210. Singles €85. Apartment €290–€360.
Rooms	14: 8 doubles, 2 twins, 1 triple, 2 singles, 1 apartment (no kitchen).
Meals	Breakfast €14. Dinner €39–€65. Restaurant closed Mondays & Tuesdays October-May.
Closed	January.
Directions	A29 exit 'La haie tondue' for Falaise & Bonneboscq, then D16 to Cambremer. In front of church, on left 150m.

Madame Harfaux
Route du Cadran,
14340 Cambremer, Calvados

Tel	+33 (0)2 31 32 22 45
Fax	+33 (0)2 31 32 22 58
Email	contact@chateaulesbruyeres.com
Web	www.chateaulesbruyeres.com

Château du Mesnil d'O

The approach to this 18th-century chateau lifts the spirit. Stone pillars and tall iron gates mark the entrance from the road, a tree-lined avenue set in five hectares of garden and parkland leads to the front door. The four bedrooms, one with listed wallpaper from 1905, are on the first floor up a beautiful staircase in white stone from Caen, the wrought-iron handrail and balustrade are listed. A square landing at the top with a long view over the park is a perfect place to spread your newspaper on a lovely old dining table; bookshelves burst with literature and line the length of one wall. Family portraits abound in the corridor along with the odd antique; fresh flowers are lovingly placed in the bedrooms and on the landings. Breakfast in the dining room is a feast for the eye: blue velvet chairs, chevron parquet floor, panelled walls with painted scenes above the doors and a wonderful Louis XVI buffet displaying its collection of old plates. One might feel overawed by such splendour, but the warm welcome of Monsieur Chanbaneix makes the visitor feel instantly at home. You will be loath to leave. *No credit cards.*

Price	€110.
Rooms	4: 3 doubles, 1 suite for 4.
Meals	Breakfast included. Restaurants within 5km.
Closed	Rarely.
Directions	From Caen N13 to Paris. In Vimont, right on D47 then D40 towards St Pierre sur Dives 7km; on right.

	Guy de Chanbaneix 14270 Vieux Fumé, Calvados
Tel	+33 (0)2 31 20 01 47
Fax	+33 (0)2 31 20 32 87
Email	lemesnildo@wanadoo.fr
Web	www.lemesnildo.com

Château La Cour

Warm and charming hosts, David and Lesley's attention to detail is impressive. Not everyone can take a 13th-century château, once part of the estate of the Ducs of Harcourt, and so successfully blend history with comfort. Expect a bold décor — striped yellow wallpaper with pink and blue curtains — and a subdued luxury: Lloyd Loom chairs, marble fireplaces, Egyptian cotton. One room has a curved wooden staircase that leads to a superb bathroom above. A house for feasting, too: fine English china, damask and candelabra set the table in the charming dining room. David grows for Lesley to cook, and his organic potager (three varieties of potato, 50 of vegetable) is a delightful diversion. High stone walls shelter it from unkind winds, fruit trees shade the lawn, and long narrow beds make for easy harvesting. Lovely traditional bedrooms face south and look over the garden; the apartment is stunning. The Cravens are keen conservationists; barn owls nest in the end wall of the house and there is good birdwatching. The Normandy beaches, Bayeux and its tapestry are within easy reach. *No credit cards.*

Price	€140–€150.
	Apartment €750 per week.
Rooms	4 + 1: 3 doubles, 1 twin.
	Apartment for 2.
Meals	Breakfast included. Hosted dinner with
	wine €35–€50, book ahead.
Closed	Rarely.
Directions	D562 south from Thury Harcourt for
	5km; right onto D133 for Culey le Patry;
	left onto D166; 2nd right onto D211.
	Château on right approaching village.

David & Lesley Craven
14220 Culey le Patry,
Calvados

Tel	+33 (0)2 31 79 19 37
Fax	+33 (0)2 31 79 19 37
Email	info@chateaulacour.com
Web	www.chateaulacour.com

Bois Joli

You are bang in the middle of pretty, fashionable Bagnoles de L'Orne, the only spa town in the area and with waters that flow at 24 degrees; boating lake, casino and spa remain. Bois Joli was a pension built in the mid-1800s for those seeking the cure; it sits on the edge of the Fôret d'Andaine in an acre of lawn, shrubs and sequoias. It has always been a smart getaway – Pompidou and Rommel stayed here; Rommel never paid for his room. Décor is traditional, understated, elegant. In the salon: comfortable chairs, books, newspapers, flowers in pewter vases and a piano you may play; in the dining room, fine rush-seated chairs and stiff white napery. The food is good: homemade brioche and orange pressé for breakfast; oysters, magret de pigeon and apricot tart for dinner. Slip off your shoes in a carpeted bedroom, immaculate with matching wallpaper and bedcover in toile de Jouy or pale flower. Old country wardrobes add character; staff are discreet. The hotel arranges mushroom-picking weekends in the woods, and there's masses to do in town: golf, cycling, riding, swimming, tennis.

Price	€72–€152.
Rooms	20 twins/doubles.
Meals	Breakfast €11.
	Lunch & dinner €20–€50.
Closed	Never
Directions	From Argentan, D916 for Mayenne, follow signs for Bagnoles Lac. Signed.

Yvette & Daniel Mariette
12 avenue Philippe du Rozier,
61140 Bagnoles de L'Orne, Orne

Tel	+33 (0)2 33 37 92 77
Fax	+33 (0)2 33 37 07 56
Email	boisjoli@wanadoo.fr
Web	www.hotelboisjoli.com

Auberge de la Source

Using reclaimed beams and stone, Christine and Serge built the auberge on the site of his parents' 18th-century apple press. Unfortunately that means no more cider, but they serve a superb one made just down the road. Both the restaurants – one smaller and cosier, the other with huge sliding windows – and the bedrooms were designed to make the most of the view down to the lake, which is the hub of a huge sports complex. Apart from windsurfing and a sailing school, there's riding, a climbing wall, archery, fishing and something called 'swing-golf', easy to learn, apparently. Children have a play area, pony rides, mini-golf and pedal boats. If you want real nature the forest is nearby where you will see huge stags without too much searching. The auberge has big rooms catering for families, all with huge beams and chunky antiques mixed in with more modern furniture. The food is simple, centring on steaks cooked over a wood fire, and fresh farm produce to go with them. A sensible choice for families with small children – or sporty teenagers. *This is a farming family, please book ahead for dinner.*

Price	€54–€90.
Rooms	5: 1 double, 4 family rooms.
Meals	Breakfast included. Picnic €10. Lunch & dinner from €14. Book ahead.
Closed	Rarely.
Directions	From La Ferté Macé, D908 for Domfront Mont St Michel. After 2km right to auberge. Signed.

Christine & Serge Volclair
La Peleras,
61600 La Ferté Macé, Orne
Tel   +33 (0)2 33 37 28 23
Fax   +33 (0)2 33 38 78 83
Email   source@orange.fr
Web   perso.orange.fr/auberge.lasource

Le Pavillon de Gouffern

More mansion than lodge, Gouffern was built 200 years ago by a wealthy gentleman
with plenty of fellow hunters to entertain. But the scale of this elegant 'pavilion' is
perfect for today's traveller. It stands in an estate of 80 hectares and guests can walk,
cycle or ride in the private forest in peace and seclusion. Big windows let in lots of soft
light to illuminate the newly renovated décor: hunting themes, an Edwardian salon with
leather chairs and oak floors, an unfussy elegance that gives a sense of the quiet class of
a good country house. Recently renovated bedrooms, some of them in the well
converted outbuildings, are big and eminently comfortable (smaller on the top floor),
new bathrooms have all the necessary bits and meals are served in the handsome dining
room – the food has been much praised. In the grounds, the delightful Doll's House,
built for children of another age, is now an idyllic suite (honeymoon specials
arranged)… and you may play billiards by the fire in the bar. A nearby stable delivers
horses to the door and, if you are lucky, the chef will cook your freshly caught trout.

Price	€80–€200. Cottage €250.
Rooms	20 + 1: 19 doubles, 1 single.
	Cottage for 2-4.
Meals	Breakfast €10. Picnic available.
	Lunch & dinner €25–€50.
Closed	24-25 December.
Directions	Exit Argentan on N26. Hotel 7km from
	Argentan in the forest of Silly en
	Gouffern. Signed.

Karelle Jouaux & Vincent Thomas
61310 Silly en Gouffern,
Orne

Tel   +33 (0)2 33 36 64 26
Fax   +33 (0)2 33 36 53 81
Email   pavillondegouffern@wanadoo.fr
Web   www.pavillondegouffern.com

Moulin de Villeray

Emerging through a beguiling creeper-covered entrance, the scale of this grand old 16th-century mill in pleasant riverside grounds is unexpected and thrilling. The big paddle wheel sits behind a huge arched window in a dining room that trumpets excellent food and unlimited French wines – the pride of Christian. Naturally there are beams galore, all stripped to natural tones to form a union with soft furnishings; in the sitting rooms, age-old satin flagstones with hues of brown, fawn and mushroom; in cosy, wood-clad bedrooms, beds dressed in checks, florals and plain natural tones. Under weathered old terracotta runs a storey of roof windows each providing plunging river views; ground-floor areas are an evocative mix of beam and old exposed stone. A cavernous bread oven converted into an open fireplace is the epitome of rusticity at its warmest and a fine symbol of this family's welcome and dedication. Enjoy the informality from beneath colourful umbrellas on the large terrace, or from the lawns that run all along the banks of the river. The village is untouched, the countryside magical.

Price	€90-€170. Suites €160-€250.
Rooms	26: 12 twins, 7 doubles, 3 suites, 4 suites for 3-4 (6 rooms in village house next to Moulin).
Meals	Breakfast €15. Lunch €28-€69. Dinner €36-€69.
Closed	November-Easter. Open for groups and at the New Year.
Directions	From Chartres on N23 dir. Nogent Le Rotrou. 14 km after Montlandon, right on D203 to Condé Sur Huisne; D10 dir. Remalard for 3km, left to Villeray. Le Moulin at bottom of hill on right.

Monsieur Christian Eelsen
Villeray,
61110 Condeau, Orne

Tel	+33 (0)2 33 73 30 22
Fax	+33 (0)2 33 73 38 28
Email	moulin.de.villeray@wanadoo.fr
Web	www.domainedevilleray.com

Château de Villeray

Magnificently perched to command acres of parkland, this Renaissance château — with its full complement of pepperpot towers, noble windows, terrace, belvederes and old moat — could scarcely be more French. The deep country quiet is extraordinary. For a place that has seen many of the highs and lows of French history, it invites you quite informally into oak-panelled reception rooms: to one side a comfortable sitting room with open log fire, to the front, a splendid stone and marble staircase lit by windows trimmed with stained glass. Another endearing touch is the frivolously pretty ceiling light in the very grand restaurant; you may expect an agreeable mix of attentive service, haute cuisine and Christian's superb 'directoire' of French wines. Bedrooms spread in all shapes and sizes over the first two floors, united by a sense of easy elegance. Soft furnishings set neutral tones for antiques: Art Deco armchairs, polished boards interspersed with oriental carpets, the odd four-poster. Most bathrooms sport white tiles hand painted with Muriel's own natural designs, one of many welcoming family touches.

Price	€90–€290. Suites €170–€390.	
Rooms	13: 9 doubles, 4 suites for 2	
Meals	Breakfast €15. Lunch & dinner €28–€69. Half-board mandatory €47 €70 p.p. supp. May to mid-Sept. Restaurant closed Nov-Easter; meals can be taken at the Moulin.	
Closed	November-Easter; 1 week in January.	
Directions	From Chartres on N23 dir. Nogent Le Rotrou. 14 km after Montlandon, right on D203 to Condé Sur Huisne; D10 dir. Remalard for 3km, left to Villeray. Château on right.	

Monsieur Christian Eelsen
Villeray,
61110 Condeau, Orne

Tel	+33 (0)2 33 73 30 22
Fax	+33 (0)2 33 73 38 28
Email	moulin.de.villeray@wanadoo.fr
Web	www.domainedevilleray.com

Domaine de la Louveterie

From the forested road, the drive descends to glorious views over the hills of the Perche. And there is the house, a 17th-century longère in 32 acres of peacefulness, rescued and restored by Carol and Pietro. A charming couple, well travelled and fluent in several languages, they moved from Paris two years ago and are enchanted with their new life. A gravelled courtyard sets the scene (beyond are two gîtes). No short cuts have been taken in the renovation; no ostentation either – what you get is an overwhelming feeling of comfort and well-being. Pietro oversees pasture and woodland, potager and pool; Carol, a culinary photographer, stars in the kitchen. Good wines and food are ferried to a room where logs smoulder; hosts join guests for after-dinner coffee and digestifs. And so to bed… the Chambre Fifties is caught in a cosy time warp (in spite of the flat-screen TV), Chinoise and Voyage rest warmly under the eaves, and the suites spread themselves impressively over two floors, the grandest with wooden panelling, choice antiques and a real fire. *No credit cards. Ask about cookery & watercolour courses & riding weekends.*

Price	€80–€100. Suites €120–€140.
Rooms	5 + 2: 3 doubles, 2 duplex suites for 2. 2 apartments for 2.
Meals	Breakfast included. Dinner with wine, €35–€65.
Closed	Rarely.
Directions	From Rouen A13, A154, N154 to Evreux; N12 to Dreux; D828 then D928 to La Loupe. Ask for detailed directions.

Carol & Pietro Cossu-Descordes
61110 Moutiers au Perche,
Orne

Tel	+33 (0)2 33 73 11 63
Fax	+33 (0)2 33 73 05 16
Email	domainedelalouveterie@wanadoo.fr
Web	www.domainedelalouveterie.com

Hôtel de la Cathédrale

In one of the cobbled streets of historic old Rouen with the cathedral looming over it – is this half-timbered hotel in a city of timber-frame houses. There is a large breakfast/tearoom with a non-working but imposing stone fireplace, exposed beams with their joists and comfortable armchairs. Views go straight through to the delightful little cobbled courtyard which is set with garden furniture, potted plants, small shrubs, a riotous creeper and geraniums that tumble from window boxes – a lovely spot for breakfast (an excellent one at that) or afternoon tea. Rooms are spotless and simple; the ones overlooking the street are the biggest, with old style double windows and elaborately moulded cupboard doors. From some bedroom windows you see two Gothic marvels: the cathedral towers and the magnificent tracery of Saint Maclou – your soul will be safe here. Do remember this is an old building so insulation between the rooms can be thin. Laurent is running a remarkable-value hotel plumb in the middle of a city that cries out to be explored. *Car park: Hôtel de Ville.*

Price	€66–€76.
Rooms	26 twins/doubles. Rooms can connect for family suites.
Meals	Breakfast €7.50. Tea room for snacks. Meals available locally.
Closed	Never.
Directions	In Rouen centre to Rue St Romain; 1st street along east side of Cathedral to unload luggage. Pedestrian street so park in 'Parking Hôtel de Ville', a 5-minute walk from hotel.

Laurent Delaunay
12 rue St Romain,
76000 Rouen, Seine-Maritime
Tel   +33 (0)2 35 71 57 95
Fax   +33 (0)2 35 70 15 54
Email contact@hotel-de-la-cathedrale.fr
Web   www.hotel-de-la-cathedrale.fr

Château de Requiécourt

Discreetly in the heart of the landscaped settlement of Requiécourt – awash with cedars, horse chestnuts, sequoias, shrubs and ornamental lake – towers a wall. At the press of a button, tall gates swing open and invite you into the château grounds. Madame Milon, friendly and well-informed, receives you, then ushers you from smart reception counter to the bedrooms upstairs. Here, pastel colours and tall windows combine to create calm, light-filled spaces; elegant too, with crisp white bed linen and bare polished parquet. Paintings from local artists hang on pristine walls; dig into your pockets and you may take one home. Each room is different; Rose Velours, with its fourposter bed, pivoting antique wash basins and corner balcony surveying the park, is particularly pleasing. Back downstairs is a long oval table for breakfast and a furnished gravelled terrace the other side of the French windows. Kayak along the Epte, motor to Giverny in a vintage car – the tourist leaflets reveal all. With so much to do and Paris nearby you may find yourself booking for one night and staying for more. *Shiatsu available.*

Price	€85–€125.
Rooms	5: 4 doubles, 1 twin.
Meals	Breakfast included. Restaurants within 10km.
Closed	Rarely.
Directions	From A13, junc. 16 to Vernon. D181 for Gisors, 14km; D9 to Cahaignes; D9 to Requiécourt. On village square, signed. Ring bell.

Emmanuelle Milon
Hameau de Requiécourt,
5 rue de la Chartreuse, 27420 Cahaignes, Eure

Tel   +33 (0)2 32 55 37 02
Fax   +33 (0)2 32 27 27 28
Email   welcome@chateauderequiecourt.com
Web   www.chateauderequiecourt.com

Le Moulin de Connelles

Bring your boater, hop in a green and red-trimmed flatboat right out of a Monet painting and punt along a quiet arm of the Seine after a morning at Monet's garden, 30 minutes away. Watery greens, pinks and that scintillating veil of haze that is particular to this part of Normandy intensify the impressionist mood. Then look up at the extraordinary half-timbered, chequer-boarded, turreted manor house and you will have to pinch yourself, hard. Part of the house is on an island; hidden paths lead through flowering bushes to a private pool. Young Karine keeps up the family tradition of quiet hospitality here while bringing the park and its flowerbeds up to snuff. Bedrooms and restaurant have been renovated with fine materials: oak, mosaics, weathered marble, granite and limestone. Step around to the garden and peek at rows of copper pots through the kitchen windows, reflections of the lovely meals served in the restaurant. Reserve a room with a balcony overlooking the river or splurge on the suite, with its jacuzzi for two in the tower. Bring your paintbrushes. *Boats for trips upriver.*

Price	€130–€170. Suites €170–€310.
Rooms	13: 7 doubles, 6 suites.
Meals	Breakfast €13. Lunch & dinner €33–€56. Children's meals €13
Closed	Rarely.
Directions	From A13 exit 10 Louviers on N15 towards Pont de l'Arche for 4km; right to St Pierre du Vauvray, Andé & Connelles. Signed.

Karine Petiteau
40 route d'Amfreville sous-les-Monts,
27430 Connelles, Eure

Tel	+33 (0)2 32 59 53 33
Fax	+33 (0)2 32 59 21 83
Email	moulindeconnelles@moulindeconnelles.com
Web	www.moulindeconnelles.com

Château d'Emalleville

An elegant, listed 18th-century château, Emalleville has it all: perfectly landscaped and formal gardens, vast woodlands for walking (and autumn shooting), a tennis court, an ancient fallen mulberry that has rebuilt itself, a cosy suite in the converted beamed dovecote (a favourite) and fine rooms in the orange brick and limestone coach house and outbuilding. There is perfect toile de Jouy in some of the rooms and most beds are canopied. Contemporary touches here and there work nicely: photos and drawings dedicated to the dancer who took Paris by storm in 'Josephine', a colourful bullfighting theme in 'Seville', while 'Giverny' is floral and feminine. All open directly to the lawns. Tucked away behind the precious vegetable garden and orchard is the pool. Breakfast is served in the *salle de chasse*: try the mulberry or wild plum jam. The lady of the manor's exquisite taste has woven a magic from floor to ceiling, from Jouy print to antique wardrobe: you will feel like prince and princess here. And you're only 30 minutes' drive from Giverny.

Price	€80–€120. Suites €140–€230.
Rooms	8: 6 doubles, 2 suites for 4–5.
Meals	Breakfast included. Restaurant 8km.
Closed	Never.
Directions	From Evreux, D155 for Louviers & Acquigny. Through Boulay Morin, 500m after village, left to Emalleville. 2nd road on right; château opposite church; ring bell.

Frédérique & Arnaud Tourtoulou
17 rue de l'Église,
27930 Emalleville, Eure

Tel   +33 (0)6 14 49 24 20 (mobile)
Fax   +33 (0)2 32 34 30 27
Email ftourtoulou@aol.com
Web   www.chateaudemalleville.com

Château de la Puisaye

In their own 20-hectare heaven, two cats, two dogs, horses and a fleet of farmyard fowl. You'll like it here, too. A scatter of shuttered windows in a classically pale façade, this house oozes 19th-century country-house elegance. Large and airy, rooms are lightly furnished with antiques, huge mantelpiece mirrors and glass-panelled doors flooding spaces with light. The salon and library have elaborate woodwork while the dining room, with its gleaming table and silver candlesticks, invites a lingering breakfast – a feast of homemade pastries, jams and cooked dishes. On request, Diana – a stylish cook – will make dinner, perhaps some foie gras followed by truffle stuffed guinea fowl, ingredients come fresh from the potager and 19th-century greenhouse. In the bedrooms, creamy paintwork and old-fashioned French wallpaper, marble fireplaces and snowy bed-linen create an ordered calm. Welcoming and relaxed, Diana, a former English solicitor, and her French husband moved here to indulge her love of horses. With carp in the pond, mushrooms in the forest and croquet in the garden, it's just about perfect.

Price	€85–€110. Suite €125–€175. Cottage €400–€700.
Rooms	5 + 1. 3 doubles, 1 twin, 1 suite for 4. Cottage for 8.
Meals	Breakfast included. Dinner €30; menu gourmand €45; Normandy platter with cider, €14.
Closed	One week in winter.
Directions	From Verneuil/Avre on D839 towards Chartres; D56 twds Senonches for 1.5kms; right onto C19 for Château.

Bruno & Diana Costes
Lieu-dit la Puisaye,
27130 Verneuil sur Avre, Eure

Tel	+33 (0)2 32 58 65 35
Fax	+33 (0)2 32 58 65 35
Email	info@chateaudelapuisaye.com
Web	www.chateaudelapuisaye.com

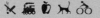

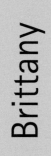
Brittany

Château du Launay

A dream of a place, another world, another time, beside bird-swept pond and quiet woods. Launay marries austere grandeur with simple luxury, fine old stones with contemporary art, rich minimalism with exotica. In the great white hall, a large decorated Indian marriage chest shares the Persian rug with two bronze stags. The staircase sweeps up, past fascinating art, to big light-filled rooms where beds are white, bathrooms are plainly, beautifully modern, light and colour are handled with consummate skill. The second floor is more exotic, the corridor punctuated with an Indian gate, the rooms slightly smaller but rich in carved colonial bed, polo-player armchairs, Moghul prints. For relaxation, choose the gilt-edged billiard room, the soberly leather-chaired, book-filled library or the stupendous drawing room with a piano (concerts are given) and many sitting corners. A house of a million marvels where you take unexpected journeys and may find yourself on a horse on old Roman roads or pike fishing on the pond. Your hosts are charming.

Price	€160–€240. Apartments €125–€140 (€750–€850 per week).
Rooms	8 + 2: 6 doubles, 2 twins. 2 apartments for 2-4.
Meals	Breakfast included. Restaurant 5km.
Closed	December–March.
Directions	From Pontivy, D782 for 21km to Guémené; then D1 for Gourin to Toubahado for 9km. Don't go to Ploërdut. In Toubahado right on C3 for Locuon for 3km. Entrance immediately after Launay sign.

Monsieur & Madame Bogrand
Launay,
56160 Ploërdut, Morbihan

Tel	+33 (0)2 97 39 46 32
Fax	+33 (0)2 97 39 46 31
Email	info@chateaudulaunay.fr
Web	www.chateaudulaunay.com

Hôtel Le Lodge Kerisper

Claudie and her young family moved from Paris to open this chic, charming, buckets-and-spade hotel. Huge mirrors reflect white walls, pale floors and seaside touches as you enter. There is more than a touch of the French 'Hamptons' about these converted stone buildings perched high above steep little lanes leading down to the harbour; sunhats, toys, kites and beach paraphernalia are the order of the day. The bedrooms in this cleverly adapted building, complete with giddy, architect designed conservatory on stilts, look inward to a small, prettily lawned garden and a pool, while antique gilt chairs chit-chat with modern sofas as you sip aperitifs at the ultra smart, zinc-topped bar. Bedrooms, many with terraces, are comfortably understated. Linen and voile curtains float on polished floors, white painted wood ceilings are discreetly contemporary. A hard day's cycling the coastal paths (or bikini gazing on a sandy beach) leads, inevitably, to supper at one of the pretty harbourside restaurants… fairy lights twinkle, halliards click and yachts bob gently in the stylish little port. *Spa & treatments.*

Price	€95–€255. Suite €180–€290.
Rooms	20: 12 doubles, 3 suites, 5 family suites.
Meals	Breakfast €15 (adults), €8 (children). Restaurant 100m.
Closed	Never.
Directions	100m north of main harbour street La Trinité Sur Mer. Well signed.

Claudie & Philippe Favre
4 rue du Latz,
56470 La Trinité sur Mer, Morbihan

Tel	+33 (0)2 97 52 88 56
Fax	+33 (0)2 97 52 76 39
Email	contact@lodgekerisper.com
Web	www.lodge-kerisper.com

Le Logis de Parc er Gréo

The neat new building is a metaphor for Breton hospitality. The front is a high north wall
– it may seem forbidding but once inside you know that it shelters house and garden
from the wild elements, that fields, woods, sea and the coastal path are just yards away.
Eric prepares itineraries for guests, boating is on the spot, swimming a little further
away or in the pool. Warm colours, oriental rugs and fine family pieces sit easily on the
tiled floors of the many-windowed ground floor. Eric's father's watercolours lend
personality to all the rooms, and the unusual candlesticks in the hall and ancestral
portraits, including a large Velazquez-style child in a great gilt frame, are most appealing.
Salon and dining room open widely onto terrace and garden — wonderful places to relax
or play with the children on the big lawn. Rooms, attractive in shades of red, green and
salmon, are functionally furnished. Your hosts, their charming young family and their
enthusiasm for their project — to stop being clients in boring hotels and do things
properly themselves — make this an easy, friendly place to stay. *You can charter Eric's boat.*

Price	€75–€138. Suite €155–€299.
Rooms	15. 7 doubles, 7 twins, 1 suite.
Meals	Breakfast €12. Restaurants 3km.
Closed	Mid November–mid-March. Sometimes open Christmas.
Directions	From Vannes D101 for Ile aux Moines. Ignore left turns to Arradon. Left to Le Moustoir then on to Le Gréo & follow signs.

Eric & Sophie Bermond
9 rue Mané Guen, Le Gréo,
56610 Arradon, Morbihan

Tel	+33 (0)2 97 44 73 03
Fax	+33 (0)2 97 44 80 48
Email	contact@parcergreo.com
Web	www.parcergreo.com

Villa Kerasy Hôtel

Bamboos and cherry trees, koi carp and stone statues – the presence of the East is strong. Influenced by an East India Company trading post nearby (now a small museum), Jean-Jacques has taken the Spice Route as a theme. The 1914 building, once a factory, is attractive enough from the outside; inside it is captivating. From the moment you pass the sentinel stone elephants, you're enveloped in luxury. The bedrooms are all different, with muted, subtle colours, lovely fabrics, intriguing pictures, fresh flowers… Some overlook the street, others the entrancing Japanese garden. Thoughtfulness and attention to detail are apparent throughout – even the buddha has a fresh camellia dropped into his capacious lap – but there's no hint of pretentiousness. Jean-Jacques has experience in the hotel trade and knows exactly how to make you feel cherished without impinging on your space. The day begins with a fabulous breakfast and you're just a five-minute walk from the centre of Vannes, where there are any number of good restaurants. *Ayurveda spa opens in May 2008.*

Price	€118-€165. Suite €288-€330.
Rooms	12: 6 doubles, 5 twins, 1 suite for 2-4.
Meals	Breakfast €12.
Closed	Mid-November–mid-December; January.
Directions	From N165 exit Vannes centre; follow signs to Hôpital or Gare SNCF; hotel signed.

Jean-Jacques Violo
20 avenue Favrel et Lincy,
56000 Vannes, Morbihan

Tel	+33 (0)2 97 68 36 83
Fax	+33 (0)2 97 68 36 84
Email	info@villakerasy.com
Web	www.villakerasy.com

Château de Talhouët

Your arrival is straight out of a Wilkie Collins' novel. Up a gloomy, bumpy, muddy lane smelling of moss and fungi, then wow! The imposing 16th-century granite manor house has views that reach all the way to the Aze valley and the cliffs of Rochefort en Terre. Jean-Pol bought the 1562 ruin — originally built by the crusading Talhouët family — 16 years ago, thus fulfilling a long-held dream. He's also restoring the grounds: woodland, terraced fields, wildflower meadow and a series of fascinating walled gardens, English and French. Floors are wonderful: either stone worn to satin or polished wood with Persian rugs. The sitting room manages to be both cosy and vast, with its old rose panelling, antique chairs and soft, deep sofas. There's a giant bookcase for browsing through, and a tempting selection of magazines. Jean-Pol will join you for a drink as you discuss the menu; delicious dinners are cooked by a charming young chef. Then to bed up an impressive stone stair; you will sleep under fancy florals and softly painted beams. Be woken by birdsong and a gentle view

Price	€135-€220.
Rooms	8 doubles.
Meals	Breakfast included. Dinner €48.
Closed	15-30 November; 5 & 25 January.
Directions	From Redon D775 through Allaire 9km; right D313 through Malansac to Rochefort en Terre; D774 for Malestroit 4km. Left onto small road for 2km. Entrance on left; château another 500m.

Monsieur Jean-Pol Soulaine
56220 Rochefort en Terre,
Morbihan

Tel	+33 (0)2 97 43 34 72
Fax	+33 (0)2 97 43 35 04
Email	chateaudetalhouet@libertysurf.fr
Web	www.chateaudetalhouet.com

Domaine de Bodeuc

A taste of Paris in the country. Jean and Sylvie, escapees from the city, have restored, most glamorously, this 19th-century manor house in its own park surrounded by woodland. The roomy hall is dominated by a glass chandelier, wall colours are earthy and cool – mushrooms, aubergines – and a bold mix of good antiques with striking modern art gives a dramatic impression. Salons are small but bedrooms are large; whether in the house or stables, they are decked out in similar style giving a pleasing sense of space: beds large and crisply white with colourful spreads and proper sheets and blankets; bathrooms elegant and pampering. Relax with a drink on the small terrace overlooking the park or in the piano bar, dine well on locally sourced wild salmon, venture out to one of the good local restaurants. It's supremely tranquil here, yet you're close to wild beaches, a huge choice of golf courses, and excellent shopping in the fortified port of Vannes. Wine tasting and mushroom weekends are planned for the future, along with the development of the organic potager and the original walled garden.

Price	€78-€152. Singles €70 -€95. Family room €124-€168. Suite €140-€192.
Rooms	14: 10 twins/doubles, 1 single, 2 family rooms for 3-4, 1 suite.
Meals	Breakfast €12. Dinner €27, book ahead.
Closed	Mid-November-mid-December; mid-January-mid-March.
Directions	N165 from Nantes or Vannes, exit 16 towards St Dolay. After 3km left in Izernac. From Rennes near Redon, right in Izernac, 4km before La Roche Bernard.

Sylvie & Jean Leterre
Route de Saint Dolay,
56130 Nivillac, Morbihan
Tel   +33 (0)2 99 90 89 63
Fax   +33 (0)2 99 90 90 32
Email   contact@hotel-bodeuc.com
Web   www.hotel-bodeuc.com

Hôtel La Désirade

Everyone loves an island and this one, with its wild windswept coast, is especially enticing. Battered by storms in winter, it is hot and gorse-scented in summer and the roads are silent. La Désirade, sheltered in its parkland, is made up of a new village of colourwashed houses around a pool. If leafy gardens, comfortable hotelly bedrooms and super bathrooms (white bathrobes, lashings of hot water) don't bring instant relaxation, the spa and massages surely will. Breakfast is served buffet-style in the breakfast room or by the pool; dinner, formal but excellent, is in the hotel restaurant across the lane. The young chef specialises in local dishes and the presentation is impeccable; wines are first class too. Research the island's possibilities curled up in a wicker chair in the reception salon with its unexpectedly blue fireplace: there are lots of illustrated books. You have 104 kilometres of coastal paths and cycle routes to choose from, while the beaches are a 20-minute walk away. Take your paintbox and you'll be in good company: Monet and Matisse both came to the island to paint.

Price	€122–€164. Family rooms €230–€350.
Rooms	32: 14 doubles, 14 twins, 4 family rooms for 4.
Meals	Breakfast €14.50. Dinner from €29.
Closed	12 November–29 December; 4 January–17 March.
Directions	From Quiberon, ferry to Belle Île (45min) then taxi or bus (7km). Well signed.

Pierre & Bénédicte Rebour
Le Petit Cosquet, Bangor,
56360 Belle Île en Mer, Morbihan

Tel	+33 (0)2 97 31 70 70
Fax	+33 (0)2 97 31 89 63
Email	hotel-la-desirade@wanadoo.fr
Web	www.hotel-la-desirade.com

Entry 113 Map 2

Château de Kerlarec

The plain exterior belies the 19th-century festival inside – it's astonishing. Murals of mountain valleys and Joan of Arc in stained glass announce the original Lorraine-born baron ("descended from Joan's brother") and the wallpaper looks great, considering it too was done in 1834. In the gold brocade-papered salon, Madame Avelange, an expert on interiors of the previous centuries, lavishes infinite care on every antique and painting. There may be furnishings from 1842 to 1865 in one room while in another, only Louis XV will do. The rooms are lavish. One suite is fresh in yellow and white with soft voile curtains at the window and draped from a coronet over the bed; the largest suite has an original peacock blue panelling. Expect excellent English along with porcelain and silver at breakfast. Specialities are homemade rhubarb and ginger, melon and star anise conserves. The set menu from local produce is innovative and original; clients who dine by candlelight once usually do again. Your enthusiastic hostess lavishes the same attention on her guests as on her house. *No credit cards.*

Price	€110-€145.
Rooms	6: 5 suites for 2, 1 suite for 2-3.
Meals	Breakfast included. Dinner €30-€50.
Closed	Never.
Directions	From Quimperlé D22 NE towards Pontivy for 6km; château on left – take care on entry!

Françoise & Dominique Avelange
29300 Arzano,
Finistère

Tel	+33 (0)2 98 71 75 06
Fax	+33 (0)2 98 71 74 55
Email	chateau-de-kerlarec@wanadoo.fr
Web	www.chateau-de-kerlarec.com

Château-Hôtel Manoir de Kertalg

So many contrasts. Through thick woods of majestic trees and up a magical entrance drive, you expect the old château in its vast estate, but the hotel is actually in the big, blocky stables, built in 1890 for racehorses (who even had running water): it became a hotel in 1990 when the tower was added. The salon is formal and glitzy with its marbled floor, modern coffered ceiling, red plush chairs – and intriguing dreamscapes. You will be welcomed with polished affability by the charming young owner, and possibly by visitors come for tea and ice cream (a favourite summer outing). Even the 'small' bedrooms are big; walls are covered in lined fabric, cream with textured design, a combination of two fabrics above and below the dado rail. There is a feeling of being cocooned and wrapped up away from the world. The suite with the four-poster has windows looking out over both garden and château and acres of carpet. The tower rooms are cosier but have space for a couple of armchairs. Wild woodland walks with hundreds of hydrangeas beckon and, yet, there's a helipad – somehow the two worlds meet and embrace.

Price	€105–€195. Duplex €240.
Rooms	9: 6 doubles, 2 twins, 1 duplex for 4.
Meals	Breakfast €13. Five restaurants 2–8km.
Closed	November–Easter.
Directions	From N165 west exit Quimperlé Centre to Moëlan sur Mer. There, right at lights for Riec & follow signs (12km from N165).

M Le Goamic
Route de Riec sur Belon,
29350 Moëlan sur Mer, Finistère

Tel	+33 (0)2 98 39 77 77
Fax	+33 (0)2 98 39 72 07
Email	kertalg@free.fr
Web	www.manoirdekertalg.com

Manoir du Stang

There is ancient grandeur in this 'hollow place' (*stang*) between the remarkable dovecote arch and the wild ponds. On the tamed side: a formal French courtyard, a blooming rose garden, an avenue of mature magnolia grandiflora, some masterly old stonework. But the welcome is utterly natural, the rooms not at all intimidating. The eighth generation of the Huberts like guests to feel at home in their family mansion with a choice antique here, an original fabric there, an invigoratingly pink bathroom to contrast with a gentle Louis Philippe chest – always solid, reliable comfort and enough space. Views are heart-warming, over courtyard, water and woods, the peace is total, bar the odd quack. Communal rooms are of stupendous proportions, as befits the receptions held here: the dining room can seat 60 in grey-panelled, pink-curtained splendour, its glass bays looking across to the gleaming ponds. Masses of things sit on the black and white salon floor – a raft of tables, fleets of high-backed chairs, a couple of sofas, glowing antique cupboards – and you still have space and monumental fireplaces.

Price	€75–€150.
Rooms	24: 22 twins/doubles, 2 family rooms.
Meals	Breakfast €10. Dinner for large parties only. Restaurants 1km.
Closed	20 September–mid May; open by arrangement for groups.
Directions	From Quimper, N165 exit Concarneau & Fouesnant on D44 then D783 for Quimper. Entrance left on private road. Parking a little away from hotel.

Hubert Family
29940 La Forêt Fouesnant,
Finistère

Tel	+33 (0)2 98 56 97 37
Fax	+33 (0)2 98 56 97 37
Email	manoirdustang@wanadoo.fr
Web	www.manoirdustang.com

Hôtel du Centre

You can tell that this place has a young owner – there's such a fresh and refreshingly un-pompous atmosphere. It's right on the seafront in the old port of Roscoff, with a lively bar called Chez Janie looking out over the boats. It was here that the onion-sellers used to come to sign their contracts with Janie; her photo, in Breton costume, still hangs on the wall. Black and white stairs take you up to the hotel reception (at ground level on the street side). All is chic, uncluttered and colourful, ranged on the panelled walls are pictures of traditional local costumes and the furniture is blond wood and ultra modern. Also on this floor, overlooking the port, is a stylish, inexpensive and good bistro-style restaurant. More stairs, this time with red and grey bannisters and a red carpet, to whisk you up to bedrooms. These have a naïve charm, and are perfect: reclaimed furniture has been sandblasted and sprayed dove-grey; fabrics are warm red or striped tawny; sheets are white and crisp; bathrooms are simple, modern and very good. All in all, tremendous value and well-nigh irresistible.

Price	€59–€118.
Rooms	16: 15 doubles, 1 suite for 5.
Meals	Breakfast €8.
	Lunch & dinner from €10.80.
Closed	Mid November–mid March.
Directions	From Morlaix D58 to Roscoff.
	Hotel on sea front over bar 'Chez Janie'.

Jean Marie Chapalain
Le Port,
29681 Roscoff, Finistère

Tel	+33 (0)2 98 61 24 25
Fax	+33 (0)2 98 61 15 43
Email	contact@chezjanie.com
Web	www.chezjanie.com

Grand Hôtel des Bains

Marine purity on the north Brittany coast: it's like a smart yacht club where you are an old member. The fearless design magician has waved a wand of natural spells – cotton, cane, wood, wool, seagrass: nothing synthetic, nothing pompous. Sober lines and restful colours leave space for the scenery, the sky pours in through walls of glass, the peaceful garden flows into rocks, beach and sea. Moss-green panelling lines the deep-chaired bar where a fire leaps in winter. Pale grey-panelled bedrooms have dark mushroom carpets and thick cottons in stripes and checks. Some have four-posters, some balconies, others are smaller, nearly all have the ever-changing sea view. Bathrooms are lovely – with bathrobes to wear to the magnificent indoor seawater pool and treatment spa. Staff are smiling and easy, the ivory-panelled dining room with its sand-coloured tablecloths is deeply tempting. Spectacular coastal paths, a choice of beaches, yoga and spa retreats, even a writer's workshop – the luxury of space, pure elegant simplicity and personal attention are yours. *Excellent wine cellar.*

Price	€130–€280.
Rooms	36 twins/doubles.
Meals	Breakfast included. Dinner €34–€50.
Closed	Never.
Directions	From Rennes-Brest N12 exit Plouégat & Moysan then Plestin les Grèves, continue to Locquirec. Hotel in centre. Through gate to private car park.

Madame Nicol
15 bis rue de l'Eglise,
29241 Locquirec, Finistère

Tel	+33 (0)2 98 67 41 02
Fax	+33 (0)2 98 67 44 60
Email	reception@grand-hotel-des-bains.com
Web	www.grand-hotel-des-bains.com

Ti al Lannec

With dozens of English antiques, it is superbly French – soft and fulsome: an Edwardian seaside residence perched on the cliff, its gardens tumbling down to rocky coves and sandy beaches; only waves and breezes through the pines can be heard (the beach club closes at midnight). Inside, a mellow warmth envelops you in armfuls of drapes, bunches, swags and sprigs. Each room is a different shape, individually decorated as if in a private mansion with a sitting space, a writing table, a good bathroom. Besides the florals, stripes and oriental rugs, there is a sense of space with the use of white fabric and with views onto the sea or ancient cypresses. Some bedrooms are big, with plastic-balconied loggias, some are ideal for families with convertible bunk-bed sofas. Salons are cosily arranged with little lamps, mirrors, old prints; the sea-facing restaurant serves excellent food. The Jouanny family are deeply part of their community and care immensely about guests' welfare: they create a smart yet human atmosphere, publish a daily in-house gazette and provide balneotherapy in the basement.

Price	€162–€363. Singles €88–€113.
Rooms	33: 22 twins/doubles, 3 singles, 8 family rooms for 3-5.
Meals	Breakfast €17. Lunch & dinner €25–€70. Children's meals €16–€23.
Closed	December-February.
Directions	From N12 Rennes-Brest road, exit 3km west of Guingamp for Lannion onto D767. In Lannion, follow signs to Trébeurden. Signed.

Jouanny Family
14 allée de Mézo-Guen,
22560 Trébeurden, Côtes-d'Armor

Tel	+33 (0)2 96 15 01 01
Fax	+33 (0)2 96 23 62 14
Email	contact@tiallannec.com
Web	www.tiallannec.com

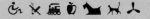

Château Hôtel de Brélidy

From upstairs you can see across bucolic fieldscapes to Menez-Bré, Armor's highest spot
at 302m. The old guest rooms here are cosy, quilty, family-antiqued; a newly refurbished
one shows off its blue and while toile de Jouy draped round an iron four-poster bed and
a marble surround to sink in the new bathroom. Below are the beamed salon and billiard
room, their vast carved fireplaces built above the two great dining-room fireplaces –
such strength. The worn stone staircase and an iron man fit well; so will you, enfolded
in the personal attention that is Brélidy's keynote. In the west wing, on the site of the
original open gallery, guests in the suite can parade before waist-high windows like lords
and ladies of yore. More modest rooms lie below, carefully decorated with soft colours,
enriched with antiques; four have private entrances with little terraces and there's a huge
terrace for all up above. In the gentle garden, the converted bakery is ideal for families
and there's an indoor jacuzzi. Beyond are two rivers, two ponds with private fishing, and
everywhere is utter peace. You can hire mountain bikes, too.

Price	€100–€186. Suites €148–€168. Cottage €122–€143.
Rooms	13 + 1: 7 doubles, 4 twins, 1 suite, 1 suite for 4. Cottage for 4.
Meals	Breakfast €13. Dinner €30–€36.
Closed	20 December–1 April.
Directions	From N12 exit Lannion-Tréguier to Tréguier. D712, D8 then D15 to Brélidy; signed.

Carole & William Langlet
Brélidy, 22140 Bégard,
Côtes-d'Armor

Tel	+33 (0)2 96 95 69 38
Fax	+33 (0)2 96 95 18 03
Email	chateau.brelidy@worldonline.fr
Web	www.chateau-brelidy.com

Manoir de la Hazaie

Chunks of Breton history – violence, greed and bigotry – happened here where country peace now reigns. The Marivins, she an artist/pharmacist, he a craftsman/lawyer, cherish every minute of its past and have filled it with family treasures: they call it their museum house. The salon combines grandeur and warmth, ancient stones, antiques and a roaring fire. Ancestral portraits hang beside Madame's medieval paint and pottery scenes. Tournemine's red ceiling inspired a powerfully simple colour scheme, plain furniture and a great canopied bed. Airily feminine Tiffaine has wildly gilded, curlicued Polish furniture and a neo-classical bathroom romp: statues, pilasters, a mural of *Girl in Hat*. Baths have sybaritic jacuzzi jets. Rooms in the mill house, separate to the main building, with fine old floor tiles and lovely rugs, open onto the garden – ideal for families. Glide from Hadrian's Villa into the pool, listen to the underwater music and whale sounds, sleep in luxury. Past owners have all left their mark: the admiral's anchors, the priest's colours. Live like royalty and enjoy it all.

Price	€145–€240. Suite €214–€240.
Rooms	6: 5 twins/doubles, 1 suite for 4.
Meals	Breakfast €14.
	Restaurants within 8km.
Closed	Never.
Directions	From St Brieuc N12 towards Rennes for 12km then D786 towards Le Val André for 8.5km. In Planguenoual D59 direction Lamballe; house signed after 2.5km.

Jean-Yves & Christine Marivin
22400 Planguenoual,
Côtes-d'Armor

Tel	+33 (0)2 96 32 73 71
Fax	+33 (0)2 96 32 79 72
Email	manoir.hazaie@wanadoo.fr
Web	www.manoir-hazaie.com

Manoir du Vaumadeuc

Paradise. The approach down a long drive through mature trees leads to the impressive granite exterior of this 15th-century manor. As you enter through the old, massive wooden door which leads into the manorial hall the whole place seems untouched by time. A huge stone fireplace dominates the far end, there's a high vaulted beamed ceiling, an enormously long banqueting table and hunting trophies on the walls. It is easy to imagine former guests feasting and making merry after the hunt. A magnificent staircase leads to bedrooms on the first floor, decorated and furnished in period style. They are magnificent and comfortable, with no frills, quite masculine, à la hunting and shooting fraternity. All rooms are large and some are enormous; one of them has stairs leading down into a room the size of a tennis court. The bathrooms are smart and spotless. Such a courteous, warm welcome from Monsieur O'Neill; his family has owned this listed house with its superb dovecote, a keep pond for fish, a garden and acres of woods for generations.

Price	€90-€195. Suites €135-€225.
Rooms	13: 10 twins/doubles, 3 suites.
Meals	Breakfast €12. Picnic available. Dinner for groups of 10 or more.
Closed	Occasionally.
Directions	From Plancoët D768 towards Lamballe for 2km. Left on D28 for 7km to Pleven. Manoir 100m outside village.

M & Mme O'Neill
22130 Pleven,
Côtes-d'Armor

Tel   +33 (0)2 96 84 46 17
Fax   +33 (0)2 96 84 40 16
Email   manoir@vaumadeuc.com
Web   www.vaumadeuc.com

Hôtel Manoir de Rigourdaine

At the end of the lane, firm on its hillside, Rigourdaine breathes space, sky, permanence. The square-yarded manor farm, originally a stronghold with moat and all requisite towers, now looks serenely out over wide estuary and rolling pastures to the ramparts of Saint Malo and offers a sheltering embrace. The reception/bar in the converted barn is a good place to meet the friendly, attentive master of the manor, properly pleased with his excellent conversion. A double-height open fireplace warms a sunken sitting well; the simple breakfast room – black and white floor, solid old beams, plain wooden tables with pretty mats – looks onto courtyard and garden. Rooms are simple too, in unfrilly good taste and comfort: Iranian rugs on plain carpets, coordinated contemporary-chic fabrics in good colours, some good old furniture, pale bathrooms with all essentials. Six ground-floor rooms have private terraces onto the kempt garden – ideal for intimate breakfasts or sundowners. Good clean-cut rooms, atmosphere lent by old timbers and antiques, and always the long limpid view. We like it a lot. *9-hole golf course 10km.*

Price	€62–€82.
Rooms	19: 10 doubles, 4 twins, 3 triples, 2 quadruples.
Meals	Breakfast €7.50 Snacks & wine can be provided. Restaurants in Plouër sur Rance.
Closed	Mid-November–Easter.
Directions	From St Malo N137 for Rennes. Right on N176 for Dinan & St Brieuc; over river Rance. Exit for Plouër sur Rance for Langrolay for 500m; lane to Rigourdaine.

Patrick Van Valenberg
Route de Langrolay,
22490 Plouër sur Rance, Côtes-d'Armor
Tel   +33 (0)2 96 86 89 96
Fax   +33 (0)2 96 86 92 46
Email   hotel.rigourdaine@wanadoo.fr
Web   www.hotel-rigourdaine.fr

Villa Reine Hortense

A mysterious Russian prince, poet and aesthete, Nikolas de Vlassov, built this house at the turn of the last century as a tribute to Reine Hortense de Beauharnais, daughter of Empress Joséphine and mother of Napoléon III. It is the only property of its type with direct access to the beach; in fact, it is on the beach with its feet firmly planted on the rocks below. The entrance leads straight into a Versailles parqueted salon with views over the sandy Dinard bay and across to St Malo. A ceiling-height green and white ceramic stove from 1850 is there for beauty only, as is the grand piano. Memorabilia and portraits line the trompe l'oeil marbled staircase topped with a 17th-century Cordoba leather trunk. All bedrooms are named for queens: you can play Reine Hortense and sit in her silvered copper bath tub, then dry off on the balcony overlooking the bay; be yellow and sunny in Anne d'Autriche with access to the veranda; or Elisabeth in blue and white with a canopy and draped bed. The warm, friendly Benoists will take good care of you here — all is charm, all is light. *Three flights of steep steps to hotel.*

Price	€150–€235. Suite €295–€385.
Rooms	8: 5 doubles, 2 twins/doubles, 1 suite for 4.
Meals	Breakfast €15. Restaurants 5-min walk across beach.
Closed	5 October–25 March.
Directions	From Rennes, N157 for Dinard, follow signs Centre Ville & Plage. Left around beach. Signed. Parking opposite.

Florence & Marc Benoist
19 rue de la Malouine,
35800 Dinard, Ille-et-Vilaine

Tel	+33 (0)2 99 46 54 31
Fax	+33 (0)2 99 88 15 88
Email	reine.hortense@wanadoo.fr
Web	www.villa-reine-hortense.com

Hôtel Alba

The English aristocrat who built Hotel Alba as his seaside mansion in 1850 chose the site well. Only the sweep of the esplanade separates the elegant terrace from the beach; sitting in the bar when the tide's in, you feel you're at sea, gazing on an infinity of water. The hotel was bought by Monsieur Robert two years ago; since then it has been overhauled and redecorated. The results are fresh and inviting. You'll feel glad to be here, from the moment you drive down the narrow quiet street at the back to park beside the vivid flower beds under the palms. The reception area is manned 24 hours a day and Monsieur is warm and outgoing, with a decided sense of humour. The bedrooms are comfortable: soft lighting, restful colours – cream, oatmeal, terracotta – and natural fabrics. Headboards and wardrobes are lime-washed pine. If you're lucky you'll have a room with its own small balcony and wonderful views over the beach. Wander along the sand and you reach the old walled part of St Malo, the Intra Muros, and its maze of shops and restaurants. *Sister hotel is in centre of town.*

Price	€70–€171. Triples & family rooms €130–€200.
Rooms	22: 7 doubles, 9 twins/doubles, 4 triples, 2 family rooms for 4.
Meals	Breakfast €12. Restaurants nearby.
Closed	Never.
Directions	N137 for Saint Malo. Follow signs Thermes Marin, Hôtels, Gare. Right at beach front on D155. On left, before Thermes Marin.

	Monsieur & Madame Robert 17 rue des Dunes, 35400 Saint Malo, Ille-et-Vilaine
Tel	+33 (0)2 99 40 37 18
Fax	+33 (0)2 99 40 96 40
Email	info@hotelalba.com
Web	www.hotelalba.com

Le Valmarin

The gracefully proportioned *malouinière* was built in the early 18th century by a wealthy ship owner. Very close to the ferry terminal, and in the centre of town, this hotel has an unexpectedly large rose-filled garden with sunloungers and tables dotted around under mature cedars and a copper beech. Most bedrooms — light-filled with high ceilings, tall windows carefully draped to match the bed covers — overlook the garden: lovely. Second-floor rooms have sloping ceilings and a cosier feel, with exposed beams, white walls and pale blue carpets and paintwork. There are lavender bags in the wardrobes, plenty of books in French and English, and breakfast at the small yellow and blue dining tables. Or, have a lie-in and ask for your café au lait in bed — before exploring the fabulous ramparts of the city or sunning on the nearby beaches. There are equestrian facilities and excellent thalassotherapy spas nearby or take an ocean ride to the islands of Jersey, Guernsey, Sark or Herm. Dinan, the 'Nice of the North', is a very short drive. Great value. *Secure parking.*

Price	€95–€145.
Rooms	12: 9 twins/doubles, 3 family rooms for 3-4.
Meals	Breakfast €10.
Closed	January-February. Call for out of season reservations.
Directions	In St Malo follow signs for St Servan & town centre. Left at r'bout 'Mouchoir Vert' for St Croix Church; right at church; 20m to hotel.

Gérard & Françoise Nicolas
7 rue Jean XXIII, St Servan,
35400 Saint Malo, Ille-et-Vilaine

Tel	+33 (0)2 99 81 94 76
Fax	+33 (0)2 99 81 30 03
Email	levalmarin@wanadoo.fr
Web	www.levalmarin.com

Château de Bonaban

The imposing gateway gives you a hint of what's in store long before the avenue of trees
ushers you into the presence of this austerely splendid building. History weighs heavy:
the first castle here was built in Roman times, the present one was pillaged during the
Revolution. Climb the stately flight of steps to the main door and enter a vast hall with
a sweeping marble staircase. Chandeliers, elegantly upholstered antique chairs,
magnificent curtains and paintings set the tone of grandeur for the rest of the hotel. The
'Prestige' bedrooms are big, high-ceilinged and sumptuous; the 'Romantics' (on the top
floor) are fractionally smaller, with sloping ceilings and a cosier, more modern feel. (If
you're on a lower budget, there are simpler, cheaper rooms out in the old coach house,
now converted into the Pavillon.) The restaurant — either in the full panoply of a state
room or in the more intimate surroundings of a circular turret — is excellent. Madame
is a gentle, thoughtful hostess. The grounds, flanked by the river, are wonderfully quiet.

Price	€85–€195.
	Suite & family rooms €235–€300.
Rooms	32: 20 doubles, 3 twins,
	8 family rooms for 3, 1 suite for 4.
Meals	Breakfast €14.
	Lunch & dinner €28–€50, book ahead.
	Restaurant closed Wednesdays.
Closed	Rarely.
Directions	N137 exit Chateauneuf; D76 to
	Cancale, La Gouesnière. Through
	village on D4 towards Dol. Hotel on
	right after leaving village.

Madame Vlasta Siler
35350 La Gouesnière,
Ille-et-Vilaine

Tel	+33 (0)2 99 58 24 50
Fax	+33 (0)2 99 58 28 41
Email	chateau.bonaban@wanadoo.fr
Web	www.hotel-chateau-bonaban.com

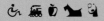

La Foltière

Come for the gardens — and Monsieur! He loves having guests, and the gardens, all 20 hectares, are his pride and joy. They date from 1830 when the château was built, designed to be fashionably informal. The château has the usual sweeping drive and imposing stairway and hall. Rooms are vast. The feel is hushed stately home, yet it's not at all precious and children are welcomed, even spoiled, with mazes and bridges, slides and surprises. Bedrooms have tall windows and are big enough to dance in: peachy 'Degas' with its own dressing room, deep-red 'Renoir' (these two interconnect — ideal for families); blue 'Monet' with its original porcelain loo; 'Sisley', a symphony in yellow; 'Pissaro', ideal for wheelchair users. Breakfast on homemade croissants (and, when Madame is around, Breton crêpes) or charcuterie and cheese. Then seek out the grounds — magnificent from March to October. Paths meander round the huge lake and past groves and secret corners bursting with camellias and narcissi, azaleas and rhododendrons, old roses and banks of hydrangea. *Tea room & garden shop open afternoons.*

Price	€130-€140. Suite €160.
Rooms	5: 4 doubles, 1 suite.
Meals	Breakfast €12.
	Many restaurants nearby.
Closed	20-28 December.
Directions	From Rennes/Caen A84; exit 30 towards Fougères; Parc Floral 10km from Fougères towards Mont St Michel & St Malo.

Alain Jouno
35133 Le Châtellier,
Ille-et-Vilaine

Tel	+33 (0)2 99 95 48 32
Fax	+33 (0)2 99 95 47 74
Email	foltiere@parcfloralbretagne.com
Web	www.parcfloralbretagne.com

Château du Pin

Painter and photographer, the brave, artistic Ruans have launched with passionate enthusiasm into renovating a small château with a ruined chapel, antique stables and a thrilling atmosphere. Traces of seigneury date from the 15th century; the owners' sense of space and colour will triumph. The original staircase curves up to the 'literary' guest rooms – mauve/silver Proust, ochre/gold Georges Sand, theatrical suite Victor et Juliette, Oriental for Pierre Loti – and each shower is behind a great rafter. The vastly magnificent drawing/billiard room wears rich reds, has two large windows back and front plus a small window on a gable wall which sits on top of the mantelpiece; it's great fun. A small cottage with a romantic garden and interior courtyard sits in the nine-hectare park. Your gentle hosts love cooking; breakfast is a treat with crêpes, homemade jams and cakes, fruit and yogurt; they then share dinner and stimulating talk with you. This is a land of legends; the Brocéliande forest, the Emerald coast, the gulf of Morbihan, Dinard and Saint Malo all nearby for exploration.

Price	€85–€90. Suites €110–€150. Cottage €358–€520 per week (long weekends possible).
Rooms	5 + 1: 2 twins/doubles, 1 suite for 2, 2 family suites for 4. Cottage for 3-4.
Meals	Breakfast €10. Dinner €25, book ahead.
Closed	Rarely.
Directions	From Rennes N12 west to Bédée 23km; D72 to Montfort sur Meu; D125 for St Méen le Grand; château 3km on left.

Catherine & Luc Ruan
35370 Iffendic près de Montfort,
Ille-et-Vilaine

Tel	+33 (0)2 99 09 34 05
Fax	+33 (0)2 99 09 03 76
Email	luc.ruan@wanadoo.fr
Web	www.chateaudupin-bretagne.com

Château des Tesnières

Wonderful, fairytale Château des Tesnières, with turrets that look like they could reach the stars, is set amid venerable trees, with far-reaching views and six hectares of parkland to explore. Inside is perfection. No chintz in sight, but contemporary design merging perfectly with 19th-century features and fireplaces, soft hues contrasting with rich colours and bathrooms stylishly dramatic, two with claw-foot baths. You might spot barn owls on the window ledge of Sud – they nest in the turret of this suite. Downstairs, the Louis XVI drawing room, library and dining room have elegant furniture, marble fireplaces, sofas so deep that you won't want to rise, gilt-edged mirrors, seagrass floors, parkland views. The energetic, enthusiastic Dutch owners have done a fabulous job restoring this place; prepare to be wickedly spoilt. Breakfast is a sumptuous feast, served in your private salon, in the dining room or on the terrace. In the surrounding area are numerous lovely walks, water sports on the Villaine river, and historic Vitre, a market town with an 18-hole golf course. Superbe!

Price	€110–€160.
Rooms	5: 1 double, 4 suites. Extra bed & cot available.
Meals	Breakfast included. Restaurants in Vitré, 10-min drive.
Closed	December–January.
Directions	From Vitre, D178 for La Guerche. 2nd r'bout, right to Torcé, D33, 3km, left, D108 to Domalain. Through estate to countryside, 2nd left.

	John & Siebren Demandt Boon
	35370 Torcé,
	Ille-et-Vilaine
Tel	+33 (0)2 99 49 65 02
Fax	+33 (0)2 99 49 65 66
Email	info@chateaudestesnieres.com
Web	www.chateaudestesnieres.com

Western Loire

Le Château de l'Abbaye

In endlessly flat countryside, set back from the main road in its own walled grounds, this 'castel romantique' has been graciously managed by Danielle Renard for more than 20 years. Now she is joined by the new generation: son Renaud-Pierre and daughter-in-law Korakot. So many visual enticements the moment you arrive: bibelots and boxes, photo frames and fresh flowers, small items embroidered by Korakot, furniture antique and new, even a vintage Belgian stove. Roosters are a family passion and can be found in every medium, shape and size; take a peep at the bulging scrapbooks of drawings sent in by previous guests and their children. Continental breakfast with homemade jams is served on the veranda in summer; dinner at candlelit tables reflects the best seasonal produce (French regional menus from Danielle, Thai from Korakot). Bedrooms, not huge, lie off the corridor on the second floor and are individually decorated to create cocoon-like spaces; extras include children's books and embroidered needlecases – typical touches from these charming, thoughtful hosts.

Price	€69–€159.
Rooms	5 + 1: 2 doubles, 1 twin, 2 suites/family rooms for 3. Apartment for 2–4.
Meals	Breakfast €12. Dinner €36.
Closed	Rarely.
Directions	A83 exit 7 towards La Rochelle; through Moreilles; château at end of village with large red gate.

Danielle, Korakot &
Renaud-Pierre Renard
85450 Moreilles, Vendée

Tel	+33 (0)2 51 56 17 56
Fax	+33 (0)2 51 56 30 30
Email	daniellerenard@hotmail.com
Web	www.chateau-moreilles.com

Château de la Cacaudère

The 19th-century, golden-stone château had been abandoned for 50 years when the Montalts discovered it. Madame has a fine eye for colour and a lightness of touch; music and châteaux are her passions. (She also produces fine fruit tarts for breakfast.) Original wood panelling is there but much of the furniture has been picked up on postings abroad then put together with French flair. Bedrooms range from smallish to large with sumptuous sashed canopies; one has steps down to a pretty pink room for a child, another a reading room in a turret. Bathrooms are similarly stylish, one with an old curvy tub with Savoy taps, another with a trompe l'oeil ceiling of the sky. Pass the kitchen on your way to breakfast and catch a glimpse of polished copper pans — immaculate, spotless. There's a big, comfy sitting room with long windows looking to the garden; it's large and leafy, filled with copper beeches and pines, walled orchard and pool. Sheep graze peacefully, and there's an old garage for bikes and ping-pong. Delightful. *No credit cards. Minimum stay two nights.*

Price	€85-€130.
Rooms	5: 2 doubles, 1 twin, 1 family room for 3, 1 quadruple.
Meals	Breakfast included. Barbecue available for guest use. Restaurants 5km & 15km.
Closed	September-April.
Directions	From La Rochelle A11 towards Poitiers for 8km; at r'bout exit N137 (E03) for Nantes to Ste Hermine, right at monument Clémenceau to centre ville.

M & Mme Montalt
Thouarsais-Bouildroux,
85410 La Caillère, Vendée

Tel   +33 (0)2 51 51 59 27
Email   chris.montalt@wanadoo.fr
Web   www.chateau-sud-vendee.com

Château de la Flocellière

You really need to see La Flocellière from a helicopter. The aerial view is the most striking; the battlemented castle was built around 1090 and is listed. Hotel guests stay in the château, where bedrooms are vast, gracious and opulent, with huge windows on two sides onto the gardens and park. Overseeing this vast dominion is the Vicomtesse and her meticulous eye misses nothing, from the topiary in the grounds to the maids' attire. All is opulence and beauty and beeswax infuses every room. You can lounge around in the sitting room in the gallery, play a game of billiards, admire the magnificent potager below the ruined walls, visit the library or be taken on a full tour. This is living at its most sedate and children are welcome providing they behave impeccably. Snacks are no-go in the secluded swimming pool area ("a terrace, not a beach"). If you choose to dine, tables d'hotes for 14 takes place two to three times a week – your chance to meet the hosts. Weddings and receptions are not limited to weekends, and the setting is sensational. Historic, magnificent, hospitable.

Price	€125-€205. Suite €225-€305. Houses €1,900 per week.
Rooms	4 + 2: 2 twins/doubles, 1 family suite for 4-5. 2 houses for 10-12.
Meals	Breakfast €12. Dinner €54-€61, book ahead.
Closed	Rarely.
Directions	From Paris A11 for Angers, then A87 to La Roche sur Yon; exit 28 for Puy du Fou, then to Pouzauges until St Michel Mt Mercure. Left at traffic light to La Flocellière and main church; left on rue du Château.

Vicomte & Vicomtesse Patrice Vignial
85700 La Flocellière,
Vendée

Tel	+33 (0)2 51 57 22 03
Fax	+33 (0)2 51 57 75 21
Email	flocelliere.chateau@wanadoo.fr
Web	www.flocellierecastle.com

Hôtel du Martinet

Madame Huchet describes the Martinet as a modest country hotel. It's a fair description; sitting in the garden the atmosphere is bucolic. Just down the road, halfway down the Vendée coast, Bouin is a working seaside village with a pretty church built in the 14th and 15th centuries; it is not somewhere that has sprung up for the tourists. Madame Huchet's son Jean-François runs oyster beds; busy little fishing ports are clustered along the coast. This is a real family hotel: Emmanuel, an absolute delight, is the chef and kitchen gardener specialising, not surprisingly, in fresh fish and seafood. His wife Christelle lends a hand at mealtimes, either in a cosy blue-panelled dining room or in a more summery room with a veranda giving onto the garden. The rooms are very basic, some in the main house and some alongside the swimming pool. So, a good little place to bring children for a holiday: the hotel is relaxed and informal, there are country walks as well as beaches and Jean-François will be happy to take you to see his oysters. *House aperitif offered to Sawday readers.*

Price	€54–€70. Half-board €55–€77 p.p; duplex €100.
Rooms	30: 23 twins/doubles, 1 triple, 6 duplexes for 4-6.
Meals	Breakfast €7–€10. Picnic lunch €10. Lunch & dinner from €23.
Closed	Rarely.
Directions	51km south-west of Nantes on D751 past Bouaye, then D758 through Bourgneuf en Retz towards Noirmoutier for 9km. Signed. Ignore 'no entry' sign.

Françoise Huchet
Place de la Croix Blanche,
85230 Bouin, Vendée

Tel	+33 (0)2 51 49 08 94
Fax	+33 (0)2 51 49 83 08
Email	hotel.martinet@wanadoo.fr
Web	www.lemartinet.com

Hôtel Fleur de Sel

Noirmoutier has a personality all its own: this group of simple white buildings in its Mediterranean garden is typical. Built in the 1980s, it sits peacefully between sea and salt marsh, long sandy beach and little yachting harbour. It is perfect for family holidays, with tennis court, golf driving range, big pool and outdoor jacuzzi. Bedrooms are good too, some in classic cosy style with country pine furniture and fabrics, others more bracing with ship-shape yew furniture and yachting motifs; several have little ground-floor terraces. The delightful, caring owners have humour and intelligence; their daughter's paintings are sometimes shown here. The chef has worked with the very best in Paris and meals are served by courteous waiters in the airy, raftered dining room or on the oleander-lined terrace. It is all clean-cut, sun-warmed, impeccable and welcoming. There is a bridge, but try and come by the Passage du Gois causeway, open three hours round low tide: an unforgettable four kilometre drive 'through the sea' where shellfish-diggers cluster. The island is, of course, very popular in summer.

Price	€89–€175.
Rooms	35: 30 doubles, 5 family rooms.
Meals	Breakfast €12. Lunch €27.50. Dinner €38–€49.
Closed	4 November–mid-March.
Directions	From Nantes ring road south-west D723, D751, D758 to Beauvoir sur Mer. Road to Noirmoutier via Le Gois only possible at low tide. Otherwise take bridge. Hotel 500m behind church.

Pierre Wattecamps
Rue des Saulniers,
85330 Noirmoutier en l'Île, Vendée

Tel	+33 (0)2 51 39 09 07
Fax	+33 (0)2 51 39 09 76
Email	contact@fleurdesel.fr
Web	www.fleurdesel.fr

Hôtel Villa Flornoy

Villa it is, a large one, in a quiet road just back from the vast sandy beach and protected from the sea-front bustle. Built as a family boarding house in the 1920s, Flornoy still stands in the shade of a quieter age: high old trees, nooked and crannied seaside villas in stone, brick and wood. Inside it is just as peaceful. After being greeted by the delightful new and young owners – enjoy sitting in the salon: garden view, four tempting 'corners', well-chosen prints and the occasional interesting *objet*. Rooms – mostly a good size, a few with balconies – have a pretty, fresh feel, nothing frilly, just plain or Jouy-style wall fabrics, coordinated colours and patterns, good modern/traditional furniture, excellent beds and white bathrooms with fine new fittings. Sylvie has refreshed some rooms in tones of ivory and string adding wood panelling for a more by-the-seaside feel. It is simple, solid, attractive and in the morning you will enjoy a generous breakfast in the light dining room or under the trees in the green and blooming garden. Really good value and a relaxed welcome. *Walking distance to beach.*

Price	€60–€108.
Rooms	30: 22 twins/doubles, 8 triples.
Meals	Breakfast €9. Dinner €20–€22. Restaurant closed October–March.
Closed	Mid-November–January.
Directions	In Pornichet to Centre Ville, right onto Avenue Général de Gaulle for 300m. Avenue Flornoy on right just after Hôtel de Ville on left.

Sylvie & Sébastien Laurenson
7 avenue Flornoy,
44380 Pornichet, Loire-Atlantique

Tel	+33 (0)2 40 11 60 00
Fax	+33 (0)2 40 61 86 47
Email	hotflornoy@aol.com
Web	www.villa-flornoy.com

Le Tricot

Sunshine pours in past cream shutters and bathes the house in light. In the living room, windows face east and west so dawn and sunset are heavenly; once the last rays ebb away, the marble fireplace, piano and coat of arms come into their own. The dining room is as impressive; doors lead out to the garden, there's a black and white tiled floor and a splendid portrait of the Duke of Anjou – later Philip V of Spain. Bedrooms have exquisite Japanese fabric on the walls, polished boards and old rugs; French antiques are dotted about. Bathrooms are new, with showers or deep tubs and oodles of towels. The pale stone house dates from 1642 and is the largest inside the city ramparts, surrounded by a walled garden of box-trimmed flowerbeds and mature trees. Guérande is a fascinating medieval city and all the sights are within walking distance, the beach just a short drive. The rest of the peninsula could occupy you for weeks; go sea fishing, ride, explore the bustling harbours – and do visit the salt marshes, its fascinating salt museum and waterways of The Grande Brière, a haven for bird life. *No credit cards.*

Price	€100-€140. Suite €175-€200.
Rooms	3: 1 double, 1 twin, 1 suite for 4.
Meals	Full English breakfast included. Restaurants in town.
Closed	Mid-November-March.
Directions	Enter Guérande through Porte Bizienne, 1st right on rue du Tricot; house on right at end of cul de sac.

Loïc & Andréa de Champsavin
8 rue du Tricot,
44350 Guérande, Loire-Atlantique

Tel	+33 (0)2 40 24 90 72
Fax	+33 (0)2 40 24 72 53
Email	chambresdhotes@letricot-guerande.com
Web	www.letricot-guerande.com

Château de Cop-Choux

The name refers to the old lime kilns on the estate and comes from 'couper la chaux' — so, nothing to do with cabbages. Where to start: the elegant house built just before the French Revolution with towers added on either side in the early 20th century, the huge park of 18 hectares, the pool, the rolling lawns and ancient trees? Or the 17 marble chimneys, the original parquet floors and your friendly hosts? Patrick has just taken over the château and is full of enthusiasm and plans for the future. The park is huge, with chestnut trees lining the approach. A river runs through the grounds which contain lakes for fishing, woods for taking a country ramble. The house is full of light; several rooms have windows on three sides; bedrooms are big and dreamy and named after herbs. Violette has filmy blue fabric floating at tall windows, Romarin has exquisite carved twin beds (and an interconnecting room), bathrooms are gorgeous. You can have a just laid egg for breakfast in a pretty panelled room, or on the terrace; then amble across lawns to the pool. *Large cottage for 6 for weekly rental.*

Price	€110–€120. Suite €150.
Rooms	5: 4 twins/doubles, 1 suite for 4.
Meals	Breakfast €8. Hosted dinner €32.50. Restaurants in Ancenis, 12km.
Closed	Rarely.
Directions	A11 exit 20 for Ancenis; N23 for Nantes; D164 towards Nort sur Erdre for 11km, right after Pont Esnault. Signed.

Patrick Moreau
44850 Mouzeil,
Loire-Atlantique

Tel	+33 (0)2 40 97 28 52
Email	chateau-cop-choux@orange.fr
Web	www.chateau-cop-choux.com

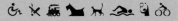

Le Palais Briau

A glorious Palladian house perched high on the hillside overlooking the Loire valley. Built in the 1850s by François Briau, an early industrialist who made his fortune building railways, the house is palatial, lovingly restored and saved from commercial modernisation by the present owners. Faithful to the era, they have even held on to Briau's original furniture and fittings (of which he was immensely proud). Madame radiates exuberance and charm; Monsieur is an artist and designer whose impeccable taste has been stamped on every interior. A remarkable colonnaded stair sweeps up to the guests' sitting and dining rooms – pure Napoleon III. Bedrooms are light and large with separate dressing-rooms; all have magnificent views on the park or Abbey. Exquisite wallpapers, brocade canopies above polished mahogany beds, fine linen, flowers – all elegant and glamorous. Bathrooms are sumptuous and Italian-tiled. The grounds too are fabulous; large areas are completely wild and overgrown and contain the remains of a vast orangerie; herons return to nest every year. Breathtaking.

Price	€120-€180. Single €90.
Rooms	4: 3 doubles, 1 suite for 3 + child bed.
Meals	Breakfast included. Restaurants 1.5km.
Closed	24-25 December.
Directions	A11 after Angers, exit Beaupréau, N23 for Nantes, left on r'bout at entrance of Varades. Signed. Rue Madeleine is small and behind industrial area.

Thérèse & François Devouge
Rue de la Madeleine,
44370 Varades, Loire-Atlantique

Tel	+33 (0)2 40 83 45 00
Fax	+33 (0)2 40 83 45 00
Email	devouge@palais-briau.com
Web	www.palais-briau.com

Château d'Yseron

Olivier de Saint-Albin has recently redecorated his ancestral home in Directoire style. The salon is large with a blazing fire at one end and full-length windows looking over fields and lake. The hall is distinguished by delicate murals of dancing girls. The dining room has rich ruby walls and a fine copy of da Vinci's last supper by Alfred Heurtaux, the great-grandfather that built the château. Delicious breakfast – fruit, croissants, homemade jams – is served here or on the terrace, almost at any hour. Monsieur is a welcoming and accommodating host; an oenologist, he also arranges tastings of local wine including his own – a prize-winning muscadet. Interiors are light and airy, the style uncluttered and elegant; expect high ceilings, wooden floors, gilt mirrors, ancestral paintings. Each bedroom is different, from the romantic rose-red 'Chambre Jouy' to the serene 'Louis XVII'. There is also a suite of two rooms with a bathroom between: ideal for a family group. This is a place to unwind – a library for wet days, parkland for fine ones, fishing in the lake, horse riding nearby.

Price	€80–€120. Family room €160.
Rooms	4: 3 doubles, 1 family room for 1–4.
Meals	Breakfast included. Restaurant 3km.
Closed	Never.
Directions	Nantes-Poitier/Cholet N249, exit Vallet. Cross Vallet to Ancenis on D763; right to ZI Est, 500m after Vallet at r'bout. Yseron 1.5km.

Olivier de Saint-Albin
44330 Vallet,
Loire-Atlantique

Tel	+33 (0)2 51 71 70 40
Fax	+33 (0)2 51 71 70 11
Email	ostalbin@wanadoo.fr
Web	www.yseron.net

Le Chai de la Paleine

Despite doing all the restoration in a 19th-century bourgeois manor house, opening a new hotel in the old wine warehouse *(chai)* and having five children, Caroline and Philippe are unfailingly relaxed and welcoming. Perhaps their secret is that they want everyone to fall in love with La Paleine, as they did. Old buildings are scattered here and there: a hen house with nesting holes in its walls now used as a bike store, an old wash-house in the middle of the lawn with a stone trough and fireplace: all sorts of hide-outs can be found in semi-secluded corners of the grounds. The brand new rooms are simple, uncluttered, stylish. Children will love having breakfast sitting inside one of two enormous wine casks – *foudres* – big enough for six. There are two sitting rooms with soft green and beige sofas, bookcases for browsing, a fully equipped kitchen and an honesty bar. You are on the edge of an interesting village and there's a good little auberge down the road for supper. Come for a great family atmosphere, homemade jam and yogurt for breakfast and a bag of walnuts to take home.

Price	€58–€78. Singles €49.
Rooms	12: 11 doubles, 1 suite for 4 (some with kitchens).
Meals	Breakfast included. Auberge 200m (closed Monday).
Closed	5-25 January.
Directions	From A11 onto A85 exit Saumur for Poitiers; N147 exit Le Puy; 2nd right (Toutes Directions); house opposite Stop sign.

Philippe Wadoux
10 place Jules Raimbault,
49260 Le Puy Notre Dame, Maine-et-Loire

Tel	+33 (0)2 41 38 28 25
Fax	+33 (0)2 41 38 42 38
Email	lapaleine@wanadoo.fr
Web	www.paleine.fr

Le Domaine de Mestré

History oozes from every corner of Mestré. A Roman road, a cockleshell for the pilgrims who stayed en route to Compostella, part of a 13th-century chapel – and the mill and tithe barn remind us that monks farmed here when Mestré was part of the vast Abbey. Most of the present building is 18th century: the family have farmed here for 200 years and keep alive the traditions of French country hospitality. Monsieur runs the eco-conscious farm, milking by hand. Madame makes fine natural soaps, and cooks; two daughters help out. All take pride in providing delicious home-grown food and elegant service. Big, rustic-style rooms are furnished with lovely family antiques – huge sleigh or brass beds with wool-stuffed mattresses and fluffy eiderdowns, no TV; some have great views over the wooded valley. The sitting room is 'Victorian parlour' with dark panelling, red wallpaper, a card table and leather-bound books, the dining room is simply delightful. A sense of timeless welcome and class enfolds the privileged guest to this family-run chambres d'hôtes. *Cash only.*

Price	€60–€70. Singles €50. Suites €110–€120.
Rooms	12: 8 doubles, 2 singles, 2 suites.
Meals	Breakfast €8. Dinner €25 (not Thurs & Sun), book ahead.
Closed	16 December–March.
Directions	From Saumur D947 for Chinon. Right in Montsoreau for Fontevraud l'Abbaye. 1st right 1.5km after Montsoreau; signed.

Dominique & Rosine Dauge
49590 Fontevraud l'Abbaye,
Maine-et-Loire
Tel   +33 (0)2 41 51 75 87
Fax   +33 (0)2 41 51 71 90
Email domaine-de-mestre@wanadoo.fr
Web   www.dauge-fontevraud.com

Château de Verrières

The château was built in 1890 by a certain Général Baillou de La Brosse to host the balls and grand soirées that he so enjoyed. It has been passionately, authentically, lavishly restored. The house is in huge grounds – unusually so since it is right in the old town of Saumur – and aristocratic French cavalry officers used to hone their equestrian skills here. Your hosts speak impeccable English, are very welcoming and love to talk about the château's restoration. Every trace of necessary updating – central heating, rewiring – has been carefully concealed. Big bedrooms have huge windows; some look onto the park, others the elegant Academy of Cavalry or the Château de Saumur; the Japanese top-floor suite is extraordinary. Bathrooms are as luxurious as you'd expect, each one unique. Swim in the heated pool or be whisked off by a horse and carriage for a trot around the town (and don't miss the wonderful market). Yolaine, a refined and accomplished cook, makes homemade jams for beautiful breakfasts in the sunny courtyard or the vaulted cellars. Readers are full of praise.

Price	€120–€280.
Rooms	10: 8 doubles, 1 twin, 1 suite.
Meals	Breakfast €14. Occasional dinner €39.
Closed	Christmas.
Directions	A85 exit Saumur for Saumur-Centre, over 2 roundabouts. Left for Château de Saumur at 2nd set of lights. Verrières 100m on right.

Yolaine de Valbray–Auger
53 rue d'Alsace,
49400 Saumur, Maine-et-Loire

Tel	+33 (0)2 41 38 05 15
Fax	+33 (0)2 41 38 18 18
Email	chateaudeverrieres@wanadoo.fr
Web	chateau-verrieres.com

Château de Salvert

This highly sculpted neo-Gothic folly is home to a couple of unselfconscious aristocrats and lots of cheerful children. While the baronial hall is properly dark and spooky, the dining room and salon are elegant bordering on plush: pink and gilt chairs and sparkling chandeliers, golden mirrors and white-draped tables, ancestors on eau-de-nil walls. The double bedroom has its shower in one turret, the loo in another (off the corridor), and is decorated with modern fabrics and fine French pieces. The vast suite, thrice the price, is really quite something, with its five tall windows and two perfect beds clasped under a green and gold coronet. In the huge park where wild boar roam and spring boarlets scamper are two gîtes restored by the indefatigable Monsieur: one, a 14th-century farmhouse, the other, an old pressoir. Both are a luxurious combination of old and new. Not the cheapest address but a grand one, in an area impossibly rich in culture... and on the banks of the Loire broods old Saumur, a 20-minute drive.

Price	€90. Suite €250.
	Gîtes €1,500–€1,600 per week.
Rooms	2 + 2: 1 double, 1 suite for 2-5.
	2 gîtes: 1 for 6, 1 for 8.
Meals	Breakfast €12. Dinner €55.
	Wine €22–€35.
Closed	Rarely.
Directions	From A85 exit 'Saumur' on D767 for
	Le Lude. After 1km, left on D129 to
	Neuillé. Signed.

Monica Le Pelletier de Glatigny
Salvert,
49680 Neuillé, Maine-et-Loire

Tel	+33 (0)2 41 52 55 89
Fax	+33 (0)2 41 52 55 89
Email	info@salvert.com
Web	www.chateau-de-salvert.fr

Château des Briottières

This heavenly little château has been in the same family for 200 years and is now occupied by the relaxed and endearing Monsieur de Valbray, his wife and six children. Your hosts manage to envelop you in elegant living, while providing a family atmosphere. A magnificent library/billiard room leads into a small sitting room; if it's grandness you're after, share your pre-dinner aperitif with Monsieur in the huge, and hugely aristocratic salon, replete with family portraits, tapestries and fine antiques. Sweep up the marble staircase to the bedrooms on the first floor, feel the comfort of the beds (the newest are king-sized), gaze on park views. Several bedrooms have been recently redecorated but traditional furniture and fabrics prevail. Some beds are charmingly canopied, and the sumptuous family suite includes a small governess's room. Some bathrooms are marbled; the more expensive sport extras such as towelling robes. In the grounds is a delightful country-style orangerie built in 1850 which can be rented for two nights or more.

Price	€160–€350.
Rooms	9 + 1: 4 twins/doubles, 3 doubles, 1 single, 1 family room for 3. Cottage for 12.
Meals	Breakfast €13. Candlelit dinner €50, book ahead.
Closed	3 days at Christmas; 2 weeks in February.
Directions	From A11, exit 11 Durtal to D859 for Châteauneuf sur Sarthe. D770 to Champigné; D768 for Sablé; left at Marigné sign; 4km further.

François de Valbray
49330 Champigné,
Maine-et-Loire

Tel	+33 (0)2 41 42 00 02
Fax	+33 (0)2 41 42 01 55
Email	briottieres@wanadoo.fr
Web	www.briottieres.com

Château du Plessis Anjou

You can sail off from the grounds in a balloon; two of the best sons et lumières are within easy reach, and so are the châteaux and wineries of the Loire. Built in the 16th century, Le Plessis has always been in the family and has been taking guests for years. Though large and very elegant, the château, set in 14 hectares of wooded park, is inviting rather than imposing, with curving tiled roofs, white walls and creeper-covered shutters. Dinner, at a long table in a rather ornate dining room with Roman friezes, could include salmon, duck with apricots, cheese and a crisp fruit tart; fruit (masses of raspberries) and vegetables come directly from a walled potager. One bedroom is striking, with a lofty beamed ceiling and beds set in a deep turquoise alcove. Beds are turned down at night: water and chocolates placed on bedside tables. The Renouls have two children of their own hence the hen house, sheep and rabbits along with a playground and trampoline. There's a small pond brimming with fish and lilies, Pinup the pony for rides, and Atchoum, the fox terrier. *A guide available for many activities.*

Price	€130–€160. Suites €200–€250.
Rooms	8: 6 doubles, 2 suites.
Meals	Breakfast €12. Hosted dinner €48, book ahead.
Closed	Never.
Directions	From A11 exit Durtal on D859 to Châteauneuf sur Sarthe; D770 for Le Lion d'Angers for 18km. Right on N162 for Château Gontier. After 11km right on D189 for La Jaille Yvon.

	Valérie & Laurent Renoul
	49220 La Jaille Yvon,
	Maine-et-Loire
Tel	+33 (0)2 41 95 12 75
Fax	+33 (0)2 41 95 14 41
Email	plessis.anjou@wanadoo.fr
Web	www.chateau-du-plessis.com

Hôtel Haras de la Potardière

François Benoist's mother inherited La Potardière from her father and in 1990 entrusted her son with taking care of it – and making it pay for its keep. Luckily, François is an architect specialising in restoring old buildings. They live in a creeper-covered wing of the château with their four children: Camille, Alexis, Noëlle and Emeline. In fact, one of the most appealing features of La Potardière is a brochure history written in the form of a letter from all six of them. François's grandfather built up a successful centre for training show jumpers alongside an established thoroughbred stud. In 1992, after ten years of empty stables, La Potardière began taking in stallions for the summer months, when owners bring mares from all over France; most of the rooms look out onto grazing horses. Bedrooms are just what you would hope for: a graceful mixture of pretty and elegant, wood and flowers. What a place for a horse-mad child! But all children will love it here: fields, a safe pool, a Wendy house full of toys. A superb welcome. *Group dinners by arrangement.*

Price	€90–€130. Triples €130–€150. Suites €130–€185.
Rooms	Château: 7 twins/doubles, 1 triple, 3 suites for 4-5. Stables: 4 twins/doubles, 1 triple, 2 suites for 4-5.
Meals	Breakfast €10. Cold platter €23, order ahead.
Closed	16 February–3 March 2008.
Directions	From Paris, A11 exit 10; D306 for Sablé la Flèche and Bazouges sur la Loire. Right in village of Crosmières; signed.

Francois & Marie-Yvonne Benoist
Route de Bazouges,
72200 Crosmières, Sarthe

Tel	+33 (0)2 43 45 83 47
Fax	+33 (0)2 43 45 81 06
Email	haras-de-la-potardiere@wanadoo.fr
Web	www.potardiere.com

Auberge du Port des Roches

If you can see yourself sitting at the edge of slow green water of an evening, perhaps watching out for the odd fish, this is the place for you. Not grand – this is the Loir not the Loire, an altogether less glamorous river – but we can hear you saying: "Oh, what a pretty spot". Valérie and Thierry have been here about eleven years, are young, very friendly though a touch shy, and full of enthusiasm for their auberge. Their main business is probably the restaurant – they can seat about 50 people in two rooms and the riverside terrace heavy with roses and perfumed plants– but Valérie is justly proud of the effort she has put into the bedrooms and into the way everything positively sparkles. Rooms are not large but done in fresh colours, sky blue, for example, with crisp white bedcovers. At the front you will have a view over the Loir. A small lane does run past the hotel, but windows are double glazed. This is a very quiet, very French place to stay, within easy reach of the châteaux and very good value.

Price	€46-€60.
Rooms	12: 9 doubles, 2 twins, 1 family room for 3.
Meals	Breakfast €7. Picnic available. Lunch & dinner €24-€48. Restaurant closed Sunday evenings, Mondays & Tuesday lunchtimes.
Closed	February; 1 week in autumn.
Directions	From La Flèche, N23 to Le Mans for 5km; right on D13 to Luché-Pringé. Through village for 2km, right on D214. Signed.

Valérie & Thierry Lesiourd
Le Port des Roches,
72800 Luché Pringé,
Sarthe

Tel   +33 (0)2 43 45 44 48
Fax   +33 (0)2 43 45 39 61

Château de l'Enclos

The Guillous welcome you into their grand château in its elegant setting as long-lost friends. Sociable and fun – they own a red 1933 Citroen – they will whisk you around their parkland with its fine trees, llamas, a pair of donkeys, goats and chickens. Inside, a staircase sweeps up to the handsome bedrooms of parquet floors and rich carpets, writing desks and tall windows. Two have balconies. The charming salon opens to a stage-set-perfect garden, and you dine with your hosts in best table d'hôtes style. Opt for the dreamy treehouse and you will take another staircase up and around a giant sequoia; amazingly built between three trees that form a triangle, it is barely visible among the branches. Made of fine grained spruce and modelled after the typical hunting cabin from the Finnish Laplands, it has two rooms and a tall hand railing which circles the deck. Live close to nature and drink in the views at the break of dawn – or sunset. Breakfast will be delivered to your door. Masses to do in little Brûlon or in medieval Le Mans, and a marvellous home to return to. *No credit cards.*

Two wells help water the animals, whose manure in turn feeds the vegetable garden, along with compost from the kitchen. Rain is harvested in rooftop containers that hold 4,000 litres; this too ends up in the garden, thus completing the cycle. The heating system, fuelled by natural gas, is based on a clean and energy-efficient method of condensation. In the park the Guillous have created a nature trail and documented 50 species of trees, two of which are rare. Happy hens scratch around under the trees so there are fine eggs for breakfast, and everything that can be recycled is.

Price	€95. Treehouse €130 for 2.
Rooms	3: 2 doubles, 1 twin, 1 treehouse for 3.
Meals	Breakfast included Dinner with wine, €30.
Closed	Never.
Directions	From A81 Le Mans-Laval; exit 1 to Brûlon. Château on right at end of town. Signed.

Annie-Claude & Jean-Claude Guillou
2 ave de la Libération,
72350 Brûlon, Sarthe

Tel	+33 (0)2 43 92 17 85
Email	jean-claude.guillou5@wanadoo.fr
Web	www.chateau-enclos.com

SPECIAL
GREEN ENTRY
see page 12

Château de Vaulogé

A fairytale place! The Radinis, from Milan, wanted their children to have an international education so moved to Geneva, then found Vaulogé. Marisa and her daughter now run the hotel, and Marisa devotes herself to the garden, her latest project being the horseshoe-shaped potager for fresh dinner produce. The original part of the château was built in the 15th century: this is where the family lives. Later Vaulogé was remodelled in a troubadour style, giving it two circular towers with conical slate roofs; when the shock waves of the Revolution had faded, the aristocracy reclaimed their houses. If it's space you're after, stay in Casanova: a huge round tower room, with terracotta floor and amazing, near-vertical beams – excellent for propping books on. (There are plenty of books: Marisa feels a house is not properly furnished without them.) There are other round rooms – La Petite Tour is smaller, and ravishingly pretty. The whole place is enticing with flowers and little nooks and crannies, often put to good use as wardrobes or cupboards. The grounds are lovely, with lilies on the moat and a delicate stone chapel.

Price	€230. Suites €250.
Rooms	5: 1 double, 4 suites for 2-3.
Meals	Breakfast included.
	Dinner with drinks €60, book ahead.
Closed	2 January-31 March.
Directions	A11 exit 9 Le Mans Sud. D309 for Noyen via Louplande, Chemiré le Gaudin. 1.5km after Fercé sur Sarthe, right at small chapel.

Marisa Radini & Micol Tassan Din
72430 Fercé sur Sarthe,
Sarthe

Tel	+33 (0)2 43 77 32 81
Fax	+33 (0)2 43 77 32 81
Email	vauloge@mail.com
Web	www.vauloge.com

Château de La Barre

Immerse yourself in ancient grandeur. Resplendent in 40 hectares of parkland, the château has been in the family since 1421. The portraits and furniture in the Grand Salon are as they were in 1784; join the Comte and Comtesse for welcome drinks under the vast chandelier. She is English, he French and both are young and enthusiastic hosts. Book in for a candlelit dinner (and special wines) served on fine china; move on to a brandy and a chaise-longue in the Salon Rose – or billiards in the medieval 'fire room' (living room), under the watchful eye of Kakou the parrot. And sweep up to bed. In one immense wing are five bedrooms, all different. Expect golden fabric walls and grand oils in Chambre Jaune; red and white stripes in the twin-bedded Suite des Fleurs; heaps of toile de Jouy and polished parquet in the serene Chambre Bleue; in the vast Chambre Marin, a canopied suite fit for a king. Some windows have balconies overlooking the grounds, bathrooms have antique tubs or jacuzzis, outside are bicycles from which you may discover the bucolic Perche. *Children over eight welcome.*

Price	€130–€220. Suites €310.
Rooms	5: 2 doubles, 3 suites for 3.
Meals	Breakfast €15.
	Hosted dinner with wine, €60; book
	ahead. Restaurants 3km & 12km.
Closed	15 January–10 February.
Directions	A11 Le Mans & Rennes, exit
	La Ferté-Bernard. D1 for St Calais.
	Château 3km before St Calais,
	to right directly off D1.

Comte & Comtesse de Vanssay
72120 Conflans sur Anille,
Sarthe

Tel	+33 (0)2 43 35 00 17
Email	info@chateaudelabarre.com
Web	www.chateaudelabarre.com

Château de Monhoudou

Your aristocratic hosts are keeping the ancestral home alive in a dignified manner – 19 generations on. Something special inhabits a place when it has been treasured by the same family for so long and you'll find it here. This is a jewel set in rolling parkland; sheep and ewes, graze under mature trees, there are horses in the paddock, swans on the moat, the occasional call of peacock, deer or boar. And there's endless scope for biking and hiking. Inside are antiques on parquet floors, modern beds, bathrooms and loos in turrets, a small library, intriguing alcoves, hunting trophies, a dining room elegant with family silver. Dinner, prepared by Madame, can be a romantic affair for two or you can join other guests for home-prepared foie gras, coquilles Saint Jacques, duck with peaches, braised leeks, apple and calvados sorbet. Then bask in front of the log fire in the sitting room under the gaze of family portraits. And do ask to see the chapel upstairs. Timeless tranquillity and a charming hostess.

Price	€100–€155.
Rooms	6: 4 doubles, 1 twin, 1 suite for 3.
Meals	Breakfast €18. Hosted dinner with wine, €39; dinner (separate tables) with champagne & wine, €69. Book ahead.
Closed	Rarely.
Directions	From Alençon N138 S for Le Mans about 14km; at La Hutte left D310 for 10km; right D19 through Courgains; left D132 to Monhoudou; signed.

Michel & Marie-Christine de Monhoudou
72260 Monhoudou, Sarthe

Tel	+33 (0)6 83 35 39 12 (mobile)
Fax	+33 (0)2 43 33 11 58
Email	info@monhoudou.com
Web	www.monhoudou.com

Château de Saint Paterne

A 21st-century fairy tale: a 500-year-old château was abandoned by its owners for 30 years, then rediscovered by the heir who left sunny yellow Provence for cool green pastures to resurrect the old shell. He and his wife are a charming young couple and have redecorated with refreshing taste, respecting the style and history of the building, adding a zest of southern colour to panelled, antique-filled rooms, pretty country furniture before ancient fireplaces and hand-rendered, rough and 'imperfect' finishes nothing stiff or fixed. Sitting, dining and first floor bedrooms are in château style; the Henri IV room (he had a mistress here, of course) has thrillingly painted beams; ancestors and objets adorn but don't clutter. The attic floor is fantasy among the rafters: nooks, corners and split levels, a striking green and red bathroom, another bath sunk below the floor. Your host, an excellent cook, uses exotic vegetables from his kitchen garden and calls his cookery courses Laisons Délicieuses. An attractive mixture of past and present values and superb hosts.

Price	€135–€230.
Rooms	10: 6 doubles, 4 suites.
Meals	Breakfast €12.
	Dinner with apéritif and coffee, €45,
	book ahead.
Closed	January–March.
Directions	A28 exit 19 towards St Peterne then
	St Paterne centre. Entrance on right
	opposite garage.

Charles–Henry & Segolène de Valbray
72610 Saint Paterne, Sarthe

Tel	+33 (0)2 33 27 54 71
Fax	+33 (0)2 33 29 16 71
Email	chateaudesaintpaterne@wanadoo.fr
Web	www.chateau-saintpaterne.com

Hôtel Oasis

Efficient anglophile Monsieur Chedor runs a happy ship. You couldn't fail to feel well cared for: bedrooms are spotless and well-equipped, there are leather settees in the bar and a personal trainer in the gym. The cosy, woody reception sets the tone: all the beams, joists, exposed stones and wafer-brick walls you'd expect from a restored farmhouse with outbuildings. Bedrooms are in the stable wing: some off a raftered corridor upstairs, some at ground-floor level. White walls and old timbers, attractive repro country furniture, comfy armchairs, writing desks and super bathrooms. The bar has an English pubby feel and serves decent food (there's also pizzeria/grill in the courtyard), the lounge is snug with plants, pool and piano and the breakfast room is a treat: red-clothed tables on a flagged floor and a big stone fireplace crackling with logs in winter. A shame to stay just a night, there's so much to see in the area, from the 24-hour race at le Mans to the 14th-century château at Carrouges. And you could squeeze in a round of mini-golf before breakfast. Excellent value.

Price	€41–€69.
Rooms	13: 10 doubles, 1 twin, 2 family rooms for 3.
Meals	Breakfast €6.80. Light meals available.
Closed	Never.
Directions	From N12 at Javron, D13 to Villaines La Juhel. On right entering village.

Steve Chedor
La Sourderie,
53700 Villaines la Juhel, Mayenne

Tel	+33 (0)2 43 03 28 67
Fax	+33 (0)2 43 03 35 30
Email	oasis@oasis.fr
Web	www.oasis.fr

Loire Valley

Hôtel Diderot

In the large sunny courtyard, contentment radiates from the very walls; climbers romp merrily up pergolas, roses peek around the olive tree, tables and chairs rest in shady corners. You'll want to linger here over breakfast, and the 66 varieties of homemade jam are the perfect excuse. In winter you have a low-beamed and charming dining room with a vast fireplace lit on cool days – a survivor from the original 15th-century house. Bedrooms feel like beautiful rooms in a family home and each is different in style: Napoleon III, Art Deco, contemporary. All have simple, elegant fabrics, pretty pictures, fresh flowers, a good supply of books. Those facing the courtyard are light and airy, those at the back overlook a quiet street, darker but cool and appealing. Further (ground-floor) rooms in the new 'Pavillon' are modern with cheerful colours, those in the 'Annexe' are more functional. Françoise and brother Laurent are naturally, delightfully hospitable, and having lived in this town all their lives they know its history well. Castle, churches, restaurants and river lie just beyond the door.

Price	€53–€75.
Rooms	27: 17 doubles, 10 twins.
Meals	Breakfast €8.
	Choice of restaurants within 10 minutes.
Closed	21 January–7 February.
Directions	From Paris, A10 exit 24 after Tours.
	D751 to Chinon. Signed.

Françoise & Laurent Dutheil
4 rue Buffon & 7 rue Diderot,
37500 Chinon, Indre-et-Loire

Tel	+33 (0)2 47 93 18 87
Fax	+33 (0)2 47 93 37 10
Email	hoteldiderot@wanadoo.fr
Web	www.hoteldiderot.com

Domaine du Château d'Hommes

A tit had just made its nest in the post box and Madame was hoping that the guests wouldn't disturb it. No hunting, no shooting on this 178-hectare estate; lots of deer and birdsong and a posse of baby wild boar when we visited. The courtyard setting is certainly splendid: the moat and the ruins of the old castle, with one little tower still standing, make a thoroughly romantic setting for this great house, originally the tithe barn built just outside the castle wall. Inside, a vast baronial hall and fireplace welcome you and the atmosphere becomes more formal with a huge dining table, candelabra at either end. Antique furniture in the bedrooms (beautifully Italian in one case) goes hand-in-hand with lavish, impeccable bathrooms. Two rooms give onto the fine courtyard bounded by outbuildings; two look out to open fields and woods. In contrast, honeymoon couples ask for the Tower Room where the view overlooks the moat. Watch the friendly donkey follow Monsieur when he takes his morning ride or relax on the large lawned area starring a huge walnut tree. Very peaceful, very charming.

Price	€87–€117.
Rooms	5: 2 twins, 3 doubles.
Meals	Breakfast included. Hosted dinner on 1st night, with wine, €30; book ahead. Restaurant 4km.
Closed	Rarely.
Directions	From Le Mans for Château du Loir & Château La Vallière. From there to Rillé & Hommes. D64 for Gizeux. Château on right as you leave village.

Hardy Family
37340 Hommes,
Indre-et-Loire

Tel	+33 (0)2 47 24 95 13
Fax	+33 (0)2 47 24 68 67
Email	levieuxchateaudehommes@wanadoo.fr
Web	www.le-vieux-chateau-de-hommes.com

Château de la Bourdaisière

A superlative, princely experience: a history-laden estate with formal gardens and native woods, a Renaissance château on the foundations of a medieval fortress, vaulted meeting rooms and a little boudoir for intimacy as well as a bright, floral breakfast room onto the garden. Guest rooms? François I has a bathroom the size of a bedroom, rich dark green beams and quantities of old books in his magnificent terrace suite; Gabrielle d'Estrées is gorgeously feminine as befits a mistress of Henri IV, who wears rich, regal red; Jeanne D'Arc has amazing beams and a loo in a tower (smaller rooms are less grand). The drawing room is the princes' own – they drop by, their books lie around, their family antiques and paintings furnish it. Authenticity and good taste are rife, the place is genuinely special yet very human and your hosts are charmingly friendly. The brothers de Broglie grow 200 aromatics and 500 types of tomato. Celebrate the real thing at lunch with a glass of Château Bourdaisière.

Price	€124–€224. Apartments €254.
Rooms	20: 8 doubles, 3 twins, 1 family room for 3, 2 apartments for 3-5 (without kitchen). Pavilion: 6 doubles.
Meals	Breakfast €12. Dinner for groups only €41, book ahead.
Closed	2 November-26 March.
Directions	From A10, exit Tours Centre for Amboise, then D751 to Montlouis sur Loire. Signed.

Prince P.M. de Broglie
25 rue de la Bourdaisière,
37270 Montlouis sur Loire, Indre-et-Loire

Tel	+33 (0)2 47 45 16 31
Fax	+33 (0)2 47 45 09 11
Email	contact@chateaulabourdaisiere.com
Web	www.chateaulabourdaisiere.com

Château de l'Hérissaudière

Wander through wild cyclamen under giant sequoias, take a dip in the elegant pool, enjoy an aperitif on the flowery terrace. You could get used to country-house living here, French-style. Madame, charming, cultured, welcomes you as family to her home. The classic manor house, built in creamy tufa stone, wrapped in 18 acres of parkland, is all light, elegance and fresh flowers. Walls are hung with gilded mirrors and bold paintings, tables covered with interesting *objets*. Relax in the sunny salon or the clubby library with its books and games table. Bedrooms, overlooking the park, are large, gracious and subtly themed, perhaps with rich Louis XV furnishings or a blue and yellow Empire style. The Chinon suite, tucked away, is good for children; the former hunting room is wheelchair-friendly; bathrooms are grand with original tiling and marble floors. Breakfast is a gourmet feast. Madame offers light suppers, weekend summer buffets or will recommend local restaurants. Loire châteaux, golf and cycling trails (bikes to hire) are nearby; tennis, ping-pong, croquet are in the grounds. *Cash or cheque only.*

Price	€150–€160. Suites €160–€220.
Rooms	5: 3 suites, 2 doubles.
Meals	Breakfast included
	Occasional light supper, €25.
Closed	Rarely.
Directions	Leave Tours for Angers/Laval. 7km after La Membrolle sur Choisille, left onto D48, direction Langeas/Bernay.

Madame Claudine Detilleux
37230 Pernay,
Indre-et-Loire

Tel	+33 (0)2 47 55 95 28
Email	info@herissaudiere.com
Web	www.herissaudiere.com

Hostellerie de la Mère Hamard

Watch the world from your window, the locals clutching their baguettes on their way home from the boulangerie. You are in the middle of a little village and it's peaceful here – yet Tours is no more than a ten-minute drive. The old *hostellerie* sits opposite the church and was built as a presbytery in the 18th century; Monique and Patrick have done it all up in a light, modern way. The two ground-floor rooms are large, each have their own tasteful colour scheme and matching bed covers and curtains. The bathrooms are bright and crisp with pretty friezes, some with showers, others with bath. Smaller rooms on the first and second floors have pale walls, light, bright fabrics. The two largest rooms, over the restaurant in another building, are under the eaves with sofas that can double as beds. Dine on the terrace in summer: another reason to stay is the food, traditional but with original touches. Enjoy leek flan with mussels, roasted pigeon with stewed onions, a stuffed saddle of rabbit with crayfish. Popular with the locals: book your table at weekends.

Price	€68-€92.
Rooms	11: 7 twins/doubles, 4 family rooms for 3.
Meals	Breakfast €11.50. Lunch & dinner €27-€53 (closed Sun eve & Monday). Restaurants 5km.
Closed	15 February-15 March.
Directions	From Tours, N138 for Le Mans, then left for Semblançay. Hotel in centre of village, opposite church.

M & Mme Pegué
37360 Semblançay,
Indre-et-Loire

Tel	+33 (0)2 47 56 62 04
Fax	+33 (0)2 47 56 53 61
Email	reservation@lamerehamard.com
Web	www.lamerehamard.com

Entry 159 Map 4

Château de l'Aubrière

Even before the Comtesse greets you, the fairytale turrets and sweeping lawns drop polite hints that you are among the aristocracy. Yet the 1864 château has a family feel, its ornate towers good-humouredly at odds with the kids' bikes by the back door – evidence of the Lussacs' five children. Rest assured, it is sumptuous inside. The bedrooms are magnificent, each named after a Loire château — caress the beautiful old elm wardrobe in Langeais, sink into the deep blue and red comfort of enormous Chenonceau, compose your postcards at the Napoleon III writing desk of Villandry. One bathroom is faux-black marble with red carpets while others have jacuzzi baths; all sparkle with gilt-framed mirrors. Downstairs dine at individual tables surrounded by some magnificent portraits. Scallop salad, duck confit, vegetables from the garden and lavender ice cream may tempt you – but save room for bacon and green-tomato jam at breakfast. There's plenty to do here: swim in the heated pool, admire the formal gardens or explore the 15 hectares of grounds with views.

Price	€110–€150. Single €80. Suites €175–€210. Family suite €210 for 4. Triple €170–€210.
Rooms	13: 4 doubles, 3 twins, 1 single, 3 suites, 1 family suite for 4-5, 1 triple.
Meals	Breakfast €12. Dinner from €40. Restaurant closed Wednesdays.
Closed	October-end April.
Directions	A10 exit 19 to Tours Nord & Le Mans. Follow signs for Le Mans on N138; exit La Membrolle & Choisille. Signed.

Comte & Comtesse Régis de Lussac
Route de Fondettes,
37390 La Membrolle sur Choisille, Indre-et-Loire
Tel +33 (0)2 47 51 50 35
Fax +33 (0)2 47 51 34 69
Email aubriere@wanadoo.fr
Web www.aubriere.fr

Château du Vau

Lanky, relaxed, philosopher Bruno has turned his family château into a delightful, harmonious refuge for the world-weary traveller. The cosy, book-lined, deep-chaired sitting room is a place where you find yourself irresistibly drawn into long conversations about music, yoga, art… The sunny breakfast room is charming with its stone-coloured tiles and pretty fabrics. Generations of sliding children have polished the banisters on the stairs leading to the large, light bedrooms that are beautifully but unfussily decorated — splendid brass bedsteads, Turkish rugs on parquet floors, old family furniture, pictures and memorabilia — the spirit of zen can be felt in the search for pure authenticity. A flock of sheep graze peacefully in the newly planted orchard, and there's a dread-locked donkey called Omega. Deer can often be seen bounding across the meadow. With 118 hectares of grounds it is very hard to imagine that you're only 15 minutes from the centre of Tours. On fine summer evenings you can take a supper tray à la Glyndebourne in a favourite corner of the vast grounds. *Golf course opposite.*

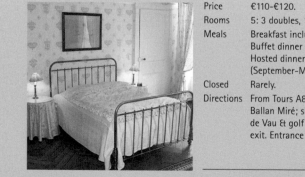

Price	€110-€120.
Rooms	5: 3 doubles, 1 triple, 1 family room.
Meals	Breakfast included. Buffet dinner €26 (June-August). Hosted dinner with wine, €42 (September-May).
Closed	Rarely.
Directions	From Tours A85 (Saumur); 1st exit for Ballan Miré; signs for Ferme-Château de Vau & golf course at motorway exit. Entrance opp. golf course.

Bruno Clément
37510 Ballan Miré,
Indre-et-Loire

Tel	+33 (0)2 47 67 84 04
Email	info@chateau-du-vau.com
Web	www.chateau-du-vau.com

Château de Reignac

A remarkably balanced restoration is this four-star hotel, full of elegance and charm, where the 'old' is underplayed and the 'new' is discreet. So many personalities stayed or were connected with this château that Erick decided to theme the rooms adding a portrait or special object – and a biography. 'Lafayette', who inherited the château and visited until 1792, is a small suite with two bathrooms all in subtle greens and yellows with an attractive writing desk for your historical novel and a private terrace for a balmy evenings. Axel de Fersen, a Swedish nobleman who swooned for Marie Antoinette, is in pale blues and yellows with a statue of his beloved and a claw-foot bath. Lime and mauve work wonders in the *grand salon* – enormous sparkling mirrors and flower-dressed chimney – while the exotic smoking room/bar – Zanzibar – is in dark browns with cane furniture. Books can be borrowed from the properly sober library where an Egyptian theme runs through the art on the walls. The guests-only restaurant serves a daily changing menu, full of spicy, original touches. We think you will like it here.

Price	€150–€190. Suites €240. Apartment €280–€320.
Rooms	12: 6 doubles, 2 twins, 3 suites for 3, 1 apartment for 4 (without kitchen).
Meals	Buffet breakfast €14. Dinner with wine from €44.
Closed	January.
Directions	A10 towards Bordeaux, exit 23 Tours Sud; N143 toward Loches for 22km; Reignac on left; château next to church.

Erick Charrier
19 rue Louis de Barberin,
37310 Reignac sur Indre, Indre-et-Loire

Tel	+33 (0)2 47 94 14 10
Fax	+33 (0)2 47 94 12 67
Email	contact@lechateaudereignac.com
Web	www.lechateaudereignac.com

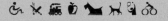

Domaine de la Tortinière

It seems unreal, this pepperpot-towered château on a hill above the Indre, the bird-filled woods where wild cyclamen lay a carpet in autumn and daffodils radiate their light in spring. Then there's the view across to the stony keep of Montbazon, so this is an exceptional spot with tennis, a heated pool, fishing or rowing on the river, too. Bedrooms are decorated with flair and imagination, be they in the château or in one of the several outbuildings. One of these, an adorable Renaissance doll's house, has two smaller rooms and a split-level suite; the orchard pavillion, for playing shepherdesses, is big and beautifully furnished – the desk invites great writings. Bathrooms are luxurious, some smaller than others. For wet nights there's an underground passage to the orangery where you dine – with a dining terrace for summer. Soft lighting, panelled reception rooms, deep comfort and discreet friendliness here in this real family-run hotel: the warm, humorous owners are genuinely attentive, their sole aim is to make your stay peaceful and harmonious. Discover the mills and villages of the Indre.

Price	€140–€300. Suites €280–€340.
Rooms	Château: 7 doubles, 4 suites. Pavillions: 16 doubles, 3 suites.
Meals	Breakfast €16. Dinner €42–€72. Restaurant closed Sunday evenings November-March.
Closed	20 December-February.
Directions	2km north of Montbazon. From Tours D910 south for Poitiers for 10km. In Les Gués, right at 2nd set of lights. Signed.

Xavier & Anne Olivereau
Les Gués de Veigné,
37250 Montbazon, Indre-et-Loire

Tel	+33 (0)2 47 34 35 00
Fax	+33 (0)2 47 65 95 70
Email	domaine.tortiniere@wanadoo.fr
Web	www.tortiniere.com

Domaine des Bidaudières

Sylvie and Pascal Suzanne have made their mark on this classic, creamy-stoned ex-wine-grower's property. Unstuffy and outgoing, this stylish young couple lend sophistication to the place and produce a small quantity of their own wine, having planted new vineyards to the terraced rear. Cypress trees stand on the hillside behind and give an Italianate feel. Bedrooms are fresh and contemporary, each immaculate and carpeted and decorated in Designers Guild fabrics. All are light, south-facing and have valley views. The sitting room, where the kitchen used to be, was actually built into the rock — a hugely attractive, stone-floored room with a low rocky ceiling and an open fire at one end. Guests can idle away the afternoon in the elegant swimming pool on the lower terrace which lies alongside the carefully restored orangerie. Sun beds are separated by small bushes for more privacy. There is even a direct access to the pool via the lift in the main house. Families are welcome to stay in the more rustic 'troglodyte' apartment nearby. *Cash or euro cheque only.*

Price	€125. Suite €140. Cottages €110–€170. Apartment €110.
Rooms	8 + 1: 4 doubles, 1 twin, 1 suite for 3, 2 cottages for 4-5 (without kitchen). Apartment for 5.
Meals	Breakfast included. Restaurants 10-15km.
Closed	Rarely.
Directions	From Paris, A10 exit 20 Vouvray onto N952 for Amboise. In Vouvray D46 for Vernou sur Brenne; 2nd street on left after r'bout.

Monsieur & Madame Pascal Suzanne
Rue du Peu Morier,
37210 Vouvray, Indre-et-Loire

Tel	+33 (0)2 47 52 66 85
Fax	+33 (0)2 47 52 62 17
Email	contact@bidaudieres.com
Web	www.bidaudieres.com

Hôtel du Bon Laboureur et du Château

This little hotel, a stroll from the château of Chenonceaux, started life as a coaching inn in the 18th century. Now in the hands of the fourth generation, it has expanded into an adjoining building (the old village school) and into a somewhat grander building with a rather pretentious tower, known tongue-in-cheek as 'The Manor'. The bedrooms are light and airy with plenty of space and are kept in tip-top condition. In an 18th-century house there are four; up a narrow wooden staircase tiled in terracotta is a double in pretty cream and red toile de Jouy. The heart of the hotel is in the original building, with its elegant 18th-century style dining room and a simpler, more relaxed one next to it. In summer, tables with starched white cloths, candles and flowers are set on the terrace under the trees. A good spot for seeing the châteaux; Amboise, Chaumont, Chambord and others are within easy reach so you can make your visits and return with time for a swim and a cocktail before dinner. A large potager behind the hotel supplies vegetables. Charming owners, delightful cuisine.

Price	€115-€155. Suites €190-€230.
Rooms	25: 20 doubles, 5 suites.
Meals	Breakfast €12. Picnic €9. Lunch & dinner €30-€85. Restaurant closed for lunch Tuesday.
Closed	Mid-November-mid-December; January.
Directions	From Blois, cross Loire onto D751 then D764 to Montrichard. Follow signs to Chenonceaux; on right.

Isabelle & Antoine Jeudi
6 rue du Docteur Bretonneau,
37150 Chenonceaux, Indre-et-Loire

Tel	+33 (0)2 47 23 90 02
Fax	+33 (0)2 47 23 82 01
Email	laboureur@wanadoo.fr
Web	www.bonlaboureur.com

Le Vieux Manoir

Just imagine visiting Amboise, doing a whistle-stop tour of the magnificent château, a spot of lunch, and then staying in a beautiful manoir from whose wine cellars runs a secret tunnel to the château's very grounds. Gloria ran a wonderful B&B in Boston before resettling in France with her husband to fulfil a dream of restoring a 17th-century jewel. Rooms are filled with fascinating French flea market finds and family antiques, and bedrooms bow to the ladies: Colette is beamed and bright in a red and white theme, Madame de Lafayette's hand basin sits in an antique dresser, bevelled mirrors and hand-made tiles sparkle in the bathrooms. There's a salon, a snooze-friendly library and a convivial conservatory for fine breakfasting which opens onto a cheery French-formal town garden. The little two-storey guardhouse has become an impeccable cottage for four with a sitting room and a kitchen only Americans know how to do – perfect for families with children over five. With 30 restaurants nearby, your only problem will be in choosing where to step out for dinner.

Price	€115-€190. Cottages €210-€295.
Rooms	6 + 2: 5 doubles, 1 triple, 2 cottages for 2-4.
Meals	Breakfast included. Restaurants in town.
Closed	November-February. Call for out of season reservations.
Directions	In Amboise, from Quai Général de Gaulle, onto Ave des Martyrs at post office. Rue Rabelais left after 150m, one way, narrow.

Gloria & Bob Belknap
13 rue Rabelais,
37400 Amboise, Indre-et-Loire

Tel +33 (0)2 47 30 41 27
Fax +33 (0)2 47 30 41 27
Email info@le-vieux-manoir.com
Web www.le-vieux-manoir.com

Le Manoir Les Minimes

You can stay in either the manor itself or in the small pavillion across the courtyard. Every detail has been thought out care, lovingly chosen antiques and *objets* placed to create a light sophistication. A far cry from the Minimes order who had a convent here until it was destroyed in the French Revolution; this noble townhouse took the site. Between majestic Loire and historic castle, the manor has 18th-century grace and generous windows that look onto its big courtyard, the castle and the lustrous river. The charmingly young and enthusiastic Eric Deforges was a fashion designer, hence his faultless eye for fabric, colour and detail. Exquisitely decorated rooms are big – slightly smaller on the top floor, with beams and river views from their dormers – and have luxurious bathrooms. The masterpiece is the suite where the toile de Jouy wall fabric seems to be one single piece. There is a terrace outside where you can take an aperitif in the late afternoon under yellow umbrellas, gazing up at the royal château of Amboise, while Olga, the elegant Brie sheepdog, sleeps in the sun nearby.

Price	€119-€190. Suites €270-€460.
Rooms	15: 13 twins/doubles, 2 suites.
Meals	Breakfast €12-€17. Will provide menus & make reservations in local restaurants within walking distance.
Closed	Never.
Directions	From A10 for Amboise. Over Loire, then right on D751 for town centre. On left approaching town centre.

Patrice Longet & Eric Deforges
34 quai Charles Guinot,
37400 Amboise, Indre-et-Loire

Tel	+33 (0)2 47 30 40 40
Fax	+33 (0)2 47 30 40 77
Email	reservation@manoirlesminimes.com
Web	www.manoirlesminimes.com

Château des Ormeaux

The view's the thing. From the turreted 19th-century château built around a 15th-century tower, you take in the glories of 27 hectares. Corner rooms on two floors – original panelling on the first floor, sloping ceilings on the second – have tiny little boudoirs off the main room in the turret. A decent size, bedrooms have elaborate bedcovers and drapes; bathrooms are grand in a turn-of-the-century way. One room, blue and gold, has a marble fireplace and an 'armoire à glace', a wall of mirrors hidden behind an apparently ordinary cupboard, another, decorated in ochre and maroon, a crystal chandelier and plushly canopied bed. Two new rooms have been carefully restored in the 18th-century manoir, with visible beams and lime rendering. Best of all, from wherever you stand (or swim) those valley views are superb. Everyone dines at a table laden with china, crystal and candles, on fabulous food served by your fabulous hosts – Eric, Emmanuel and Dominique – enhanced by background Bach. A hugely welcoming place.

Price	€115–€165.
Rooms	8: 5 doubles, 3 twins.
Meals	Breakfast included. Dinner with wine, €48 (min. 8), book ahead.
Closed	15 January-15 February.
Directions	From Paris A10 exit 18 Amboise, D31 for Amboise. Right at Autrèche to D55 to Montreuil en Touraine; D5 to Nazelles; right on D1 for Noizay; Château end of village after La Bardouillère.

Emmanuel Guenot & Eric Fontbonnat
Route de Noizay (D1), Nazelles,
37530 Amboise, Indre-et-Loire

Tel	+33 (0)2 47 23 26 51
Fax	+33 (0)2 47 23 19 31
Email	contact@chateaudesormeaux.fr
Web	www.chateaudesormeaux.fr

Le Fleuray Hôtel & Restaurant

Peter and Hazel have created a haven of peace in the middle of the countryside surrounded by fields and grazing cows. The raw material was ideal: a solid, handsome old manor house with duck pond and barns, mature trees and bushes: all that was needed to persuade them to settle. The rooms in the barn are just right for families; slightly cut off from the rest, their French windows open onto the garden with their own individual patios. Those in the main building are slightly smaller but cosy and immaculate with queen size or twin beds. The Newingtons are unstuffy and easy-going, genuinely enjoying the company of visitors. Truly a family affair; Jordan and Cassie, the older children, are a big part of the picture and are rapidly becoming professionals. They have created a slightly English mood, with lightly floral sofas into which you can sink, bookcases, flowers and prints. It must be fun to dine outside on the patio under parasols, on crisp white tablecloths and green chairs. Lovely in winter, too, with an open fire and fine inventive cooking. The guest book sings their praises.

Price	€78–€124.
Rooms	21:10 twins/doubles, 9 family rooms for 2-5, 2 duplex suites for 4-6.
Meals	Breakfast €13. Dinner €29–€48. Child meal €17.
Closed	One week during November; Christmas & New Year.
Directions	From A10 exit 18 Amboise & Château Renault. D31 to Autrèche. Left on D55 to Dame Marie Les Bois. Right on D74 for Cangey. 8km from exit.

Newington Family
Route Dame Marie les Bois (D74),
37530 Cangey-Amboise, Indre-et-Loire

Tel	+33 (0)2 47 56 09 25
Fax	+33 (0)2 47 56 93 97
Email	lefleurayhotel@wanadoo.fr
Web	www.lefleurayhotel.com

Hôtel Château des Tertres

Artist in residence. A classic mid-19th-century nobleman's house surrounded by mature wooded parkland in the Loire valley – but not all is traditional inside. The young, energetic Monsieur Valois is an inventive soul, and his sense of fun pervades this lovely place. Many of the rooms *are* period pieces, including the sitting rooms and the largest of the bedrooms, and some are remarkably ornate. The smallest rooms, though, are minimalist – symphonies of creamy yellow and white with suspended glass basins. That a creative spirit is at work is evident, too, in the gardener's lodge whose four guest rooms have been furnished with panache: one with a massive Italian four-poster, another with a perspex bedhead and a row of medieval steel helmets lined up on the wall! The stereo systems are cleverly disguised. Your host is extremely hospitable and will let you in on the secrets of the château if you ask: before it was restored to its original elegance it had an amazingly chequered career, having been a German military headquarters, a school for metal workers and a chicken farm in three of its former lives.

Price	€75–€112.
Rooms	17: 11 doubles, 3 twins. Lodge: 2 family rooms for 3–4, 1 suite for 4.
Meals	Breakfast buffet €10. Restaurant 1km.
Closed	23 October–Easter.
Directions	From A10 exit Blois. N152 for Amboise & Tours. Right to Onzain opp. bridge to Chaumont. Left in village for Monteaux. Château 1.5km on right.

	Bernard Valois 11 rue de Meuves, 41150 Onzain, Loir-et-Cher
Tel	+33 (0)2 54 20 83 88
Fax	+33 (0)2 54 20 89 21
Email	contact@chateau-tertres.fr
Web	www.chateau-tertres.com

Château du Guerinet

Peering over sumptuous bedcovers beneath golden canopies, you can imagine how a humble woodcutter's daughter must have felt when married to a Prussian prince prepared to build her such a magnificent château. He even brought the forest – acres and acres of it. Hunting scenes playing over its walls and with its own private terrace, the downstairs bedroom is snugly majestic. Stepping lightly up the broad turning staircase on chequered trompe l'oeil marble brings you to a four-poster bedroom, a seemingly effortless mix of rich dark wood and original panelling. In a smaller double, the blue-purple tones of curtains, canopy and Chinese rug all blend in style, while elegantly furnished suites trumpet William Morris designs. You could hold a party in the Greco-Roman bathrooms, chambers of mirrors, some with lion-footed tubs. Pause to grace the impressive hall, before entering the striking salon – or the dining room flanked by tall, bright windows and giant mirrors. Enjoy a wholesome dinner here in the company of Corina and Dave, your two friendly Australian hosts. *Infra-red sauna.*

Price	€130–€195. Suites €165–€195. Family suite €165–€195. Whole château (summer) €6,500–€7,500 per week.
Rooms	6: 4 doubles, 1 family room for 3, 1 family suite for 4.
Meals	Breakfast included (based on 2 adults sharing). Dinner €45 with wine, book ahead. No meals Tues & Wed.
Closed	July & Aug (whole château rental only).
Directions	From Blois D766 for Angers/Château Renault. Pass Orchaise, 2km for Herbault. Signed.

Clemence Family
41190 Orchaise,
Loir-et-Cher

Tel	+33 (0)2 54 70 10 13
Fax	+44 (0)20 7691 7575
Email	corina@loirechateau.com
Web	www.loirechateau.com

Château de la Voûte

Mmes Pompadour and Du Barry — the room names are a giveaway. You sleep in a bedroom whose windows and beds are voluptuously draped, whose parquet floors have been burnished to perfection and whose furniture is swaggeringly ornate. Off the red and gold guest salon, with grand piano, is a library lined with turquoise shelves; breakfast is taken in a striped, light-filled room with an enamelled 17th-century stove and a fresco of the Bay of Naples. It may sound overwhelming but somehow it works; the grandeur is neutralised by flashes of wit. The château has been restored by the hospitable Marie and Jean-Pierre, who abandoned Parisian life after their children left home. Take the opportunity of dining with them one evening: they're good company. The château flourishes a 15th-century tower slept in by Henri IV, but mostly dates from the 17th and 18th centuries. The grounds, with magnificent trees, run down to a watermill and the Loir (a lowly relation of the Loire), while the hill behind is topped by the lovely historic town of Trôo. Delightfully off the tourist track.

Price	€85–€135.
Rooms	6: 2 doubles, 1 twin, 3 suites for 2-3.
Meals	Breakfast included.
	Hosted dinner €48, book ahead.
Closed	Never.
Directions	From Paris A11 exit La Ferté Bernard, then Savigny Bessé, then Trôo.

Monsieur J.P. Roussel
Trôo, 41800 Montoire sur le Loir,
Loir-et-Cher

Tel	+33 (0)2 54 72 52 52
Fax	+33 (0)2 54 72 48 18
Email	info@chateaudelavoute.com
Web	www.chateaudelavoute.com

Château de Boisrenault

Built by a 19th-century aristocrat as a wedding present for his daughter – well overdue, she'd had two sons by the time it was finished – this may be turreted, noble and imposing on the outside, but it's a family home within. Furniture, objects, pictures, all have a tale to tell and there's no shortage of hunting trophies and stags' heads on the walls. Reception rooms are lofty, with huge fireplaces. One sitting room has a baby grand; another, smaller and cosier, is lined with books. As for the bedrooms, each is an adventure in itself. Named after the family's children and grandchildren, they feature a hotchpotch of pieces from different periods, including some excellent antiques. A couple of stuffed pheasants make unusual lampshades in Hadrien's room and offset the yellow walls; two apartments upstairs have their own equipped kitchens. A delicious pool is discreetly tucked away behind trees in the lovely grounds; table tennis and table football are a godsend on rainy days. Meals are taken at a vast table in the dining room; be sure to book if you'd like dinner. A good place for a family stay.

Price	€79–€100. Family rooms €100–€130. Apartments €312–€486 per week.
Rooms	7 + 2: 2 doubles, 1 twin, 4 family rooms for 4. 2 apartments for 4-5.
Meals	Breakfast included. Dinner €23, book ahead.
Closed	Rarely.
Directions	From A20 exit 11 on D8 to Levroux; D926 for Buzançais. Château on left 3km before town.

Florence du Manoir
36500 Buzançais,
Indre

Tel	+33 (0)2 54 84 03 01
Fax	+33 (0)2 54 84 10 57
Email	boisrenault@wanadoo.fr
Web	www.chateau-du-boisrenault.com

La Petite Fadette

Just off the main road, this tiny unspoilt village takes you back two centuries to Georges Sand's quiet country childhood, whence she proceeded to make her name, rather noisily, as an early advocate of feminism and free love (with Chopin, Musset, et al). Opposite her elegant château with perfect strolling gardens, this pretty country inn amongst a cluster of village houses of age and character fits the scene perfectly. Arched doors open into the simple tea room where pink-clothed tables lead to the grand piano and the old oak stairs up to the bedrooms. Under the stairs is a luxurious log for diners and beyond is a sophisticated restaurant whose vaulted wooden ceiling and magnificent fireplace frame elegantly laid tables, ready for the chef's tempting dishes. The staff is attentive and friendly, the wine list extensive. Bedrooms are all different, done in traditional style with antiques, good fabrics and up-to-date bathrooms. As breakfast is only served till 9am, you may want to take it in the village. An inn, a château and a town of exceptional atmosphere – evocative and memorable.

Price	€65–€140.
Rooms	9: 6 doubles, 2 twins, 1 suite.
Meals	Breakfast €12. Lunch & dinner €19–€50.
Closed	Rarely.
Directions	From Chateauroux, D943 for La Châtre. 5km before La Châtre, left into Nohant. Hotel in village centre opposite church.

M Bernard Gabriel Chapleau
Place du Château,
36400 Nohant, Indre

Tel	+33 (0)2 54 31 01 48
Fax	+33 (0)2 54 31 10 19
Web	www.aubergepetitefadette.com

Prieuré Notre Dame d'Orsan

Art as nature or nature as art? Go ahead, pinch yourself, your feet are still on the ground even though your spirit has been miraculously lifted by the harmony and elegance of this priory and its gardens. Patrice, an architect and landscape designer, saved the house from abandonment 15 years ago; originally built in 1107 as a convent, it stands in rural France at its most unspoilt. The oldest remaining buildings, probably the refectory and dormitory, are from the 16th century and form three sides of a square, enclosing beautifully restored gardens, open to visitors. There is no 'hotel' feel to the place at all, and the visitors to the gardens don't make it feel busy either. The reception rooms on the first floor are an interconnecting series of sitting rooms integrating the professional kitchen at one end; contemporary unfussy chic. Dine on homemade bread and home-grown produce under a leafy pergola when it's warm. Bedrooms have pine-panelled walls with shutters, windows and doors painted in a soft grey-green. You will look out onto the wonderful garden; serenity and contemplation are yours.

Price	€180-€280.
Rooms	6: 3 doubles, 3 triples.
Meals	Breakfast €18. Lunch €38. Dinner €62.
Closed	November-March.
Directions	Directions on booking.

Patrice Taravella
18170 Maisonnaes,
Cher

Tel	+33 (0)2 48 56 27 50
Fax	+33 (0)2 48 56 39 64
Email	prieuredorsan@wanadoo.fr
Web	www.prieuredorsan.com

Château de Charly

There's a sunny, southern feel to this gorgeous place. Sweep through large iron gates and up the drive to find a pretty château, attractive outbuildings, orchard and woodland, set in a 32-acre private walled park. Jason and Philippa, young, energetic, ex-engineers, are indulging their passion for life in France and their warmth is infectious. A delightful broad entrance hall with a stone-flagged floor invites you in, a gracious oak and metal-balustraded staircase ushers you up. Beautiful long windows fill bedrooms with light, large beds are well dressed, and formal wallpapers, curtains, hand woven rugs, coverlets and cushions give an elegant feel. Bathrooms sport large separate showers, twin sinks and roll top baths; gaze onto parkland as you wallow. Then it's back downstairs for table d'hotes in the gracious dining room or on the candlelit terrace – breakfast well too on the finest fresh pastries and jams from the orchard. The village is charming and has a 12th-century church with a remarkable painted ceiling.

Price	€150–€160.
Rooms	5: 4 doubles, 1 twin.
Meals	Breakfast included. Dinner €40.
Closed	Rarely.
Directions	From Paris A6/A77 exit Nevers. At La Charité sur Loire N151 for Bourges. Left at Sancergues on D6 to Nérondes. At Charly drive through village. 150m past bar and x-roads on right are gates to the château.

Philippa & Jason Park
1 route de Nerondes,
18350 Charly, Cher
Tel   +33 (0)2 48 74 99 62
Email   info@chateaudecharly.com
Web   www.chateaudecharly.com

Château d'Ivoy

Every antique bed is appropriately canopied ('Kipling': frothy mosquito net on carved Anglo-Indian bed; 'Lord Drummond': the olde English feel), every superb bathroom a study in modern fittings on period washstands, enhanced by Hermès toiletries. Ivoy is home to an interior designer who has achieved miracles since buying it from a famous entomologist who had planted a near tropical rainforest in one stateroom, now the fine-furnished, Spode dining room. It was built for Mary Stuart's purser: the Stuarts were allowed to create a Scottish duchy here that lasted 200 years and it became the Drummond family seat after the battle of Culloden. The front is stern, the back opens wide onto sweeping lawns, park and hills – all bedrooms face this way. The house radiates refinement and your hostess's infectious delight. She will welcome you in her grey-green hall with its lovely sandstone floor, invite you to use the library (home to a huge spider... imprisoned in a glass paperweight) or the salon, and will then retire discreetly. Monsieur is a whisky connoisseur – a final delight. *Children over 12 welcome.*

Price	€160-€195.
Rooms	5: 4 doubles, 1 twin.
Meals	Breakfast included. Restaurants nearby.
Closed	Rarely.
Directions	From A10 exit Salbris D944 for Bourges to Neuvy sur Barangeon; left on D926 to La Chapelle d'Angillon; D12 to Ivoy. Château on right 300m after church, entrance through L'Etang Communal.

	Marie France Gouëffon-de Vaivre
	18380 Ivoy le Pré, Cher
Tel	+33 (0)2 48 58 85 01
Fax	+33 (0)2 48 58 85 02
Email	chateau.divoy@wanadoo.fr
Web	www.chateaudivoy.com

Château de la Verrerie

Live the life of a gentle aristocrat, or his mistress if you prefer. Tucked deep in a forest, this 15th-century château was once the home of Charles II's lover, the Duchess of Portsmouth. The current Count — whose family have been owners for 150 years — is a charming, cultured, amiable aristocrat who enjoys sharing his good fortune. It has everything a good château should have: courtyard, Gothic chapel, Italian loggia, music room (for concerts), grazing horses, lawns sweeping to a lake and fleets of grand but comfortably furnished rooms. As well as a gracious salon, there are intimate sitting areas between the bedrooms — heaped with sofas, books and games. Guest rooms, overlooking the park or lake, are outrageously stunning — rich fabrics, soft carpets, vast windows, family antiques. Some have four-posters, others painted ceilings, one has a veranda, another two claw-foot baths. Yes, two. There's canoeing and horse riding nearby or woodland walks on your estate. Dine gastronomically on local produce in the Hansel & Gretel style cottage restaurant. Service is impeccable, warm and friendly.

Price	€155-265. Suites €360.
Rooms	12: 5 twins, 4 doubles, 2 suites.
Meals	Breakfast €14-€18.
	Lunch & dinner €25-€40.
	Restaurant closed Tuesdays.
Closed	20 December-January.
Directions	From Paris A6 & A77 exit Vierzon &
	Bourges. D940 to Aubigny sur Nère.
	Signed.

Comte Béraud de Vogüé
Oizon,
18700 Aubigny sur Nère, Cher

Tel	+33 (0)2 48 81 51 60
Fax	+33 (0)2 48 58 21 25
Email	info@chateaudelaverrerie.com

Poitou – Charentes

Le Logis d'Antan

Blue shutters against pale walls, faded terracotta roofs – the long façade suggests a simple country elegance. Once a wine merchant's house, then part of a farm, it basks in gardens full of beeches and wild poppies, fruit trees and figs. There's even a little pavilion. Bruno and Annie, ex-journalists with a young family, have created a friendly, unpretentious atmosphere – you'll like their style. Meals (Bruno has been on a cookery course) are eaten at a table seating up to 16 in a typically French dining room – or out on the veranda in good weather. Upstairs, where a mezzanine and maze of passageways make for great hide-and-seek, you can prepare picnics in a communal kitchen. Up here, too, are two double rooms, one with a bunk-bedded children's annexe. The triples are on the ground floor: big, traditional rooms, with their own entrances off the drive. Les Pictons, overlooking the front lawn, has exposed stone walls and a grandfather clock; La Pibale, its own terrace. Bruno and Annie work closely with a company called Cycling for Softies, so grab the bikes and explore the country. *No credit cards.*

Price	€65–€81. Family rooms €65–€113. Suite €97.
Rooms	5: 1 double, 2 family rooms for 3, 1 family room for 4–5, 1 suite for 4.
Meals	Breakfast included. Dinner with wine, €25.
Closed	27 October–5 November.
Directions	From A10 (Paris-Bordeaux) exit 33. Approx. 8km after toll, left to 'Vallans'; Logis on exit dir. Epannes.

Annie & Bruno Ragouilliaux-Di Battista
140 rue Saint-Louis,
79270 Vallans, Deux Sèvres

Tel	+33 (0)5 49 04 86 75
Fax	+33 (0)5 49 32 85 05
Email	info@logisdantan.com
Web	www.logisdantan.com

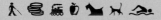

Le Logis Saint Martin

Run with efficiency by the Pellegrins this 17th-century *gentilhommerie* offers that most attractive combination for travellers – solidly comfortable rooms and an excellent restaurant. It is set conveniently on the outskirts of town in a little wooded valley with a small stream running just outside. The bedrooms are smallish, beamed, elegantly furnished and very comfortable; the bigger rooms, with lovely old rafters, are on the top floor. The tower has been converted into a charming apartment: a sitting area downstairs; a smallish stone-walled bedroom up steepish stairs. Food is the point here and as you would expect in France, the menu is local and seasonal, served with panache in the elegant restaurant or in the pleasantly shaded and tranquil garden. The chef has worked with the best and there is a classic feel to the place; the waiters here know how to carve, fillet and flambé at your table. Add an attentive, helpful staff, an excellent wine list, homemade ice creams and breads and you will be glad you came.

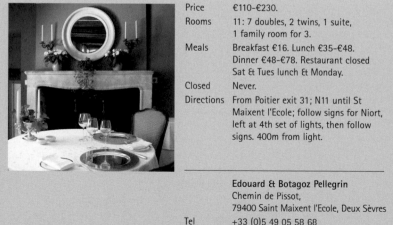

Price	€110–€230.
Rooms	11: 7 doubles, 2 twins, 1 suite, 1 family room for 3.
Meals	Breakfast €16. Lunch €35–€48. Dinner €48–€78. Restaurant closed Sat & Tues lunch & Monday.
Closed	Never.
Directions	From Poitier exit 31; N11 until St Maixent l'Ecole; follow signs for Niort, left at 4th set of lights, then follow signs. 400m from light.

Edouard & Botagoz Pellegrin
Chemin de Pissot,
79400 Saint Maixent l'Ecole, Deux Sèvres

Tel	+33 (0)5 49 05 58 68
Fax	+33 (0)5 49 76 19 93
Email	contact@logis-saint-martin.com
Web	www.logis-saint-martin.com

Château de Saint Loup sur Thouet

This château inspired Perrault to write *Puss in Boots*! It has an ancient and fascinating history. The Black Prince incarcerated John the Good here after the Battle of Poitiers in 1356 and it was rebuilt in the 17th century by the Marquis of Carabas, whose magnificence so impressed the fairytale writer. Charles-Henri de Bartillat visited the château on Christmas Eve 1990, fell in love with it and ten days later had bought it. Saint Loup is a listed monument, open to the public. The count, charming and passionate about his home, is painstakingly restoring the house, 50 hectares of grounds and kitchen garden (using 18th-century plans drawn up by Jacques Boyer de la Boissière). Rooms are lofty and light in the château, medieval in the keep: the Black Prince room in the old kitchens has two vast fireplaces and thick red stained beams; the Bishop's room in the château has a splendid canopied bed between two big windows overlooking the garden. Aperitifs are taken in the winter garden on the other side of the moat – Charles-Henri makes sure guests get to meet each other before dinner. A stunning place.

Price	€150–€220.
Rooms	18. 16 doubles, 2 singles. Entire château (or 8-bedroom keep) can be rented.
Meals	Breakfast €15. Dinner with wine, €75, book ahead.
Closed	Rarely.
Directions	From Airvault D46 to St Loup Lamairé. Château visible on entering village.

Comte Charles-Henri de Bartillat
79600 Saint Loup Lamairé, Deux Sèvres

Tel	+33 (0)5 49 64 81 73
Fax	+33 (0)5 49 64 82 06
Email	st-loup@wanadoo.fr
Web	www.chateaudesaint-loup.com

Hotel le Pigeonnier du Perron

René Descartes once owned this little *seigneurie*; its deeds go back to the 15th century. The Thiollet family has only been here for 150 years. Father and son are fully occupied in their wine laboratory in Cahors, Emilie, in her early 20s, fresh from hotel school, now prepares the meals – fish is her speciality – and runs the place smoothly with help from Fridda. Family connections guarantee an excellent selection of wines from Cahors – of course – but also from Poitou and the Val de Loire. Sun-ripe tomatoes, green and red peppers, cucumber and courgettes are home-grown along with essential herbs for the kitchen; a stone-flagged terrace with good outdoor furniture makes an inviting spot for al fresco dining. Farm buildings are grouped around a sunny courtyard and hollyhocks push up from every imaginable nook and cranny. Bedrooms are smallish but simply and pleasantly decorated with the odd splash of colour; floors are pale pine, walls soft-sponged or of pale exposed stone. One in the dovecote has a little balcony, many look over the fields and valley. Good value. *Advanced notice please for vegetarian fare.*

Price	€79–€84.
Rooms	14: 9 doubles, 4 twins, 1 family suite for 4.
Meals	Breakfast included. Dinner €17–€19.
Closed	Rarely.
Directions	A10 exit 27 for Chatellerault. At 2nd roundabout for Cenon; through Cenon for Availles; 1st right after village sign. Signed on right after approx. 1km.

Emilie Thiollet
Le Perron,
86530 Availles en Chatellerault, Vienne

Tel	+33 (0)5 49 19 76 08
Fax	+33 (0)5 49 19 12 82
Email	accueil@lepigeonnierduperron.com
Web	www.lepigeonnierduperron.com

Le Relais du Lyon d'Or

In one of France's most beautiful villages, this old hotel is finally taking shape with new owners. Diana, American, brings her previous hotel and restaurant experience and Dominique, French, sings hymns to the grape. He is a full-fledged wine expert and dealer who will suggest the perfect bottle for dinner. Each common room has been rebuilt round its old flagstones, doors and beams, then decorated in warm natural colours with paint effects (ragged, distressed, veiled), patinas and stencils. Bedrooms have intriguing details and individuality; rafters for the ones under the roof, high ceilings and beams for the others. Some are big, some are smaller, not overdone, with sparkling bathrooms. The menu is varied and emphasis is on traditional dishes using much local produce; meals can be served on the pretty parasoled terrace in summer. Just opened to the public and not to be missed is the Roc aux Sorciers with its breathtaking prehistoric bas reliefs. For birdwatching, turtle-spotting and orchid-peeping there's La Brenne, a magnificent regional park nearby.

Price	€75–€125. Suites €125–€135.
Rooms	10: 8 doubles, 1 suite for 4, 1 suite for 5.
Meals	Breakfast €12. Lunch & dinner €25–€40.
Closed	December–February.
Directions	A10 exit Châtellerault Nord D9/D725 east through La Roche Posay onto D5 to Angles sur l'Anglin. In village centre.

Dominique Fuscien & Diana Hager
4 rue d'Enfer,
86260 Angles sur l'Anglin, Vienne

Tel	+33 (0)5 49 48 32 53
Fax	+33 (0)5 49 84 02 28
Email	contact@lyondor.com
Web	www.lyondor.com

Hôtel Les Orangeries

Even before you step inside, the long cool pool beneath the trees will convince you that these people have the finest sense of how to treat an old house and its surroundings. The harmony of the deep wooden deck, raw stone walls, giant baskets and orange trees draws you in, and candles create magic by night. The young owners fell in love with the place and applied all their talent – he's an architect – to giving it an 18th-century elegance in contemporary mood. Stripped oak doors, exposed stone walls, cool stone floors glow with loving care, like valued old friends. Olivia has given each bedroom its own sense of uncluttered harmony; the quietest face the garden, the split-level suites are a delight. The Gautiers' passions include the old-fashioned games they have resuscitated for you: croquet and skittles under the trees, two kinds of billiards, backgammon and mahjong. Ask for Olivier: she speaks wonderful English and her enthusiasm for house, garden, animals – and you – is catching. Breakfast in the garden is bliss, and the hot chocolate (organic, naturally) the best you will ever have tasted.

Hats off to the Gautiers: theirs is the first hotel in France to have won the Ecolabel Européen stamp of approval. The whole place echoes a commitment to combining eco-technology and ethical responsibility with traditional hospitality and charm; the buildings are insulated, water leakage management systems have been introduced, everything that can be recycled and composted is, food is sourced within a 60km radius and coffee is Fair Trade. Staff are 100% involved with the ethos, car sharing is encouraged and the welcome guide for guests reveals how the smallest gestures can make a difference.

Price	€65–€115. Apartments €95–€170.
Rooms	11: 7 doubles, 4 apartments for 4–5 (without kitchen).
Meals	Breakfast from €13.50. Lunch snacks. Dinner from €30.
Closed	Mid-December–mid-January.
Directions	Exit Poitiers for Limoges on N147 to Lussac les Châteaux (35km from Poitiers). Ask for route via Châtellerault if arriving from north.

Olivia & Jean-Philippe Gautier
12 avenue du Docteur Dupont,
86320 Lussac les Châteaux, Vienne

Tel	+33 (0)5 49 84 07 07
Fax	+33 (0)5 49 84 98 82
Email	orangeries@wanadoo.fr
Web	www.lesorangeries.fr

SPECIAL
GREEN ENTRY
see page 12

Château de Nieuil

François I built the château as a hunting lodge in the 16th century, but swapped Nieuil for a bigger plot when he opted for the grander Chambord on the Loire. A gambling Count sold it to grandparents of the Bodinauds. Its hunting days are now over and Luce and her husband have instead created an exciting hotel and a hommage to our feathered friends with a magical birdwatching walk round the outside of the moat. Each room is named after a bird and if you are not awoken by real ones, an alarm will sing 'your' song. The château is grand and beautifully decorated: one room has a small children's room up a spiral stair, another a tiny reading room in a turret; most look onto the handsome formal garden at the back. The stunning breakfast room has views of the vast grounds through stained-glass windows. Luce, a chef in her own right, has well trained a young trio who run the restaurant in the old stables. A chandelier hung with love letters and a stainless-steel bar are touches of modern elegance in this country retreat. Open-hearted, open-armed – these people love what they do, and it shows.

Price	€125-€265. Singles €113-€238. Triples €187-€290. Suites €245-€400.
Rooms	27 + 4: 11 doubles, 6 singles, 7 triples, 3 suites. 3 gîtes; 1 gypsy caravan.
Meals	Breakfast €16. Lunch €25-€50. Dinner €46-€60. Rest. closed Sun eves, Mon/Tues lunchtimes Sept-June.
Closed	1 November-5 April.
Directions	From Angoulème N141 to La Rochefoucauld then Chasseneuil. 6.5km after C, in Suaux, left on D739 to Nieuil. Signed.

Monsieur & Madame Bodinaud
16270 Nieuil,
Charente

Tel	+33 (0)5 45 71 36 38
Fax	+33 (0)5 45 71 46 45
Email	chateaunieuilhotel@wanadoo.fr
Web	www.chateaunieuilhotel.com

Château de la Couronne

A contemporary château built in the 19th century on the edge of the Charente and Dordogne. It was a residential college before Mark and Nicky left jobs in fashion and TV to ease it into the 21st century. Leaving the comfortable shapes of the courtyard behind, step through the Gothic wrought-iron entrance into a thrillingly modern living space: a vast hallway with giant sculptures the shape of egg-timers and doors that lead to the back terrace. From here, a row of pretty bistro tables with lanterns look over a sleek black-walled swimming pool. Gardens beyond are topiaried and secluded and wooden carvings, once the props for a window display, now serve as a peaceful resting place to soak up the afternoon sun. Mark and Nicky's style is industrial and spectacular; bedrooms have an urban feel with retro fabrics and swirling glassware. Many have original papers with rustic limewashes. Bathrooms are elegant with original floors and revamped turrets, some with two baths. Outside: a private cinema, a brilliant 1930s fridge and a dinky pool table. Quaint Marthon is a stroll away.

Price	From €145.
Rooms	5 suites: 4 doubles, 1 twin.
Meals	Breakfast €15. Child €10.
	Restaurant 6 minute walk.
Closed	Rarely.
Directions	At Angoulême D939 towards Périgueux, D4 to Marthon. Left in village centre towards Montbron, left at war memorial. Château ahead.

Nicky Cooper & Mark Selwood
16380 Marthon,
Charente

Tel	+33 (0)5 45 62 29 96
Email	info@chateaudelacouronne.com
Web	www.chateaudelacouronne.com

Château de l'Yeuse

A delightful conceit: a miniature folly of a Charente château, dazzlingly striped in brick and creamy stone, with a modern extension in flamboyant style. It is just five minutes from Cognac yet is wrapped in parkland with views to the Charente river – utterly charming. Bedrooms are in the newer part – with fun, trompe l'oeil-flourished corridors – large and light in bold country-house style and with ultra-modern bathrooms. Book a room overlooking the river. By contrast, the 'old' château is all classical proportions, elegant furnishings and traditional comfort. Wallow in the cigar salon with its deep armchairs and glass-fronted cabinets, work your way through the 100-year-old cognacs. It's posh frocks for dinner in the chandelier-hung dining room, all stiff white napery and black jacketed waiters. The excitement over chef Pascal Nebout's cuisine is palpable. Céline, the young manageress, energetic yet ever-calm, will advise on visiting distilleries and music festivals. Discover the secret garden, relax by the pool, find a shady terrace or treat yourself to a massage in the hamman. Sophisticated living.

Price	€100–€170. Suites €223–€343.
Rooms	24: 18 doubles, 3 twins/doubles, 3 suites.
Meals	Breakfast €64. Lunch €30–€75. Dinner €46–€75. Restaurant closed Mon, Tues & Sat lunchtimes; also Sunday evenings off-season.
Closed	2-12 January.
Directions	From Paris A10 exit 34. Follow signs St Jean d'Angély & Cognac then for Angoulème; D15 to St Brice & Quartier de l'Echassier.

Céline Desmazières & Pascal Nebout
65 rue de Bellevue, Châteaubernard,
16100 Cognac, Charente

Tel	+33 (0)5 45 36 82 60
Fax	+33 (0)5 45 35 06 32
Email	reservations.yeuse@wanadoo.fr
Web	www.yeuse.fr

Logis du Fresne

The Butler family came to France 100 years ago to make cognac and Tone's husband Christophe has been in the business all his life. She is from Norway, and had a children's clothing label there; they are the loveliest hosts. They bought the old, elegant Logis five years ago and opened in 2003, fulfilling their vision of a refined place to stay with a bed & breakfast feel. The façade is wonderful and inside just as good. The whole feel is light and fresh and the style turn-of-the-century Norwegian: old terracotta tiles on the ground floor, pale painted beams, a cosy library, an elegant salon. Bedrooms are as serene. Those on the first floor have uncluttered chic: a gilded mirror hangs above an open fire, an oriental rug graces a limed floor… those above are more modern. The two-room suite has its own stairs; bathrooms are well-lit and beautifully modern. Breakfast is romantic, expect a fresh cut rose and quintessential silver tea set at tables forged by the village blacksmith. The grounds, with hidden pool and 15th century tower, look across to terracotta roof tops against a cornflower blue sky. Stunning.

Price	€100–€125. Suite €185. Half-board option.
Rooms	11: 10 twins/doubles, 1 suite.
Meals	Breakfast €12. Dinner €34. Restaurants 4km.
Closed	November–February. Call for out of season group reservations.
Directions	From Cognac, D24 for Segonzac then D736 for Juillac le Coq. 500m after village on right.

Tone Butler
16130 Juillac le Coq,
Charente

Tel	+33 (0)5 45 32 20 74
Fax	+33 (0)5 45 32 29 53
Email	logisdufresne@wanadoo.fr
Web	www.logisdufresne.com

Hôtel du Donjon

Centre ville is on the doorstep and surprisingly busy; the warm frontage expresses the charm of a country-style hotel. Armelle and Stephane left Normandy in search of adventure and stumbled across a townhouse in need of love and care. Now olive green woodwork and neatly trimmed privet announce the entrance. Your hosts are always to hand, the service is simple and friendly, people come and go and everything ticks over harmoniously. Polished staircases are lit with spots; corridors have creamy stone and exposed natural beams on split levels. The downstairs lobby, bustling, bright and scented with fresh cut garden flowers, has neutral furnishings and a central stone fireplace. Bedrooms are quiet and simple with views to the pretty terrace where honeysuckle creeps up the walls; the bedroom for guests with limited mobility is superbly equipped. Wine tasting tours can be arranged and, for animal lovers, there's the Charentais Donkey Protection Society to visit. Discover the rare 'dreadlocks' Poitou donkey: one of the region's best-kept secrets. A great little place.

Price	€54–€75.
Rooms	10: 7 doubles, 2 triples, 1 family room for 4.
Meals	Breakfast €6.50. Occasional meals. Restaurant 50 metres from hotel.
Closed	Never.
Directions	Paris to Bordeaux on A10, exit Niort Sud or Saint Jean d'Augely. D950 to Poitiers Saintes.

Armelle & Stephane Gras
4 rue des Hivers, 17470 Aulnay de Saintonge,
Charente-Maritime

Tel	+33 (0)5 46 33 67 67
Fax	+33 (0)5 46 33 67 64
Email	hoteldudonjon@wanadoo.fr
Web	www.hoteldudonjon.com

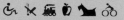

Château des Salles

A pretty little château with great personality, Salles was built in 1454 and scarcely touched again until 1860, when it was 'adapted to the fashion' (profoundly). One hundred years later, the enterprising Couillaud family brought the estate guest house, its vineyard and farm into the 20th century. Behind its fine old exterior it exudes light, harmony, colour and elegant informality with spiral stone stairs, boldly painted beams and warm, well-furnished bedrooms bathed in soft colours and gentle wallpapers. Salles is a friendly family affair: sister at guest house reception, brother at vines, mother at her easel – her watercolours hang in the public rooms, her flowers decorate bedroom doors – and in the kitchen. At dinner, refined food made with local and home-grown produce is served with estate wines. Sylvie Couillaud will help you plan your stay – she knows it all and is almost a mini tourist office. It's a congenial, welcoming house: people come back again and again and one guest said: "She welcomed us like family and sent us home with goodies from her vineyard". *Château produces pineau & cognac.*

Price	€78–€130.
Rooms	5. 4 doubles, 1 triple.
Meals	Breakfast €10. Dinner €37.
Closed	November–March.
Directions	From A10, exit 27 at Mirambeau then D730 for Royan. Château between Lorignac & Brie sous Mortagne; signed at D730 & D125 junction.

Sylvie Couillaud
17240 Saint Fort sur Gironde,
Charente-Maritime

Tel	+33 (0)5 46 49 95 10
Fax	+33 (0)5 46 49 02 81
Email	chateaudessalles@wanadoo.fr
Web	www.chateaudessalles.com

Château de la Tillade

You can tell that Michel and Solange like people and love entertaining. Their château sits at the end of an avenue of lime trees alongside the family vineyards that have produced grapes for cognac and pineau de Charentes for over two centuries. Much of the original distillery equipment is on display and well worth a visit. Your hosts make you feel instantly at ease in their comfortable, friendly home, even if you're secretly terrified of dropping the fine bone china. Solange's talents as an artist (she also holds painting courses in her art studio) are reflected in her choice of fabrics. Each bedroom is like a page out of Michel's memory book; one was his parents room, the other where he had his early schooling – a pinky double with toile de Jouy paper. His grandmother's bed is fit for a princess, as is the claw-foot bath. The smartly striped, dusky grey tower room belonged to his mother, its own terrace looks down to the pretty pinks in the front garden. Meals are a delight, with good conversation (in English or French) round the family table while you are waited on lavishly but without stuffiness.

Price	€80–€120. Extra bed €23.
Rooms	4: 1 twin, 3 family rooms for 3-4 (1 room with wc in corridor).
Meals	Breakfast included. Dinner €38, book ahead.
Closed	Rarely.
Directions	From A10, exit 36 right for Gémozac. At roundabout take Gémozac bypass for Royan, right on D6 for Tesson. Entrance approx. 3km on left, signed (château not in village, but on D6).

Vicomte & Vicomtesse Michel de Salvert
Gémozac, 17260 Saint Simon de Pellouaille, Charente-Maritime

Tel	+33 (0)5 46 90 00 20
Fax	+33 (0)5 46 90 02 23
Email	contact@la-tillade.com
Web	www.la-tillade.com

Ma Maison de Mer

Sink into a cream sofa with a chilled après-plage beer and soak up the cool, nautical chic. Built in the 1920s in a quiet tree-lined street (150m from the beach, 400m from the busy town centre) the hotel has recently been renovated by bubbly young Emma. More home than hotel, Ma Maison opened in April 2004. An intimate bar greets you as you enter and the open-plan living and dining rooms are separated by an elegant archway. Wooden floors are painted white as are the walls which draw your attention to Emma's vibrant paintings; other charming touches, from seashell collages and knitted cushions to a model gaff-rigged yacht, enhance the house. The same soothing shades are used in the bedrooms which have seagrass floors, cane chairs and sumptuous taupe-coloured bedspreads and white linen. Some of the rooms have mosquito nets and some central ceiling fans. The four-course set menu changes daily but expect plenty of seafood and superb quality. If you need an excuse to stay here, there are wine and music festivals in Saint Palais in July and August.

Price	€65–€155. Family suite €120–€200.	
Rooms	5: 2 doubles, 1 twin, 1 suite, 1 family suite for 4.	
Meals	Breakfast included. Dinner with wine, €30 (Jul/Aug only).	
Closed	Rarely.	
Directions	From A10 exit 5 Saintes to Royan on N150; in Royan D21 to St Palais; at r'bout, 4th exit, house on right, signed.	

Emma Hutchinson
21 ave du Platin, 17420 Saint Palais sur Mer,
Charente-Maritime

Tel	+33 (0)5 46 23 64 86
Fax	+33 (0)5 46 23 64 86
Email	reservations@mamaisondemer.com
Web	www.mamaisondemer.com

Le Moulin de Châlons

The Bouquets are a family of perfectionists, and their beautiful stone mill house sits gracefully at the water's edge, its sun terrace overlooking the mill race. The restaurant, with its crisp white dining tables and tankful of lobsters, has earned itself a reputation for finesse; the family hotel is charming. Enter a relaxed salon with a pretty stone fireplace, cosy leather chairs and fresh flowers peeping from vases. Spotless gleaming bedrooms with ultra-sound insulation (against the main road) are traditional; those in the new wing, designed by the Bouquets' charming daughter, ultra-modern. So you may choose between blue toile de Jouy and bold pebble stencils, or elegant antique settees and rust and grey spots and swirls. Bathrooms too are immaculate and gorgeous, the newest with a serene eastern feel. Neatly tendered gardens line the entrance while thoughtful resting places invite you to admire the birds bobbing downstream. Close by are the chic islands of Ré and Oleron; more traditional visitors may catch a slow boat up the Marais to the Venise Verte.

Price	€95–€160. Family room €120–€140.
Rooms	10: 5 doubles, 2 twins, 2 suites for 2, 1 family room for 3.
Meals	Breakfast €13. Lunch & dinner €25–€45.
Closed	Rarely.
Directions	From Royan on D25; left on D733, right on D241. Moulin is 500m after leaving Gua.

Bouquet Family
2 rue du Bassin,
17600 Le Gua, Charente-Maritime
Tel   +33 (0)5 46 22 82 72
Fax   +33 (0)5 46 22 91 07
Email moulin-de-chalons@wanadoo.fr
Web   www.moulin-de-chalons.com

Design Hôtel des Francs Garçons

The street was named after the young bachelors who used it as a meeting place for their sweethearts. The modern day Francs Garçons are Hervé Audinet and his six fellow architects; find each one's name inscribed above a bedroom door. The owners found their hotel in a state of disrepair and now each room stands testament to their passion for old buildings. While the exterior still wears its pretty façade, the interiors have been sculpted with effortless style. From the restaurant's glass tables you gaze onto sleek decking and a small black pool with a church view; Madame serves exquisite fresh food on simple white china. She's also a fan of Parisian teas, and gives you the finest blends accompanied by delicate biscuits. It is modern, unique, surprising, a marvel of crisp lines and primary colours, designer wallpapers and creamy stone walls, round black basins and beds in white cotton. Arper chairs from Italy, a chandelier from Paris, dazzling sheets of coloured glass... All this and St Sauvant just below, its lovely winding streets meeting in a peak outside the hotel's front door. *Gym & sauna.*

Price	€80–€95. Suite €115–€135.
Rooms	7: 5 doubles, 2 suites.
Meals	Breakfast €10. Brunch €15. Dinner from €22, on request
Closed	Never.
Directions	N141 from Saintes direction Cognac-Angouleme. In Coran, left on D134 direction St. Sauvant, hotel in centre of village. Ask about parking.

Monsieur & Madame Audinet
1 rue des Francs Garçons,
17610 Saint Sauvant, Charente-Maritime

Tel	+33 (0)5 46 90 33 93
Email	contact@francsgarcons.com
Web	www.francsgarcons.com

Château Mouillepied

The stream-fed moat is now mostly dry but this is how the house got its name – 'wet feet'. Many springs still gurgle in the nearby meadows, often flooded by the Charente. The oldest part of the house, the tower, was built in the 15th century, and significant bits added later. Martine and Pierre rescued Mouillepied from a few sorry years and are now restoring the house and grounds; they are a delightful pair. Large airy bedrooms are charming and uncluttered, with original wooden floors or new boards suitably wide; walls are white, curtains cotton. There are more rooms in the cottage beyond the lily pond, these with terracotta floors and chicken nesting holes in an exposed stone wall! Breakfast – stewed fruit, croissants, all the coffee or tea you'd like – is in the vast orangery overlooking the gardens. (or have it delivered to your cottage door.) The beautiful grounds contain the old laundry, bread oven and wine store. Pick up a fishing licence at the bakery and stroll along the banks of the Charente to visit the Roman city of Saintes, and the castle said to inspire *Puss in Boots*.

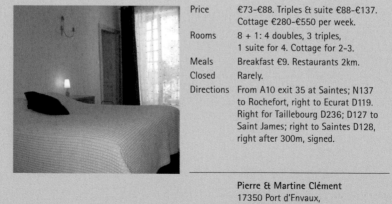

Price	€73-€88. Triples & suite €88-€137. Cottage €280-€550 per week.
Rooms	8 + 1: 4 doubles, 3 triples, 1 suite for 4. Cottage for 2-3.
Meals	Breakfast €9. Restaurants 2km.
Closed	Rarely.
Directions	From A10 exit 35 at Saintes; N137 to Rochefort, right to Ecurat D119. Right for Taillebourg D236; D127 to Saint James; right to Saintes D128, right after 300m, signed.

Pierre & Martine Clément
17350 Port d'Envaux,
Charente-Maritime
Tel   +33 (0)5 46 90 49 88
Fax   +33 (0)5 46 90 36 91
Email   info@chateaumouillepied.com
Web   www.chateaumouillepied.com

Château de Crazannes

Near sleepy Crazannes sits a fairytale castle with shiny slate turrets and a moat full of water. The remains of some of the original building are still in the grounds, dividing the garden into ornamental areas with luscious lawns, teeming roses and luxurious pool. Sylvain Fougerit is the manager and jolly host, whose enthusiasm and energy has filled the ancient building with all the comforts of a modern hotel. (A museum feel too: open for guided tours, the château has some fully costumed dummies downstairs!). Francois I stayed here for a night in 1519; bedrooms, still old fashioned, have four-posters, rich fabrics and Persian rugs on parquet; ask for one in a tower. Downstairs in the main hall are an enormous stone fireplace, a quiet library and heavy furnishings shiny with beeswax. Across the pretty garden is a barn conversion where pilgrims once dined under sturdy beams; here delicious breakfast is served at pretty tables. If you are lucky you may come across the owners – Monsieur is a keen chasseur who occasionally leaves the city to play the hunting horn in the chapel. Marvellous.

Price	€70–€160.
Rooms	8: 5 doubles, 1 twin, 1 suite, 1 family room for 2-4.
Meals	Breakfast €10. Dinner €35, book ahead. Restaurant 3km.
Closed	Rarely.
Directions	Exit Saintes, N35 for 5km; N137 towards Rochefort; right towards Plassay N119. Signed.

Monsieur Fougerit
17350 Crazannes,
Charente-Maritime

Tel	+33 (0)6 80 65 40 96 (mobile)
Fax	+33 (0)5 46 91 34 46
Email	crazannes@worldonline.fr
Web	www.crazannes.com

Hôtel de l'Océan

Seasoned travellers, Martine and Noël tried to find a hotel that felt like a home. Although they had worked in antiques and interior design, they realised after a spell running a restaurant that this was what they should be doing – but where? They knew it had to be on an island; they stumbled upon a hotel on the Ile de Ré and realised they had found it. Set back from the street in a quiet little town, the hotel has 24 bedrooms: some around an inner courtyard pungent with rosemary and lavender, others like tiny cottages among the hollyhocks. Children will love the curtained cabin bed set in a buttercup yellow alcove. Two brand new rooms in a wing are large and colonial looking, with very modern bathrooms and a calming zen feel. Floors are covered in sisal matting; ships, lighthouses and shells are dotted around against cool, soothing colours. After your pastis, your supper will involve fresh fish and herbs. The dining room is another success, with cream boards on walls and ceiling and palest greeny-grey carved chairs. It gets better every year. *Beach a 15-minute walk.*

Price	€72–€180.
Rooms	28: 21 doubles, 4 twins, 2 triples, 1 quadruple.
Meals	Breakfast €10. Lunch & dinner €23–€50. Restaurant closed Wednesdays except during school holidays.
Closed	January.
Directions	A10 exit 33 for La Rochelle. N248 then N11 Rocade round La Rochelle for Pont de l'Ile de Ré. At Le Bois Plage hotel in town centre.

Martine & Noël Bourdet
172 rue St Martin, 17580 Le Bois Plage en Ré (Ile de Ré), Charente-Maritime

Tel	+33 (0)5 46 09 23 07
Fax	+33 (0)5 46 09 05 40
Email	info@re-hotel-ocean.com
Web	www.re-hotel-ocean.com

Hôtel de Toiras

It is three years old and already studded with stars. Exquisite is the first word, refined is the second, then you stop thinking and let the senses rule. Revel in the soul of this quayside hotel, inspired by the illustrious figure of Jean de Caylar de Saint Bonnet de Toiras who protected the island from the English in 1627. Thus the arts of navigation and hunting set the tone and imbue the rooms with memories of 17th-century ship owner's houses. Linking the old part with the new is a cool and fragrant garden with three palms. Then a reception room that resembles a study, black and white tiles in an elegant living room/library, open fires, a small bar, soothing music, happy young staff. Each gracious, immaculate bedroom (some large, some small, named after writers, botanists, socialites, sailors; the detail in fabrics, paintings, *objets* and books is both rich and meticulous. This is an island of not only of big skies and beaches but bicycles too: 60 miles of cycle paths criss-cross its vineyards and pine forests. Bliss.

Price	€165–€330. Suites €320–€610.
Rooms	17: 8 doubles, 2 twins, 7 suites.
Meals	Breakfast €18–€20. Dinner from €65.
Closed	Never.
Directions	From La Rochelle, over bridge to île de Ré; on quay. In summer season, call for code.

Olivia Mathé
1 quai Job Foran, 17410 Saint Martin de Ré (Ile de Ré),
Charente-Maritime

Tel	+33 (0)5 46 35 40 32
Fax	+33 (0)5 46 35 64 59
Email	contact@hotel-de-toiras.com
Web	www.hotel-de-toiras.com

Domaine du Bien-Etre

This magnificent manor house was in its last stages of renovation when we visited, so we admired its fine bones: two arched doorways where carriages once pulled in; a double outside staircase off the reception area in the building's embrace; a terrace leading to a big, long, walled garden where a fine pair of 18th-century iron gates have already found their spot. We were whispered plans for an additional vine-covered pergola in a separate hidden courtyard. And the Pallardys have done such an exquisite makeover for La Barronie across the street (see entry 200) that we have no doubts about the Bien-Etre's future charms. The gardens have already been filled with potted lavender, jasmine, figs and roses: perfume is as important as colour. Secure parking will be at the end of the long garden with a door code so that you may enter this way, and there is so much space inside and out there is a chance that you might not ever meet the other guests. The bathrooms have fine fittings and marble basins, and the bedrooms are country chic. It will be better than we can imagine – and deliciously private.

Price	€160-€230.
Rooms	7: 4 twins/doubles, 1 suite. Garden: 2 suites.
Meals	Breakfast €15. Restaurants walking distance.
Closed	November-March.
Directions	Over bridge from La Rochelle to St Martin harbour. Street on left going down to port.

Pierre & Florence Pallardy
17 rue Baron de Chantal, 17410 Saint Martin de Ré
(Ile de Ré), Charente-Maritime

Tel	+33 (0)5 46 09 21 29
Fax	+33 (0)5 46 09 95 29
Email	info@domainedelabaronnie.com
Web	www.domainedelabaronnie.com

Domaine de la Baronnie

This secluded retreat is only 100 metres from the bustling nightlife and fun beaches of Saint Martin, but once through the beautiful old iron gates you would never know it. Down a side street from the port, built as government premises in the 18th century, La Baronnie was rescued in 1996 by Pierre and Florence who came for a seaside holiday. Enter through a delightful courtyard garden with ancient cobbles and a glorious scent of honeysuckle, jasmine, lavender and mint. The front of the house, with its pretty wooden shutters, is smartly painted, and beside the front door terracotta pots bloom with colourful flowers. Inside are fresh flowers, wooden panelling, black and white tiled floors and an ornate cast-iron staircase leading upstairs. Light, large bedrooms are smartly turned out in gorgeous colours with thick curtains and cushions, pale carpets or stripped wooden floors, some good pieces of furniture and excellent bathrooms. You are minutes from all the seaside bustle, but beyond are endless, more peaceful, sandy beaches bordered by cycle paths, dunes and pines. *Minimum stay two nights.*

Price	€160–€210.
Rooms	6: 3 doubles, 3 suites.
Meals	Breakfast €15.
	Many restaurants in town.
Closed	November–March.
Directions	Over bridge from La Rochelle to St Martin harbour. Street on left going down to port.

Pierre & Florence Pallardy
21 rue Baron de Chantal,
17410 Saint Martin de Ré (Ile de Ré), Charente-Maritime

Tel	+33 (0)5 46 09 21 29
Fax	+33 (0)5 46 09 95 29
Email	info@domainedelabaronnie.com
Web	www.domainedelabaronnie.com

Aquitaine

Villa Prémayac

The house is down a quiet back street of Blaye, a bustling little town with a pretty hilltop citadel. There's not a huge amount to do here – apart from quaff some famous wines – but the place is perfect for golfers. There are six courses within a putt of the villa and Roger, your host, was a player of repute. He now edits a golfing magazine. This is a new enterprise for him and Léa who have furbished five bedrooms for guests in the oldest part of the house. It's a bit of a rabbit warren, albeit a well-renovated one. Big bedrooms, named after Greek gods, are plushly carpeted. Ceres is golden with a flowery canopied bed, Aphrodite spring-green with rose-strewn drapes; they overlook small enclosed terraces. Bathrooms are tiled, with shiny fittings, and are vast – big enough to swing a club in. There are two small gardens, one Roman and one zen, with bonsai trees. The south-facing hills of Blaye, on the banks of the Gironde, have been lined with vines since the Romans came. Set off for the châteaux of Pauillac and Medoc or catch the ferry from Blaye. Cognac is even nearer.

Price	€90.
Rooms	6 doubles
Meals	Breakfast included.
	Restaurants within walking distance.
Closed	Rarely.
Directions	In Blaye, follow Centre Ville signs.

Léa Golias
13 rue Prémayac,
33390 Blaye, Gironde

Tel	+33 (0)5 57 42 27 39
Fax	+33 (0)5 57 42 69 09
Email	premayac@wanadoo.fr
Web	www.villa-premayac.com

Château Julie

Even if bordeaux is not your favourite tipple, this is a superb place to stay. Viticulture is the business here and if you come at the right time you have a grandstand view. Château Julie is Dutch-owned, run by Jos and Wim. Rebuilt in the 18th century to charming proportions, the house is surrounded by 80 hectares of land, half of them glistening with vines. Stay in the château – rooms are simple and uncluttered, with big bathrooms and oodles of towels – or in the self-catering cottage opposite; it sleeps six comfortably, has a big kitchen and two shower rooms. Breakfast is on the terrace in summer, or in the more sombre setting of the hall, beside an impressive wooden staircase. Pop into Bordeaux for dinner where you will be spoiled for choice. In the day play tennis, fish or explore the grounds, on foot or by mountain bike. Children can swim in the lake; they even have their own playroom if it rains. Jos and Wim can also arrange for you to visit a sister château near Saint Emilion. A great place for an active break. *Cash or French cheque only. French, Dutch, English & German spoken.*

Price	€75–€125.
	Cottage €500–€550 per week.
Rooms	5 + 1: 3 twins, 1 family room for 3,
	1 family room for 4. Cottage for 6.
Meals	Breakfast included.
	Restaurants nearby.
Closed	Rarely.
Directions	A10 Paris/Bordeaux, past toll Virsac.
	1st exit for Angoulême; signed.

Jos & Wim van der Eijk
1 Naudonnet, 33240 Virsac
(Nr St André de Cubzac), Gironde

Tel	+33 (0)5 57 94 08 20
Fax	+33 (0)5 57 94 08 23
Email	josvandereijk@wanadoo.fr
Web	www.chateau-julie.com

Château Saint Aignan

Enter a charming small 18th-century château based on a design by the architect of the Bordeaux Opera House. And the opera gets into full swing once inside: note the first reception room, its ceiling upholstered into a thousand pleats, its grand displays of china, its central sparkling chandelier. More reception rooms follow, the largest seating 200 for dinner: the château's raison d'être is its parties and weddings (check when you book that you won't bump into one). At other times peace reigns... and outside is a mature park of ancient magnolias, clipped hedges and a fabulous pool. The Saint Aignan estate has been in Madame's family for three generations; she is sad the vines have gone but she puts her energies into her guests now and is full of plans for Rolls Royce vineyard tours and courses in table decoration. Drapes soar, walls are papered and patterned, parquet gleams; there's an unbelievably long shag-pile rug in the honeymoon suite and nymphs dance over a circular beige bathtub under the eaves. Exuberantly, unashamedly French — with a hostess attractively hands-on.

Price	€95-€170.
Rooms	3: 2 doubles, 1 suite.
Meals	Breakfast €12. Light meals €28.
Closed	Christmas-2 January.
Directions	A10 Bordeaux/Paris exit 42, follow signs to Saint Loubès. Avenue on right facing church; château 300m on left.

Cloé Viralès
Rue St Aignan,
33450 Saint Loubès, Gironde

Tel	+33 (0)5 57 97 16 70
Fax	+33 (0)5 57 97 16 71
Email	virales@orange.fr
Web	www.chateau-saint-aignan.com

Château Lamothe Prince Noir

Turn off a suburban road into the pages of a fairy tale. A creeper-clad, stone château framed by two towers sits serenely in the middle of a moat. Knights on white chargers, at the very least Rapunzel, should soon appear. Or possibly Edward, the Black Prince, who used it as a medieval hunting lodge. Slip between the trees, over the bridge and be welcomed by the Bastide family. Warm and charismatic, they have given the château a stylish opulence without detracting from its character. Large bedrooms have canopied beds, strong colours, antique bed linen and a rich but comfortable assortment of furniture. One suite has a Mexican theme, another, overlooking the moat, has murals of the seasons. Bathrooms are grand with gold taps, Venetian glass and most have windows. Breakfast on the rose-covered terrace or in the elegant, chandelier-hung salon. Light suppers or, for groups, slap-up dinners with family silver and lacy napery can be arranged. Visit Bordeaux, beaches, play golf, fish in the moat. The Bastides can arrange riding, wine tastings, even a massage. You will be treated as family guests.

Price	€175–€230. Singles €85. Family room €310.
Rooms	8: 2 doubles, 1 single, 3 suites for 2, 1 suite for 3, 1 family room for 3-5.
Meals	Breakfast included. Light supper with wine €35–€45, book ahead. Restaurant 5-min drive.
Closed	Rarely.
Directions	From Bordeaux N89 exit 5; D13 to St Sulpice. There, 2nd right across from bakery towards stadium. Gate 800m on left. Signed.

Jacques & Luce Bastide
33450 Saint Sulpice et Cameyrac,
Gironde

Tel	+33 (0)5 56 30 82 16
Fax	+33 (0)5 56 30 88 33
Email	chat.lamothe@wanadoo.fr
Web	www.chateaux-france.com/lamotheprincenoir

Château Coulon Laurensac

If you have a passion for wines and want to know more about them, your time here, above the Garonne overlooking Bordeaux, will be delightfully spent. Ronald, who's knowledgeable and enthusiastic, organises exclusive tours. He and Margaret came to this pretty, compact, 18th-century château with their two young sons and a Jack Russell – aptly named Bouchon – two years ago. They have converted the outbuildings into guest accommodation: 'Pomerol' was once the cellar master's house; 'Margaux' and 'Pauillac' are in the *chai à barriques*. They have a roomy elegance: pale walls, dark beams and heavy wooden doors contrast with stylish modern furniture and exquisite modern bathrooms. Breakfast is in the château's conservatory, overlooking the pool, but the apartments have their own excellent kitchen facilities. Make sure you book a table for one of Margaret's sumptuous weekend meals, though. She describes her cooking as "a hobby gone mad" but in fact it's a delicious fusion of French and Italian. And, of course, the wines are superb.

Price	€135-€165. Gîtes €125-€165 (€575-€1,250 per week).
Rooms	1 + 3: 1 suite. 3 gîtes: 1 for 4; 2 for 2.
Meals	Breakfast included. Hosted dinner €35-€55, book ahead.
Closed	Rarely.
Directions	Rocade Bordeaux exit 22 to Latresne. Right at r'bout to 'Le bord de l'eau', left at river. On left, 800m.

Ronald & Margaret Rens
1 chemin de Meydieu,
33360 Latresne, Gironde
Tel +33 (0)5 56 20 64 12
Fax +33 (0)5 56 21 79 44
Email coulonlaurensac@wanadoo.fr
Web www.clbx.com

Le Relais de Franc Mayne

Drive through the vineyards to meet the golden-stoned U-shaped 18th-century château at the centre of a wine estate. This is vine-surrounded château life at its most plush; on one side is the magnificent wine 'chai', where visitors taste and learn, on the other is the building where you sleep and gently indulge. The vast, vibrant bedrooms are of a luxury unheard of in 'normal life'. One, the Indian room, has a four-poster with a purple bedcover and an Indian screen for a headboard. The bathrooms are sumptuous: fat towels and dressing gowns, rivers of hot water. If you insist on dining, they will summon a chef for a meal in a dining room fit for kings. The central table, handsome with white crockery and flowers, is a showcase for meals washed down with remarkable estate wines. If you have time to play you can explore, with a guide, the two hectares of underground graves used as wine cellars. Join the bustle of the vineyard visitors, retreat to your château, or walk to hilltop St Emilion through the vineyards. The owners live elsewhere, but the managers are delightful.

Price	€150–€220.
Rooms	9 doubles.
Meals	Breakfast €10. Dinner for groups only, from €30. Restaurants 1km.
Closed	Never.
Directions	From Libourne D670 to St Emilion; D243 for 1km. Entrance on left before three flags.

Griet & Hervé Laviale
14 La Gomerie, Route départementale D243,
33330 Saint Emilion, Gironde

Tel	+33 (0)5 57 24 62 61
Fax	+33 (0)5 57 24 68 25
Email	welcome@relaisfrancmayne.com
Web	www.relaisfrancmayne.com

Château de Carbonneau

Readers are full of praise. Big château bedrooms done in safe pastels over classic dados, a fine old bed in the beige room, huge bathrooms dressed with rich tiles - here is a quiet, self-assured family house where quality is natural, history stalks and there's plenty of space for four young Ferrières and a dozen guests. There's more space in the surroundings; 50 hectares of farmland, some of which are planted in vineyards under the appellation Sainte Foy Bordeaux and the rest are used for grazing the herd of Blondes d'Aquitaine (no, not ladies, lovely cows and a handsome bull). Visit Wilfred's winery and taste the talent handed down by his forebears; you may want to leave with a case or two. Jacquie, a relaxed dynamic New Zealander, does all the interior stuff, wields a canny paintbrush and has created a guest sitting room of comfortable furniture, old family pieces and modern lampshades. Breakfast is served on the main terrace or in the dining room. Relaxing can be had in the Napolean III conservatory. Oh, and they breed gorgeous Bernese dogs.

Price	€65–€90.
Rooms	5. 2 doubles, 3 twins/doubles.
Meals	Breakfast included. Dinner €22, book ahead.
Closed	December–February.
Directions	D936 to Castillion la Bataille-Bergerac; from Réaux, right to Gensac, Pessac; at r'bout, D18 to Ste Foy le Gde; 2km on right.

Madame Jacquie Franc de Ferrière
33890 Pessac sur Dordogne,
Gironde

Tel	+33 (0)5 57 47 46 46
Fax	+33 (0)5 57 47 42 26
Email	carbonneau@wanadoo.fr
Web	www.chateau-carbonneau.com

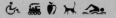

(handwritten in left margin: max 60)

Château de Sanse

You are in Bordeaux wine country looking at a château more Tuscan than 18th-century French. The stunning entrance hall sets the tone: clean lines and a palette of pale creams and whites set off with splashes of mauve – fabulous. No fuss, no swags, only the necessary accessories: a teak desk, a wickerwork sofa strewn with white cushions. The off-white and oatmeal theme continues upstairs with sisal in the corridor and coir in some of the bedrooms; a play of texture rather than colour. Thought has been given to families – triples can be arranged and some rooms interconnect; there's a child-friendly pool and early suppers for the little ones. Most rooms have private balconies with lovely views, big enough to sit out on in comfort. Christian, talented and experienced, heads the kitchen and delivers some inventive dishes, but nothing overly pretentious or complicated. Enjoy such treats on as terrine of foie gras *mi-cuit* with spiced bread and pear chutney, and lemon and ginger crème brulée. Peaceful seclusion and a special place – book early in season.

Price	€100-€135. Suites €165-€195. Apartment €700-€1,200.
Rooms	16 + 1: 12 twins/doubles, 4 suites. 1 apartment for 4-5.
Meals	Breakfast €12. Lunch from €18. Dinner €35.
Closed	January-February.
Directions	A10 exit St Andre de Cubzac to Libourne; towards Castillon La Bataille; D17 right Pujols; D18 left Gensac; D15e right to Coubeyrac. Hotel signed on right.

33350 Sainte Radegonde,
Gironde

Tel	+33 (0)5 57 56 41 10
Fax	+33 (0)5 57 56 41 29
Email	contact@chateaudesanse.com
Web	www.chateaudesanse.com

Les Baudry

Steeped in 500 years of history, the four solid wings of this distinguished château enclose a grand central courtyard where a water feature shimmers and tinkles with a fountain and tiny fish. Entering through the hall, veer to the left for the salon, to the right, through large wood-panelled doors, for the intimate dining room: a room wrapped in blue wallpaper bearing a flower and ribbon motif. Seated at one of the tables, you'll discover that Hélène's wonderful cuisine 'à la grande-mère' is more than delicious; it's a reason to be here. To the north is the Italian-themed orangerie where breakfast is served among terracotta and citrus trees; to the south and east, guest rooms are large, traditional, framed by lofty beams and supported by equally solid stone pierres. Fireplaces bring out the earthy colours, the glow of antiques and the softness of cotton and boutis coverings. From bedroom windows, views of formal Italiante gardens and a long drive of hornbeam hedges give way to more untouched countryside, even as pillars by the pool guide the eye to Dordogne and Bordeaux vistas beyond.

Price	€120–€150.
Rooms	5: 2 twins/doubles, 3 suites.
Meals	Breakfast €10. Dinner €30.
Closed	Rarely.
Directions	From Bergerac, D936 for Bordeaux until Gardonne (12 km); left on D4 towards Saussignac (5 km). In Saussignac continue on D4 for Monestier. Château 2km from Saussignac on left.

Hélène Boulet & François Passebon
Les Baudry, 24240 Monestier,
Dordogne

Tel	+33 (0)5 53 23 46 42
Fax	+33 (0)5 53 61 14 59
Email	chateaudesbaudry@orange.fr
Web	www.chateaudesbaudry.com

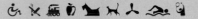

Château Les Farcies Du Pech'

The neat and tidy winery a mile from Bergerac makes a leafy out-of-town stay. The tone is set by the impeccable cream and French-grey façade: here is a chambres d'hôte that is both elegant and homely. The Dubards, who took over 10 years ago, live in a separate wing, work hard at their enterprise and are developing a shop to promote the wine. (Do not go home empty-handed from one of the oldest vineyards in the world: this predates Bordeaux.) Inside, whitewashed walls rub shoulders with polished timbers, all is immaculate and not a thing out of place. Big, nicely proportioned bedrooms have high ceilings and gleaming floors, pale sponged walls, striped curtains, traditional lamps and the odd choice antique; windowless bath and shower rooms are halygon-lit. White cotton duvet covers trimmed with beige linen have matching pillows, but nothing is busy or overdone. Windows overlook gentle parkland and grazing deer, all feels settled, there's no one to rush you at breakfast and Madame Vidalencq, your courteous hostess, helps you plan your day.

Price	€100.
Rooms	5 doubles.
Meals	Breakfast included. Restaurants in town.
Closed	Rarely.
Directions	From Bergerac N21 towards Périgueux; right after Centre Leclerc. Signed 'Les Farcies'.

Serge Dubard
Les Farcies, 24100 Bergerac,
Dordogne

Tel	+33 (0)5 53 82 48 31
Fax	+33 (0)5 53 82 47 64
Email	vignobles-dubard@wanadoo.fr

Château Les Merles

The 19th-century French façade conceals an interior of Dutch minimalism suffused with light. Old and stylish new march hand in hand and a Dutch chef heads the kitchen bringing skill and finesse to the cooking: great spit roasts, Bergerac wines, fresh vegetables from the organic garden. A rustic-chic bistro (Philippe Starck chairs on charming old flags), a restaurant in the stables, two light-streamed sitting rooms, a bucolic nine-hole golf course to one side… A golfers' haven it is, but everyone would love it here. This family-run hotel – two sisters in charge – brims with generosity and professionalism. A black and white theme runs throughout – matt-black beds, white bedspreads, black frames, white lamp shades, black towels, white roses – the austerity offset by a rich gilt-framed mirror or a fuchsia fauteuil. Outside is a vast gravelled courtyard with striking white dining chairs and black parasols, a terrace looks south to the shimmering pool and the hills are braided with vines. Civilised, classy, welcoming. *Children's daycare available by arrangement.*

Price	€120-€160. Single €140-€120. Suites €150-€205. Apartment €220-€290.
Rooms	15: 11 twins/doubles, 1 single, 2 suites, 1 apartment for 4.
Meals	Breakfast €14. Lunch & dinner €22.50-€42.50.
Closed	Never.
Directions	From Bergerac D660 for Sarlat. At Tuilières, left onto D36 for Pressignac. Château 800m.

Judith Wagemakers & Karlyn van Grinsven
Tuilières, 24520 Mouleydier,
Dordogne
Tel   +33 (0)5 53 63 13 42
Fax   +33 (0)5 53 63 13 45
Email info@lesmerles.com
Web   www.lesmerles.com

36 mins

La Métairie

If you love horses you'll be in your element: you can relax on the terrace and watch them in the next field. You can also ride close by. La Métairie was built as a farm at the turn of the last century and converted into a hotel some 40 years ago, a U-shaped building smothered in wisteria and Virginia creeper. There's no road in sight and you really do feel 'away from it all' – yet the Dordogne and its cliff top villages are just minutes away. Borrow bikes if you're feeling energetic! Bedrooms are small but cheerful, full of sunshiney yellows; beds are huge. They have room for a couple of comfy chairs, too. Bathrooms match – large and cheerful – and three ground-floor rooms have French doors and a semi-private patio. The pool is big enough for a proper swim and when you come out you can read under the trees – there are plenty right by the pool. In summer you can eat out here, or on the flowery terrace. The dining room has black and white floors, washed stone walls and well-spaced tables. Go ahead, indulge, order the four-course Périgourdine menu. You can swim it off later.

Price	€115-€150. Suite €175-€230. Half-board mandatory in high season, €123-€173 p.p.
Rooms	10: 9 doubles, 1 suite.
Meals	Breakfast €16. Lunch €18-€25. Dinner €38; Périgourdine menu €45.
Closed	November-March.
Directions	From Lalinde, D703 for Le Bugue. At Sauveboeuf, D31 through Mauzac. Signed.

Monsieur Heinz Johner
24150 Mauzac et Grand Castang,
Dordogne

Tel	+33 (0)5 53 22 50 47
Fax	+33 (0)5 53 22 52 93
Email	metairie.la@wanadoo.fr
Web	www.la-metairie.com

$23 men

Domaine de la Barde

A sensational place. Once a weekend cottage for the 13th-century nobility who owned it, the Domaine has now become a luxurious but immensely friendly and easy-going hotel. The owner, unlike most restorers of ancient buildings, began with the grounds which they arranged as a perfect French garden saving several centuries-old trees in the process, before they tackled the mill, the forge and the manor house. There is an informal 'family' feel about the place which in no way detracts from the professionalism of the management: the priority is your comfort, and it shows in their staff and in the immaculate, lavish but personal decoration and furnishing of the bedrooms. They also have a flair for the dramatic visual touch – witness the glass floor under which flows the millstream in the old mill, the *oeil de boeuf* window in the forge and the 'menacing Eros' who surveys you as you stroll through the gardens. There's plenty to do; the swimming pool has a jet-stream massage, there's table tennis and, in the orangerie, a sauna.

Price	€100–€200. Suites €203–€240.
Rooms	18: 15 twins/doubles, 3 suites for 2-3.
Meals	Breakfast €15. Lunch & dinner €39–€55.
Closed	3 January–March.
Directions	From Périgueux N89, exit 16; D710 to Le Bugue. 1km before Le Bugue, Domaine signed on right.

Monsieur Patrick Dubourg
Route de Périgueux, 24260 Le Bugue, Dordogne

Tel	+33 (0)5 53 07 16 54
Fax	+33 (0)5 53 54 76 19
Email	hotel@domainedelabarde.com
Web	www.domainedelabarde.com

Hôtel Les Glycines

Potential for name-dropping here: Prince Charles stayed for several days in the 60s with his Cambridge tutor. Les Glycines has been lodging people since 1862, when it was a *relais de poste*. It has been enlarged over the years, with the stables being turned into more rooms once they were no longer needed for horses. The gardens are fabulous: they were planted by the son of a head gardener at Versailles. You meander down to the pool under arches laden with roses and honeysuckle and there is even a vegetable garden too. Just past the lobby you enter the dining room which runs the breadth of the building and overlooks the garden. The Lombards took over seven years ago, threw themselves into decoration and have even added another terrace last year. Pascal leads the orchestra in the kitchen; do try his roast veal with choice local ham and truffled polenta. Don't be put off by the busy road and the station nearby: once in the garden you could be in the country, though you might ask for a room at the back or in the annexe. Families can have interconnecting rooms, which sleep five comfortably.

Price	€84–€160. Family rooms €180–€230. Extra bed €24.
Rooms	27: 23 doubles, 4 family rooms for 3.
Meals	Breakfast €12. Picnic lunch €12-24. Lunch €22–€47. Dinner €37–€77. Restaurant closed Monday noon.
Closed	November-Easter.
Directions	From Périgueux, D47 to Sarlat. Over river, on left immediately before Les Eyzies station.

Pascal Lombard
4 avenue de Laugerie,
24620 Les Eyzies de Tayac, Dordogne
Tel   +33 (0)5 53 06 97 07
Fax   +33 (0)5 53 06 92 19
Email   glycines.dordogne@wanadoo.fr
Web   www.les-glycines-dordogne.com

Auberge de la Salvetat

Locals believe this area to be 'saved land' and there are 12th-century church ruins on the estate that pre-date the cloisters at Cadouin down the road. Part of the building that makes up the restaurant and some bedrooms was the presbytery and the views from the terrace are sublime: across the woods and pastures with not another building in sight. Bedrooms are not huge but perfectly comfortable and have terraces; those in the main house are the best and one has a mezzanine - good for families. The restaurant with its beamed and covered terrace is now overseen by Fabien, a chef with a local reputation for excellent, French country cooking, and Ann still makes the puddings. She and Steve are loving their change of career and everything is done with a smile; there's not a trace of pomposity here. Children will adore the space to play in the pretty gardens and the good-sized swimming pool; you may have to tear them away to do any sightseeing but there are some exciting water sports in the area and a different market almost every day. Walkers will be happy too: routes run from the door.

Price	€70–€95.
Rooms	14: 7 doubles, 3 twins, 4 family rooms for 3.
Meals	Breakfast €9.75. Lunch & dinner €20–€36. Restaurant closed Sun eve & Mon lunch.
Closed	1 November–23 March.
Directions	2km from Cadouin on the Belvès road.

Steven & Ann Jordan
Route de Belvès, 24480
Cadouin, Dordogne

Tel	+33 (0)5 53 63 42 79
Fax	+33 (0)5 53 61 72 05
Email	contact@lasalvetat.com
Web	www.lasalvetat.com

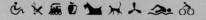

Hôtel du Manoir de Bellerive

The manoir was built by Napoleon III for one of his *belles*, and used as a stopover on the route to Biarritz. The entrance hall is huge with a double staircase leading to a gallery; in a niche behind reception is a saintly statue, one of several that came with the house. Off the hall is a cosy English-style bar, panelled head to toe in golden wood scattered with glass tables atop huge oriental ginger jars; such is the sumptuousness of the place. The owners, are charming and omni-present, overseeing an ever-helpful staff. Bedrooms come in three categories – Traditional, Privileged and Exclusive – and are deliciously decorated. Swags and padded walls are the order of the day, floors wear Turkish rugs, bathrooms are sizeable and full of mirrors, the newest, in the orangery, fashionably tiled in earthy shades. The gourmet cuisine has been bestowed with stars, plates and crowns; the bistro with its lighter fare provides an alternative. Breakfast on the terrace overlooking the river, a perfect beginning to each day: chocolate croissants, hot rich coffee. Grand, intimate, brilliantly placed.

Price	€155–€240.
Rooms	21: 3 doubles, 14 twins/doubles, 2 suites for 2, 2 apartments (without kitchen) for 3-4.
Meals	Breakfast €18. Lunch & dinner €45–€90. Restaurant closed for lunch Mon-Thurs.
Closed	January–mid-March.
Directions	From Toulouse A10 exit 55 for Souillac, then Bergerac. From Périgueux head for Le Bugue & Sarlat on D710, D703, D31e.

Karina & Rudi Madalijns
Route de Siorac,
24480 Le Buisson de Cadouin, Dordogne

Tel	+33 (0)5 53 22 16 16
Fax	+33 (0)5 53 22 09 05
Email	manoir.bellerive@wanadoo.fr
Web	www.bellerivehotel.com

Café de la Rivière

In honey-stoned Beynac, a restaurant with rooms and a terrace with dreamy views of the Dordogne overlooks four châteaux and the gentle river – cross the road and catch a canoe. It is owned and run by John, an affable semi-retired businessman, and his wife Tricia, a teacher, and is enhanced by a talented chef. On south-facing terraces hewn out of the rock you are served food that goes beyond the usual magret de canard. There's something different every day according to the freshest and best of what the market provides and always a vegetarian option; great value. Rooms, too, are well-priced. You get one at the back (very quiet) overlooking the village roofs and others on the top floor with super views over the river. Expect space and simplicity in rooms that are more for sleeping than spending time in: white walls, comfy beds, rugs on waxed wooden floors, voile drapes, double-glazing at the front, air conditioning for summer. Beautiful, bustling Beynac, whose château was stormed and captured by Richard the Lionheart, is a historic treat, best in May, June and September. *Minimum stay two nights.*

Price	€50 €65.
Rooms	3: 1 double, 2 twins.
Meals	Breakfast €7. Lunch & dinner from €20. Restaurant closed Nov-March.
Closed	November-March.
Directions	A20 From Brive to Souillac, D704 to Sarlat. D57 to Beynac.

John & Tricia Apps
Le Bourg,
24220 Beynac et Cazenac,
Dordogne

Tel	+33 (0)5 53 28 35 49
Email	info@cafedelariviere.com

Le Relais du Touron

Such a nice approach up the drive lined with box hedges and spiræa, surrounded by lawns and handsome mature trees. A friendly reception is in the main entrance hall, by the high open fireplace. Only the big family bedroom is actually in the main house, all the other rooms and the dining room are in the modern converted barn and stable block with the pool just below. The dining room has one all-glass wall overlooking the pool and garden beyond and is flooded with light. The Viala family is building a reputation for good, interesting food; choose the five-course half-board menu or go à la carte. Most bedrooms are above the dining area and have the same decoration in straightforward style: plain carpets and walls, bright bedcovers and curtains, decent lighting. The nearby road is well screened by thick trees and shrubs. Indeed, the three-hectare garden, which also contains a small pond, is a great asset with lots of private corners to be explored. A delightful path of six kilometres will take you by foot or by bike right into Sarlat. Low-key, good value with a warm family welcome.

Price	€50–€62. Family room €90–€100.
Rooms	18: 1 family room for 4.
	Outbuildings: 13 doubles, 4 twins.
Meals	Breakfast €9.
	Lunch & dinner €16–€34.
Closed	15 November–March.
Directions	From Sarlat, D704 to Gourdon.
	Hotel signed on right before Carsac.

Viala Family
Le Touron, 24200 Carsac Aillac,
Dordogne
Tel   +33 (0)5 53 28 16 70
Fax   +33 (0)5 53 28 52 51
Email   contact@lerelaisdutouron.com
Web   www.lerelaisdutouron.com

Les Maisons d'Antan

Isabelle has created a heavenly escape, lost in the countryside between Montignac and Sarlat. She has bought two houses in a restored hamlet, created a central courtyard, added terraces screened by voile and introduced a cool pool – shielded by a 'preserved' tumbledown wall. This is the essence of her design philosophy: to fuse the finest of the old and the loveliest of the new. In the first house are three big rooms on three luminous floors: ground, first and attic. Walls are rendered lime – buttermilk, gris nuage, taupe – floors are tiled with terres cuites from Morocco, wash basins are of beaten silver, bed linen is delicious. Be seduced by an immense fireplace, a limed door, bathrobes sporting giant tassels. The *bergerie*, the second house, holds a rustic family room on the ground floor: a pebblestone floor, a prune velours sofa. The treats continue at table, where dates and spiced eggs partner breakfast coffee and gâteaux. You are left to your own devices but Isabelle knows you may gravitate to her kitchen – such is the hotel's atmosphere and her charm. *Available for weekly rental.*

Price	€180–€240. House €2000–€4000.
Rooms	4 + 1: 1 double, 2 suites, 1 family room for 3. House for 8 for weekly rental.
Meals	Breakfast €15. Brunch €27. Restaurant 13km.
Closed	October–April.
Directions	A20 exit 51 Périgueux on N89; Le Lardin D62 to St Genies; Cross St Genies to Montignac D704; 1st left for La Brousse; 1.5km.

Isabelle Hossein
La Brousse, 24590 Saint Genies,
Dordogne

Tel   +33 (0)5 53 31 98 17
Email   contact@maisons-antan.com
Web   www.maisons-antan.com

La Roseraie

Built as the country residence for a Parisian family, it is now a sparkling hotel. Experienced, enthusiastic hoteliers, the Nourrissons have brought their good chef with them. Pretty dining rooms dotted with yellow-clothed tables and posies set the scene for celery and truffle millefeuille and braised guinea fowl with pumpkin and chestnuts; such is their devotion to food there is an 'Initiation à la Gourmandise' menu for children. In summer you spill onto a terrace edged with clipped box… which leads to a garden of mature trees, roses and 19th-century formality, and a delicious palm-fringed pool. The gardens edge the river, prone to flood in winter (one good reason why La Roseraie closes in November). Bedrooms, comfortably pattern-carpeted with traditional furniture soon to be updated, have sweet river and garden views, while two apartments sit privately across the square revealing an unusual mix of the rustic and the frou-frou: fine old beams, stone walls, rococo-style chairs and a fancy four-poster. Medieval Montignac has it all – including the caves at Lascaux.

Price	€78-€120. Family room €130-€160. Apartment €250. Half-board €80-€140 p.p.
Rooms	14 + 2: 7 doubles, 3 twins, 4 family rooms for 4. 2 apt for 4.
Meals	Breakfast €12. Lunch from €19. Dinner €22-€47. July/August: half-board only.
Closed	November-Easter.
Directions	A20 & A89 to La Bachellerie, follow Montignac then Montignac centre.

Vincent & Isabelle Nourrisson
11 Place d'Armes,
24290 Montignac Lascaux, Dordogne
Tel   +33 (0)5 53 50 53 92
Fax   +33 (0)5 53 51 02 23
Email   hotelroseraie@wanadoo.fr
Web   www.laroseraie-hotel.com

Stwin

Auberge de Castel Merle

This hidden paradise has been in Anita's family for five generations. Her grandfather archaeologist added stones from his own digs; Eyzies, the capitol of prehistory, is nearby. Husband Christopher is British and also devoted to this atmospheric place. They have renovated the old buildings with consummate care, keeping the traditional look, using wood from their own land to restore walnut bedheads and doors. Christopher is an enthusiastic truffle hunter and head chef; there's a vast cast-iron cauldron in the banquet room in which he once conjured up a cassoulet for the entire village. This is wild boar country and cooking the beast is one of his specialities. Flowery curtains, pelmets and hand-painted flowers on the walls prettify the dining room; bedrooms have a straightforward country look, with Provençal prints and stone walls. Some rooms overlook the courtyard, others the woods. And the views. the glory of the place is its position, high above the valley of the Vézère, with river, forests and castles beyond – best admired from one of the check-clothed tables on the large, leafy terrace.

Price	€55–€60
Rooms	7: 6 doubles, 1 twin.
Meals	Breakfast €8. Dinner €19–€27. Half-board only in July & August. Restaurant closed lunchtimes.
Closed	Mid-October–March.
Directions	A89 to Montignac, then D706 for Les Eyzies. At Thonac left over bridge then right to Sergeac. Signed.

Anita Castanet & Christopher Millinship
24290 Sergeac, Dordogne

Tel	+33 (0)5 53 50 70 08
Fax	+33 (0)5 53 50 76 25
Email	hotelcastelmerle@yahoo.fr
Web	www.hotelcastelmerle.com

La Commanderie

Off the medieval street, through the stone archway and the gently-treed gardens, into the steep-roofed *commanderie*. The Commanders of the Order of Malta put up here 700 years ago en route to Santiago de Compostella and a low curved toll passage still forms part of the house, its black slate slabs gloriously intact. This is not so much a hotel as a houseful of guests overseen by diminutive Madame, a correct but considerate hostess. An uncontrived collection of antiques warms the friendly bedrooms, each with its own personality – convent-white walls are set off by touches of dark blue, ceilings soar, floors of varying ages and patterns are softened by Indian rugs, maybe there's a crucifix or a pink glass chandelier. Downstairs, guests gather at round tables set with antique cane chairs, floral curtains hang at tall windows and you get two choices per gastronomic course – just right for this unassuming, atmospheric place. There's a pool in the shade of the cedars and the Lascaux Caves are a mile down the road.

Price	€85.
Rooms	7: 5 doubles, 2 twins.
Meals	Breakfast €10. Lunch €20–€45. Dinner €35–€45. Restaurant closed Monday.
Closed	August.
Directions	N89 between Brive & Périgueux. At crossroads at Lardin, towards Condat, right to La Commanderie, 50m after church.

Mme Annick Roux
245 Condat sur Vezère,
Dordogne

Tel	+33 (0)5 53 51 26 49
Fax	+33 (0)5 53 51 39 38
Email	hotellacommanderie@wanadoo.fr
Web	www.best-of-perigord.tm.fr

56mins

Manoir d'Hautegente

The ancient manor, first a smithy, later a mill, has been in the family for 300 years but is paradoxically just 50 years old: burned down in the Second World War, it was rebuilt. The millstream has become a fabulous waterfall feeding a pond that shimmers beneath the bedroom windows and the thoroughly kempt garden is a riot of colour. Hautegente is rich inside too, like a private house, with two sumptuous dining rooms clothed in silk and hung with well-chosen paintings and prints. There's a cosy drawing room where a large fireplace and a vast array of cognacs summon the sybarite. Lavishly decorated bedrooms have fine thick curtains, antiques and pretty lamps; some are small, some enormous and the soft, expensive feel of padded wall fabrics contrasts with the lovely old staircase leading up from the hall. The rooms in the converted miller's house are more modern; four have mezzanines and the ground-floor room is vast. Bathrooms are all beautifully tiled and properly equipped. A splendid and peaceful place.

Price	€90–€250. Half-board option June to mid-September, €95–€183 p.p.
Rooms	17. 12 doubles, 5 triples.
Meals	Buffet breakfast €14. Dinner €48–€70. Picnic available.
Closed	Mid-November–Easter.
Directions	From Brive N89 for Périgueux through Terrasson. Left at Le Lardin on D704 for Sarlat, then left at Condat on D62 to Coly.

Patrick & Marie Josée Hamelin
24120 Coly,
Dordogne

Tel	+33 (0)5 53 51 68 03
Fax	+33 (0)5 53 50 38 52
Email	hotel@manoir-hautegente.com
Web	www.manoir-hautegente.com

Château de Siorac

Soaring ceilings, glowing parquets, intricate plasterwork, noble furnishings. Grand, yes, but never intimidating, thanks to the couple who run it, sweet sunny Jose and Diana. He, a scientist, she, an ex-stockbroker, gave up New York for this honey-hued château and have worked their socks off to bring it back to life. They and their family (horses, dogs) inhabit a smaller house in the grounds, and the grounds are worth a wander just for the pom poms of box skirting lawns and terraces. Built on a small rise overlooking a Perigordian plain, the mainly 19th-century château is solidly handsome and sports two fairytale turrets. Inside, a monumental Renaissance fireplace dominates a dining room where breakfast is exquisitely presented and dinners are graced by silver candelabra. Paper carrying the initials of the Beaupoil family lines the living room walls, and the bedrooms on the first floor are stupendous. Be seduced by huge beds, damask curtains, sombre tapestries and sweeping parquet; four of the bathrooms are breathtakingly grand, one embellished with Roman urns and mosaics. Formidable!

Price	€105–€120. Suite €150.
Rooms	6: 5 doubles, 1 suite.
Meals	Breakfast included. Dinner €45, book ahead.
Closed	5-12 April; 27 September-7 October.
Directions	From Bordeaux to St Astier, D3 for Périgueux. 1km after Gravelle, left for château.

Jose & Diana Serrano
24430 Annesse et Beaulieu,
Dordogne

Tel	+33 (0)5 53 07 64 53
Fax	+33 (0)5 53 07 64 53
Email	serrano@chateaudesiorac.com
Web	www.chateaudesiorac.com

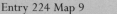

Hostellerie Les Griffons

The setting is the sort of thing one dreams of in a harsh winter. It is impossibly lovely: a handsome 16th-century stone house, once a mill, beside a medieval bridge over the river, bright and inviting with blue shutters… the views of the château tip the dream beyond reality. One look at their website and you want to be there. Many of the old features have been nurtured – the big stone fireplaces, the lovely old windows – and every room has a medieval flavour. Some may find the mood on the first floor a touch sombre, though colours are fashionably bold; on the second, windows and timbers are white. From most bedrooms the views over the little town are wonderful; bathrooms are fine rather than magnificent; paintings by a local artist add personality. You dine and breakfast stylishly at the river's edge, a place where you would want to picnic if you were passing through. The food is, by all accounts, excellent (the owner's son is a pastry chef). Bourdeilles is enchanting, and close to equally lovely Brantôme, 'Venice of the Perigord.' Come to be spoiled by such places as only France can provide.

Price	€110–€120. Family rooms €130.
Rooms	10: 6 doubles, 2 twins, 2 family rooms for 3.
Meals	Breakfast €12. Lunch & dinner €30–€40.
Closed	31 October–7 April.
Directions	From Périgueux dir. Angoulème. Just before Brantôme, left for Bourdeilles (village médiéval) for 5km. L'Hostellerie is in centre of village.

Cathy & Dominique Robert
24310 Bourdeilles,
Dordogne

Tel	+33 (0)5 53 45 45 35
Fax	+33 (0)5 53 45 45 20
Email	griffons@griffons.fr
Web	www.griffons.fr

Château Le Mas de Montet

A nose for fine living brought John and Richard to this serene place. At the end of an avenue guarded by plane trees – gloriously French – is the château, slate-topped and turretted in Renaissance style. Once frequented by Mitterrand and his labradors – one suite is named in his honour – it has been extravagantly restored. Reception rooms lined with eau-de-nil brocade are sated with auction house finds, richness and softness bring instant seduction and bedrooms, named after Corneille, Voltaire, Madame de Lafayette, have all you'd hope for the price (British electrical sockets included!). Beds are big and supremely comfortable, four-posters canopied and draped, bathrooms Deco-white… the one in the tower has its own chandelier. Copious breakfasts are served at tables in the orangery where later you dine on Perigordian delicacies; doors open in summer to a big terrace; 50 hectares of parkland, wildlife and pool sweep down to the fish-rich Dronne. Grand yet easy, this is the perfect place for stressed city souls to unwind… uncommercial, full of charm, heaped with readers' praise.

Price	€145–€225. Suites €225–€395.
Rooms	10: 4 doubles, 1 twin, 5 suites.
Meals	Breakfast €19. Lunch €20. Dinner €49.
Closed	Never.
Directions	A10 then N10 to Angoulême, south towards Libourne, then Montmoreau, then Aubeterre. Signed on D2/D20 between Aubeterre & Ribérac.

John Ridley & Richard Stimson
Petit Bersac, 24600 Ribérac,
Dordogne

Tel	+33 (0)5 53 90 08 71
Fax	+33 (0)5 53 90 66 92
Email	reception@lemasdemontet.com
Web	www.lemasdemontet.com

Domaine du Moulin de Labique

Ducks on the pond, goats in the greenhouse and food *à la grande-mère* on the plate – the Domaine du Moulin de Labique glows with warmth and humour. Shutters are painted with *bleu de pastel* from the Gers and the 13th-century interiors have lost none of their aged charm. The lucky new owners, Christine and Patrick, cook up a super dinner (seasonal, local, delicious) for guests. Bedrooms are a match for the rest of the place and are divided between those in the main building above a vaulted *salle d'armes*, those in the barn, reached via a grand stone stair, and an apartment in the old bread and prune-drying ovens. There are chunky roof beams, seagrass mats on ancient tiles, lovely old iron bedsteads, antique mirrors and papers flower-sprigged in positive colours (raspberry, jade green). The suite in the barn has its own terrace, some bathrooms have Portuguese tiles: there's much to captivate and delight. Outside, old French roses, young alleys of trees, a bamboo-fringed stream and an exquisite pool. Book a long stay, you won't regret it.

Price	€90. Suite & apartment €140.
Rooms	7 + 1: 4 doubles, 2 twins, 1 suite for 4. Duplex apartment for 4.
Meals	Breakfast €8. Dinner €31.
Closed	Rarely.
Directions	From Cancon N21; D124 for Monflanquin; D153 at Beauregard to St Vivien; on right 1km after St Vivien.

Patrick & Christine Hendricx
St Vivien, 47210 Villeréal,
Lot-et-Garonne

Tel	+33 (0)5 53 01 63 90
Fax	+33 (0)5 53 01 73 17
Email	moulin-de-labique@wanadoo.fr
Web	www.moulin-de-labique.fr

Villa le Goèland

It is lush, lavish, inviting. Dominating the ocean, yards from the beaches of glamorous Biarritz, the only privately owned villa of its kind to have resisted commercial redevelopment has opened its arms to guests. Turrets were added in 1903; Paul's family took possession in 1934; now he and his wife, young, charming, professional, are its inspired guardians and restorers. They live in an apartment upstairs and know all there is to know about the pleasures of Biarritz: casino, museums, boutiques, golf, spa. Be ravished by oak floors, magnificent stairs and sunshine-filled balconies that go on for ever; the salon and dining room each have one so fling open the tall French windows. From the wonderful family bedroom is a *tour d'observation* with the finest view in Biarritz. Bedrooms, not cosy but lofty, are panelled and parquet'd, beds are king-size, two suites have terraces, bathrooms date from the 1900s to the 1960s, and breakfasts flourish sunshine and *viennoiseries*, served by Paul with a smile. Amazing.

Price	€150–€270.
Rooms	4: 3 doubles, 1 suite for 3.
Meals	Restaurant 20m.
Closed	November-February, but check.
Directions	From Place Clemençeau in Biarritz centre follow signs for place Ste Eugénie by Rue Mazagran; after pharmacy 1st right Rue des Goèland. House between antique shop & bar, narrow street.

Paul & Elisabeth Daraignez
12 plateau Atalaye, 64200 Biarritz,
Pyrénées-Atlantiques

Tel	+33 (0)5 59 24 25 76
Fax	+33 (0)5 59 22 36 83
Email	info@villagoeland.com
Web	www.villagoeland.com

Maison Garnier

In glamorous Biarritz, playground of royalty and stars, a jewel of sophisticated simplicity. Pristine-white bathrooms have huge showerheads, bedrooms are done in subtle white, eggshell, dark chocolate and soft coffee with the occasional splash of brilliant colour. The bright breakfast room has Basque floorboards setting off pale walls, red and white striped curtains; white linen is a perfect foil for lovely regional tableware in a red and green stripe and light pours in from great windows. Guests are enchanted by hotel and owners: both have real charm and warmth. In 1999, this old boarding house was turned into a smart and friendly little hotel. So, no hall counter, just a gorgeous wrought-iron stair rail, a 1930s-feel salon with a deep sofa, an old fireplace and a magnificent oriental carpet – the tone is set the moment you arrive. And you will soon be at ease with your delightful, engaging hosts. On the lively Rue Gambetta a five-minute walk from that fabulous surfing beach it is close enough to do everything by foot. Remarkable value, book early.

Price	€90–€140.
Rooms	7: 5 doubles, 2 twins.
Meals	Breakfast €9. Lunch & dinner available locally.
Closed	Rarely.
Directions	From A63 exit Biarritz & La Négresse for Centre Ville & Place Clémenceau. Straight ahead for large, white bank building with clock; left onto Rue Gambetta. Free parking on side street.

Anne & Yves Gelot
29 rue Gambetta, 64200 Biarritz,
Pyrénées-Atlantiques

Tel	+33 (0)5 59 01 60 70
Fax	+33 (0)5 59 01 60 80
Email	maison-garnier@hotel-biarritz.com
Web	www.hotel-biarritz.com

Les Almadies

In the heart of busy Basque Saint Jean de Luz, this cool little find. From the discreet street entrance off the tree- and flower-filled square to the understatedly modern furnishings, everything is calm, relaxing and quietly stylish. Jean Jacques and Patricia, a young, gentle, friendly couple, have a clear eye for clean lines and harmony. The wooden floor and Philippe Starck-style chairs in the breakfast room create a lovely bright space in which to start the day; take your fill of fresh fruits, compotes, yoghurts, cheeses and pastries. If it's sunny, eat outside on the balcony overlooking a charming little town square. Bedrooms, with French windows and balconies onto quaint side street or square, have an easy-going simplicity – soft colours, embroidered bed covers, white-painted furniture. Bathrooms are a glistening contemporary mixture of wood and white tiles. Spend the day at the beach, hop over to the glorious Guggenheim in Spanish Bilbao, or stay put and explore this border town. No dinners but plenty of restaurants close by. A simple, restful spot – made for lingering.

Price	€75–€125.
Rooms	7: 4 doubles, 1 single, 2 triples.
Meals	Breakfast €10. Restaurants in town.
Closed	3 weeks in November.
Directions	In Saint Jean de Luz follow signs for Centre Ville/La Poste; with La Poste on left, 2nd right on Rue d'Esslissagaraiy which becomes Rue du Midi. Parking behind hotel.

Jean Jacques Hargous
58 rue Gambetta, 64500 Saint Jean de Luz, Pyrénées-Atlantiques

Tel	+33 (0)5 59 85 34 48
Fax	+33 (0)5 59 26 12 42
Email	hotel.lesalmadies@wanadoo.fr
Web	www.hotel-les-almadies.com

Hotel

Château d'Urtubie

The Château d'Urtubie was built in 1341 with permission from Edward III. The keep is still intact, except for the roof which was changed in 1654 to resemble Versailles, using the expertise of local boat builders. Your host, Laurent, is a direct descendant of the builder of the castle, Martin de Tartas, and opened Urtubie as a hotel in 1996 to make sure he can keep it alive. The castle is classified and also operates as a museum: *The Antiques Roadshow* could run an entire series here. You can have a 'prestige' bedroom on the first floor, very grand and imposing: not 'light and airy' which we often praise, but a touch sombre and totally in keeping with the age and style. On the second floor, you have the 'charm' bedrooms, which are slightly smaller. Bathrooms are a mix of ancient and modern, with stylish touches such as airy mosquito nets draped over traditional baths. On the outskirts of a pretty little Basque town, only five minutes' drive from the beach, Urtubie is also set in beautiful gardens. Don't be worried it might be stuffy: Laurent couldn't be more friendly and families are most welcome.

Price	€70-€150.
Rooms	10: 8 twins/doubles, 1 double, 1 single.
Meals	Breakfast €11. Restaurant 500m.
Closed	November-March.
Directions	A63 Bayonne & St Sebastien, exit St Jean de Luz Sud, first on left, N10 for Urrugne. Right just before roundabout entering Urrugne. 3km from St Jean de Luz.

Laurent de Coral
Urrugne, 64122 Saint Jean de Luz,
Pyrénées-Atlantiques

Tel	+33 (0)5 59 54 31 15
Fax	+33 (0)5 59 54 62 51
Email	chateaudurtubie@wanadoo.fr
Web	www.chateaudurtubie.fr

Hôtel Laminak

Relaxed, smiling and friendly, Philippe and Chantal are enchanted with their new project. They had just taken over when we visited so the style is still country cottage, but with less emphasis on floral designs. The setting is gorgeous, with all the lush greenery of the Basque countryside at your feet and views up to the mountains. The hotel is on a quiet road outside the village of Arbonne, with a few discreetly screened neighbours and a big, handsome garden filled with mature shrubs and trees. In summer it is a delight to eat breakfast on the terrace. Rooms are neat and attractive, carpeted, wallpapered and with antique pine furniture. You will sleep well here, and be looked after with a quiet and warm efficiency by the owners for whom this place has been a long-cherished dream. You can, too, settle round the open fire in the evenings, warmed by the easy comfort of the place and the satisfying sag of the leather furniture. It is an easy hop to the coast and the throbbing vitality of Biarritz. Those mountains are worth a week's effort in themselves; just below them, the fish await your line.

Price	€71–€99. Children under 2 free.
Rooms	12 twins/doubles.
Meals	Breakfast €10. Light dinner €11–€17, book ahead.
Closed	7-23 January.
Directions	A63 exit 4 La Négresse & follow signs to Arbonne; signed.

Philippe & Chantal Basin
Route de St Pée, 64210 Arbonne,
Pyrénées-Atlantiques

Tel	+33 (0)5 59 41 95 40
Fax	+33 (0)5 59 41 87 65
Email	info@hotel-laminak.com
Web	www.hotel-laminak.com

Domaine des 3 Baudets

High on a hill live French Véronique and her husband Werner, whose reputation as an inspired cook is making headlines. Tucked behind the village of Issor and with views that stretch to the Pyrénées is a 17th-century manor house dressed in pretty yellow and reclining in a smart garden. Guests stay in the auberge, a converted barn to the side of the main house: an open fire, a small bar, tablecloths in sprightly checks and stripes, French windows flung open to a terrace for warmer nights. Langorous hours will be spent here eating exceptional food, drinking the finest local wines, winding down. Stumble back to fresh and pretty bedrooms, each with a wall of warm colour — mango orange, deep yellow — and new beds with crisp linen in whites and greys; tiled shower rooms have riverstone floors. Saunter through wrought-iron gates to explore lawns, mature trees, shrubs and a swimming pool for wallowing. It would be cossetting to just hang around here most days, but you are surrounded by spectacular walking, skiing and canyoning country — and Lourdes and Biarritz can be visited in a day. *No credit cards.*

Price	€55-€75. Family room €110-€135.
Rooms	6: 4 doubles, 1 twin, 1 family room for 4.
Meals	Breakfast included. Dinner €25.
Closed	November, January.
Directions	From Orlon St Marie, towards Saragosse, through Gurmencon, Asasp. After 3km, right for Lourdios Et Issor, signed.

Véronique & Werner Stich
64570 Issor,
Pyrénées-Atlantiques

Tel   +33 (0)5 59 34 41 98
Fax   +33 (0)5 59 34 41 98
Email 3baudets@wanadoo.fr
Web   www.3baudets-pyrenees.com

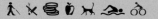

Domaine de l'Aragon

Winged cherubs, buxom wenches, handsome lovers greet you at breakfast – and flicker provocatively in the candlelight over dinner. The wall panels of the dining room of this 19th-century hunting lodge charm with their friskiness. Helmut and Eva, the young, friendly Austrian owners (perfect English), have retained the mini-château style of the house and lost the pretension – grand living in extremely laid-back fashion. Heaps of chandeliers, gilded mirrors, oil paintings, wooden panelling, and no-one to mind if you curl up in front of the fire. Bedrooms are comfortably and traditionally furnished, with boldly coloured walls and floating curtains. First-floor rooms have grand windows, top-floor rooms sit prettily under the eaves. Helmut cooks dinner – he runs an e-commerce business *and* is a trained chef – delivered to an intimate dining room; summer meals are served on a prettily tiled veranda beneath a stripy awning. Pop into Pau, borrow bicycles and explore Béarn, take a day trip to Biarritz. Or relax among the garden's venerable trees and raise a glass to the snow-topped Pyrénées.

Price	€70–€90.
Rooms	9: 7 doubles, 2 twins.
Meals	Breakfast €8.
	Dinner €28, book ahead.
Closed	Rarely.
Directions	From Pau, N134 to Oloron Ste Marie & Saragosse for 27km; hotel on left entering Herrère.

Eva Kratky & Helmut Fritz
Route de Pau, 64680 Herrère,
Pyrénées-Atlantiques

Tel   +33 (0)5 59 39 24 63
Fax   +33 (0)5 59 39 24 84
Email   info@domaine-aragon.com
Web   www.domaine-aragon.com

La Benjamine

Treat your taste buds to fresh tomato and mascarpone tart paired with just-cut salad; wild river fish and gambas with ginger and coriander; and Roussane peaches oozing with Jurancon wine. The food is as mouthwatering as the place. Cedric and Dawn opened their 18th-century doors in 2005. At the end of a lane, surrounded by fields of vines and within view of the Pyrénées, are four restful bedrooms, a sitting room with chocolate sofas and bread-oven fireplace (logs crackling in winter), a limestone-flagged kitchen with a farmhouse table. 'From garden to plate' is the philosophy and what they can't produce themselves they source from local farmers. It's friendly and generous, for grown-ups not children, fragrant with Dawn's flowers and Mamie's orchard jams (Cedric's granny is a discreet helper). Bedrooms and bathrooms have wooden floors and natural colours, showers you can drown in and dimmer switches "for reading or romance". Breakfast in the shade of white parasols, in a secluded courtyard; swim in a pool framed by lavender, vineyards and wild flowers. *Cookery weekends.*

Price	€85–€110.
Rooms	4: 3 doubles, 1 twin.
Meals	Breakfast included.
	Dinner with wine, €42 (not Tuesday).
Closed	Rarely.
Directions	A64 exit 9 Artix; at r'bout follow Monein, then through village to island with stone arch; straight over 3km, right on Chemin Augas. House 3rd on left at top of lane.

Cédric L'Herbier & Dawn Russell
Quartier Candeloup, Chemin Augas,
64360 Monein, Pyrénées-Atlantiques

Tel	+33 (0)5 59 21 48 27
Email	cedric@labenjamine.net
Web	www.labenjamine.net

Château de Méracq

Madame will give you a warm welcome in excellent English and is always happy to help or just to chat. She is very proud of her château, her dog, her hens and her husband's cooking. He has established a menu that combines the south-west's predilection for foie gras and duck with exotic sprinklings of spices and rose petals. If you take the half-board option, you can juggle your meals around as you like: even by eating more the next day if you miss one. The pretty château is at the end of a long and inviting driveway through large grounds with chairs under shady trees. One oak is 200 years old, perhaps planted by proud new owners. The eight bedrooms are an unusual mix: some in fresh stripes or flowers, others with bold turquoise or rose walls, with contemporary patterns on the beds. The first-floor rooms are grander, with bath and shower, while those on the second floor are simpler but all have their own shower. Rooms have lace-trimmed sheets and bowls of fruit and flowers. There are no numbers on the doors. As Madame says: "It wouldn't feel like home".

Price	€95-€125. Suites €250.
Rooms	8: 5 doubles, 1 twin, 1 suite for 3, 1 suite for 4.
Meals	Breakfast €12. Casual 'country' meal €16. Lunch or dinner €29-€39, book ahead.
Closed	Mid-December-mid-January.
Directions	N34 for 12km towards Aire from Adour & Bordeaux & Mont de Marsan then left on D944 through Thèze, then 1st right. Château on edge of Méracq.

Mr & Mme Guerin-Recoussine
64410 Méracq Arzacq,
Pyrénées-Atlantiques

Tel	+33 (0)5 59 04 53 01
Fax	+33 (0)5 59 04 55 50
Email	chateau-meracq@wanadoo.fr
Web	www.chateau-meracq.com

Limousin • Auvergne

Domaine des Mouillères

A small backwater of a village, a big clearing in the Limousin forest – here is a walker's paradise. On a south-facing slope with only distantly rolling hillsides, fine trees and a couple of donkeys to disturb the eye, the long stone hotel was built in 1870 as a farmhouse for Madame's great-great-grandfather and feels as solid as her lineage. Inside, you get that sense of long-gone days of endless country peace: leather-bound tomes, gilt-framed sepia photographs of Grandmamma or great-aunt Gladys as a baby, palely gentle floral designs on wallpapers and bedcovers. But the warm carpeting, the neat little bathrooms, the stripily plush modern furniture in the lounge betray a thoroughly contemporary care for comfort. And there's a lovely terrace outside. The delightfully friendly owners and their children, the geese and their goslings, the donkeys and their foals (summer population, of course) welcome you and your family into their rural world and Madame will serve you dinners of high authenticity: old family recipes made with fresh local produce. After which, peace will descend.

Price	€55–€87.
Rooms	5: 2 doubles, 2 twins; 1 double with shower & separate wc.
Meals	Breakfast €8.50. Picnic available. Dinner €15–€30. Two restaurants 3km & 7km.
Closed	October–March.
Directions	70km from Limoges for Bourganeuf & Aubusson N141. Left at Charbonnier to St Georges la Pouge.

Madame Elizabeth Blanquart–Thill
23250 Saint Georges la Pouge,
Creuse

Tel	+33 (0)5 55 66 60 64
Fax	+33 (0)5 55 66 68 80
Email	mouilleres@aol.com

Au Rendez-Vous des Pêcheurs

It isn't called Fishermen's Lodge for nothing and there's a spectacular, steep winding decent. The house and its exquisite riverside setting are intimately linked. Fifty years ago, the Fabrys built a house on the banks of the Dordogne; at the same time a dam was started just downstream. Madame opened a kitchen for the site workers – and the house became an inn. This being the Corrèze, food looms as large as the river. The restaurant, a fine room full of light and plants and Limoges china, overlooks the view reaching off to the distant wooded hills of the gorge. A reader describes his meal: "I had a set menu comprising of a *mise en bouche*, a feuilleté of sea scallops, a superb fillet steak with gratin potatoes and asparagus and four types of chocolate dessert that defy description". Bedrooms are differently decorated in simple, pleasing country style with coordinated bathrooms. The terrace is generous, the garden pretty, the view to treasure. Remarkable value in one of France's gentlest, loveliest pieces of countryside. A treasure. *Take a trip down the river in a traditional long boat.*

Price	€44–€49. Half-board mandatory in summer, €44 p.p.
Rooms	8. 5 doubles, 1 twin, 2 triples.
Meals	Breakfast €7. Picnic available. Lunch & dinner €16–€45. Restaurant closed Sun eve & Mon, 20 Sept-15 June.
Closed	12 November–mid-February.
Directions	42km east of Tulle: D978 to St Merd de Lapleau via Marcillac la Croisille; D13 to lieu-dit Pont du Chambon.

Madame Fabry
Pont du Chambon,
19320 Saint Merd de Lapleau, Corrèze

Tel	+33 (0)5 55 27 88 39
Fax	+33 (0)5 55 27 83 19
Email	contact@rest-fabry.com
Web	www.rest-fabry.com

La Maison des Chanoines

Originally built to house the cannons (les chanoines) of Turenne, this ancient restaurant-hotel has been in Monsieur Cheyroux's family for 300 years. No wonder the family held on to it – the 16th-century, mellow-stoned house with its steep-pitched slate roof is one of the loveliest in a very lovely village. Madame, young, charming, gracious, is a fan of fine English fabrics and has used them lavishly for curtains and cushions. Bedrooms are divided between this house and another (equally ancient) opposite, approached via a little bridge from the garden. Well-lit rooms have plain carpets and white walls; bathrooms ooze fluffy towels. The breakfast room is stone-flagged with wickerwork chairs padded in duck-egg blue. The dining takes place in the old cannon cellar – small and cosy, with white-clothed tables and vaulted ceiling – or under a fairylight-strewn pergola in the garden amid honeysuckle and roses. The food is a delight; Monsieur is chef and will use only the freshest, most local produce for his regional dishes. Ask about their three-day gourmet stay. Great value.

Price	€65–€90.
Rooms	6: 2 doubles, 2 twins, 1 triple, 1 family room.
Meals	Breakfast €9. Lunch & dinner menu €32–€40. Open for lunch Sundays & holidays. Closed Wednesdays in June.
Closed	15 October–week before Easter.
Directions	From Brive, D38 to Monplaisir; D8 for 8km to Turenne. Left uphill following château sign. On left before church.

Chantal & Claude Cheyroux
Route de l'Eglise, 19500 Turenne, Corrèze

Tel	+33 (0)5 55 85 93 43
Fax	+33 (0)5 55 85 93 43
Email	maisondeschanoines@wanadoo.fr
Web	www.maison-des-chanoines.com

Auberge de Concasty

Half a mile high stands the river-ploughed plateau: strong air, wild country, immense space. Built 300 years ago, the family mansion stands prouder than ever, and the utterly delightful Causse family have brought everything thoroughly up to date: jacuzzi, hammam and organic or local produce to keep you blooming (veg from the sister's farm next door). The dining room, with its vast inglenook fireplace where some fine plants live in summer, and the covered patio overlooking the pool and the view, are the stage for lovingly prepared shows of foie gras and asparagus, scallops and confits, the supporting cast an impressive choice of estate wines; great breakfasts, too. Guest rooms, some in the main house, some in a restored barn, two in the newly renovated chestnut dryer, are stylishly rustic with space, good floral fabrics and an evocative name each – no standardisation here, except for that view. The magnificent new family room in pale ivory and soft blue is the height of sophistication. You will love the smiling, attentive staff and the warm family atmosphere they generate. *Some rooms with balcony or terrace.*

Price	€63-€90.
Rooms	13: 10 doubles, 3 twins/doubles.
Meals	Breakfast €9. Brunch €16. Picnic available. Dinner €32-€42.
Closed	December-March.
Directions	From Aurillac, N122 for Figeac, left to Manhès on D64. From Figeac, N122 then D17 after Maurs.

Martine & Omar Causse-Adllal
15600 Boisset,
Cantal

Tel	+33 (0)4 71 62 21 16
Fax	+33 (0)4 71 62 22 22
Email	info@auberge-concasty.com
Web	www.auberge-concasty.com

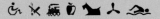

Château de Sédaiges

A crumbling old château such as children dream of, Sédaiges has it all: 14th-century turrets and crenellations, stairs and corridors galore, a crazily high neo-Gothic hammer-beamed hall built to house the tapestries given by Louis XIV, elegant 18th-century drawing rooms, open to the public, where Marie-Antoinette's lookalike holds court. Delightful Bab tells the tales with all her passion for this microcosm of a vanishing way of life: remote Auvergne is more unspoilt than any other part of old France; the family chapel bears witness. In the creaky old warren upstairs, among the antiques, beneath the aristocratic ceilings, are the endearingly unpretentious family-château bedrooms, two of them just refurbished: marble and muslin, florals and plush frame some fine furniture; bathrooms vary in style. You will feel you belong to the place and damask-clothed silver-served breakfast among the gleaming copper pans in the old kitchen is as atmospheric as it can get. Don't miss the re-engineered Barbie-doll show or the wonderful botanical walk through the park and its stupendous specimen trees.

Price	€100–€140. Extra bed €20.
Rooms	5: 3 doubles, 1 suite for 3, 1 suite for 4 (without lounge). Overflow room for children.
Meals	Breakfast included. Restaurant in village.
Closed	October–April.
Directions	From Aurillac D922 for Mauriac 10km. At Jussac right onto D59 to Marmanhac. Château signed.

Bab & Patrice de Varax
15250 Marmanhac,
Cantal

Tel	+33 (0)4 71 47 30 01
Fax	+33 (0)1 53 96 02 77
Email	bdevarax@netcourrier.com
Web	www.chateausedaiges.com

Hostellerie de la Maronne

In the quiet rolling green meadows where the little Maronne hurtles towards its gorge and brown cows echo the russet of autumn, this much-extended 1800s manor looks out to wooded hills. You will meet its energetic, subtly humorous owner and be well fed by his wife and budding chef son in the soft quiet restaurant. They have just totally redone all their rooms to four-star level. The lovely double drawing room has deep sofas, two fireplaces, good rugs, some intriguing Madagascan furniture. Bedrooms, all with excellent bedding, vary in size and spread over a small warren of buildings, past flowering corners. Nearly all have the sweeping valley view (three rooms at the back are up against the hillside); the best are the terrace rooms. Luxury fabrics are muted in blue and coffee or ivory and terracotta, enlivened by exotic pieces – framed textiles from India, a solitaire table from Madagascar – and bathrooms are excellent. The pool is ideal for landscape-gazing, there's fabulous walking and you will find rest in this house of silence: no seminars, no piped music and headphones for telly – bliss.

Price	€85–€135. Suites €140–€200. Half-board €85–€145 p.p.
Rooms	21: 18 twins/doubles, 3 suites.
Meals	Breakfast €11. Lunch & dinner €25–€45.
Closed	November–Easter.
Directions	From Aurillac, D922 north for 33km to St Martin Valmeroux; D37 for Fontanges. Do not go towards St Paul de Salers.

M & Mme Decock
Le Theil, 15140 Saint Martin Valmeroux,
Cantal

Tel	+33 (0)4 71 69 20 33
Fax	+33 (0)4 71 69 28 22
Email	maronne@maronne.com
Web	www.maronne.com

Entry 242 Map 10

Hôtel Saluces

The ancient house in the twisty centre of atmospheric Salers is built of dark volcanic rock and grounded in endurance: mineral vibes that sing in tune with the raucous ghost of erudite, dissipated Governor Saluces, who just escaped the guillotine in 1791, and the new owners' brilliantly sensitive conversion. Jeannette's sure talent with natural fabrics and original decorative finishes, Daniel's love of knotty woods, rough marble and the beauty created by those who went before, have produced a superb little hotel. First, the lava-grey polished cement floor and its subtle marble mandalas, then the inimitable tones of Farrow & Ball paints, a giant granite fireplace, a chestnut-shaded courtyard for breakfast or teatime crêpes. Beamed and floorboarded, each bedroom is a delight. Mostly big to very big, they are done in pale Louis XVI and the prettiest quilted flowers, or country antiques and gentle linen, or blocky modern timber and earth-brown flannel with fiery orange bindings; they also have fine big bathrooms. Add a tremendously friendly welcome, great value and blackbird song: a great find.

Price	€58–€136.
Rooms	8: 4 doubles, 2 twins, 1 family room for 4, 1 suite for 2.
Meals	Breakfast €8.
Closed	Never.
Directions	From Aurillac D922 for Mauriac 35km; right D680 to Salers to centre ville. Rue de la Martille is small street on right, off Place de la Mairie.

Daniel & Jeannette Gil
Rue de la Martille,
15140 Salers, Cantal

Tel	+33 (0)4 71 40 70 82
Fax	+33 (0)4 71 40 71 70
Email	contact@hotel-salers.fr
Web	www.hotel-salers.fr

Domaine de Gaudon – Le Château

The contrast could scarcely be greater. Out in the wilds of deepest Auvergne with nature bounding free all round, you find new Venuses and urns lining the edges of a great park. Inside the 19th-century splendour of glossy oak panelling, ceiling roses and original wall coverings, this totally natural, endearing couple have created a setting of unexpected glamour, all brass and satin and gilt and quilting, for their superb French antiques. Gleaming luxuriously, big bathrooms are in keeping. Alain is a dab hand at wall panels and mouldings, Monique knows exactly what she likes in fabrics and drapes and colour combinations (prussian blue and gold, canary yellow and gold, green and orange), they simply love having guests and breakfast is designed to dazzle you as your bedroom did. Gaudon is a Gîte Panda in a wildlife conservation area with some superb specimen trees, a wetland observation spot and innumerable frogs, bats, birds and insects (there are samples in frames indoors). Herons fish in the pond, children love the place and your hosts have been breeding Connemara ponies for 40 years. Astonishing.

Price	€98. Extra person €20.
Rooms	5: 3 doubles, 1 twin, 1 suite.
Meals	Breakfast included.
	Supper trays available.
Closed	Rarely.
Directions	From Montpellier, exit 9.
	D229 then D996 to St Dier d'Auverge.
	At end village, D6 for Domaize for
	3km. Right for Ceilloux, 1km.

Alain & Monique Bozzo
63520 Ceilloux,
Puy-de-Dôme

Tel	+33 (0)4 73 70 76 25
Email	domainedegaudon@wanadoo.fr
Web	www.domainedegaudon.fr

Château de Maulmont

This extraordinary place, built in 1830 by Louis Philippe for his sister Adélaïde, has long views and architecture: medieval crenellations, 16th-century brick patterning, Loire-Valley slate roofs, neo-Gothic windows, even real Templar ruins – a cornucopia of character. The owners provide activities on 23 hectares of parkland – a golf driving range, riding nearby, fishing, outdoor and indoor pools – and cultivate a certain 'formal informality'. They have preserved original features – carved inside shutters, the original spit in the kitchen, the panelled banqueting hall with its stained-glass portraits of Adélaïde in various moods – and collected some stunning furniture. Bedrooms go from small to very big, from plain honest comfortable with simple shower room to draped and four-postered château-romantic in the tower (the luxury rooms are worth the difference). And do visit the King's Room, a round blue and white tower 'tent', for a brilliant whisper-to-shout effect. Eating is simple in the Templars Tavern, gastronomic in the elegant dining room; Frederika and her staff are alert and eager.

Price	€80-€180. Suite €195-€220. Apartments €200-€275.
Rooms	19 + 3: 12 doubles, 6 twins, 1 family suite for 3-4. 3 apartments for 4-6.
Meals	Breakfast €12-€14. Lunch & dinner €34-€60; with wine €65-€80. La Taverne weekday menu €20.
Closed	Rarely.
Directions	N209 for Vichy; D131 for Hauterive; there, right to St Priest Bramefant; D55 then right at r'bout on D59 to Randan.

Mary, Théo & Frederika Bosman
St Priest Bramefant, 63310 Randan,
Puy-de-Dôme

Tel	+33 (0)4 70 59 03 45
Fax	+33 (0)4 70 59 11 88
Email	info@chateau-maulmont.com
Web	www.chateau-maulmont.com

Auberge de Chassignolles

The old village lay untouched in the pure green air, its 1930s inn decaying gently behind the medieval church; then along came two charming, colourful young Londoners, bringing oodles of talent and baby Fred. The place now hums with good looks and seriously delicious food. It is simplicity incarnate: upstairs, light from tall windows falls on herring-bone parquet, bounces off white walls onto perfectly appropriate old furniture – a 1930s carved and inlaid bedroom suite dressed in pure white linen, a deep and friendly armchair – and Ali's artistic eye sees to all the details. One room above the restaurant is a resident's library/sitting room and there's a big private garden over the road. Bathrooms are perfectly adequate with good extras. The pretty, old-style restaurant – country furniture, checked cloths, crinkly lamps, a fascinating mixture of old crockery – is the ideal frame for Harry's finely honed *cuisine de terroir*, all fresh local produce and real taste. An antidote to urban frenzy, with a small grocery shop by the bar, this is a perfect focus for revived community life and a boon for travellers.

Price	€45–€55.
Rooms	8: 6 doubles, 1 family room for 4; 1 twin sharing bathroom.
Meals	Breakfast €6.50. Lunch €15. Dinner €18. Picnic lunch €8.
Closed	October–mid-May.
Directions	From A75, exit 18 onto D76, thro' Brassac les Mines towards Brioude. Left onto D5, thro' Auzon, on for 8km. Left onto D52 to Chassignolles. Auberge in main square.

Harry Lester & Ali Johnson
Le Bourg, 43440 Chassignolles,
Haute-Loire

Tel	+33 (0)4 71 76 32 36
Fax	+33 (0)4 71 76 36 84
Email	info@aubergedechassignolles.com
Web	www.aubergedechassignolles.com

Midi – Pyrénées

Le Domaine de la Borie Grande

The 18th-century house in two hectares of parkland combines understatedly elegant luxury with a country B&B mood – wholly delightful. It is a beautifully kept home where you will find artistic flair and a love of cooking (vegetables from the neighbour, a stock of local wines and produce). A place of friendly proportions and lovingly collected antiques, where soft yellow cushions and gilt-edged fauteuils add sparkle to a palette of taupe, cream and soft grey. Enter a square hall off which lead three reception rooms: a cosy one for contemplation, a tranquil drawing room for tea and a grand salon for aperitifs and conversation. A stunning carved armoire – from the owner's great grandmother – takes pride of place, the deep cream sofa could seat a dozen, a big pale rug warms a terracotta floor and Cordes is perched high on the hill: magical. You will be guided up a sweeping stair to large and luminous bedrooms where antique rugs strew polished parquet, crisp linen enfolds new beds and white bathrooms have big mirrors and oodles of towels. And the garden has tennis and a pool. *Cash or cheque only.*

Price	€95–€100.
Rooms	3: 1 double, 1 twin, 1 suite.
Meals	Breakfast included. Hosted dinner €35 with wine; book ahead.
Closed	Rarely.
Directions	In Cordes sur Ciel follow signs toward Laguépie. Right at bend on bottom of hill leaving Cordes; straight on 1km to church in Campes; left to St Amans. On left, 500m from church.

Alain Guyomarch
Saint Marcel Campes,
81170 Cordes sur Ciel, Tarn

Tel	+33 (0)5 63 56 58 24
Fax	+33 (0)5 63 56 58 24
Email	laboriegrande@wanadoo.fr
Web	www.laboriegrande.com

Le Manoir de Raynaudes

The simple, sunny manor house deep in the Tarn owes its life to a dream; step in to a haven of refined rusticity and stunning cuisine. In a region of earthy, hearty gastronomy, Orlando – food critic, food editor, now chef – adds a wonderfully light touch. At one big friendly table, on a terrace with glorious views, you sit down to some of the most gorgeous food in south-west France. Perhaps a salad of roasted prawns, peaches and chicory picked minutes before, pigeon breasts with crisp sage polenta, a quivering panna cotta with golden raspberries… Light floods in through beautiful windows, a metal-framed staircase links three floors, peace seeps into every corner. Bedrooms are named after local friends who supported the owners' ambitious renovation, bathrooms ooze L'Occitane soaps and oils, simplicity and serenity are enlivened by crisp colours and touches of brocante. Meadows, a hundred oak trees, a clear night sky, a willow-fringed lake with ducks and fish, cheeses to grow fat on, touches of glamour, an enclosed courtyard, a dreamy pool – and a recipe book on its way. Exceptional.

Price	€190–€265.
Rooms	4: 1 double, 1 twin/double, 2 suites.
Meals	Breakfast included. Dinner €50–€60 (not Thurs & Mon).
Closed	Mid-November-mid-March. Open Christmas & New Year.
Directions	From Cordes sur Ciel, D922 to Laguépie; right after 2km onto D91 for Carmaux & Monestiés; Salles; left onto D27 Le Ségur; left at T-junc., 1st right onto D80. Raynudes on right; Le Manoir 1st right.

Orlando Murrin & Peter Steggall
81640 Monestiés,
Tarn

Tel	+33 (0)5 63 36 91 90
Fax	+33 (0)5 63 36 92 09
Email	manoir@raynaudes.com
Web	www.raynaudes.com

Le Phénix

Like its namesake, it rose from the ashes: when Tim and Ally bought the old *maison de maître* it had almost burned to the ground. Location is everything though, and it is set in acres of gentle woods and parkland, so they set to with gusto and the results are delightful. The relaxed attitude of the owners gives a homely but stylish feel, the guest sitting room has an open fire, underfloor heating, deep comfy sofas in soft creams and taupes, plenty of books and games. The kitchen is the hub and here you may sit and chat and watch your supper being prepared; enjoy a glass of wine here, or take it to the pretty garden room with its rattan furniture and green outlook. A stone staircase leads to big bedrooms with handmade beech and oak floors, lovely rugs, a mix of florals and stripes, a fresh feel; bathrooms are ultra-modern or vintage, with generous baskets of goodies. There's even a little kitchen should you want to rustle up a picnic and dine by the pool – or lounge in a hammock in a shady corner. Cafés and bustling markets are minutes away by car; this is perfect for families. *No credit cards. Minimum stay two nights August.*

Price	€75–€95. Single €55. Suite €120.
Rooms	6: 2 doubles, 2 triples, 1 single, 1 suite for 5.
Meals	Breakfast included. Dinner €22, book ahead.
Closed	Rarely.
Directions	From Rabastens, left at cinema onto D2 direction Sálvagnac. Approx 5km then left onto D28 Condel/Grazac; 100m on right, signed.

Tim & Ally Hewett
Lieu dit La Riviere,
81800 Rabastens, Tarn
Tel   +33 (0)5 63 33 86 64
Email   info@lephenixfrance.com
Web   www.lephenixfrance.com

Hôtel Cuq en Terrasses

Even the name is appealing. Come to the Pays de Cocagne, their brochure says. Where is that exactly, you may wonder, have I drunk that wine? It is in fact an imaginary land of pleasure, from this once prosperous pastel-producing region. Brochures often stretch the truth, but this place is magical. Philippe and Andonis gave up good jobs in Paris to buy this 18th-century presbytery after coming here on holiday. Perched in a beautiful garden on the side of a hill, between Toulouse and Castres, the tall, mellow stone house with white shutters looks so inviting. All the rooms, including a two-floor suite by the saltwater pool, are full of character, all different, with old terracotta floors, hand-finished plaster, exposed beams and some antique beds. But it is worth staying here just for the bathrooms — all different, in wood and white or terracotta and with hand-painted tiles. Breakfast on a long narrow terrace which blends into the garden. If you manage to drag yourself away to do some sightseeing, come back for fantastic Mediterranean food, bought earlier at the local market. It doesn't get much better.

Price	€95–€145. Suite €185. Half-board option (min. 4 nights).
Rooms	7: 3 doubles, 3 twins/doubles, 1 suite.
Meals	Breakfast €13. Snacks available. Hosted dinner €35, book ahead.
Closed	November-Easter.
Directions	N126 to Cuq Toulza. Then D45 towards Revel. After 2km on left at top of hill in old village.

Philippe Gallice & Andonis Vassalos
Cuq le Château,
81470 Cuq Toulza, Tarn
Tel   +33 (0)5 63 82 54 00
Fax   +33 (0)5 63 82 54 11
Email   cuq-en-terrasses@wanadoo.fr
Web   www.cuqenterrasses.com

Domaine de Rasigous

The drawing room is the magnet of this exceptional house: gentle colours, fabulous furnishings and, in winter, a log fire in a marble fireplace. The soft yellow and white dining room is full of light; never twee, the tables are beautifully decorated for good-looking varied food and local wines (especially the delicious Gaillac). Natural pale, bare floorboards with fine rugs or luxurious plain carpets give that country-house feel to large, heavenly bedrooms, sensitively decorated with rich colours and interesting furniture. The three suites are elegantly unfrilly. Luxurious bathrooms have been ingeniously fitted into odd spaces – the free-standing bath is most handsome. Even the single room, with its sleigh beds, lovely linen and bathroom in a walk-in cupboard, is on the 'noble' floor, not under the eaves. The courtyard is ideal for summer breakfast; gaze at the water lilies in the water garden, eight different types of frogs will sing and jump for you. The owner's flair and hospitality make this a wonderful place to stay – try to give it at least three nights.

Price	€90–€105. Single €75. Suites €130–€140.
Rooms	8: 4 twins/doubles, 1 single, 3 suites for 2.
Meals	Breakfast €12. Dinner €28.50 (not Wednesdays). Restaurant nearby.
Closed	December–February.
Directions	From Mazamet D621 for Soual for 16km; left on D85 to St Affrique les Montagnes. 2km further on D85. Green sign on left.

Fabrice Delprat
81290 St Affrique les Montagnes,
Tarn

Tel	+33 (0)5 63 73 30 50
Fax	+33 (0)5 63 73 30 51
Email	hotelrasigous@infonie.fr
Web	www.domainederasigous.com

Château de Garrevaques

The walls were breached under fire of bombards and culverins… Then came the Revolution, then the occupation; but the family is adept at rising from the ashes and the 17th generation is now in charge. Marie-Christine has all the charm and passion to make a go of such a splendid place – slightly faded in parts but full of history. In the château are huge reception rooms, magnificent antiques, some original 18th-century wallpaper by Zuber and, up spiral stone stairs, a games room with billiards. Over in the Pavillon are modern bedrooms traditionally styled – big beds, wooden floors, fabrics in a range of colours and patterns. Downstairs, two comfortable lounges – sleek black leather sofas in one, repro fauteuils in another – a grand piano and a bar. Come to unwind; you are miles from anywhere, there's a super spa with an oriental hammam and a garden studded with old trees. Set off for a walk with Lord the family dog, return to tennis court and pool. Marie-Christine is unstoppable: cookery courses, itineraries to nearby places of interest, flying lessons next door… you are in good hands.

Price	€170–€220
Rooms	Pavillon: 14 twins/doubles, 1 duplex for 3-4.
Meals	Buffet breakfast €12. Hosted dinner in château, €35 (min. 6). Book ahead.
Closed	Never.
Directions	From Revel, D1 for Caraman. Opposite Gendarmerie in Revel, D79F to Garrevaques for 5km. Château at end of village on right.

Marie-Christine & Claude Combes
81700 Garrevaques,
Tarn

Tel	+33 (0)5 63 75 04 54
Fax	+33 (0)5 63 70 26 44
Email	m.c.combes@wanadoo.fr
Web	www.garrevaques.com

Château de Séguenville

A dream of a French family château. Restoring it is a perpetual labour of love for Marie and Jean Paul; and still it has oodles of character. She is an enthusiastic cook and he loves his wine, so they will happily prepare a menu gastronomique if you ask in advance. This is a 13th-century château, destroyed in the revolution, rebuilt in 1850, beautifully run and in the family for 40 years; Marie and Jean Paul can tell you all about both house and region. Be charmed by galleried bedrooms with marble fireplaces and creaky floors, big bathrooms that combine the old with the new, a salon Chinois with black leather sofas, a second salon with a vast open fire, and centuries-old trees in the grounds. It's still crumbling in places but you'll relish the slightly frayed charm, and your hosts, young parents, particularly love having families to stay. Decoration is simple yet elegant, and full of personality. Outside are a swimming pool and a terrace for breakfast with glorious views. In the summer spin off on a bike or visit the chateau's windmill, open to visitors and still grinding flour. *No credit cards.*

Price	€120–€125.
Rooms	5: 3 doubles, 1 family room for 5, 1 suite.
Meals	Breakfast included. Dinner, 3 courses, €25. Wine from €7.
Closed	15 December–15 January.
Directions	From Toulouse dir. Blagnac Airport, then Cornebarrieu/Cadours; on to Cox, 3rd road on right, 5km after Cox, signed Séguenville.

Marie & Jean Paul Lareng
Région de Toulouse, 31480 Cabanac Séguenville, Haute-Garonne

Tel   +33 (0)5 62 13 42 67
Fax   +33 (0)5 62 13 42 68
Email   info@chateau-de-seguenville.com
Web   www.chateau-de-seguenville.com

La Guiraude

The peaceful old farmhouse is surrounded by a warren-like garden of secret nooks and hidden terraces, mature trees and country views — and there's a swimming pool tucked away. Inside all is tranquil. French doors at both ends of the sitting room open, hacienda-like, to terraces, and the room has an Italian feel: Tuscany siennas and ochres, ironwork and terracotta. Bedrooms are large, cool and decorated in classic colours — cream and burgundy, grey and navy, royal blue and gold; two have private terraces looking to the hills. Comfortable beds look inviting in their crisp white linen; swish bathrooms have baskets of extras and an abundance of towels. When you're peckish, Janine brings you a delicious afternoon tea – and it's worth staying for dinner at the long sociable table. Cooking is Alistair's passion and he conjures up a small-choice, three-course menu every night (foie gras with fig compôte, chicken with tarragon cream, tarte au citron. Nearby, a Friday market full of farm produce and colour; beyond, forests, gorges and caves. *Minimum stay two nights.*

Price	€90–€110.
Rooms	5: 2 doubles, 2 twins, 1 family room for 4.
Meals	Breakfast €10. Dinner €28–€38.
Closed	Rarely.
Directions	From A61 exit Villefranche de Lauragais.

Janine & Alistair Smith
31290 Beauteville,
Haute-Garonne

Tel   +33 (0)5 34 66 39 20
Fax   +33 (0)5 61 81 42 05
Email   guiraude@wanadoo.fr
Web   www.guiraude.com

Château de Beauregard

Paul and Angela have created something memorable here. Paul is French, a chef by training and brimful of energy – an entrepreneur – but it is Angela's intuition and imagination that have wrought the magic inside this little hotel. The château, grafted onto a 17th-century dairy farm in 1820, was in a woeful condition when they bought it. Everyone thought them quite mad but they've saved it triumphantly, using reclaimed materials, even finding some massive old radiators; the new central heating looks perfectly at home. The rooms are full of appeal and interest, the old furniture and fabrics that Angela has tracked down have just enough shabby chic to look as though they've been there forever. Each bedroom is named after a French writer, with a corresponding shelf of their work. Breakfast is served in the pretty winter-garden or, in warm weather, out under the wisteria (the grounds are lovely). Dining at L'Auberge d'Antan is a treat: Paul has turned the stables into a rustic restaurant and you can watch the (very good) Gascon-style food being cooked over a wood fire. There's even a new spa.

Price	€60–€80. Suites €80–€200. Apartment €460–€900 per week.
Rooms	8 + 1: 4 twins/doubles, 4 suites. Apartment for 6.
Meals	Breakfast €10. Dinner €30.
Closed	November–March.
Directions	From Toulouse to Tarbes, A20 exit 20 to Salies du Salat; D117 to Saint Girons, Massat.

Angela & Paul Fontvieille
L'Auberge d'Antan, Avenue de la Résistance,
09200 Saint Girons, Ariège

Tel	+33 (0)5 61 66 66 64
Fax	+33 (0)5 34 14 07 93
Email	contact@chateaubeauregard.net
Web	www.chateaubeauregard.net

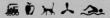

L'Abbaye Château de Camon

Camon... the name conjures up images of pious folk, wrapped in sackcloth and arriving by donkey. History and architecture buffs will swoon trying to work out which bits were built when, but it was first recorded as a Benedictine Abbey in 928. Now Peter, who managed The Samling in Cumbria, and his wife Katie, an interior designer, give you monks' bedrooms with vaulted ceilings and long windows with 28 panes; all look south over the hills and have tiny glistening floor tiles. Rooms on the second floor are squarer; all have soft colours, beautiful fabrics and spoiling bathrooms. On chilly evenings, hang out in the huge salon with its exquisite 18th-century plasterwork, floral ceiling and roaring fire, or take tea quietly to the sheltered cloister garden. Breakfast is served, most elegantly, on a long high terrace running the whole length of the château and overlooking formal park gardens with lawns, mature trees and swimming pool. Chef Tom will thrill bon viveurs with his rather grand menu, the estate wine is superb and you are 30 minutes from grand skiing at Mont D'Olmes. Stunning.

Price	€110-€180. Suite €240.
Rooms	11: 9 doubles, 2 suites for 4.
Meals	Breakfast €16. Dinner €36.
Closed	2 January-15 March.
Directions	From Carcassonne N13 to Bram, D4 to Fanjeaux, D119 south to Mirepoix, D625 towards Laroque, D7 for Camon. Signed.

Katie & Peter Lawton
Camon,
09500 Ariège

Tel	+33 (0)5 61 60 31 23
Fax	+33 (0)5 61 60 31 23
Email	peter.katielawton@wanadoo.fr
Web	www.chateaudecamon.com

Hôtel Restaurant Relais Royal

Arrive on a summer afternoon and you'll pass the courtyard tables set for tea. Then through the Renaissance-style gate and into the lobby where terracotta gleams, the grandfather clock ticks away the hours and pretty arched doors lead to a second courtyard and pool. The lofty dining room has a touch of gilt here and there and is a suitable setting for some serious food: guinea fowl with eight spices, roasted tuna with piperade and coriander. Dine in winter in front of a fire in the old kitchen, its walls lined with copper pans; retire with a cigarello to the clubby haze of the Blue Room. Then up the grand ironwork staircase to bedrooms with a modern décor that allows the original features to shine: glorious 18th-century windows, high ceilings and beams (these painted a fashionable white). Fabrics are coordinated, bathrooms are large and luxurious. Gerwin and Rogier, cultured and charming – as are their staff – will help you explore. You are in the heart of Mirepoix so the cathedral is a must; there's hiking and biking in the Pyrénées, and Carcassonne is worth at least a day.

Price	€160–€240. Suites €245–€340.
Rooms	8: 5 twins/doubles, 3 suites for 2-4.
Meals	Breakfast €20. Lunch €35-€87. Dinner €35-€87, except Mon & Tues. Children's menu €18.
Closed	2 January-7 February.
Directions	From Toulouse A66 towards Foix. Exit Pamiers, Mirepoix & Carcassonne. D20 to Mirepoix & Bram. In centre of Mirepoix, nr post office.

Mr Gerwin Rutten & Mr Rogier Van Den Biggelaar
8 rue Maréchal Clauzel,
09500 Mirepoix, Ariège

Tel	+33 (0)5 61 60 19 19
Fax	+33 (0)5 61 60 14 15
Email	relaisroyal@relaischateaux.com
Web	www.relaisroyal.com

La Grande Combe

An energetic, lovable couple live in this astonishing old place, built on a hillside before a heart-stopping view. You go from level to delightful level: the ancient timber frame holds brilliantly restored rooms done in a simple, contemporary style that makes the old stones glow with pride. The emphasis is on communal living and Nelleke is a passionate and skilful lady in the kitchen. Professional presentation and inventive menus converge in the warmly atmospheric dining room; start, perhaps, with duck terrine, move on to salmon on a bed of sauerkraut with chorizo sausage, then finish with a platter of local cheeses and a lemon tart. Hans prides himself on picking the perfect wine to accompany the meal. Sitting rooms have original paving and bedrooms have ingenious bathrooms, walk-in showers and incredible views – all including the singles, which are small yet fresh. Care is given to a huge organic garden and there are little terraces and a library for quiet times. Don't pay much attention to the bumpy road up; once here you will unwind. No frilly bits, no clutter, an exceptional place.

Price	€80. Singles €40. Studio €378-€406 per week.
Rooms	7: 3 doubles, 2 twins, 2 singles.
Meals	Breakfast included. Hosted dinner with wine €29, book ahead.
Closed	Rarely.
Directions	D902 between Brousse-le-château and Faveyrolles; at iron bridge onto D200 but do not cross bridge; take forest road, signed.

Hans & Nelleke Versteegen
12480 Saint Izaire,
Aveyron

Tel	+33 (0)5 65 99 45 01
Fax	+33 (0)5 65 99 48 41
Email	grande.combe@wanadoo.fr
Web	www.la-grande-combe.nl

Le Murier de Viels

You won't meet a soul on the drive to get here – but you may meet a wild deer. This small, intimate hotel, a sprinkling of 18th-century Quercy buildings on many lush levels, hides amongst the oak woods and gazes down upon the river. Come for a smiling welcome and an atmosphere of relaxed comfort: Josephine and Oz have left stressful lives in the UK to realise their dream of owning a small hotel in France. The layout of the place is charming, with reception, restaurant and guest rooms scattered among terraces, entwined by secret corners. The pool area has a great view – *everywhere* has a great view; there's space and there's tranquillity. In the bedrooms, exposed stone walls rub shoulders with white plaster, there is stylish modern French furniture and soothing colours, big walk-in showers and fluffy white towels, excellent reading lamps and luxurious pillows. One suite has a fitted wardrobe with antique doors, a comfy raffia sofa and a stunning view through a huge window. Every room is pristine. Make the most of 'international cuisine' in a dining room bright with yellow leather chairs.

Price	€65-€95. Family rooms €75-€90. Suite €105-€130. Cottage €400-€700.
Rooms	7 + 1: 3 doubles, 1 twin, 2 family rooms for 3, 1 duplex suite for 3. Cottage for 4.
Meals	Breakfast €9.50. Picnic on request. Dinner €25-€30.
Closed	November–mid-March.
Directions	From Figeac to Villefranche de Rouergue, cross river then immed. right onto D86 towards Cajac. 2km, follow signs.

Oz & Josephine Osman Shariff
12700 Causse et Diege,
Aveyron

Tel	+33 (0)5 65 80 89 82
Fax	+33 (0)5 65 80 12 20
Email	info@le-murier.com
Web	www.le-murier.com

Villa Ric

Jean-Pierre built his house some 20 years ago, high on a steep hill covered in "proper" trees (not conifers). The view from the terrace, where you eat when it's warm, is of rolling hills as far as the eye can see. Food is an important part of your stay here: Jean-Pierre discusses the menu each evening with guests, most of whom choose half-board. Others do drop by to dine, but the emphasis is very much on a restaurant for residents, and food is fresh and inventive. Bedrooms are Laura Ashley-pretty, perhaps with broad striped wallpaper and fresh white wicker chairs; many have exposed beams. Bathrooms gleam; each matches its flower-themed bedroom. The hotel is at a crossroads, ideal as a stopover for the Auvergne, Dordogne or the journey down to Spain. But why not linger a little longer? In July and August the old timbered market town hosts a well-established music festival: opera, music in the streets, processions and art exhibitions. Elisabeth is a passionate collector of the ceramics of Jean Lurçat, who settled here in 1945 and whose work is shown at a special workroom-museum in town. *Inventive cuisine.*

Price	€75–€105. Half-board €75–€105 p.p.
Rooms	5 twins/doubles.
Meals	Breakfast €10. Dinner €35–€58.
Closed	November–Easter.
Directions	From Paris, A20 exit 52 for St Céré, then Leyme. From Toulouse exit 56. Hotel 2km from St Céré.

Elisabeth & Jean-Pierre Ric
Route de Leyme, 46400 Saint Céré, Lot

Tel	+33 (0)5 65 38 04 08
Fax	+33 (0)5 65 38 00 14
Email	hotel.jpric@libertysurf.fr
Web	www.jpric.com

Manoir de Malagorse

You get more than you pay for here, so enjoy it to the hilt. The refined manoir in the idyllic setting was once a farmhouse whose occupants fell on hard times. Now the place smiles again, thanks to Anna and Abel's loving restoration. Off the central staircase, spread over two floors, the bedrooms are statements of simple luxury and the great kitchen is a wonder to behold: a massive fireplace, a vaulted ceiling. This is where you dine at one long table — unless you choose the privacy of the dining room, or the terrace among the immaculate pom-pom hedges. Anna's table decorations are a match for Abel's exquisite food: napkins tied with twine, candles tall and dramatic. Now this delightful pair have twins of their own they love the idea of entertaining families and have created two contemporary suites in an outbuilding. Colours are muted, bed covers quilted, your hosts are unintrusively present and Anna can offer a professional massage after Abel's demanding wine-tastings. There are cookery courses in summer; in winter they close to run an Alpine restaurant. Special. *Gastronomic discovery weekends.*

Price	€120–€140. Suites from €250.
Rooms	6: 3 doubles, 1 family room, 2 suites.
Meals	Breakfast included. Dinner with wine, €45. Restaurants 6km.
Closed	Mid-November–April.
Directions	From Souillac 6km; N20 for Cressensac, on dual c'way, 1st right to Cuzance & Église de Rignac; 1st right in Rignac, signed. Detailed directions on booking.

Anna & Abel Congratel
46600 Cuzance, Lot

Tel	+33 (0)5 65 27 15 61
Fax	+33 (0)5 65 27 14 83
Email	acongratel@manoir-de-malagorse.fr
Web	www.manoir-de-malagorse.fr

Hôtel Relais Sainte Anne

If conversation should flounder, the saying goes, *un ange passe* – an angel is passing overhead. Perhaps there is one in the tiny chapel of Sainte Anne, at the centre of this beautiful cluster of ancient buildings, a reminder of another, quieter time when the hotel was a girls' convent. The chapel is intact and is used occasionally for small concerts and art exhibitions and the whole ensemble has been lovingly and sensitively restored with no jarring architectural mishaps. The large pool is discreetly tucked away and the walled garden, a cunning combination of formal French structure and English informality, manages to retain a strong feeling of the past – young charges playing hide-and-seek in the shrubbery, or gathering in the little courtyards or around the fish pond. Inside is equally evocatively atmospheric; warm old stone, fine wallpapers, opulent curtains, heavy rugs and proper attention to lighting. Most of the perfect ground-floor bedrooms have their own terraces, too. Sophisticated surroundings without any self-consciousness – a rare treat. *New restaurant opposite, Le Patio.*

Price	€70-€160. Suites €135-€245.
Rooms	16: 7 doubles, 4 twins, 1 single, 4 suites.
Meals	Breakfast €12-€15. Lunch & dinner €18-€65.
Closed	Mid-November-mid-March.
Directions	From Brive A20 for Cahors exit 54 for Martel; rue du Pourtanel; hotel on right at town entrance.

	Madame Ghislaine Rimet-Mignon
	Rue du Pourtanel,
	46600 Martel, Lot
Tel	+33 (0)5 65 37 40 56
Fax	+33 (0)5 65 37 42 82
Email	relais.sainteanne@wanadoo.fr
Web	www.relais-sainte-anne.com

Hôtel Restaurant Le Vert

The alchemy of family tradition – three generations and 25 years for this young couple – has rubbed off onto the very stones of this unpretentious, authentic country inn where Bernard's skills shine from the kitchen. All is simplicity with fresh flowers, glowing silverware and old flagstones leading you from the small lobby to the dining room. Glance at the blackboard for the day's special to get your appetite going and if the weather is as it should be, head for a table on the terrace. The local food cognoscenti are greeted as friends here, always an auspicious sign. You might chose a warm goat cheese, golden roasted with a lavender honey, then a prune-stuffed quail followed by a cherry-studded tiramisu. This is Cahors wine territory; Eva will advise. The rooms in the garden annexe are big, cool and elegant with beamed ceilings, stone walls and antique furniture lightened by simple white curtains and delicate bedspreads. The pool is hidden on the far side of the garden. In a country where politicians are authors and cooks are philosophers, Bernard's ivory tower is in the kitchen.

Price	€55–€130.
Rooms	7: 6 twins/doubles, 1 single.
Meals	Breakfast €9. Dinner €38–€45. Restaurant closed Thursday.
Closed	November–March.
Directions	From Villeneuve sur Lot, D911 for Fumel; south of Fumel D139 for Montayral. On past Mauroux towards Puy l'Evêque for approx. 500m. Hotel on right.

Bernard & Eva Philippe
Le Vert,
46700 Mauroux, Lot

Tel +33 (0)5 65 36 51 36
Fax +33 (0)5 65 36 56 84
Email hotellevert@aol.com
Web www.hotellevert.com

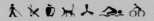

Domaine de Saint Géry

The beauty of the old farm buildings were enough to inspire this remarkable young couple to purchase a very run-down property in 1986. Now the grassed and paved areas between the buildings are decorated with loads of large-scale exotica – lemon trees, bays, oleanders, olives – and a fountain. A truffle-rich oak and hazelnut forest spreads out behind the buildings. The Dulers also seem to ably manage small children, a 80-acre cereal farm, an organic vegetable garden and a restaurant – in addition to making and marketing their own sausages, hams, confits, and truffle-enhanced foie gras. You can sample all of these delectables and more, as Patrick performs superbly in the kitchen and Pascale handles the divine desserts. Bedrooms are traditionally furnished with solid old wooden bedframes, generous curtains, no frilly bits or clutter – and all come with their own terrace or sitting out space. The delightful pleasures of the table and genuine hospitality are united here in such an intimate and peaceful setting that you may find it difficult to leave. *12km of walking paths.*

Price	€186–€364. Suite €396–€515.
Rooms	5: 4 doubles, 1 duplex suite for 5.
Meals	Breakfast €25. Dinner €91.
Closed	5 October–mid-May.
Directions	Exit 58 on A20 direction Cahors. At first roundabout left D653 direction Agen for 500m. D7 left for Labastide Marnhac & on to Lascabanes. Signed.

Pascale & Patrick Duler
46800 Lascabanes, Lot

Tel	+33 (0)5 65 31 82 51
Fax	+33 (0)5 65 22 92 89
Email	duler@saint-gery.com
Web	www.saint-gery.com

Domaine de Cantecor

Whether you are in the main house or in the outbuilding with its garden-level patio, all the rooms are bright, cheerful, uncluttered, charming. The 18th century property has masses of character and the owners make it clear that they want you to feel at home. On summer nights the floodlit pool is enchanting and during the day you may well be unable to resist a game of boules on the lawn or just relax in the quiet garden. Comfortable sofas around an open fireplace, bookshelves stacked with paperbacks, a country kitchen (the central meeting place) and samples of wine bought from local growers complete this charming picture. Lydi will cook dinner if the group is big enough and if she feels all the guests would enjoy mingling. This is a great base for exploring the subterranean caves or sampling the full-bodied wines from this area, and mountain bikes are on hand for the sporty. Lydi and René keep a good supply of information on all the activities in the area and, between them, can hold their own in English, German, Spanish and Dutch, of course. Great people, great value. *No credit cards.*

Price	€65-€80.
Rooms	6: 4 twins, 1 double, 1 family room for 4
Meals	Breakfast included. Restaurant 2km. Occasional dinner on request.
Closed	October-March.
Directions	A20 exit 58; N20 towards Montauban for 7km; left on D250 for La Madeleine; left after 600m. Signed.

Lydi & René Toebak
La Madeleine, 82270 Montpezat de Quercy,
Tarn-et-Garonne

Tel	+33 (0)5 65 21 87 44
Email	info@cantecor.com
Web	www.cantecor.com

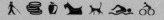

Hostellerie du Manoir de Saint Jean

Hats off to Anne-Marie, who, after three years, has impressed the locals (we asked around) with her renovations and her cuisine. This might not have been so difficult for another native from the town, but she is a transplant from Nice and an ex-antique dealer to boot. The dining room is, of course, outstanding; soft yellow and cream, full of enormous gilt framed mirrors and beautiful drapes framing huge windows. The terrace is particularly lovely and overlooks the formal garden – gradually establishing itself – and the side of the pool. There is a 'menu of the day' based on seasonal produce with the addition of two choices for each course. Anne-Marie hand-picks her wine suppliers and makes sure that they are among those who are producing the most 'natural' product possible; the same philosophy governs the chef's choice for his local produce. Space and more space – from the entrance hall to the corridors to the bedrooms where well-chosen antiques rest in just the right places adding warmth and colour. Bathrooms are bright and airy. A fine beginning, the patina will come: this is a place to watch.

Price	€100-€120. Suites €150-€200.
Rooms	10: 1 double, 9 suites for 2-4.
Meals	Breakfast €15. Lunch & dinner €38-€70. Restaurant closed Sunday evenings & Mondays.
Closed	Rarely.
Directions	A62 exit 9; in Moissac, D7 to Bourg de Visa. 9km; well signed.

Anne-Marie Morgadès
Saint Jean de Cornac,
82400 Saint Paul d'Espis, Tarn-et-Garonne
Tel   +33 (0)5 63 05 02 34
Fax   +33 (0)5 63 05 07 50
Email info@manoirsaintjean.com
Web   www.manoirsaintjean.com

Château de Goudourville

Medieval splendour without the draughts and with hot showers, lashings of atmosphere and romance: Hughes de Gasques established a stronghold here in the 11th century, Simon de Monfort laid siege to Goudourville – in vain – and it was here, after the battle of Coutras, that Henri IV laid 22 flags at the feet of the Countess of Gramont, 'la belle Corisande'. Bedrooms are vast and dramatic with massive old four-posters – Clement V, done up in red silk, Charles IX, all stone walls and cream hangings; d'Andouins, with subtle blue-and-cream wallpaper and a pretty, painted four-poster, Gasques, a lighter room in white and cream with a rosy terracotta floor. Baths are deep and bathrooms laden with towels. Dinner is served at small tables in a stone-vaulted dining room with a huge fireplace and you can choose from a selection of local specialities. There's a tree-filled terrace overlooking the Garonne, a large swimming pool and masses to do and visit nearby. Start with the château's beautifully preserved 11th-century chapel. *Nearby Moissac is well worth a visit.*

Price	€98–€140.
Rooms	8. 3 doubles, 3 triples.
Meals	Breakfast included. Dinner from €46, book ahead.
Closed	Mid-November–March.
Directions	From Valence, D953 towards Lauzerte. Signed.

Jacqueline Bazire
Goudourville,
82400 Tarn-et-Garonne

Tel	+33 (0)5 63 29 09 06
Fax	+33 (0)5 63 39 75 22
Email	goudourville@wanadoo.fr
Web	www.goudourville.com

L'Arbre d'Or

The 'Golden Tree' is Chinese and turn-of-the-century (the previous one); it's a ginkgo biloba and probably the finest in France. David will tell you its story and will explain why he believes Beaumont de Lomagne to be the finest example of a bastide town in south-west France; it's certainly very handsome and the Saturday market is not to be missed. He and Ann obviously love the place and are doing it up little by little and take great care of their guests; they've given thought to disabled access and are happy to look after cyclists and walkers. Ann's a keen cook and has adopted traditional, regional recipes — adding the occasional English crumble — which you can eat outside in the shaded, pretty garden or in the dining room with its exposed beams. A comfortable, old-fashioned atmosphere reigns in the bedrooms too, with their marble fireplaces, large windows, interesting old furniture and pretty decorative touches. Two of the bedrooms have walk-in showers; the quietest overlook the garden at the back. A 17th-century gentleman's residence-turned-hotel with plenty of character.

Price	€60-€70.
Rooms	5: 4 doubles, 1 twin.
Meals	Breakfast included. Dinner with aperitif, wine & coffee, €24; book ahead.
Closed	Rarely.
Directions	From A62 exit Castel Sarrasin. From A20 exit Montauban. D928 towards Auch. L'Arbre d'Or opposite Beaumont post office.

Ann & David Leek
16 rue Despeyrous,
82500 Beaumont de Lomagne,
Tarn-et-Garonne

Tel	+33 (0)5 63 65 32 34
Email	info@larbredor-hotel.com
Web	www.larbredor-hotel.com

Castelnau des Fieumarcon

Getting there is almost an initiation. Pass through a large Renaissance portal and spot a music stand and a welcome sign; then ring the gong. If all you hear is birdcall, you are in the right place. Built in the 13th century by local feudal lords – who for a time during the Hundred Year War pledged allegiance to the English crown – this stronghold was left to crumble until 25 years ago when the owners moved in. They restored the ramparts, renovated the houses, creating gardens for each one and left much of the creeper-clad old stone untouched. The houses are not 'interior decorated', but simple, clever touches lend sophistication: framed dried herbs on the painted walls; fairy-light baldaquins; terracotta tiles; a massive Louis XV armoire; antique Gascony treasures. Many have their own kitchens. Castelnau is on high ground so the views from every window – and the pool – are astounding, giving off a timeless hazy glow from the low-lying hills and surrounding fields. Stendhal called it the French Tuscany. He would be at home here: no cars, no TVs, no telephones. A rare pearl.

Price	€90–€250.
Rooms	13 small houses for 2-9.
Meals	Breakfast €15. Picnic available. Hosted dinner €38–€70, book ahead Restaurant 4km.
Closed	Rarely.
Directions	A61 exit for Auch on N2. From Astaffort right onto D266 after police station, continue on D266 until Castelnau. After 1km left to Lagarde Fieumarcon, on for 4.5km; on right just after church; ring gong.

Frédéric Coustols
32700 Lagarde Fieumarcon, Gers

Tel	+33 (0)5 62 68 99 30
Email	office@lagarde.org
Web	www.lagarde.org

Hôtel Les Fleurs de Lees

Barbotan has the only baths in France where you can be treated for arthritis, rheumatism and varicose veins – all at the same time. But if you need a holiday, not an overhaul, come to this beautifully-run hotel. Michael is half English, half Chinese and he and Jean have spent their married life working in five-star places in Dubai, Iran, London, Paris, picking up up a few tips along the way. Now they have their own clutch of rooms, a lovely pool lined with loungers and a restaurant in which Michael can put into practice his international cooking. Interesting bits and pieces brought back from travels dot the décor; bedrooms are rag-rolled and named after flowers. Double rooms are on the first floor, all but one with a large covered terrace, table and chairs; the suites are on the lower ground floor and open to a terrace that leads to the pool. These are themed – African, Oriental, Indian… the honeymoon suite, with drapes over the bed, is a semi-circular symphony in white. If you still need a spin at the spa, now offering anti-stress treatments, Jean will point you in the right direction.

Price	€65–€85. Suites €115.
	Full-board option November-March.
Rooms	16: 11 doubles, 5 suites.
Meals	Breakfast included.
	Lunch & dinner €19–€31.
Closed	November-March.
	Call for out of season reservations.
Directions	From A62 towards Toulouse, exit 3 Langon for Mont de Marsan; D932 Capitieux; left for Gabarret via D124E, D379, D303 through Maillas & Losse on D24.

Michael & Jean Lee
24 avenue Henri IV, 32150
Barbotan les Thermes, Gers

Tel	+33 (0)5 62 08 36 36
Fax	+33 (0)5 62 08 36 37
Email	contact@fleursdelees.com
Web	www.fleursdelees.com

Château de Projan

Fascinating is the story of how an eccentric world-traveller and painter restored this 18th-century château to house his art collection. Eclectic and successful is the mix of the original pieces – mirrors, commodes and armoires – with paintings, tapestries and sculpture from the pre-Raphaelite, Cubist and Art Deco periods. Bedrooms are all on the first floor with wide oak boards and tomette tiles at the intersections of the passageways. One fabulously large room has a 15 metre high ceiling with the original moldings, others have their preserved timber frames, antique writing desks and modern oak. Most astonishing are the 20th-century panelled bathrooms, built for a king's ransom we imagine, designed to harmonise with the rooms: sparkling white porcelain, modern taps, massive mirrors, huge showers. There are two terraces with views across to the Pyrénées for dining, a hall-cum-piano room and fireplaces for chilly evenings. The kitchen opens to the ground-floor hall so you can watch Richard prepare his duck or pigeon specialities for dinner. Perfect for the jazz festival in Marciac.

Price	€100–€130. Family €130–€180.
Rooms	8: 6 doubles, 1 suite for 3, 1 family room for 4.
Meals	Breakfast €10. Dinner €31–€50.
Closed	February; the week before All Saints Day; 21–28 December (open 31 December).
Directions	A64 exit Pau; N134 to Sarron; D646 to Riscle, St Mont & Projan. Signed.

Christine & Richard Poullain
32400 Projan, Gers

Tel	+33 (0)5 62 09 46 21
Fax	+33 (0)5 62 09 44 08
Email	chateaudeprojan@libertysurf.fr
Web	www.chateau-de-projan.com

Château Le Haget

There is a love story behind those Alsatian-style turrets in the middle of the Gers. The young master of the château (built in 1850 on the foundations of a 15th-century château, a stopover for pilgrims en route for Santiago de Compostella) fell for a maiden from eastern France and took great measures to make her feel at home. But it is the southern side, the original formal front facing the park and the Pyrénées, that is the most imposing and beautiful. Stretching out before it is a park of 12 hectares, complete with orangerie and two giant sequoias. The uncluttered, modern finish in the bedrooms is in sharp contrast to the dark wood of the Alsatian baroque; rooms under the roof have a bit more character. Marc, French, organises airport transfers, takes care of green fees for golfers, books meetings with winegrowers *and* lends a hand in the kitchen. Give him a head's up and he can set up a wine tasting for you at the château. His maiden, Annemieke, a warm, delightful Dutch lady and a mother of three, is a most gracious hostess and keeps the place humming. *19 small chalets available in summer.*

Price	€75–€110.
Rooms	10 + 19: 3 doubles, 7 twins. 19 chalets in the park (summer rental only).
Meals	Breakfast included. Dinner €20–€35. Restaurant closed Mon-Thurs.
Closed	February; 1st two weeks of November.
Directions	NE of Tarbes, N21 dir. Miélan; 12km after Miélan, D261 for Haget; 1.5km from Montesquiou, signed.

Marc & Annemieke Passera
Route de Miélan,
32320 Montesquiou, Gers

Tel	+33 (0)5 62 70 95 80
Email	info@lehaget.com
Web	www.lehaget.com

Just 2 Suites

Come for the largest, loveliest bathrooms in the book. Turn-of-the-century double basins and tubs, a grey-painted armoire, a rattan recliner, vintage taps (but lashings of hot water), cherubs and candles. The spreading suites in the solid old farmhouse are a gorgeous example of Dutch sobriety: Janneke's style is "minimalist abundance". Your hosts live in the converted stables; in the house are the suites, one up, one down – plus a library of 1,000 books and DVDs. Imagine white walls and a huge bed, four elegant spears, a framed nude propped on an antique *chiffonnier*; then a room with a sofa, a country table, logs in a vast hearth. Skies are big here and views long, to fields and blue mountains. You eat in the open-sided barn at a long table – the neighbours call it the party room – and the pool is flanked by loungers from an East German spa... There are many surprises, all of them good. It's peaceful, and beautiful. Spain and Toulouse are an hour, skiing closer, local restaurants offer four course lunches for €10, dinner is a half-hour drive. But please dine in at least once! *No credit cards.*

Price	€175–€260.
Rooms	2 duplex suites for 2-4.
Meals	Breakfast included. Lunch €25. Dinner, 6 courses, €42.50. Book ahead.
Closed	Rarely.
Directions	A64 exit for Lannemezan, D393 to Galan. Call owners who will meet you at the Mairie (town hall).

Janneke & Peter Schoenmaker
13 chemin de Campuzan,
65220 Puydarricux, Hautes Pyrénées

Tel	+33 (0)5 62 33 68 03
Email	info@just2suites.com
Web	www.just2suites.com

Le Relais de Saux

A dream of a place. Three to five hundred years old, high on a hill facing Lourdes and some dazzling Pyrenean peaks, the house still has a few unregenerate arrow slits from sterner days. You come in through the leafy multi-coloured garden that spreads across lawns and terraces with corners for reading or painting, a splendid first impression, and enter a house where you feel instantly at home. Bernard Hères inherited Saux from his parents and, with the help of his wife's flair and energy has opened it to guests. They are an enthusiastic and interesting couple who can guide you to fabulous walks, climbs or visits before welcoming you back to deep armchairs in the dark old-timbered salon with its peaceful garden view, or a refined meal in the elegant dining room. Bedrooms are in the same traditional, elegant mood with draped bedheads and darkish carpeted or flock-papered walls. One has no fewer than four tall windows, another has a gorgeous old fireplace, the two second-floor rooms are big yet cosy with their lower ceilings. And carpeted, well-fitted bathrooms for all.

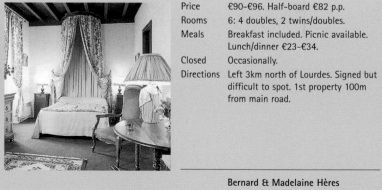

Price	€90–€96. Half-board €82 p.p.
Rooms	6: 4 doubles, 2 twins/doubles.
Meals	Breakfast included. Picnic available. Lunch/dinner €23–€34.
Closed	Occasionally.
Directions	Left 3km north of Lourdes. Signed but difficult to spot. 1st property 100m from main road.

Bernard & Madelaine Hères
Route de Tarbes, Le Hameau de Saux,
65100 Lourdes, Hautes-Pyrénées
Tel   +33 (0)5 62 94 29 61
Fax   +33 (0)5 62 42 12 64
Email   contacts@lourdes-relais.com
Web   www.lourdes-relais.com

Languedoc – Roussillon

Guest house

Relais des Monts

Monsieur had an unusual start, for a hotelier; a hunting guide in central Africa, he established a reserve for monkeys, lions and giraffes. All a far cry from this old stone hamlet, settled among the woods and fields like a sleepy head on a feather pillow. It is blissfully private. All three bedrooms are impeccable, only one betraying the owner's exotic past: 'Victoria' is decorated in colonial style, has a wall light fashioned from a spearhead and rich yellow walls and sisal floors to evoke hot sand. In contrast, 'Estelle' is pretty with red and white gingham curtains, white furniture and a lovely bow window that fills the room with light. The toile de Jouy suite has frou-frou lamps and curtains and big views. Two rooms have private terraces, one its own entrance, bathrooms are marble. Downstairs, the vaulted breakfast room is embracing and light; your continental breakfast is served on pretty porcelain and the big glass door gives tempting glimpses of the countryside. The Lozère air is pure, the nights silent, there's a good restaurant a mile away and hiking from the door.

Price	€180–€210.
Rooms	3: 1 double, 1 twin, 1 suite.
Meals	Breakfast €15. Restaurants 3km.
Closed	November–March.
Directions	A75 exit 40 La Canourgue, Gorges du Tarn, La Malène. 3km before La Malène, left for Les Monts.

M & Mme Laboureur
Les Monts, Route de la Canourgue,
48210 La Malène, Lozère
Tel   +33 (0)4 66 48 54 34
Fax   +33 (0)4 66 48 59 25
Email   relaisdesmonts@aol.com
Web   www.relaisdesmonts.fr

La Lozerette

In September 1878, Robert Louis Stevenson set off from Le Monastier with his donkey, Modestine, to walk the 220km to St Jean du Gard. Towards the end of his journey he stopped off at the Cevennes village of Cocurès, on the river Tarn, just above the National Park. Here Pierrette runs the country inn started by her grandmother and passed on to her by her parents; her father still advises on the best walks. Staff are especially warm and friendly and cope smilingly with all comers to this busy hotel. Pierrette is very much hands-on, running the reception, taking orders in the restaurant and managing the wine cellar: she is a trained sommelier and will pick you out just the right bottle. Bedrooms are fairly large, with wooden floors and headboards and are done in stripes, checks or flowers: colour co-ordinated but not twee. All have balconies with flower boxes. The whole hotel is spotless without looking clinical. Play boules in the garden, walk in the National Park or follow Stevenson's trail, either on foot, donkey or horseback. The chestnut in all its forms is a speciality here. One of our favourites.

Price	€53–€90. Half-board €54–€68 p.p.
Rooms	21 twins/doubles.
Meals	Breakfast €7.80. Lunch & dinner €18.50–€49. Children's menu €11. Restaurant closed Tuesday & Wednesday lunchtimes out of season.
Closed	November–Easter.
Directions	From Florac, N106 for Mende. Right on D998 for Le Pont de Montvert. After 4km hotel on left, signed.

Pierrette Agulhon
Cocurès,
48400 Florac, Lozère

Tel	+33 (0)4 66 45 06 04
Fax	+33 (0)4 66 45 12 93
Email	lalozerette@wanadoo.fr
Web	www.lalozerette.com

Mas de l'Hospitalet

Perhaps a stopping place for pilgrims, the 900-year-old mellow stone mas is a former commanderie of the Knights Templar. In the foothills of the Cevennes National Park, by a main road but in its own spacious grounds, it comes with a saltwater pool, a long sheltered sun terrace, and two courtyards, one for summer breakfasts in the shade, the other vast and perfect for weddings. Bedrooms and apartments border the main courtyard, the cottage is near the pool and every space exudes a luxurious rusticity. It took four years to bring the mas back to life and to put the final touches to the décor: fine old bedheads and wardrobes, crisp white sofas and linen, garnet-red drapes. A new enterprise so floors are gleaming oak and bath and shower rooms unpolished marble – but large exposed beams show their elegant bones. A Bali canopied bed lives in one of the apartments; white china gleams as perfect foil for the night-blue tiles in the kitchens. In the cottage are old tiles and a pretty terrace. A family of quince-coloured Anduze vases dots the courtyard; the new vaulted restaurant is stunning.

Price	€85–€105. Apartments & cottage €100–€130.
Rooms	7 + 3: 6 doubles, 1 twin. Cottage for 2, 2 apartments for 2.
Meals	Breakfast €7. Lunch €15–€25. Dinner €20–€35.
Closed	Rarely.
Directions	From Alès on N110 south. At St Christol La Pyramide continue towards Bagard; on left before village, long stone building & tower.

Harvey Baker & Eva Strom
30140 Bagard,
Gard

Tel	+33 (0)4 66 60 61 23
Email	evastrom@wanadoo.fr
Web	www.masdehospitalet.com

Villa Saint Victor

This frightfully grand looking, 1880s building, all towered and pillared and stone-staircase'd, is actually very friendly and twinkly on the inside. Run as a proper family business, Geoffrey taking great care of you and Stephane and his wife in the kitchen, the feel is smaller and cosier than you might imagine. A salon with lovely antiques and paintings has space for mingling extroverts as well as corners for cosier chats; the dining area has an arched ceiling, an open fire and big wicker chairs to linger in. Bedrooms on the first floor are grander, with upholstered chairs, views over the park and generous bathrooms, some tower-shaped with bidets like thrones; the rooms above are simpler and more contemporary, with rope carpeting, lighter colours and excellent bedding. Fresh, generous food is beautifully prepared and presented; afterwards you can wander through doors to the garden with its old palm trees and parasols, sloping lawns and silent lily pond. Children will adore the space to run around and you're near to Uzès with its stunning market — and Roman Orange.

Price	€90–€140. Suites €180–€230. Apartments €200–€230.
Rooms	19: 7 doubles, 5 twins, 5 suites, 2 apartments.
Meals	Breakfast €15. Lunch €18. Dinner €39. Restaurant closed Sun eve & Mon.
Closed	January–February.
Directions	From Uzès D982 to Bagnol sur Ceze for 6km; right on D125 to Saint Victor des Oules. Signed.

Geoffrey & Stéphane Vieljeux
Place du Château,
30700 Saint Victor des Oules, Gard

Tel	+33 (0)4 66 81 90 47
Fax	+33 (0)4 66 81 93 30
Email	info@villasaintvictor.com
Web	www.villasaintvictor.com

Entry 278 Map 16

Hôtel Le Saint Laurent

A sparkle of château-living sweeps through this quiet hotel, tucked down one of the town's medieval streets. Not surprising; Thierry and Christophe worked in grand establishments before injecting the 14th-century farmhouse-turned-hotel with a sense of élan. From the sun-trapped courtyard, steps lead to a covered veranda, invitingly spread with deep sofas. Inside, stone-flagged spaces show off their statues, gilded mirrors and heavy candlesticks. Bedrooms are intimate – some a slight squeeze – and lavish with antiques, cushions and pretty *objets*. Some have padded bedheads, others romantic canopies, one has a terrace, another is startling in black and white. All very boudoir, and delicious chocolates to welcome you. Large, white bathrooms want for nothing. You will be spoilt by the owners and bubbly staff; breakfast late (great pancakes!) in the vaulted dining room or the Moroccan-tabled courtyard. A beauty salon is planned. Avignon, Uzès and vineyards are close; enjoy the town's music concerts. No evening meals but plenty of local restaurants. *Private locked parking nearby.*

Price	€95–€138. Singles €75–€95. Suites €135–€195.
Rooms	10: 5 doubles, 2 singles, 3 suites (1 with terrace).
Meals	Breakfast €15. Restaurant 20m from hotel.
Closed	Never.
Directions	A9 exit 22 Roquemanne. Left on N58 to Bagnols sur Cèze; 4km left for St Laurent des Arbres. Hotel in old town centre, signed.

Thierry Lelong & Christophe Bricaud
1 place de l'Arbre,
30126 Saint Laurent des Arbres, Gard

Tel	+33 (0)4 66 50 14 14
Fax	+33 (0)4 66 50 46 30
Email	info@lesaintlaurent.biz
Web	www.lesaintlaurent.biz

Château Beaupré Deleuze

The massive wooden door (so satisfying to knock on!) opens into a secret cobbled courtyard. It's cool here, and delightful among the arches and massive urns. Carla (erudite, blonde, full of laughter) and Pia (an archaeologist) love China, and the rooms of their 18th-century château are dotted with stunning antiques picked up on travels: oriental rugs, lacquered wardrobes, pottery jars, calligraphy. Karl, the chef, cooks Provençal dishes and brilliantly presides over the dining room, beautifully stone-flagged and vaulted, with a long table, leather-seated chairs and a big fire. The bedrooms, all simplicity and light, have fine parquet or glowing tiles, white walls and deliciously crisp bed linen; one has a grey-painted mezzanine for two extra beds, another a fantastic anthracite bath. The sweetest place for breakfast is up on the ballustraded terrace: intimate, peaceful, overlooking the garden's rustling trees and the rooftops of St Laurent. The house is close enough to town for a stroll, a summer concert or a trip to the Saturday flea market. Well-nigh perfect. *Minimum stays in certain seasons.*

Price	€90–€140. Family room €90–€160. Apartments €150–€260 (€1,100–€1,800 per week).
Rooms	4 + 2 . 1 double, 1 twin/double, 1 family for 2–4. 2 apartments for 2–4.
Meals	Breakfast included. Dinner €25, on request.
Closed	Rarely.
Directions	A9 exit 22 Roquemaure for Bagnols sur Cèze. After 4km continue past turn for St Laurent les Arbres. Left at Rubis, follow road. On right, signed.

Pia Pierre & Carla Copini
Chemin de la Bégude,
30126 Saint Laurent des Arbres, Gard

Tel   +33 (0)4 66 50 31 21
Fax   +33 (0)4 66 50 28 78
Email   chateau.beaupre@free.fr
Web   www.chateau-beaupre.com

Domaine du Moulin

The little luxuries of a good hotel and the personality of a B&B in Antoinette's renovated 12th-century mill. She and Otto, both Dutch and multi-lingual, have been respectful of age and style: old parquet floors and doors have been revived, a wooden stair polished to glow. Big modern flower paintings and a Belgian tapestry look good on white walls. The river Nizon flows beneath the house and criss-crosses the grounds, several hectares of them – a mill pond flanked by cherry trees (spectacular in spring), an alley of poplars, a lavender field, a pool. And there are swings and slides for the grandchildren, which yours may share. Breakfast is a Dutch feast of hams, cheeses and cherry jams, served at the big table under the tented pergola, or in the all-white dining room with chandelier. Antoinette is lovely and fills the place with flowers. Bedrooms, named after her daughters, have piles of pillows and fine English florals; bathrooms are swish with big showers or two basins; some are air conditioned, one has a sun terrace of its own. There's a cosy library full of books, and you and the chef choose the menu for dinner.

Price	€80–€185. Apartment €1,200–€2,200 per week.
Rooms	4 + 1: 4 twins/doubles. Apartment for 7.
Meals	Breakfast €15. Dinner by arrangement. Restaurants nearby.
Closed	Rarely.
Directions	A9 exit 22 Roquemaure for Bagnols sur Cèze. After 4km continue past left turn for St Laurent les Arbres. Left at Rubis, follow road.

Antoinette Keulen & Otto Van Eikema Hommes
Chemin de la Bégude,
30126 Saint Laurent des Arbres, Gard

Tel	+33 (0)4 66 50 22 67
Fax	+33 (0)4 66 50 22 67
Email	laurentdesarbres@aol.com
Web	www.domaine-du-moulin.com

Guesthouse Felisa

Abandon yourself to your senses in this delightfully restored house, run with Swiss friendliness and calm efficiency. Find clever, minimalist bedrooms in whites and creams, arty photographs on the walls, flashes of colour from fresh flowers and cushions, painted concrete floors and cool stone tiles. Bathrooms are redolent of candles and incense, towels are thick and fluffy – all you might expect of a grown-up pampering place with ayurvedic treatments for face and body, and yoga classes free every day. Food is a fusion of Provençal and far-flung influences, and all is fresh and artfully presented on white china; if you long to cook like this, there are cookery classes twice weekly. The garden is leafy and calm, with shade for sun dodgers and a gorgeous pool for stately low-key swims – it's utterly peaceful and quiet. Out and about there's tons to do – tennis, riding, canoeing, golf. Uzés has a wonderful medieval garden and a thriving market on Saturdays, Roman Nîmes has truffle markets, brocante and a museum of contemporary art. *Yoga, jacuzzi & oils on the house. Min. stay two nights.*

Price	€120–€150.
Rooms	10: 5 doubles, 4 twins/doubles, 1 family room for 3.
Meals	Breakfast included. Dinner €28 (min. 6), Fri & Sat only. Restaurants in village.
Closed	3 January–30 March.
Directions	Exit 22 Roquemaure. N580 to Bagnols sur Cèze for 5km. Left, enter village, left before solid stone house on right, sign for Domaine du Moulin. House on 1st right corner.

Isa & Philippe Lichtenthurn
6 rue des Barris,
30126 Saint Laurent des Arbres, Gard

Tel	+33 (0)4 66 39 99 84
Fax	+33 (0)4 66 39 99 84
Email	information@maison-felisa.com
Web	www.maison-felisa.com

La Maison

No noise, just the hoot of an owl and a flutter of doves around the roof tops. An 18th-century mellow-yellow stone house sits in the heart of the village. Church, tower and château stand guard over it, and beyond, vines, fields and woodlands. The views are magical. Old vaulted ceilings, shuttered windows and terracotta floors are a stunning foil for contemporary décor; this is a grand old house infused with an informal spirit. Bedrooms are mostly large: the red room has a small private terrace that looks onto the château walls, the suite has a roof terrace with 360° views. Expect warm sandy walls, Indonesian wall hangings, ethnic fabrics, a fireplace or two. Breakfast is taken leisurely in the walled garden where an ancient tree casts generous shade, or at a long table in the library with other guests. There's a piano in the salon and a swimming pool in the garden. It's no distance at all to restaurants downhill and you can strike out further and visit Nîmes, Avignon, Arles or medieval Uzes. A most welcoming place.

Price	€110–€190. Singles from €90.
Rooms	5: 4 doubles, 1 suite for 4.
Meals	Breakfast included.
	Two bistros in village, more in Uzès.
Closed	15 November–15 March.
Directions	From Nîmes, D979 for Blauzac 16km; after Pont St Nicolas, left for Blauzac; enter village, house behind church.

Christian Vaurie
Place de l'Église,
30700 Blauzac, Gard

Tel	+33 (0)4 66 81 25 15
Fax	+33 (0)4 66 81 25 15
Email	lamaisondeblauzac@wanadoo.fr
Web	www.chambres-provence.com

L'Enclos des Lauriers Roses

The tiny reception gives no clue as to what lies beyond; a secret village within a village. Step across a sunny dining room, through French windows – and blink. Scattered around three swimming pools is a cluster of cottage rooms. Built in stone (from rescued village houses) with pantiled roofs, most have a private terrace or garden. Large, airy, with tiled floors, low beamed ceilings and pretty painted Provençal furniture, each has a different character – perhaps bright saffron or cool Mediterranean colours, a bed tucked under a stone arch or family-friendly extra beds on a mezzanine level. Bathrooms are large, modern and marbled while a fridge keeps picnic food – and wine – chilled. This is a family affair: Madame Bargeton runs the restaurant, Monsieur does the wine – 500 bottles in the cellar – and the sons take care of the buildings and garden. Eat on the terrace or in the dining room, popular with locals and visitors for its good Provençal cooking. Nîmes, Avignon and beaches are less than an hour, swim in the Gorges du Gardon or walk amongst the pines and vineyards nearby.

Price	€80–€110. Triple €105–€115. Family room €130–€160. Half-board €122–€190 per room.
Rooms	18. 10 twins/doubles, 2 triples, 5 family rooms for 4, 1 family room for 6.
Meals	Breakfast €12. Lunch & dinner €23–€42.
Closed	10 November–10 March.
Directions	A9 exit 24 for N86 to Remoulins. After 3.5km left to St Gervasy for Cabrières. In village centre, signed.

Bargeton Family
71 rue du 14 Juillet,
30210 Cabrières, Gard
Tel   +33 (0)4 66 75 25 42
Fax   +33 (0)4 66 75 25 21
Email hotel-lauriersroses@wanadoo.fr
Web   www.hotel-lauriersroses.com

Jardins Secrets

The 18th-century *relais de poste* hides in a walled garden brimming with mimosa, bougainvillea and roses – yet nothing prepares you for the sensuous, flowing interiors. Annabelle's exquisite taste has weaved its magic from chic-upholstered Louis XVI fauteuil to baldaquin bath lit with candle sconces: an atmosphere of relaxed indulgence reigns. She is the smiling, elegant hostess, he is the inspired cook, bringing you *grillades* and salads to the summer pool. For breakfast you feast on homemade pains aux raisins outside, or at a big farmhouse table beneath a bejewelled chandelier. Tranquillity prevails yet this is in the town centre, so make the most of the bikes and discover the Roman treasures of Nîmes. Later return to one of three salons, comfortable with travel books, whisky or brandy as Debussy wafts into that dreamy garden. Then up the fine stone stair with iron balustrade to extravagant bedrooms with huge beds and billowing pillows, hot-water bottles tucked between crisp sheets and your own winter fire. Seductive and special.

Price	€180–€350.
Rooms	14: 9 doubles, 5 suites.
Meals	Breakfast €20. Poolside lunches. Dinner €50–€80.
Closed	Never.
Directions	5 minutes from railway station. Take Avenue Carnot, then 1st small street on right.

Madame Annabelle Valentin
3 rue Gaston Maruejols,
30000 Nîmes, Gard

Tel	+33 (0)4 66 84 82 64
Fax	+33 (0)4 66 84 27 47
Email	contact@jardinssecrets.net
Web	www.jardinssecrets.net

Domaine des Clos

When Sandrine and David returned to their Beaucaire roots, they found a worthy vessel for their creativity in an 18th-century wine domaine. All has been authentically and lovingly restored. Every room has a view to the vineyards or the central courtyard lawn, the pool is large and the family — with three children — truly charming. The beautifully designed interiors reveal lots of old beams, vibrant splashes of colour in curtains, bedspreads and tapestries and artefacts galore, many collected during the Aussets' Tunisian travels. Outside are exquisite Italianate gardens and the best of Provence… from among the olive trees, jasmine and bougainvillea, shady stone pergolas and relaxing sitting spots emerge. Consider an aperitif or, in summer, a meal on the terrace of the old écurie; in winter, keep warm by the fireplace in the communal salon, delightful with its deep fuchsia walls and ceilings hung with handcrafted fixtures. It is hugely original, wonderfully artistic, and the information booklet includes enough markets to keep the picnic bags brimming. Be as active or as idle as you like.

Price	€75–€165. Apartments €450–€1,500 per week.
Rooms	8 + 5: 5 doubles, 3 family rooms for 4. 5 apartments for 2-7.
Meals	Breakfast included. Cold plate €20. Dinner €30 with wine, twice weekly in summer; book ahead. Restaurant 6km.
Closed	Rarely.
Directions	Exit A7 at Remoulins to Beaucaire. At entry to Beaucaire 2nd exit on large r'bout then D38 to St Gilles for 6km. Domaine on left.

Sandrine & David Ausset
Route de Bellegarde,
30300 Beaucaire, Gard
Tel   +33 (0)4 66 01 14 61
Fax   +33 (0)4 66 01 00 47
Email   contact@domaine-des-clos.com
Web   www.domaine-des-clos.com

Calvisson

There's a secret to this old townhouse in the little market town: from the narrow street it looks nothing special, but enter the private courtyard and it's another world. First the courtyard, a wonderful source of light and greenery, then a biggish living area for guests and finally a vaulted dining room for candlelit dinners in a womb-like atmosphere of warm colours and stone walls. A grand piano, tuned, awaits its muse in the salon-cum-library. Summer breakfast is, of course, in the sunny courtyard. Up a spiral staircase lined with lovely tapestries, the tempting rooms fan off at different levels – there's a lovely smell of wax-polished stone floors; most are beautifully restored with old doors, original chandeliers and good windows that seem to frame pictures. You can tell that an artist – Régis will give private lessons – and an art historian are in residence here as everything has been carefully chosen, with simple, solid antique furniture that's genuinely part of the house. Your charming hostess is eager to help her guests and in summer the house is blessedly cool after the scorching sun.

Price	€55–€75.
Rooms	12: 2 doubles, 2 suites.
Meals	Breakfast included. Hosted dinner €20, with wine (min. 4; not Saturday). Book ahead.
Closed	January.
Directions	A9 exit Gallargues. N113 for Nîmes. Just after bas Rhône canal, D1 to Calvisson. In village, along main street, two doors from Town Hall.

Régis & Corinne Burckel de Tell
48 Grand'rue,
30420 Calvisson, Gard

Tel	+33 (0)4 66 01 23 91
Email	burckeldetell@hotmail.fr
Web	www.bed-and-art.com

L'Auberge du Cèdre

No wonder guests return to this big bustling house. The lively, charming Françoise and her multi-lingual husband Lutz welcome walkers, climbers, cyclists and families. Workshop groups are welcome too; there's a special space for them, separate from the big and comfy sitting room. This is a mellow-stoned auberge, adorned with green shutters, iron balustrades and orangerie windows at the rear. Bedrooms are plain, beamy, white, with the odd splash of ethnic colour and terracotta floors that gleam. Except for the new suite, bathrooms are shared; this is not the place for those looking for luxury. Sharing keeps the prices down and there have been no complaints. On the contrary, the atmosphere is one of good humour and laughter. Meals are chosen from a blackboard menu. A great place for a family to stay: a swimming pool, space to run around in, pétanque under the chestnut trees before you turn in for the night. The auberge sits in the middle of the Pic Saint Loup, one of the best vineyards in the Languedoc; Lutz's excellent wine cellar is another reason to prolong your stay.

Price	€23–€62. Half-board €34–€73 p.p.
Rooms	20: 7 twins/doubles, 9 triples, 3 quadruples, all sharing 8 bathrooms & 7 wcs; 1 suite with separate bath & wc.
Meals	Breakfast included. Light lunch €9. Á la carte €28–€37 at weekends.
Closed	Mid-November–mid-March.
Directions	D17 from Montpellier for Quissac. 6km north of St Mathieu de Tréviers, left to Lauret, 1km. Through village follow signs.

Françoise Antonin & Lutz Engelmann
Domaine de Cazeneuve,
34270 Lauret, Hérault

Tel	+33 (0)4 67 59 02 02
Fax	+33 (0)4 67 59 03 44
Email	welcome@auberge-du-cedre.com
Web	www.auberge-du-cedre.com

Domaine du Canalet

An elegant mansion, an enchanted wood and an art gallery for a bedroom. Set in dreamy parkland, this fin-de-siècle house gives nothing away – until you step inside. It is a showcase of contemporary art: sculptures, collages, light installations and paintings are set against the classical proportions of the high-ceilinged, light-filled rooms. Muriel ran a gallery in Paris and champions new artists. Three salons, scattered with artworks, sofas and glossy books, lead into one another. Then up the sweeping staircase to bedrooms that have an assured designer touch. Colours are neutral, paintings bold, furnishings minimalist but luxurious. Bathrooms are sculptural spaces of glass, chrome and wood. Yves looks after the grounds, a magical discovery of canals, secret paths, ancient trees, stone steps and shady ponds... plenty of spots to nourish the soul. And a hidden pool and terrace by the orangerie, perfect for breakfasts and candlelit suppers. Play tennis, cycle (bikes to borrow) or hike in the Cévennes, visit Lodève and the Larzac. Or enjoy a cultural evening with visiting artists and winegrowers.

Price	€185–€300. Suite €265–€350.
Rooms	4: 2 doubles, 1 twin, 1 suite for 2-3.
Meals	Breakfast included. Brunch €15. Dinner from €45, book ahead.
Closed	Never.
Directions	At Lodève, signs to Bedarieux. At r'bout (Pizza di Maïori) take Ave Joseph Vallot. On left, after small red house next to football field.

Muriel Lagneau & Yves Berliet
Avenue Joseph Vallot,
34700 Lodève, Hérault

Tel	+33 (0)4 67 44 29 33
Fax	+33 (0)4 67 44 29 33
Email	muriel@domaineducanalet.com
Web	www.domaineducanalet.com

Château de Jonquières

Isabelle met François harvesting the family grapes; now the estate is theirs, and is nurtured with passion. The château, remodelled in the 17th century, sits peacefully in the village: all you hear are church bells and the baker's horn. Isabelle has restored the guest wing with enthusiasm but without decorative excess. Up two staircases are four colour-themed bedrooms where sober beds are dressed in best family linen and new towels match bathroom tiles. A rich red carpet in the tower room, restored wallpapers in the Rose, Yellow and Blue rooms, and framed engravings raided from the attic. There's masses to do in the area, with vineyards and fine restaurants to visit and Lac Salagou close by, but why not stay put? There's an ornamental pond in the courtyard, a marble fireplace in the salon, billiards in the summer salon and cards in the playroom tower or you may lounge on the lawns in the shade of the giant bamboo groves. Or take a glass of estate wine to the delightful covered balcony above the Renaissance stairway and gaze over ancient rooftops. *No credit cards.*

Price	€85–€90.
Rooms	4: 3 doubles, 1 twin.
Meals	Breakfast included. Restaurants 2–6km.
Closed	Mid-November–mid-March.
Directions	From Montpellier to Millau & Lodève on N109. At St André de Sangonis (34km), D130 to Jonquières.

François & Isabelle de Cabissole
34725 Jonquières,
Hérault

Tel	+33 (0)4 67 96 62 58
Fax	+33 (0)4 67 88 61 92
Email	contact@chateau-jonquieres.com
Web	www.chateau-jonquieres.com

La Calade

Octon is an unspoilt little village, typical of the flavour and architecture so informed by the Languedoc sun. Right under the old church, the owners have created a colourful atmosphere within the white stone walls of the former presbytery. Don't expect great luxury – the setting is simple, the rooms and bathrooms adequate – but there is a freshness about the place when it's hot, the beds are comfortable and the pine floors are spotless. The terrace, shaded by acacia trees and an awning, is very appealing both at breakfast time and in the evenings – it also serves as the sitting area. The overall feel is bright and clean and the new owners couldn't be more friendly and helpful. They particularly enjoy welcoming families with children. The restaurant is becoming very popular with the locals – always a good sign – so book ahead. There are plenty of places to visit, good paths for hikers, excellent local wines and the fabulous Lake Salagou for swimming and sailing. In short, a great base for daily excursions, where the warm welcome and the authentic atmosphere easily make up for somewhat basic comforts.

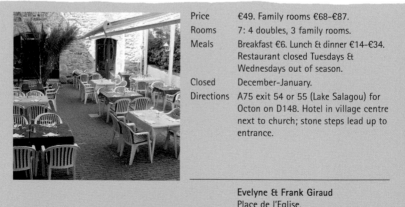

Price	€49. Family rooms €68-€87.
Rooms	7: 4 doubles, 3 family rooms.
Meals	Breakfast €6. Lunch & dinner €14-€34. Restaurant closed Tuesdays & Wednesdays out of season.
Closed	December-January.
Directions	A75 exit 54 or 55 (Lake Salagou) for Octon on D148. Hotel in village centre next to church; stone steps lead up to entrance.

Evelyne & Frank Giraud
Place de l'Eglise,
34800 Octon, Hérault
Tel   +33 (0)4 67 96 19 21
Fax   +33 (0)4 67 88 61 25
Email   lacalade-octon@wanadoo.fr
Web   www.hotel-lacalade.com

Entry 291 Map 15

Hôtel de Baudon de Mauny

Here is a very fine *hôtel privé*, its flowery façade in Louis XVI style, its position the cobbled heart of Montpellier. A vast and noble double front door opens onto a courtyard and you enter 18th-century France. Breakfast is served in the elegant hall alongside; a wide stone stair transports you to bedrooms above. On the first floor you will admire the majestic ceilings, the stone floors, the marble fireplaces, the plaster friezes and the vast windows, some with their original panes. Second-floor bedrooms have private salons and brand new shower rooms. It is sophisticated, extraordinary, and the young family whose passion this house is live above; you will be looked after beautifully. Outside the door is grand old Montpellier with its exciting young energy – its sleek designer trams, its car-free Old Town, its farmers' market under the arches, its dance festival in July, its botanic gardens – the oldest in Europe? – and its rich collection of art housed in the just-restored Musée Fabre. Strolling distance is the Jardin des Sens for extravagant dining, and the marvellous old Brasserie next to the Opera.

Price	€150 €260.
Rooms	5 doubles.
Meals	Breakfast €15.
Closed	Rarely.
Directions	Directions & parking details on booking.

Alain de Bordas
1 rue de la Carbonnerie,
34000 Montpellier, Hérault

Tel   +33 (0)6 07 47 11 23
Email mascom@wanadoo.fr
Web   www.baudondemauny.com

Le Clos de Maussanne

This is La Chamberte No.2 – country-style. Set in the vineyards off the main road, midway between Béziers and Pezenas, the 17th century house with the clock tower is smaller inside than it looks. Just one room in depth, the house is nevertheless elegant, and has been furnished as charmingly as its town cousin. The lovely dining room/salon, the heart of the place, looks onto beautiful old plane trees at the front and a walled garden at the back; there's a covered terrace full of tables and a new kitchen downstairs. Staff are delightful. Bedrooms, too, overlook the garden; the largest has white painted beams stretching to the roof, its pale floor sweeping from dressing room to terrace. All have WiFi, fridges and super flat TVs. But the biggest inspiration is the food – no menu, each night a surprise. Visit lovely old Pezenas or take a walk along the canal bank to Béziers; there are seven locks in a row. In the peaceful old quarter (no cars) are a cathedral and a market on Fridays. Return to a pool surrounded by palms – bliss. *Ask about cookery classes.*

Price	€120–€150.
Rooms	5 doubles.
Meals	Breakfast included. Lunch €30. Dinner €40.
Closed	Never.
Directions	A9 exit 35 direction Béziers. At 1st roundabout, 2nd exit direction Pezenas. At 2nd roundabout, 1st exit direction Pezenas. 2km on right.

Bruno Saurel & Irwin Scott-Davidson
Route de Pezenas, 34500 Béziers,
Hérault

Tel	+33 (0)4 67 39 31 81
Email	contact@leclosdemaussanne.com
Web	www.leclosdemaussanne.com

La Chamberte

When Bruno and Irwin set about converting this old wine storehouse, the last thing they wanted was to create a 'home from home' for guests! This is different, and special. Communal spaces are huge, ceilings high, colours Mediterranean, and floors pigmented, polished cement. Bedrooms are simpler than you might expect, but with big beds, often with a step up to them, and dressed in coloured cottons; shower rooms are in ochres and muted pinks, some with pebbles set in the cement floor. The cooking is Bruno's domain: "not my profession but my passion". He may whisk you off to the hills early one morning, stopping on the way home for a loaf of bread and a slab of paté to go with the aperitif. In summer eat on the interior patio, a glorious plant-filled space that reaches up to the original barn roof; in winter retreat to a dining room with an open fire. Guests gather for a glass of carefully chosen wine and nibbles but dine at separate tables stylishly decked with flowers and candles. Outsiders are allowed in at weekends. Bruno feels dinner is an important moment of the day, to be savoured. *Cash only.*

Price	€84–€98. Half-board option, €850 per week.
Rooms	5 doubles.
Meals	Breakfast included. Lunch €25. Dinner with wine, €35.
Closed	Rarely.
Directions	A9 exit 35 (Béziers Est) for Villeneuve les Béziers; over canal to town centre; 2nd left after Hotel Cigale; green gate on right.

Bruno Saurel & Irwin Scott-Davidson
34420 Villeneuve lès Béziers,
Hérault

Tel	+33 (0)4 67 39 84 83
Email	contact@la-chamberte.com
Web	www.la-chamberte.com

Hôtel de Vigniamont

The townhouse of the Comte de Vigniamont has been revived. Big grey shutters, a brass plaque on a sandy wall, blue wooden flower tubs to keep the cars at bay. Enter a cool flagged entrance, ascend a lovely stone-turned stair – the town is known for them – and step into an elegant, uncluttered, terracotta-tiled salon where stuffed sofas beg to be sunk into and floor-to-ceiling windows overlook 400 years of history. Large, refined bedrooms have pastel colours and pretty fauteuils, an antique wardrobe here, a touch of toile de Jouy there, perhaps French windows opening to a central courtyard. The English McVeighs have worked so hard to restore this place; outgoing and generous, they ran a tea shop, and later a pub, in California. Now they serve generous breakfasts on the sun-washed roof terrace, and, as the sun goes down, it's "raid the pantry" time: aperitifs and delectable tapas. Once weekly a mouthwatering meal is produced. A treat to be in the town of Pézenas, embraced by antiques and artisans, buildings, balconies, restaurants and bars – and with such nice people. We love this place.

Price	€100–€150.
Rooms	5: 2 doubles, 3 suites.
Meals	Breakfast included. Hosted dinner with wine, €45 (Mondays only).
Closed	November–March.
Directions	A9 exit 34 D13 to Péçzenas centre. 1st left after lights, right at x-roads, 1st left on Rue Louis Blanc, right on Joseph Cambon, left into Rue Massillon.

Robert & Tracy McVeigh
5 rue Massillon,
34120 Pézenas, Hérault

Tel	+33 (0)4 67 35 14 88
Fax	+33 (0)4 67 55 18 96
Email	info@hoteldevigniamont.com
Web	www.hoteldevigniamont.com

Les Bergeries de Ponderach

Monsieur Lentin remembers this *bergerie* when it was full of sheep; he now fills it with contented guests. The whole place is an expression of his cultivated tastes in music, painting (he has a permanent art gallery on the premises), food and wine. You enter your room through its own little vestibule; make your way to your private balcony and take a deep breath, you've arrived in a truly unspoiled part of the Languedoc. Bedrooms are spacious, bathrooms are attractively tiled. Chopin comes with the aperitif after which Monsieur Lentin offers carefully chosen regional cooking with a good selection of organic wines. Guests return again and again for the slow sports: the roasting of chestnuts over an open fire, the playing of pétanque under the big trees. Sculpting your own perfect holiday is not difficult, given all that's here for you – maybe one third exercise in the Parc Regional with its wonderful walks, one third culture visiting the cathedral and its pink marble choir, one third gastro-hedonism with your feet under the auberge's beautifully laden table.

Price	€85–€105. Half-board €70–€90 p.p.
Rooms	7: 3 doubles, 2 twins, 1 suite for 4.
Meals	Breakfast €12. Picnic available. Dinner €29–€33.
Closed	2 November–15 March.
Directions	From Béziers, N112 to St Pons de Thomières; left for Narbonne on D907. Hotel 1km further, just after swimming pool on left.

Gilles Lentin
Route de Narbonne,
34220 Saint Pons de Thomières, Hérault

Tel	+33 (0)4 67 97 02 57
Fax	+33 (0)4 67 97 29 75
Email	bergeries.ponderach@wanadoo.fr
Web	bergeries-ponderach.com

Château de Saint Michel de Lanès

Your admirable hosts have saved this utterly romantic place, a near-ruin of an ancestral château, by dint of sheer crusading aristocratic grit, intelligent research and hard manual work. The Viscount, a self-taught master builder, even regilded the lofty baroque ceilings. There are 40 rooms and four ghosts; Madame can recount pre-Revolutionary family lore for hours; every piece of furniture tells a tale; the cedars are regal, the river is peaceful, the croissants and jams are served on grandmama's fine silver. You'll love the faded, old-fashioned grandeur of the place and the refreshing nonchalence towards modern conventions… central heating in winter, air conditioning in summer – just throw the windows open instead! Guests have the privilege of the best renovations: two fine salons, huge, bright, comfortable bedrooms. There's badminton and pétanque in the park, an 11th-century church in the village, and fields of sunflowers stretching as far as the eye can see. And two Michelin stars a 20-minute drive. Exceptional. *Advance booking advisable. Arrival 5pm-7pm please.*

Price	€149.
Rooms	4: 3 doubles, 1 twin. Rooms can interconnect.
Meals	Breakfast included. Restaurant 50m.
Closed	Christmas holidays.
Directions	A61 for Carcassone; exit Villefranche de Lauragais for Gardouch; cross Canal du Midi; left D625, 10km. In St Michel left cross bridge; château on left.

Vicomte & Vicomtesse Vincent de La Panouse
1 rue du Pont de l'Hers,
11410 Saint Michel de Lanès, Aude
Tel   +33 (0)4 68 60 31 80
Fax   +33 (0)4 34 92 31 80
Email   chateausaintmichel@tiscali.fr
Web   www.chateausaintmichel.com

Château de la Prade

Lost among the cool shadows of tall sunlit trees, beside the languid waters of the Canal du Midi, is a place of understated elegance and refinement. The 19th-century house is more 'domaine' than 'château', though the vineyards have long gone. It sits in 12 acres… formal hedges, ornamental railings and impressive gates linking château to grounds. Swiss Roland runs the chambres d'hôte side of things, Lorenz looks after the gardens: generous, kind-hearted, discreetly attentive hosts. Served on pink tablecloths in a light, airy room with a crystal chandelier, dinner is a mix of Swiss, French and Italian cuisine, and breakfast a delicious treat (croissants with homemade apple and rose preserve, exquisitely prepared fruit salads). Bedrooms, too, have tall windows, polished floors and an uncluttered charm; be charmed by traditional armchairs and footstools, huge beds and fresh flowers, white bathrooms with towels to match. You are a half mile from the main road to Carcassonne and yet here there's a feeling of rare calm – disturbed only the peacocks calling from the balustrades, most vocal in late spring!

Price	€80–€115.
Rooms	4 twins/doubles.
Meals	Breakfast included.
	Dinner, 4 courses, €19.
	Restaurants 8km.
Closed	November–March.
Directions	Exit Bram 22; follow N113 dir. Villepinte & Carcassonne.

Roland Kurt
11150 Bram,
Aude

Tel   +33 (0)4 68 78 03 99
Fax   +33 (0)4 68 24 96 31
Email   chateaudelaprade@wanadoo.fr
Web   www.chateaulaprade.eu

Château de Cavanac

A quiet place, with birdsong to serenade you. The château has been in the family for six generations and dates back to 1612; Louis, *chef et patron*, has a small vineyard, so you can drink of the vines that surround you. A convivial place, with a big rustic restaurant in the old stables, where hops hang from ancient beams and there's an open fire on which they cook the grills; in summer you dine under the stars. The hotel is quiet and friendly, with comfort and an easy feel; Louis and Anne are justly proud of their food and breakfast is among the best we have had. The older bedrooms, where Chinese rugs cover terracotta tiles, are somewhat dated but the newly renovated ones are positively lavish: four-posters, dramatic canopies, plush fabrics in soft colours, parquet floors, a colonial feel. Outside you stumble upon (not into, we hope) a cool swimming pool. And there's a very pretty, sun-trapping terrace with plenty of sun loungers. Beyond the smart wrought-iron gates, Languedoc waits to beguile you; horse riding, cellars to visit, and medieval Carcassonne so close by.

Price	€85–€120. Singles €65–€95. Suites €150–€155.
Rooms	28: 19 doubles, 2 singles, 3 triples, 4 suites.
Meals	Breakfast €10. Dinner from €40 (except Mon). Restaurants in Carcassonne, 3km.
Closed	9 January–6 March; 1–15 November.
Directions	From Toulouse, exit Carsassonne Ouest for Centre Hospitalier, then Route de St Hilaire. Signed. Park in restaurant car park.

Anne & Louis Gobin
11570 Cavanac, Aude

Tel	+33 (0)4 68 79 61 04
Fax	+33 (0)4 68 79 79 67
Email	infos@chateau-de-cavanac.fr
Web	www.chateau-de-cavanac.fr

Montfaucon

A gracious spot for peace and quiet by the river Aude – strolling couples, quacking ducks – yet a short walk from lovely old Limoux with its bars, restaurants and weekend festivals throughout the year: a lively pull for musicians and artists. Enter the huge beautiful doors to this ancient house, parts of which go back to 1324, to discover a fabulous conversion has taken place. Local artisans and master craftsmen have created a stylish entrance lobby with stone walls, marble floors and a sweeping staircase in turned wood. The dining room has beautiful beams, wrought-iron wall lights and huge French doors through which light floods; the terrace, romantically lit at night, overlooks river and town. The atmosphere is one of relaxed elegance, individually designed bedrooms in 19th-century style have floral or striped bedcovers and curtains to match. Sleep deeply in a vast bed with monogrammed sheets; wake to gleaming marble, Persian rugs and walk-in showers. Marvellous. *Minimum stay two nights.*

Price	€170–€220.
Rooms	5: 2 doubles, 2 twins, 1 suite for 2.
Meals	Breakfast included. Restaurants 5-min walk.
Closed	24 December–5 January.
Directions	From Toulouse A61 exit 22; from Narbonne A61 exit 23 to Limoux. Signed.

	Joanne Payan
	11 rue Blanquerie,
	11300 Limoux, Aude
Tel	+33 (0)4 68 69 48 40
Fax	+33 (0)4 68 69 08 93
Email	joanne@montfaucontours.com
Web	www.montfaucontours.com

Château des Ducs de Joyeuse

The drive up is impressive, the castle even more so: 1500s and fortified, part Gothic, part Renaissance, standing in its own patch of land on the banks of the Aude. A large rectangular courtyard is jolly with summer tables and parasols, the stately dining room has snowy linen cloths and fresh flowers, the staff are truly charming and helpful, and the menu changes daily according to what is fresh. Vaulted ceilings and well-trodden stone spiral stairs lead to formal bedrooms with heavy wooden furniture, some beamed and with stone fireplaces; there's a heraldic feel with narrow high windows, studded doors and smart bedspreads in navy blue and bright red. Ask for a room with a watery view. Bathrooms glow with tiled floors, bright lights and stone walls – some up to two metres thick: perfect sound insulation.Historical information about the building is on display everywhere, Manager Philippe is full of ideas and can help you plan your trips out. Hearty souls can knock a ball around the tennis court then cool off in the outdoor pool – or brave that lovely river. Good value.

Price	€95-€117.
	Suites & family rooms €174-€198.
Rooms	35: 10 doubles, 11 twins,
	12 suites for 2, 2 family rooms for 4-5.
Meals	Breakfast €13.
	Dinner €36-€55, every day June-Sept.
Closed	Mid-November–February.
Directions	Directions on booking.

Dominique & Alain Avelange
Allée du Château,
11190 Couiza, Aude

Tel	+33 (0)4 68 74 23 50
Fax	+33 (0)4 68 74 23 36
Email	reception@chateau-des-ducs.com
Web	www.chateau-des-ducs.com

La Fargo

Pluck a handful of cherries on the way to breakfast; gather up the scents of rosemary and thyme. This centuries-old converted forge blends effortlessly with the unspoilt Corbières countryside. Christophe and Dominique, a gentle couple with a hippyish streak, lived the good life rearing goats, before rescuing the building five years ago. Their passion for food, nature and Indonesia – where they winter – is evident. Large, light bedrooms have a charming and simple colonial style – white or stone walls, tiled floors, dark teak, bright ikat bedcovers. Huge bathrooms glitter with mosaic tiles, the showers like tropical rainstorms. Breakfast on the terrace – homemade jams and brioches – under the shade of the kiwi fruit vines. Dine here or in the restaurant where clean, modern lines blend well with rustic stonework and food is an adventurous mix of Mediterranean and Asian. Corbières is a natural de stresser: come for birdwatching, walking, fishing, vineyards, Cathar castles and medieval abbeys. Or wander around la Fargo's potager and orchard, pluck some fruit and lie back in one of dozens of wooden loungers.

Price	€65–€180.
Rooms	6: 5 doubles, 1 family room for 4. 6 extra rooms (4 doubles, 2 triples) and a pool opening Summer 2008.
Meals	Breakfast €8. Lunch & dinner €30–€50. Restaurant closed Mondays.
Closed	15 November–March.
Directions	A61 exit Lézignan-Corbières, D611 toward Fabrezan, then D212 to Lagrasse, then St Pierre des Champs. Fargo on right exiting village.

Christophe & Dominique Morellet
11220 Saint Pierre des Champs, Aude

Tel	+33 (0)4 68 43 12 78
Fax	+33 (0)4 68 43 29 20
Email	lafargo@club-internet.fr
Web	www.lafargo.fr

Auberge du Roua

Hard to tell from the spic and span interior that this small hotel was once an 18th-century mill. But this is the south, where life is lived outdoors which here is so special: you could happily spend all day dozing or reading on the quiet garden terrace by the stone-paved pool surrounded by tropical plants. There is ample opportunity to escape the sun's dazzle under the trees, and the views of the Albères are splendid. Bedrooms have been refreshed, are comfortable and a bright modern décor has been used in the newest addition; bathrooms are a good size. This is a family-run hotel; don't be surprised to see a couple of young children about. The dining room, with its white nappery and crystal, is formal and rightly highlights the vaulted ceiling of the old mill – an appropriate setting for the chef's superb and refined cuisine. The terrace by the pool is perfect for evening dining. Unusual to find a hotel hidden away in the middle of the countryside where, in these parts, the whole world is at the beach – it's a five-kilometre hop to the ocean and a 20-minute stroll to the centre of bustling Argelès.

Price	€60–€135. Suites & family rooms €109–€189.
Rooms	20: 12 doubles, 4 twins, 2 connecting rooms for family of 4, 2 family rooms for 3.
Meals	Breakfast €10. Dinner €35–€75. Restaurant closed Wednesday evenings October–May. Sunday, lunch only,
Closed	December–mid-February.
Directions	N114, exit 10 for Argelès sur Mer. In town, right at lights, straight on after the underpass; follow signs.

Magalie Tonjum
Chemin du Roua, 66700 Argelès sur Mer,
Pyrénées-Orientales

Tel	+33 (0)4 68 95 85 85
Fax	+33 (0)4 68 95 83 50
Email	magalie@aubergeduroua.com
Web	www.aubergeduroua.com

Le Mas Trilles

There's a charming haphazard feel to the layout of this rambling, honey-coloured 17th-century farmhouse that Marie-France and Laszlo have renovated to perfection. First greeting you are the sounds of birdsong and rushing water, then, perhaps the head-spinning scent of orange or cherry blossom. There are two comfortable sitting rooms, one high-ceilinged with its original beams, both with cool terracotta tiles and places to read and relax; some of Marie-France's paintings are displayed here. Many of the pristine bedrooms, larger in the main house, are reached by unexpected ups and downs. There are fine antiques and French doors lead onto little terraces; some look onto the pool, some onto woods or mountains. The largest room has magnificent views of the Canigou mountain, the spiritual home of the Catalan nation. Breakfast on the sweet terrace with homemade fig or apricot jam or in front of a crackling fire on chilly day. Then down by the river, there are fine views of the mountains and an intoxicating feeling of space. All agree that with such a warm welcome, this is more like a home than a hotel.

Price	€104–€210. Triples & suites €188–€260.
Rooms	10: 3 doubles, 5 triples, 2 suites.
Meals	Breakfast included. Light meals on request (€15). Restaurant 200m.
Closed	8 October–28 April.
Directions	Exit 43 Boulou towards Céret on D115 but do not enter town. Le Mas is 2km after Céret towards Amélie les Bains.

Marie-France & Laszlo Bukk
Le Pont de Reynès,
66400 Céret, Pyrénées-Orientales

Tel	+33 (0)4 68 87 38 37
Fax	+33 (0)4 68 87 42 62
Email	mastrilles@free.fr
Web	www.le-mas-trilles.com

L'Orri de Planès

Not a lonely goatherd in sight but, high on the hill at 1,600m, a huge old barn of Pyrenean stone renovated simply and sustainably. No frills, just vast wooden beams, terracotta floors, stone walls and a Norwegian wood-burning stove. Small, spotless bedrooms and bathrooms are no softer - "less is more" is the motto - but this is not for softies! You're on the Cardagne plain between two mountain ranges and the hiking is superb. Look north to France and south to Spain; spring flourishes with wildflowers, butterflies swoon around them. Cool off in the outdoor pool, relax with a book from the library (or a toy from the children's corner), borrow maps to plan the next assault; Arif and Marta are experienced guides. When winter does its thing your options are snowshoeing and cross-country skiing straight from the door; downhill skiing is 3km away. You'll be well fed at long wooden tables on local pâtés and cheeses, meats, yogurts, charcuterie, honey, wine - and so at one with nature that candles and napkins will seem frivolous indulgences from another life. *Snowshoes & backpacks for hire.*

Unhappy about the steady march of the insatiable consumer society and the effect it all has on the planet, Arif and Marta decided to act instead of just worry. Common sense and sustainability have prevailed in their renovations with the installation of a thermal system to regulate temperature using very little fuel; solar panels which heat the water and produce enough electricity to cover most of their needs; and a recycling system to minimise rubbish. Water is conserved by the installation of flow reducers in the loos and showers and all cleaning materials are environmentally friendly.

Price	€30 p.p. Under twelves €20.
Rooms	10: 1 family room for 4; 4 doubles, 4 twins, sharing 4 showers; 1 dorm for 6-8 with 1 bath & 1 shower.
Meals	Breakfast included. Picnic lunch €7.50. Half-board €45 p.p.; under twelves €30.
Closed	3 weeks after Easter holidays (April or May). 3 weeks in November.
Directions	From Perpignan N116 for Prades; Mont-Louis. D32 to La Cabanasse, St Pierre des Forçats & Planès (5km from Mont Louis). Follow signs in town.

Arif Qureshi & Marta Maristany
Trailside Eco-Lodge, Cases de Mitg,
66210 Planès, Pyrénées-Orientales

Tel	+33 (0)4 68 04 29 47
Email	contact@orrideplanes.com
Web	www.orrideplanes.com

SPECIAL
GREEN ENTRY
see page 12

Rhône Valley – Alps

Le Clos du Châtelet

Washed in barely-there pink, with soft blue shutters, the house was built as a country retreat towards the end of the 18th century — by a silk merchant who must have had a thing about trees. Overlooking the valley of the Saône, with immaculate sweeping lawns, the garden is full of beautiful old ones: sequoias, cedars, chestnuts and magnolias. To one side of the house, an open outbuilding smothered in flowers is home to a collection of antique bird cages. Bedrooms are welcoming havens in elegant muted colours: 'Joubert' in pink ochre with twin wrought-iron four-posters draped in toile de Jouy; 'Lamartine' in palest aqua enhanced by grey and lilac hangings. All have polished wooden floors and gently sober bathrooms. There's much comfort here, an open fire in the sitting room, period furniture, prints, deer antlers on the wall and an air of calm. A harp stands in the corner of the elegant drawing room: we are not sure if it is played but this is the sort of place where it might be. Dinner is by candlelight in the dining room, atmospheric with its old terracotta floor and fountain in the wall. *No credit cards.*

Price	€105–€110.
Rooms	4: 3 doubles; 1 double with separate bath.
Meals	Breakfast included. Dinner €27, book ahead.
Closed	Rarely.
Directions	A6 exit Tournus for Bourg en Bresse to Cuisery. Right at Cuisery for Sermoyer & Pont de Vaux. In Sermoyer follow chambres d'hôtes signs.

Madame Durand Pont
01190 Sermoyer, Ain

Tel	+33 (0)3 85 51 84 37
Fax	+33 (0)3 85 51 84 37
Email	leclosduchatelet@free.fr
Web	www.leclosduchatelet.com

Hôtel Le Cottage Bise

Not many cottages have 35 bedrooms; not many have this fabulous setting – you might be in a Wagner opera as you gaze from the terrace at the sun setting over the Roc de Chère across the Lac d'Annecy. The three buildings which make up the hotel look, unsurprisingly, like Alpine chalets and are set in pretty, well-planted gardens in which you can wander on your way to meet one of the local millionaires or perhaps Wotan himself. Monsieur and Madame Bise run this welcoming, relaxed establishment with a quiet Savoyard efficiency, which, at its heart, has a proper concern for the comfort of guests. *Douillette* – that lovely word which is the French equivalent of 'cosy' – perfectly describes the atmosphere in the bedrooms, with their floral chintz fabrics and comfortable furniture. You are well away from the bustle of Annecy itself, but close enough to dabble if you wish; there are multifarious activities for the sporty and inspiration for the arty who wish to follow in the footsteps of Cézanne or Lamartine. Class, comfort *and* culture – what more could you want?

Price	€100–€250. Suites & family rooms €300–€450.
Rooms	35: 17 doubles, 15 twins, 3 suites. Family rooms on request.
Meals	Breakfast €16. Lunch €27–€60. Dinner €40–€60. Restaurants within walking distance.
Closed	10 October–April.
Directions	In Annecy, follow signs Bord du Lac for Thônes D909. At Veyrier du Lac follow D909A to Talloires. Well signed in Talloires.

Jean-Claude & Christine Bise
Au Bord du Lac, 74290 Talloires,
Haute-Savoie

Tel	+33 (0)4 50 60 71 10
Fax	+33 (0)4 50 60 77 51
Email	cottagebise@wanadoo.fr
Web	www.cottagebise.com

Auberge Le Chalet des Troncs

Some people get everything right, and without making a lot of noise about it. Jean-François, an architect, has skilfully renovated this wood and stone chalet built around 1780. The style is rustic, the design is contemporary. All walls in the two sitting rooms are the original wood as are ceiling and floor; an old sledge has been converted into a coffee table with a nice scatter of antiques and bric-a-brac about. Original is the design of the handsome leather and pine sofas in front of the big open fire as are the open rough-plank dividers between the beds and bathrooms. He has cleverly fashioned lamps made from branches and kept the light subdued. Christine is busy in the kitchen garden or gathering wild herbs which she uses in her excellent cooking; the pot au feu is prepared over the open fire. The indoor pool feels outside as one wall is a huge picture window onto the mountain views. You can cross-country ski from the door or catch a free bus 800 metres away for the Grand Borvand. Perfectly quiet, with a lovely rambling garden – grass, shrubs, moss, wild flowers – this is to hard to fault.

Price	€140–€190
Rooms	4: 3 twins, 1 family room for 3.
Meals	Breakfast €15–€20. Picnic lunch €10–€20. Dinner from €35.
Closed	Rarely.
Directions	In Grand-Bornand, at the church, straight ahead 5km dir. Vallée du Couchet. In Hameau des Plans, right at little chapel for Hameau.

Christine & Jean-François Charbonnier
Les Troncs, Vallee du Bouchet,
74450 Le Grand Bornand, Haute-Savoie

Tel	+33 (0)4 50 02 28 50
Fax	+33 (0)4 50 63 25 28
Email	contact@chaletdestroncs.com
Web	www.chaletdestroncs.com

Au Coin du Feu-Chilly Powder

The homeward piste takes you to the door; the cable car, opposite, sweeps you to the peaks. The chalet is named after its magnificent central fireplace… on one side gleaming leather sofas, on the other, red dining chairs at a long table. Everything feels generous here: great beams span the chalet's length, windows look up to the cliffs of the Hauts Forts, high ceilings give a sense of space. There's a reading room on the mezzanine above the living area with books, internet, antique globe and worn leather armchairs, and a small bar made of English oak by a carpenter friend. Bedrooms are Alpine-swish and themed: there's the Toy Room for families, the English Room that sports a bowler hat. The carpets are sisal, one room's four-poster is veiled in muslin and the bathrooms have Molton Brown toiletries and shower heads as big as plates. The chef produces the best of country cooking, and Paul and Francesca can organise everything, including torchlight descents. There's massage, a sauna, a hot tub outdoors, DVDs to cheer wet days – even an in-house nanny. A great spot for families. *New seven-bedroom chalet next door.*

Price	€80. Half-board mandatory in winter, €465–€1,095 p.p. per week.
Rooms	17: 6 doubles, 3 twins, 1 triple, 7 family rooms for 2-5.
Meals	Breakfast included. Picnic lunch €5. Dinner €35.
Closed	Never.
Directions	From Morzine, signs to Avoriaz, then Les Prodains; 2.8 km; on right, just before cable car.

	Paul & Francesca Eyre BP 116, 74110 Morzine, Haute-Savoie
Tel	+33 (0)4 50 74 75 21
Fax	+33 (0)4 50 79 01 48
Email	paul@chillypowder.com
Web	www.chillypowder.com

The Farmhouse

The day starts with a breakfast spread in the cattle shed – now a deeply atmospheric dining room – and ends with a slap-up dinner hosted by Dorrien. Fifteen years ago he gave up England for the oldest farmhouse in Morzine – the lovely, steeply pitched Mas de la Coutettaz at the peaceful end of town. Push open the mellow carved door to find a 1771 interior of dark chunky beams, huge polished flags and patina'd pine doors with original mouldings. Big, characterful, comfortable bedrooms, whose bathrooms promise white robes and L'Occitane lotions, are reached via a central stone stair; some have mountain views. And at the end of the garden is an exquisite little mazot: the bedroom is up a steep outside stair. Morzine is the perfect staging post for the Avoriaz and Portes du Soleil, so come for hiking, biking, swimming in the lakes; in winter, a 'ski host' at the farmhouse introduces you to the runs. Return to a hot toddy in the bar and a crackling log fire, lit at the merest hint of chill, even in summer. Final proof (as if you needed it) that you will adore The Farmhouse and hope to return.

Price	€75-€175. Singles €45-€135. Triple €105-€255. Half-board €95-€190 p.p.
Rooms	8: 3 doubles, 1 twin, 3 triples, 1 suite for 6.
Meals	Breakfast included. Dinner, 4 courses with wine, €30-€40. Half-board only, December-April, on weekly basis.
Closed	May; October-November.
Directions	In Morzine, follow signs for Avoriaz. On Ave Joux Plan, left after Nicholas Sport, then right. On left.

Dorrien Ricardo
Le Mas de la Coutettaz,
74110 Morzine
Haute-Savoie
Tel +33 (0)4 50 79 08 26
Email info@thefarmhouse.co.uk
Web www.thefarmhouse.co.uk

Chalet Odysseus

Chalet Odysseus has the lot: comfort (soft sofas, bright rugs, open fire), swishness (satellite TV, sauna, small gym), a French chef who waves his gourmet wand over the dining table once a week, and English hosts who spoil you rotten. Kate and Barry lived in the village for seven years, then built this chalet. They have the ground floor of this beautifully solid, purpose-built, new chalet, you live above, and it's the sort of place you'd be happy in whatever the weather. Cheerfully pretty bedrooms come with the requisite pine garb, beds are covered in quilts handmade by Kate, two rooms have balconies that catch the sun, and the tiniest comes with bunk beds for kids. The shower rooms and bathroom are airy and light. As for Les Carroz, most skiers pass it by on their way to high-rise Flaine – a shame, for the village has heaps of character and several fine places to eat. Your own 4x4 gets you to the lifts in minutes, tying you in with the whole of the Grand Massif. Dinners are four-course and there's a *grole* night to boot. Great for a family break, whatever the season.

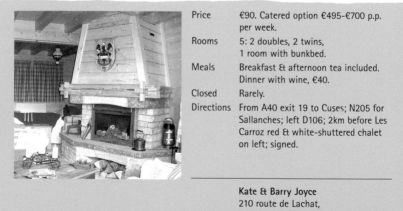

Price	€90. Catered option €495-€700 p.p. per week.
Rooms	5: 2 doubles, 2 twins, 1 room with bunkbed.
Meals	Breakfast & afternoon tea included. Dinner with wine, €40.
Closed	Rarely.
Directions	From A40 exit 19 to Cuses; N205 for Sallanches; left D106; 2km before Les Carroz red & white-shuttered chalet on left; signed.

Kate & Barry Joyce
210 route de Lachat,
74300 Les Carroz d'Araches, Haute-Savoie

Tel	+33 (0)4 50 90 66 00
Fax	+33 (0)4 50 90 66 01
Email	chaletodysseus@wanadoo.fr
Web	www.chaletodysseuslachat.com

Chalet La Vieille Forge

Pack up all your children, most of your friends, and their children too: there's room for all in this charming, rambling, 18th-century house. The huge living room has bags of character and a French homely style: scattered rugs on polished oak floors, black leather chairs around the wood-burner, plaster or wood-clad walls, old photos, ski prints, antlers. Breakfast is cooked and hearty (organic if you wish), eaten in the morning room on a rustic pine table. Satellite TV, DVD and books and games will keep children and grown-ups happy when they're not on the slopes. Bedrooms are spacious and some rather grand, the family room is perfect for hurling loads of children in together, bathrooms are beautifully tiled. Full catering in winter: you're collected at the airport, greeted with a glass of bubbly, ferried to and from ski slopes, dropped off at restaurants, picked up late at night (up to 23.30); there's a heated boot room, a sauna all of your own (robes provided), and freshly baked cake for tea. Dynamic, friendly, great fun – and the food is so good they run cookery courses. *Ski lifts six-minute walk. Transfers included.*

Price	From €65. Winter: half-board €290–€572 p.p. for 3 nights; €632–€959 per week.
Rooms	7: 2 doubles, 4 twins, 1 family room for 3–5; 7 bathrooms.
Meals	Breakfast €12. Half-board only in winter. Restaurant 1km.
Closed	Rarely.
Directions	A10 exit Les Houches/Bellevue; right at Bellevue cable car for 1km; at r'bout Route de Chavants, bearing left for 0.8km; at junc. bear right Route de la Côte du Chavants; 1st on left.

Tim & Gaby Newman
55 route de la Côte du Chavants,
74310 Les Houches, Haute-Savoie

Tel   +44 (0)20 7504 3776
Fax   +44 (0)20 7504 3776
Email   ski@huski.com
Web   www.huski.com

Hôtel Slalom Les Houches

Right by the Olympic Kandahar ski run, overlooking mighty Mont Blanc, is a sparkling hotel. It reopened in 2006 under the inspired stewardship of Tracy Spraggs, whose dream it had been to have a place of her own. Plain on the outside, it is super-stylish within, designer modern but with personality. Bedrooms have white walls, cream carpets, wooden beds, curtain-free windows to pull in the view, and plasma TVs. There's a swish little bar, all chrome and polished leather, where Joao, the Portuguese barman with the interesting Scottish accent, mixes a hit-the-spot Gin Fizz after taking you around the mountains. Best of all, you're 30 metres from the cable car and can ski back to the door. Note: the area offers the finest tree skiing in the region, but this little resort is charming all year round. Take a picnic to the pine-fringed Lac des Chavants or a step back in time on the Mont Blanc Tramway (it opened in 1904 and is still going strong). Sporty types can climb, trek, mountain bike, paraglide, play tennis, have a round of golf and there's a good choice of spas nearby, too. *Transfers can be arranged.*

Price	€86–€178.
Rooms	10 twins/doubles.
Meals	Breakfast €12. Restaurants in village.
Closed	May.
Directions	From Geneva A401 to Chamonix. N205/E25 exit Les Houches, right on D213, right on rue de Bellevue.

Tracey Spraggs
44 rue de Bellevue,
74310 Haute-Savoie

Tel	+33 (0)4 50 54 40 60
Fax	+33 (0)4 50 54 32 65
Email	info@hotelslalom.net
Web	www.hotelslalom.net

Les Campanules

An explosion of orange pine, Alpine style, in the heart of Tignes and right next to the ski lifts; views from most rooms are of mountains and snazzily dressed folk being shunted up them. Not for aesthetes then (the town is mostly modern), but perfect as a base and you'll be well fed, warm as toast and able to ease away any aches and pains in the spa. A large, airy restaurant and sitting area has little booths, a roaring fire, and timber or stone walls decorated with ancient wooden skis, dried flower arrangements and black and white pictures of old Tignes. Breakfast is enormous with bacon, eggs, cheeses, breads, cold meats and salads; suppers (buffet style and freshly prepared) are family-friendly, delicious… then retire to a clean, neat, soft-lit bedroom with crisp sheets and proper feather duvet. Sweat it out in the Finnish sauna or Turkish bath, brave the outdoor pool with its gorgeous warm water, freezing air and spectacular views over the town and hard-edged peaks. In summer those snowy folds are transformed into green pastures with waving wild flowers: perfect for walkers. *Ski lifts 50m.*

Price	Half-board €82–€167 p.p.; suites €112–€189 p.p.
Rooms	43: 33 twins/doubles, 10 suites.
Meals	Restaurants nearby. Half-board only, mid-December to mid-April.
Closed	May; September.
Directions	From Moutiers, N90 to Bourg St Maurice, D902, D87 to Tignes. Hotel in front of church.

Philippe & Thierry Reymond
Le Rosset,
73320 Tignes, Savoie

Tel	+33 (0)4 79 06 34 36
Fax	+33 (0)4 79 06 35 78
Email	campanules@wanadoo.fr
Web	www.campanules.com

Hotel Particulier de Digoine

Silk and its mythical route between China and the south of France is the theme here – and what a sensuous treat this is. Olivier, full of southeast Asian travels, has envisaged each room as a staging post: a Venetian room with a floor in parquet and silks in greys and blues; Chinese reds and yellows for Tibet; blues and reds and a bed on the mezzanine for a séjour in Samarkand; for Mongolia, smooth fabrics and rough bark and wood. It is an exotic décor and quite fitting as this lovely house was once owned by a silk merchant who produced his own cocoons. Downstairs one is enthralled by a series of interlocking reception rooms. In the grand salon, its views over a tributary of the river, the afternoon sun turns the dusty-pink walls golden; even more special is the terracotta-hued breakfast room, reached through a concealed door in the panelling. Food is simple but of high quality – freshly grilled meat or fish, fine cheeses. Breakfast is served at one table in the kitchen, more formally in the dining room, or in the courtyard in the summer. Olivier will happily concoct a picnic hamper if a hike is in the air.

Price	€87-€97. Family room €119. Apartment €135-€145. Whole house €900 incl. breakfast (€4,000 per week).
Rooms	7 + 1: 4 doubles, 1 twin, 1 single. Apartment for 3-5.
Meals	Breakfast €9. Hosted dinner €24, book ahead.
Closed	Never.
Directions	Autoroute A7, exit Montélimar Sud to Viviers; N86 to Bourg St Andéol. Quai Madier de Montjau on the river next to Mairie.

Olivier Dutreil
5 quai Madier de Montjau,
077000 Bourg St Andéol, Ardèche

Tel	+33 (0)4 75 54 61 07
Fax	+33 (0)4 75 54 61 07
Email	info@digoine.com
Web	www.digoine.com

Le Clair de la Plume

Come to feast on the 300 species of old-fashioned and English roses that spill into the winding streets of this 'village fleuri'. Pushing open the wrought-iron gates of the pink-façaded *maison de maître* brings you into something new. Jean-Luc Valadeau has created a feeling of warmth and hospitality: "a home with all the comforts of a hotel". His staff are equally attentive, ushering you through deliciously elegant rooms, antique pieces catching your eye on the way. The small terraced garden adds to the feeling of privacy and light floods in over the original staircase. The bedrooms are quiet, beautifully decorated – Louis Philippe wardrobes in some, country-style wicker chairs in others – and all with luxurious bathrooms. Washed or ragged walls, original floor tiles or shining oak planks – a combination of great taste and authenticity. After a generous breakfast, the Salon de Thé is open from noon till late for exotic selections of tea, assiettes salées, mouthwatering patisseries, locally made ice cream. Grignan is set in a sea of lavender and Jean-Luc gives you bikes to borrow – explore!

Price	€95–€165.
Rooms	15: 10 twins/doubles. Annexe: 2 doubles, 3 family suites.
Meals	Breakfast €12. Light lunch €12. Restaurants within walking distance.
Closed	Never.
Directions	From Lyon A7 exit 18 Montélimar Sud towards Nyons; D133 then D541 to Grignan. Signed.

Jean-Luc Valadeau
Place de Mail,
26230 Grignan, Drôme

Tel	+33 (0)4 75 91 81 30
Fax	+33 (0)4 75 91 81 31
Email	plume2@wanadoo.fr
Web	www.clairplume.com

Michel Chabran

A jewel, whose main attraction is neither the rooms nor the setting but the food. Michel Chabran is a delightful man and a prince among restaurateurs, and his little hotel, 50 miles south of Lyon, lies in France's gastronomic heart. Served on Limoges china dusted with gold is potato purée with Sevruga caviar, poularde de Bresse, hot soufflé of Grand Marnier — food that has won Michel many accolades. The à la carte menu stretches to four pages, the set menu two, there are 400 wines and the service is unpretentious and exemplary. It all started in 1943 when Michel's grandfather supplied sandwiches to workers heading south on the first paid holidays to the sun; the rest is history. Bedrooms are cosy and soundproofed and having a facelift; some face the road, others the garden. Come for a truffle weekend from November to March — Michel tells you all about the 'black diamonds', then sits you down to a six-course treat before a blazing fire. Work it all off the next day in the Vercors National Park, or visit Chave, producer of the Hermitage wines that may have seduced you the night before. *€15 supplement for pets.*

Price	€90–€165. Half-board on request.
Rooms	11 doubles.
Meals	Breakfast €21.
	Lunch €42 (not Wed/Thurs).
	Dinner €55–€155.
Closed	October–March: Sunday evenings.
Directions	A7 south of Lyon exit Tain l'Hermitage or Valence North to N7 for Pont de l'Isère. Restaurant & hotel on main street opp. Council House.

Monsieur & Madame Chabran
29 avenue du 45 Parallèle,
26600 Pont de l'Isère, Drôme

Tel	+33 (0)4 75 84 60 09
Fax	+33 (0)4 75 84 59 65
Email	chabran@michelchabran.fr
Web	www.michelchabran.fr

Château de la Commanderie

Grand it appears, and some of the makers of that grandeur – Knights Templar and Maltese, princes and prime ministers, presidents and financiers – look down upon you as you eat in the magnificent dining room, a favourite restaurant for the discerning palates of Grenoble. But the atmosphere is of an intimate family-run hotel. The whole place is awash with family antiques and heirlooms, the breakfasts are delicious, good taste prevails and flowers add that touch of life and genuine attention. Bedrooms are divided among four buildings, adding to the sense of intimacy. Rooms in château and chalet are the more traditional with carved wooden beds and gilt-framed mirrors, though some of them give onto a small road. The Orangerie's rooms, as you'll discover once you have negotiated the rather plain corridors, look out over fine parkland, and are deliciously peaceful. The least expensive rooms are in the Petit Pavillon, on the road side. But whichever you choose, you will be beautifully looked after – and you are in a smart suburb of Grenoble. *Signs for 'La Commanderie' indicate an area of town, not the Château.*

Price	€102–€320. Singles €92–€180.
Rooms	25 twins/doubles.
Meals	Breakfast buffet €14. Lunch & dinner €27–€70. Restaurant closed Mondays, Saturday lunchtimes & Sundays.
Closed	20 December–3 January.
Directions	From Grenoble exit 5 Rocade Sud for Eybens, immediately right at 1st lights for Le Bourg; right after Esso garage. Entrance to hotel 300m on left at turning in road.

Monsieur de Beaumont
17 avenue d'Echirolles,
38230 Eybens, Isère

Tel	+33 (0)4 76 25 34 58
Fax	+33 (0)4 76 24 07 31
Email	resa@commanderie.fr
Web	www.commanderie.fr

Collège Hôtel

Who would have thought that a school-themed hotel could be so exhilarating? Combine it with a sleek new design and you have one of Lyon's most exciting places to stay, on the edge of the charming old quarter. Built in the 30s in Art Deco style, the new renovation has introduced a quirky kind of cool and at night optical fibres light the façade all colours of the rainbow. The entrance hall has lovely 'old school' touches, a huge painting of a classroom and a vintage TV running cult school classics. Room prices are chalked onto a blackboard; the reception desk has been created from a gymnasium horse; the brown breakfast room glows with polished wooden tables, leather benches and glass-fronted bookcases. Take the lift clad in school assembly photographs to black and white corridors signposted 'the dorms'… bedrooms are pure symphonies of white (walls, beds, leather armchairs), bathrooms are relentlessly stylish, with several large triangular bathtubs. A graceful roof terrace completes the show, decked in green and jutting like the prow of an ocean liner. Bravo!

Price	€105–€140.
Rooms	40.
Meals	Breakfast €11.
	Wide choice of restaurants very close.
Closed	Never.
Directions	A6 Paris-Lyon exit Vieux Lyon, just after tunnel of Fourière; follow river on Quai Fulchiron & Quai Bondy; left at Pont La Feuillée to Pl. St Paul, opp. station. Hotel on left corner (parking €12).

Laurent Phelip
5 Place St Paul,
69005 Lyon, Rhône

Tel	+33 (0)4 72 10 05 05
Fax	+33 (0)4 78 27 98 84
Email	contact@college-hotel.com
Web	www.college-hotel.com

L'Ermitage Hôtel Cuisine-à-manger

An ultra-modern sister for Lyon's centrally sited Collège Hotel, 15 minutes by car. The architecture may be different but the swish interiors are just as cool: pale blonde wood, walls exposed brick or bright white, mocha leather sofas, a crisp dining room, beautifully designed chairs. But the real plus here is the panorama: views sweep over the city to the green foothills beyond. Locals come up here just for the view; catch it from the terrace with its shady trees and lime green seating, or from the all-weather pool with its immaculate decking. The old streets of Lyon teem with good restaurants but you have a couple here, too, one with sliding glass doors to a terrace. Indulge in a gentle game of pétanque, puff around the fitness trail, return to smart modern bedrooms with flat-screen TVs, oak floors, more views – simply stunning during the Festival of Light, thanks to the city's operatic floodlighting of monuments and bridges.

Price	€135–€185. Suite €225.
Rooms	28: 27 doubles, 1 suite for 4.
Meals	Breakfast €12, Lunch & dinner from €30.
Closed	Never.
Directions	From Paris A6 exit 33; follow signs for Limonest, then Route de la Garde, Route du Mont Verdun, Route du Mont Thou, Route des Crêtes. Free parking.

Laurent Phelip
Chemin de L'Ermitage, Mont Cindre,
69450 Saint Cyr au Mont d'Or, Rhône

Tel	+33 (0)4 72 19 69 69
Fax	+33 (0)4 72 19 69 71
Email	contact@ermitage-college-hotel.com
Web	www.ermitage-college-hotel.com

Château de la Charmeraie

Nestled into the deep quiet of the Lyonnais hills, this 19th-century estate welcomes you with fine craftsmanship into reception rooms panelled in walnut and wild cherry and exquisite even to the detail of silver door handles. The outside is beguilingly simple, a deep apricot and ochre-pink, where a long sun terrace unfolds, furnished in appealing wickerware and forming a neat lip above the pool. On fine days breakfast is served here, comprising homemade jams, breads and pastries. From its seat in a dell, the house enjoys a marvellous vista of private lake, parkland and a drive flanked by horse chestnut. Within, bedrooms are sumptuous, traditional and feminine in style, matching enticing beds and perfectly upholstered armchairs with marble or brass-framed log fires, ingeniously paired at eye-level with flat-screen televisions. One comes with a pretty conservatory, another with a bed swathed in fluffy apple-green netting – wondrously amorous. Bathrooms have sheer class. It's easy to get caught up in Brigitte's enthusiasm for her own home, particularly while seated at her excellent table d'hôtes.

Price	€68–€143.
Rooms	6: 4 doubles, 1 twin, 1 suite.
Meals	Breakfast included. Dinner €30. Restaurant 10km.
Closed	Never.
Directions	A6 Paris-Lyon exit Porte de Lyon to Centre Ville. Roanne and N7 to L'Arbreste; through La Girandiere to St. Laurent de Chamousset. At entrance r'bout follow "Complexe Sportif – Le Batie". Right at Statue of Virgin Mary, 1st left and 1st right.

Brigitte & René Trégouët
Domaine de la Bâtie,
69930 Saint Laurent de Chamousset, Rhône

Tel	+33 (0)4 74 70 50 70
Fax	+33 (0)4 74 26 59 55
Email	contact@chateaudelacharmeraie.com
Web	www.chateaudelacharmeraie.com

Château de Pramenoux

Climb up into the Mont du Beaujolais hills above Lyon. Rivers pulse down on either side and great Douglas pine trees clean the air. As you round a curve, a pair of Gothic pepperpot turrets surprisingly pop into view. The château sits in a natural clearing and views from the terrace and bedrooms sweep splendidly down the valley; a small pond in front anchors the eye. Emmanuel, a charming young escapee from the corporate world, will point out the bits that date from the 10th century up to the Renaissance; he has lovingly patched and painted a great deal of it himself. Rooms are big, hugely comfortable and have simply elegant bathrooms. Choose the cherrywood panelled room: a gold and white striped bed and Louis XVI chairs dressed in eau-de-nil. Or be King and Queen and slumber under a canopied bed in a room lined with royal blue and golden fleur-de-lys, a textile re-created by Emmanuel himself with the weavers of Lyon. Passionate opera lovers organize concerts in the summer in the vast reception hall. A wonderfully peaceful place, run by the warmest people. *Cash or cheque only.*

Price	€120 €140.
Rooms	4 doubles.
Meals	Breakfast included. Hosted dinner with wine and aperitif, €32; book ahead.
Closed	Rarely.
Directions	From A6 exit Belleville D37 for Beaujeu to St Vincent; left D9 to Quincié, Marchampt, Lamure; at end of Lamure, lane opp. 'terrain de sport' for Pramenoux.

	Emmanuel Baudoin & Jean-Luc Plasse
	69870 Lamure sur Azergues, Rhône
Tel	+33 (0)4 74 03 16 43
Fax	+33 (0)4 74 03 16 28
Email	pramenoux@aol.com
Web	www.chateau-de-pramenoux.com

Domaine du Château de Marchangy

Down a stunning avenue of oaks, through big metal gates, to a perfectly proportioned house – a 'petit château' built in the 18th century – where light pours into spacious guest quarters on the first and loft floors of one of the outbuildings. Imagine big rugs on pale wooden floors, harmonious colours, delightful armoires, gorgeous fabrics and garden flowers. Chambre de L'Allée, its bed topped by a fairy-tale coronet, is the most classical, Suite St Vincent, also lovely, has two vast single beds (or two small doubles!) and its own garden entrance, and the pretty loft suite is full of rafters. Bathrooms are immaculate. Sunlight pours into the guest dining room with leather sofas and long farmhouse table, so rise at your leisure for stylish breakfasts: croissants, jams, cheeses, orchard fruits, several teas. There's a pool for summer in whinnying distance of the horses; fields and paddock surround you, the setting is idyllic. Charming Madame opened this elegant chambres d'hôte 12 years ago and gives you the best; should she not be here, the gardienne will look after you wonderfully.

Price	€85–€110.
Rooms	3 suites.
Meals	Breakfast included. Supper from €15. Wine from €10. Restaurants within 5km.
Closed	Rarely.
Directions	From Roanne D482 north; 5km after Pouilly sous Charlieu right to St Pierre la Noaille. Signed.

Marie-Colette Grandeau
42190 Saint Pierre la Noaille, Loire

Tel	+33 (0)4 77 69 96 76
Fax	+33 (0)4 77 60 70 37
Email	contact@marchangy.com
Web	www.marchangy.com

Provence – Alps – Riviera

Le Mas de Peint

Lucille and Jacques are warm, kind and proud of their beautiful farm. Their 500 bulls, 15 horses and swathes of arable land keep Jacques busy; Lucille tends to the rest. She has introduced an elegant but sober French country-farmhouse feel – no flounces nor flummery, just impeccable style. Bedrooms are deep green or old rose; generous curtains are checked dove-grey; floors come tiled or carpeted in wool. Eye-catching quirkery everywhere – a collection of fine pencil sketches, an antique commode – and some rooms with wonderful mezzanine bathrooms under old rafters. Breakfast royally in the big family kitchen or on the wisteria-draped terrace, then discover the secluded pool, encircled by teak loungers, scented with jasmine. The demi-pension option is a must. Dine outside on summer evenings, sheltered by a muslin canopy at tables aglow with Moroccan lamps – a fairytale spot in which to linger over elegant, garden-fresh food. Drift inside for a cognac in the clubby cigar room, take a peek at the black and white photos of bullfighting in the seductive salon. Heavenly. *Minimum stay three nights.*

Price	€205-€275. Suites €335-€381. Half-board €61 p.p. extra.
Rooms	11: 2 doubles, 6 twins/doubles, 1 suite, 1 suite for 3, 1 family suite for 3-4.
Meals	Breakfast €21. Lunch à la carte. Dinner €55-€57. Restaurant closed Wednesdays.
Closed	10 January-11 March; 14 November-20 December.
Directions	Arles to St Marie de la Mer D570; 2km after 2nd r'bout, D36 for Salin de Giraud & Le Sambuc.

Jacques & Lucille Bon
Le Sambuc, 13200 Arles,
Bouches-du-Rhône

Tel	+33 (0)4 90 97 20 62
Fax	+33 (0)4 90 97 22 20
Email	hotel@masdepeint.net
Web	www.masdepeint.com

Grand Hôtel Nord Pinus

An Arlesian legend, where Spain meets France, ancient Rome meets the 21st century – the hotel is hugely atmospheric. Built in 1865 on Roman vaults, it came to fame in the 1950s when a clown and a cabaret singer owned it: famous bullfighters dressed here before entering the arena and the arty crowd flocked (Cocteau, Picasso, Hemingway...). Anne Igou keeps the drama alive today with her strong personality and cinema, fashion and photography folk – and bullfighters still have 'their' superb Spanish Rococo room. The style is vibrant and alive at this show of Art Deco furniture and fittings, great bullfighting posters and toreador costumes, North African carpets and artefacts, fabulous Provençal colours and ironwork. Colour and light are deftly used to create a soft, nostalgic atmosphere where you feel both warm and cool, smart and artistic. Rooms are big, ceilings are high, the top floor suite has a covered terrace and views over the rooftops. A well-known chef has created a gourmet menu and breakfast is a festival of real French tastes – more magic, more nostalgia. As Cocteau said: "An hotel with a soul".

Price	€160–€230. Suites €295. Apartment €570.
Rooms	26: 9 doubles, 9 twins, 6 suites for 2, 1 suite for 4, 1 apartment for 4 (no kitchen).
Meals	Breakfast €14–€20. Lunch & dinner from €35.
Closed	Never.
Directions	From A54 exit Arles Centre for Centre Ancien. Take Boulevard des Lices at main post office; left on Rue Jean Jaurès; right on Rue Cloître, right to Place du Forum.

Anne Igou
Place du Forum, 13200 Arles,
Bouches-du-Rhône

Tel	+33 (0)4 90 93 44 44
Fax	+33 (0)4 90 93 34 00
Email	info@nord-pinus.com
Web	www.nord-pinus.com

La Riboto de Taven

A most magical place. Ever slept in a cave? In a canopied bed with ornate cover and hangings, with a luxurious bathroom next door? Here you can if you book far enough ahead. The Novi-Thème family – Christine, Philippe and Jean-Pierre – have farmed here for four generations. Their 18th century mas facing the garden is full of beautiful furniture handed down the generations. The property faces the spectacular cliff-top village of Les Baux de Provence- some say the most beautiful in all of France – the light changing on the cliffs as the day moves on. Walk up stone steps from the garden to a terrace, where the view is even more amazing than from the rest of the house. It is literally built onto the limestone cliff and the overhang of the rock face form the ceilings of the two 'troglodyte' rooms. In this supremely peaceful oasis of light, stone and history, excellent is the food, warm is the welcome. You will wish that you had booked for a week. *Children over 10 welcome.*

Price	€180–€280.
Rooms	6: 3 doubles, 2 troglodyte suites, 1 apartment for 4 (without kitchen).
Meals	Breakfast €18. Poolside lunch €23. Dinner €54. Restaurant closed on Wednesdays.
Closed	Early January–early March.
Directions	From St Rémy de Provence D5 to Maussane & Les Baux. Past entrance to village & head towards Fontvieille. Hotel on D78G, signed.

Novi-Thème Family
Le Val d'Enfer, 13520 Les Baux de Provence, Bouches-du-Rhône

Tel	+33 (0)4 90 54 34 23
Fax	+33 (0)4 90 54 38 88
Email	contact@riboto-de-taven.fr
Web	www.riboto-de-taven.fr

Le Hameau des Baux

It is tempting, as you mingle on the view-filled terrace, pastis in hand, to think that these buildings and huge plane trees have been here forever. But every stone has been newly laid, every green thing recently planted – full-size! Pascale's astonishing attention to detail has resulted in a triumph of style and good taste. Bedrooms are large, fresh and individually designed, from the traditional with a fine carved headboard, to the unusual, with a pigeonnier incorporated into the wall. Bathrooms are exquisite, some with mosaic tiling; rooms with private terraces drift into gardens filled with olive trees and lavender. Breakfast is served in your room, or in the dining room; dinner is from the local market: fresh, simple and generous. The stylish 'hamlet' wraps itself around an outdoor pool and all you need is here, including tennis. A pity though not to explore; the lower hills of the Alpilles beckon and the minor roads are stunning. Elegant cypresses stand out against the white rock, fruit trees are aching with blossom in the spring, and hilltop Les Baux is popular but picturesque.

Price	€190–€300. Suites from €435.
Rooms	15: 3 doubles, 7 twins/doubles, 5 suites.
Meals	Breakfast €18. Lunch €22–€45. Dinner €48–€53. Restaurant closed Wednesdays.
Closed	Mid-February.
Directions	From Arles N590 to Avignon, right on D16 to Paradou. In village left for Les Baux. Hameau 1km.

Pascale Milani
Chemin de Bourgeac, 13520 Le Paradou,
Bouches-du-Rhône

Tel	+33 (0)4 90 54 10 30
Fax	+33 (0)4 90 54 45 30
Email	reservation@hameaudesbaux.com
Web	www.hameaudesbaux.com

Entry 327 Map 16

Mas Doù Pastré

It's a charming place, gypsy-bright with wonderful furniture, checked cushions, colourwashed walls, fine kilims. Built at the end of the 18th century, this lovely old *mas* belonged to Grandpère and Grandmère: nine months were spent here, three up in the pastures with the sheep. Albine and her sisters turned the old farmhouse into a hotel to keep it in the family – and she and her talented handyman husband, Maurice, have succeeded, brilliantly. Bedrooms have wooden or tiled floors, antique doors and comfortable beds; all are big, some with their own sitting areas. Bathrooms are original with stone floors and beautiful washbasins picked up at flea markets; a claw-foot bath peeps theatrically out from behind striped curtains. Breakfast is a delicious feast and if you want a lie-in, light meals are served all day long in the new restaurant gastronomique. The garden is the best room with long views over the Alpilles: lounge on a chaise-longue with a bright awning, swim in the dreamy pool, drift off in the jacuzzi, or have a shaitsu treatment in the hamman. Bliss. *Minimum stay three nights July & August. Unsupervised pool.*

Price	€125–€180. Suite €240.
Rooms	13 + 3: 10 doubles, 2 twins, 1 suite for 4. 3 gypsy caravans for 2.
Meals	Breakfast €14. Light meals (1pm-8pm) €17–€21. Also à la carte.
Closed	15 November-15 December.
Directions	From A7, exit at Cavaillon for St Rémy for 10km, then left for Eygalières. Mas on route Jean Moulin (dir. Orgon), opposite Chapelle St Sixte.

Albine & Maurice Roumanille
Quartier St Sixte, 13810 Eygalières,
Bouches-du-Rhône

Tel	+33 (0)4 90 95 92 61
Fax	+33 (0)4 90 90 61 75
Email	contact@masdupastre.com
Web	www.masdupastre.com

Mas de la Rabassière

Fanfares of lilies at the door, Haydn inside and Michael smiling in his chef's apron – Rabassière means 'where truffles are found' – his Epicurean dinners are a must. Wines from the neighbouring vineyard, and a sculpted dancer, also grace his terrace table. Cookery classes using home-produced olive oil, jogging companionship and airport pick-ups are all part of his unflagging hospitality, always with the help of Thévi, his serene Singaporean assistant. Michael was posted to France by a multi-national, soon became addicted, and on his retirement slipped into this unusually lush corner of Provence. The proximity of the canal keeps everything green: play on a croquet lawn, walk through a grassy olive grove or sit in the garden with masses of orange roses everywhere. Big bedrooms and drawing room are classically comfortable in English country-house style: generous beds, erudite books, a tuned piano, fine etchings and oils, Provençal antiques. Come savour this charmingly generous house and sample Michael's homemade croissants and fig jam under the wisteria-covered veranda.

Price	€125. Singles €75.
Rooms	2 doubles. Extra beds.
Meals	Breakfast included.
	Dinner with wine, €40;
	book ahead for 1st evening.
Closed	Rarely.
Directions	From A54 exit 13 to Grans on D19; right on D16 to St Chamas; just before r'way bridge, left for Cornillon, up hill 2km; house on right before tennis court. Map sent on request.

	Michael Frost
	Route de Cornillon, 13250 Saint Chamas,
	Bouches-du-Rhône
Tel	+33 (0)4 90 50 70 40
Fax	+33 (0)4 90 50 70 40
Email	michaelfrost@rabassiere.com
Web	www.rabassiere.com

Ateliers de l'Image

If you've slept under one too many flouncy coverlets with fabric-lined walls to match, here is a version of a top-class hotel with, as the brochure says, "quality service without the la-di-da". The young staff may wear black T-shirts with the name of the hotel inscribed upon it, but they all seem to swim in their element and the smiles are genuine. Curiously, Philippe opened his first tiny hotel and a black and white film processing lab at the same time – thus bringing together his twin passions. People thought him quite mad, but the idea caught on and the place filled. Some came solo, some came in groups and brought their tutors with them, delighted to find such a friendly and favourable environment in which to learn new techniques. The Ateliers is just a bigger, grown-up version of that first tiny seed. The huge park that hides behind this centre-of-town hotel will save your sanity in the summer; a morning's meditation in a treehouse off one of the bedrooms will cure your soul. A photo gallery, taï chi, organic risotto, sushi… Philippe is a young man with a vision.

Price	€165-€380. Suites €300-€600.
Rooms	32: 26 doubles, 5 suites (1 for 4-5), 1 suite with treehouse.
Meals	Breakfast €19. Lunch & dinner €22-€65.
Closed	January/February.
Directions	A7 exit Cavaillon to St Rémy de Provence, centre ville. Main road through town on right.

Philippe Goninet
36 boulevard Victor Hugo,
13210 Saint Rémy de Provence, Bouches-du-Rhô

Tel	+33 (0)4 90 92 51 50
Fax	+33 (0)4 90 92 43 52
Email	info@hotelphoto.com
Web	www.hotelphoto.com

Mas du Vigueirat

A small pool cascading into a larger pool, wisteria and honeysuckle, a walled garden with quiet corners, nothing to disturb the view but meadows, woods and grazing horses. You'll find it hard to leave this tranquil, scented spot although St Rémy – with its galleries and Van Gogh museum – is but three kilometres. Arles, Avignon, the lavender fields and olive groves of Baux de Provence are not much further. High plane trees flank the drive to this dusky pink, blue-shuttered Provençal farmhouse. Inside all is light, simplicity, gentle elegance. Bedrooms are uncluttered spaces of bleached colours, limed walls and terracotta tiled floors. Views are over the garden or meadows while ground floor 'Maillane' has a private terrace. The high-beamed dining room/salon is a calm, white space with a corner cosy with sofas and books. If the weather's warm you'll breakfast outside under the plane tree. After a dip in the pool and a doze over your book, enjoy one of Catherine's delicious lunches freshly made from the vegetable garden. No suppers, but the helpful Jeanniards will recommend local restaurants.

Price	€115–€155.
	Suite (only available Jul & Aug) €185.
Rooms	4: 3 doubles, 1 suite.
Meals	Breakfast included. Picnic available.
	Poolside meals in summer €15–€20.
	Restaurants nearby.
Closed	Christmas.
Directions	From Lyon A7 exit Avignon Sud to Noves. In St Rémy, right at 5th r'bout to Maillane. After 3km, right at sign for pepinières.

Catherine Jeanniard
Chemin du Grand Bourbourel, Route de Maillane,
13210 Saint Rémy de Provence, Bouches-du-Rhône

Tel	+33 (0)4 90 92 56 07
Fax	+33 (0)4 90 26 79 52
Email	contact@mas-du-vigueirat.com
Web	www.mas-du-vigueirat.com

Entry 331 Map 16

Mas de Cornud

Guest house, cookery school and wine courses combine in a typical farmhouse where two majestic plane trees stand guard over the boules pitch and the scents and light of Provence hover. Nito, chef and nature-lover, cares about how colour creates feeling, how fabrics comfort: she and David, the sommelier, have done a superb restoration. Discover hangings from Kashmir, old French tiles, a piano you may play, and bedrooms big and varied, warm and simple. The atmosphere is convivial and open: you are a member of a family here, so join the others at the honesty bar, choose a cookbook to drool over, take a dip in the cool pool. The kitchen is the vital centre of Cornud: here you eat if the weather is poor (otherwise the garden has some lovely spots). And there are cookery lessons for the enthusiastic: the country kitchen has granite work stations, wood-fired and spit-roast ovens. Direct from artisan suppliers come olive oils and cheeses; the garden provides herbs, vegetables and fruits. Come and be part of Provence. *Two night minimum stay . Children over 12 welcome. Credit cards accepted via PayPal only.*

Price	€140-€220. Suite €240-€395.
Rooms	6: 5 doubles, 1 suite for 2-5.
Meals	Breakfast included.
	Picnic €40 with wine. Lunch €21-€35.
	Hosted dinner €55-€65.
Closed	November-week before Easter.
Directions	3km west of St Rémy de Provence on D99 towards Tarascon. D27 for Les Baux 1km, then left at sign for Mas de Cornud on D31.

David & Nitockrees Tadros Carpita
Petite Route des Baux (D31),
13210 Saint Rémy de Provence, Bouches-du-Rhôr

Tel	+33 (0)4 90 92 39 32
Fax	+33 (0)4 90 92 55 99
Email	mascornud@cs.com
Web	www.mascornud.com

Le Mas des Carassins

You'll be charmed by the gentle pink tiles and greige shutters of the *mas* turned hotel, which settles so gently into the greenery surrounding it. The garden is massive and bursts with oleanders, lavender and lemons. Carefully tended patches of lawn lead to a pool and barbecue; after a swim, pétanque and badminton to play. Or spin off on bikes – charming St Rémy is at the end of the peaceful road. This is Van Gogh country (he lived for a time nearby) and an ancient land: the hotel lies within the preserved area of the Roman town of Glanum. In the pretty dining room, oil paintings by a friend add a splash to white walls, while meals are a fine feast of market produce accompanied by excellent local wines. Bedrooms are dreamy, washed in smoky-blue or ochre shades; dark wrought-iron beds are dressed in oatmeal linens and white quilts; those on the ground floor open to small gardens or wooden decks. The young owners have thought of everything: pick-up from the airport or train, car rental, tickets for local events. Perfect. *Unsupervised pool. Spa opens in 2008. Children over 12 welcome.*

Price	€99–€144. Suites €144.
Rooms	14: 12 twins/doubles, 2 suites.
Meals	Breakfast €11.50.
	Dinner €28 (except Fridays).
	Half board €25.50.
	Restaurants 5-minute walk.
Closed	January-March.
Directions	From St Rémy de Provence centre, over Canal des Alpilles on Ave Van Gogh, then right into Ave J. d'Arbaud. Hotel entrance on left after 180m.

Michel Dimeux & Pierre Ticot
1 chemin Gaulois,
13210 Saint Rémy de Provence, Bouches-du-Rhône

Tel	+33 (0)4 90 92 15 48
Fax	+33 (0)4 90 92 63 47
Email	info@hoteldescarassins.com
Web	www.hoteldescarassins.com

Hôtel Gounod Ville Verte

Madame and Monsieur Maurin are experienced and enthusiastic hoteliers, and are right to be proud of this latest project. Hotel Gounod is at the very centre of the lively artistic town of St Rémy. It takes its name from the composer Charles Gounod, who wrote the opera *Mireille* here in 1863. Gounod informs the theme of the whole place: each of the 34 bedrooms – discovered through a labyrinth of corridors – has been decorated to represent a phase of the composer's life. His music plays softly in the comfortable communal areas and in the loos, and a statue of the Virgin Mary reflects his religious leanings. The effect is theatrical, colourful, diverting and at times marvellously eccentric, bordering on the kitsch. Beds are voluptuous. Brightly painted mannequins are dotted here and there. Some of the rooms look out onto the garden, an oasis of calm where you can laze by the pool, surrounded by palm trees. For a gastronomic treat, pad over to the salon de thé, where Madame Maurin – an excellent patissière – serves her masterful creations beneath the wooden-beamed ceiling.

Price	€125–€185. Suites & duplex €215–€230.
Rooms	34: 20 doubles (10 with terrace), 10 twins, 3 suites for 3, 1 duplex.
Meals	Breakfast included. Tea room snacks from €11.
Closed	Christmas & New Year; mid-February–mid-March.
Directions	A7 exit Cavaillon to St Rémy, follow signs for centre ville. On main square opp. church.

Monsieur & Madame Maurin
18 place de la République,
13210 Saint Rémy de Provence, Bouches-du-Rhô
Tel   +33 (0)4 90 92 06 14
Fax   +33 (0)4 90 92 56 54
Email   contact@hotel-gounod.com
Web   www.hotel-gounod.com

Hôtel Le Cadran Solaire

A soft clear light filters through the house, the light of the south pushing past the smallish windows and stroking Sophie Guilmet's light-handed, rich-pastelled décor where simple Provençal furniture, stencil motifs and natural materials – cotton, linen, organdy and seagrass – give the immediate feel of a well-loved family home. The simplicity of a pastel slipcover over a chair, a modern wrought-iron bed frame and a white piqué quilt is refreshing and restful – and the house stays deliciously cool in the summer heat. The solid old staging post has stood here, with its thick walls, for 400 years, its face is as pretty as ever, calmly set in its gentle garden of happy flowers where guests can always find a quiet corner for their deckchairs. You can have (superb) breakfast on the shrubby, sun-dappled terrace, under a blue and white parasol, or in the attractive dining room where a fine big mirror overlooks the smart red-on-white tables. A wonderful atmosphere, relaxed, smiling staff all of whom are family. And really good value.

Price	€60–€80.
Rooms	12: 8 doubles, 4 twins.
Meals	Breakfast €8. Restaurants in village.
Closed	November March, except by arrangement.
Directions	A7 exit Avignon Sud for Chateaurenard. D28 to Graveson; signed.

Sophie Guilmet
5 rue du Cabaret Neuf, 13690 Graveson,
Bouches-du-Rhône

Tel	+33 (0)4 90 95 71 79
Fax	+33 (0)4 90 90 55 04
Email	cadransolaire@wanadoo.fr
Web	www.hotel-en-provence.com

Hôtel Mas Vidau

A proper family-run hotel, on the edge of some lovely countryside with a south-facing garden and views to the Alpilles – the hiking is fabulous. André, who was born here, has tackled the restoration with friends and his partner is an architect so there's a stylish feel, too… soft fabrics, warm colours and antiques from brocantes that have been made into bedside tables and unusual lamps. The hallway has a stone floor and is decorated with André's paintings in strong, southern colours: the head of a bull or a horse. A stone staircase with iron railings leads to colour-themed bedrooms, uncluttered with little sitting areas and a rustic feel. Delightful bathrooms are marble tiled, some with old stonework exposed, others with basin supports made from recycled wood. On fine days you breakfast in the peaceful walled garden with its small pool and running fountain; perhaps under the shady pergola, redolent with jasmine. St Rémy is near, but nip out the back door and you're in the small town with its daily market. Perfect.

Price	€50–€100.
Rooms	8: 5 doubles, 3 family rooms for 3.
Meals	Breakfast €8. Lunch €15–€32. Restaurants in village.
Closed	Rarely.
Directions	From Arles N570, then D99 towards St Rémy. Hotel in centre.

André Raffy
Impasse André Vidau,
13103 Saint Etienne du Grès,
Bouches-du-Rhône
Tel   +33 (0)4 90 47 63 71
Email   anraffy@wanadoo.fr
Web   www.masvidau.free.fr

Hotel
Provence – Alps – Riviera

Mas de l'Oulivié

Having fallen in love with the olive groves, lavender fields and chalky white hillsides of Les Baux de Provence, the family built the hotel of their dreams some years ago: a creamy-fronted, almond green-shuttered, Provence-style structure, roofed with reclaimed terracotta tiles, landscaped with cypress and oleander. The owners' taste is impeccable, and every last detail has been carefully crafted, from the locally made oak furniture to the homemade tiles round the pool. And what a pool! It is curvaceous and landscaped, with a jacuzzi and a gentle slope for little ones. Furnishings are fresh, local, designed for deep comfort. Bedrooms are creamy-coloured, country-style with an elegant twist. The bar/living-room has a rustic fireplace, filled with flowers in the summer. The Achards love to provide guests and their children with the very best and that includes a superb new massage room and lunches by the pool; they also sell their own lavender and oil. One of the *crème de la crème* of Provence's small, modern country hotels.

Price	€105–€260. Suites €305–€430.	
Rooms	27: 16 doubles, 7 triples, 2 quadruples, 2 suites.	
Meals	Breakfast €13. Poolside lunch €7–€36. Restaurants in village.	
Closed	Mid-November–mid-March.	
Directions	From north A7 exit 24 for St Rémy de Provence and Les Baux. Mas 2km from Les Baux on D78 towards Fontvieille.	

Emmanuel & Isabelle Achard
Les Arcoules, 13520 Les Baux de Provence,
Bouches-du-Rhône

Tel	+33 (0)4 90 54 35 78
Fax	+33 (0)4 90 54 44 31
Email	contact@masdeloulivie.com
Web	www.masdeloulivie.com

Entry 337 Map 16

Mas des Comtes de Provence

Homesick for the south of France and looking for a life change after a frenetic professional career in Paris, Pierre fell for this historic hunting lodge and has settled in nicely after a huge restoration. The *mas* belonged to King René whose château is just up the road; some say the Germans blocked the underground tunnel that connected the two buildings. A massive, soberly elegant stone exterior dating from the 15th century protects the big interior courtyard overlooked by grey-green shuttered windows. The rooms are regal and awesomely huge – the Royal suite measures a nice 100m². 'Roi René' is in tones of ivory, brown and beige; 'Garance' in brick and yellow; ironwork chairs and side tables add interest. The huge pool heated by the Provence sun is well hidden in the two-hectare park dominated by ancient plane trees and olives, cypresses and roses. Pierre and Elisabeth may prepare a barbecue here, serving generous pre-dinner snacks to the adults while feeding the children. Canoeing, hiking, cycling, riding – all are just minutes away. Brilliant for families. *Ask about quilt-making courses.*

Price	€130–€200. Suites €225–€380. Special high season offers.
Rooms	9: 6 twins/doubles, 3 suites for 4-6.
Meals	Breakfast €12.50. Lunch €25. Dinner with aperitif & coffee €40. Book ahead.
Closed	Never.
Directions	Tarascon towards Arles on D35 'Petite Route d'Arles'. 200m after leaving Tarascon, take small road on left. Mas 600m on left.

Pierre Valo & Elisabeth Ferriol
Petite Route d'Arles, 13150 Tarascon,
Bouches-du-Rhône

Tel	+33 (0)4 90 91 00 13
Fax	+33 (0)4 90 91 02 85
Email	valo@mas-provence.com
Web	www.mas-provence.com

La Bastide de Boulbon

The opening shot is up a tiny, quiet village street and through a wrought-iron gate, then you pan from the large garden bursting with roses to a medieval château, an old mill and the Montagnette hills, a ramblers' paradise. The main actors, Gilles and Hervé, have been working hard behind the scenes to renovate this lovely bastide; it is 19th century, as are the stone fountain, the music kiosk, the old plane trees. The entrance hall is perfect: pale tones of grey and white, a splash of red on the far wall, a few Empire-style, velvety armchairs and a throw of antique carpets on the tiled floor. The dining room walls are covered in red silk brocade and show off a large still-life Flemish style painting. There is a veranda, a small salon with marine oil paintings and a beautiful staircase leading to the good-sized bedrooms, all with superb bathrooms and views on the garden. Be prepared to indulge; meals are prepared from fresh local produce; perhaps a pot au feu of fish and vegetables and always delicious homemade desserts. The scene is set, ready for a luxurious, calm relaxing stay.

Price	€85–€145.
Rooms	10: 5 doubles, 5 twins/doubles.
Meals	Breakfast €12. Dinner from €30.
Closed	15 November–15 December; 15 January–28 February.
Directions	Between Avignon and Tarascon, D35 to Barbentane then Boulbon. Signed.

Gilles Tiberghien & Hervé Le Seac'h
Rue de l'Hôtel de Ville, 13150 Boulbon,
Bouches-du-Rhône

Tel   +33 (0)4 90 93 11 11
Fax   +33 (0)4 90 97 04 01
Email contact@labastidedeboulbon.com
Web   www.labastidedeboulbon.com

Hostellerie du Val de Sault

This landscape has been called "a sea of corn gold and lavender blue": from your terrace here you can contemplate the familiar shape of Mont Ventoux, the painter's peak, beyond. The charming, communicative Yves has gathered all possible information, knows everyone there is to know on the Provence scene and is full of good guidance. He creates menus featuring truffles or lavender or spelt, or game with mushrooms for the autumn perfectly served in the formal atmosphere of the light, airy restaurant. And… children can eat earlier, allowing the adults to savour their meal in peace. Perched just above the woods in a big garden, this is a modern building of one storey; wooden floors and pine-slatted walls bring live warmth, colour schemes are vibrant, storage is excellent; baths in the suites have jets. Each room feels like a very private space with its terrace (the suites have room for loungers on theirs): the pool, bar and restaurant are there for conviviality; the fitness room, tennis court and boules pitch for exercise; the jacuzzi space for chilling out. *Ask for room with a view.*

Price	€120-€139. Suites €149-€173. Apartments €195-€205. Half-board approx. €135 p.p.
Rooms	20: 11 doubles, 5 suites for 4, 4 apartments for 2 (no kitchen).
Meals	Breakfast €12. Lunch & dinner €39-€45. Half-board only, May-Sept. Restaurant occasionally closed for lunch.
Closed	November-Easter.
Directions	D1 Col des Abeilles for Sault for 30km, then for St Trinit & Fourcalquier. After big bend, left by fire station. 1km on.

Yves Gattechaut
Route de St Trinit, Ancien chemin d'Aurel,
84390 Sault, Vaucluse

Tel	+33 (0)4 90 64 01 41
Fax	+33 (0)4 90 64 12 74
Email	valdesault@aol.com
Web	www.valdesault.com

Villa Noria

The garden sets the scene, an exclusive enclave of mature cedars, palms, cherries, roses and manicured lawn. Within the garden is an elegant 18th-century house, run by a couple who speak three languages with ease and look after guests with immaculate professionalism. Madame greets you, then ushers you up the stone farmhouse stair to beautiful bedrooms decorated in Provençal style, the finest on the first floor. Smooth floors are cool underfoot, walls are polished with pigmented wax (cerise, blue, raspberry), overheads are beamed, beds opulently swathed in white linen and bathrooms boldly, diagonally tiled. You breakfast in an elegant, wraparound conservatory where fauteuils are dressed in red and white checks and the long oval dining table sits beneath a huge weeping fern. In summer you're under the trees. Noria rests on the edge of the peaceful village of Modène, near several burgeoning villas, and the views sweep over vineyards to mountains beyond; recline by the saltwater pool on a handsome wooden lounger and drink them in. For urban evacuees, a stylish retreat. *No credit cards.*

Price	€50–€110. Suite €90–€150.
Rooms	5: 3 doubles, 1 twin, 1 suite for 3.
Meals	Breakfast included. Hosted dinner €35. Restaurant 1.5km.
Closed	Never.
Directions	D974; Carpentras to Bedoin; after 7.5km, left onto D84 to Modène. On left on entrance to village, signed.

Phillipe & Isabel Monti
84330 Modène, Vaucluse

Tel	+33 (0)4 90 62 50 66
Fax	+33 (0)4 90 62 50 66
Email	post@villa-noria.com
Web	www.villa-noria.com

Hôtel Burrhus

In the busy market square, squeezed between a café and an art gallery, this French southern building, pale faced and many shuttered, holds ultra-modern surprises. Terracotta steps run up to the first floor where everything happens: reception, lounge, breakfast room, all filled with interest from artists' exhibits – and you can thumb through a superb collection of books on art. This minimalist, industrial feel continues into the breakfast room with white walls and white chairs – some Starck-transparent – and large windows that open onto a terrace. Here, two huge plane trees give shade and you can eat breakfast on fine days as you watch the market square below. Bedrooms, down long corridors lined with seagrass, vary in size and position (those at the back are the quietest); all have a serene modern feel with blocks of vibrant colour and unusual headboards; mosaic'd bathrooms are excellent. Discover the lovely medieval town behind you, find vineyards for wine tasting and olive oil producers, stride into the Rhône valley for fabulous walking. Refreshing, hospitable, good value. *TVs on request.*

Price	€46–€82. Suite €100–€115.
Rooms	38: 37 twins/doubles, 1 suite for 4.
Meals	Restaurants walking distance.
Closed	Rarely.
Directions	From Avignon A7 exit 22 for Vaison La Romaine. Follow signs for centre ville.

Monsieur & Madame Gurly
1 place Monfort,
84110 Vaison la Romaine, Vaucluse

Tel	+33 (0)4 90 36 00 11
Fax	+33 (0)4 90 36 39 05
Email	info@burrhus.com
Web	www.burrhus.com

Château de Massillan

In a dreamy castle with two fat towers at either end, the beautiful Diane de Poitiers was installed by her long-time lover Henry II. Now you can roam the same walled gardens, drift off to sleep in the same huge rooms, gaze on the same lovely views. The proportions are unchanged, the interiors are transformed; the owners are professional designers. It is, naturally, dazzling. A cluster of individual bedrooms is a brilliant mix of exquisite antiques and brave modern pieces, bathrooms have luscious toiletries and oversized limestone sinks, there are views from every shuttered window and two rooms have large terraces overlooking a courtyard with sunlight-dappled tables and a cool contemporary fountain. A spectacular winter garden (just one wall) is furnished with armchairs and giant mirrors; a chandeliered dining room is the background for international cuisine and elegant wines. Formal gardens and a 19th-century walled kitchen garden lead to acres of parkland; lurking in a protected corner is a pool where the beau monde reclines on wooden steamer chairs. *Soft-top cars for hire.*

Price	€185–€450. Suite €625.
Rooms	13: 12 doubles, 1 suite.
Meals	Breakfast €16. Lunch €30. Dinner €48–€130.
Closed	Rarely.
Directions	From A7 exit 19 Bollène; at r'bout D8 for Nyons, Carpentras 2km; left on D994 for Nyon, Vaison La Romaine for 1.5km; right on D12 towards Uchaux for 10km to Les Farjons, signed opposite church on right. 1km to château.

Birgit Israel
Chemin Hauteville,
84100 Uchaux, Vaucluse

Tel +33 (0)4 90 40 64 51
Fax +33 (0)4 90 40 63 85
Email chateau-de-massillan@wanadoo.fr
Web www.chateau-de-massillan.com

Les Florets

The setting is magical, the greeting from the Bernard family is from-the-heart warm and the walks are outstanding. Les Florets sits just below the majestic Dentelles de Montmirail – a small range of mountains crested with long, delicate fingers of white stone in the middle of Côtes du Rhône country. Over 40km of paths wind through here so appetites build and are satiated on the splendid terrace under the branches of plane, chestnut, maple, acacia and linden trees; the low stone walls are dressed with impatiens and hydrangeas (and the peonies were blooming in March!). You'll also be sampling some of the wines that the family has been producing since the 1880s. Bright blue and yellow corridors lead to rooms which are simply and florally decorated; all have big tiled bathrooms. We liked the tiny 50s reception desk dressed with a huge bouquet from the garden; a wonderful ceramic *soupière* brightens one corner, a scintillating collection of delicate glass carafes stands in another. Book well ahead, people return year after year.

Price	€95–€130. Apartment €125–€150.
Rooms	15: 14 doubles, 1 apartment for 2-4 in annexe (without kitchen).
Meals	Breakfast €13. Lunch & dinner €27–€42. Restaurant closed Wednesday April-October; Monday evenings & Tuesdays November-Dec.
Closed	January-March.
Directions	From Carpentras, D7 for Vacqueyras. Right on D7 to Gigondas for 2km. Signed.

M & Mme Bernard
Route des Dentelles,
84190 Gigondas, Vaucluse

Tel	+33 (0)4 90 65 85 01
Fax	+33 (0)4 90 65 83 80
Email	accueil@hotel-lesflorets.com
Web	www.hotel-lesflorets.com

Château Juvenal

From the entrance hall, peep through the double doorways at the sitting and dining rooms on either side. Stunning! With two glorious lit chandeliers reflecting in the gilt-edged mirrors at each end of this long reception suite, you are transported back a couple of centuries. Surely the chamber orchestra will be tuning up any minute for a post-prandial concert with notes floating among the exquisite period furniture, high ceilings, tall windows. Yet this 19th-century gem is lived in and loved on a daily basis, thanks to delightful Anne-Marie and Bernard who also produce an award winning wine and delicious olive oil from their 250 trees. The traditional bedrooms are all on the first floor and range from cosy to spacious: Iris, the smallest in pure white and grey; Cerise, larger, with deep pink spread; Raisin with Louis XIII chairs and marble-top dresser; Les Genêts, sunny yellow with a roll top bath. Grab your shopping basket and visit the local market, there is a summer kitchen next to the pool. There are wine visits, a pony for the kids, annual tango events, a spa and two lovely apartments for longer stays.

Price	€90-€140. Suite €100-€160. Apartments €800-€1,200 per week.
Rooms	4 + 2: 1 double, 2 twins/doubles, 1 family suite for 3-4. 2 apartments for 6-7
Meals	Breakfast included. Hosted dinner twice weekly, €36 with wine.
Closed	Never.
Directions	From Carpentras for Vaison La Romaine, Malaucène on D938 for 8km. Left to D21, towards Baumes de Venise for 700m; right just before the cemetery in Saint Hippolyte.

Anne-Marie & Bernard Forestier
Chemin du Long Serre,
84330 Saint Hippolyte le Graveyron,
Vaucluse

Tel	+33 (0)4 90 62 31 76
Email	chateau.juvenal@wanadoo.fr
Web	www.chateau-en-provence.com

Le Château de Mazan

The father and uncle of the Marquis de Sade were born here – an unexpected connection, given the luminosity of the place. Though the infamous Marquis preferred Paris, he often stayed at Mazan and organized France's first theatre festival here in 1772. The château is in a charming village at the foot of Mont Ventoux. Ceilings are lofty, floors are tiled in white-and-terracotta squares that would drown a smaller space, windows are huge with the lightest of curtains. This is a family hotel, despite its size, and Frédéric, who speaks good English, ensures you settle in. His mother, Danièle, is in charge of décor – each room an ethereal delight; pale pink walls, a velvet settee, a touch of apricot taffeta, or a flash of red. Ground-floor bedrooms have French windows opening to a private sitting area; two rooms in the house next door have terraces. There are palms outside, posies within, and secluded spots in the garden – doze in the shade of the mulberry trees. There's a large terrace for dinner; the chef has worked in Michelin-starred restaurants and is keen to win his own. An exquisite hotel.

Price	€98–€275. Suites €320–€400.
Rooms	31: 14 doubles, 14 family rooms for 3-4, 3 suites for 4.
Meals	Breakfast €15. Lunch & dinner from €35. Restaurant closed Tues (also Mon out of season).
Closed	January-February.
Directions	In Carpentras for Sault & Ventoux then Mazan. In Mazan, 1st right near Mairie, then left. Signed.

Danièle & Frédéric Lhermie
Place Napoleon,
84380 Mazan, Vaucluse

Tel	+33 (0)4 90 69 62 61
Fax	+33 (0)4 90 69 76 62
Email	reservation@chateaudemazan.com
Web	www.chateaudemazan.fr

Château du Martinet

Although Napoleon could hardly have slept in this magnificent château – it was built in 1712, burned down during the French Revolution, and rebuilt only in 1846 – one can almost see his ghost, legs stretched out before a blazing fire in the 18th-century salon, sipping a well-aged cognac named in his honour. Dutch Ronald and French Françoise left busy lives in Holland to move into and lovingly revive this superb, listed monument, set in a vast, heavily treed parkland. Their dedication shows in their friendly, sincere welcome, and in their choice of elegant decoration and 18th- and 19th-century antiques. High ceilings, tall windows and subtle colours create a light, gracious and airy feel, while special touches abound: a marble ionic column here, a tapestry there, an exquisite wood-panelled ceiling with leather insets in the dining room, sumptuous chandeliers and gilt-edged mirrors throughout. Bedrooms are luxurious; colours range from fuchsia to soft blue. Outside are swimming pool, tennis court, pétanque and a fitness run; inside, elegance, tradition and refined opulence. Special.

Price	€190–€295. Suite €260. Cottages €900–€1,100 per week.
Rooms	5 + 2: 2 doubles, 2 twins, 1 suite for 2-3. 2 cottages for 2-3.
Meals	Breakfast included. Pool lunches €15–€20. Hosted dinner, with wine, €35–€45; book ahead. Restaurant 3km.
Closed	January-February.
Directions	A7 exit Orange Sud or Avignon Nord to Carpentras; D942 for Sault/Mazan. 2km after r'bout leaving Carpentras, château on left at bend.

Françoise & Ronald de Vries
Route de Mazan,
84200 Carpentras, Vaucluse

Tel	+33 (0)4 90 63 03 03
Fax	+33 (0)4 90 30 78 96
Email	contact@chateau-du-martinet.fr
Web	www.chateau-du-martinet.fr

Domaine Le Vallon

Standing on the doorstep of the little château all you hear is the wind ruffling the majestic trees and distant tractor rumble. Just three bedrooms here: one deep orange with high ceilings, another cream with a canopied bed, another with oeil de boeuf windows; plus a separate spacious apartment with kitchen available for weekly rental. All come sprinkled with choice antiques, prints and interesting etchings; floors are sweeping ancient parquet or terracotta, bathrooms are large and well-stocked. Dutch Fred and French Michèle are lovely hosts living their dream and with three languages between them conversation flows. Dinner is *grande gastronomie*: Michèle's cooking is a treat, delectable wines from Fred's cellar are poured into engraved glasses, cookery courses are planned. Breakfast is a relaxed affair; in winter on the glass-covered veranda, in summer at pretty little tables outside. Warm scents (rosemary, jasmine, thyme), crisp lawns, an orangerie, roses and a curved seat for two, a 'bassin' pool and a summer kitchen. Beyond, two hectares of vines and all of Provence.

Price	€130–€200.
	Apartment €1,500 per week.
Rooms	3 + 1: 3 twins/doubles. 1 apartment.
Meals	Breakfast included. Restaurant 300m.
	Occasional hosted dinner with wine, €60.
Closed	November-February.
Directions	From Lyon A7 exit Bollène, D7/D8 to Carpentras. 1km after Aubignan, sharp left opposite sign "Cuisine St. Luc". Follow Chemin de Serres 600m, through the crossroads. Le Vallon 700m on left.

Michèle & Fred Vogt
Chemin de Serres,
84810 Aubignan, Vaucluse

Tel	+33 (0)4 90 62 71 27
Fax	+33 (0)8 26 42 45 14
Email	vogt@vallon-provence.com
Web	www.vallon-provence.com

Château Talaud

Lavish and elegant – a stunning place and lovely people. Hein has a wine export business, Conny gives her whole self to her house and her guests. Among ancient vineyards and wonderful green lawns – an oasis in Provence – the ineffably gracious 18th-century château speaks of a long-gone southern way of life. Enter and you will feel it has not entirely vanished. Restored to a very high standard, the finely proportioned rooms have been furnished with antiques, many of them family pieces, and thick, luxurious fabrics. Windows reach from floor to ceiling and frame a stand of plane trees or fine landscaping. The big bedrooms mix old and new (Directoire armchairs, featherweight duvets) with consummate taste and bathrooms are old-style hymns to modernity. The pool is an adapted 17th-century irrigation tank: one goes through an arch to the first, shallow cistern, leading to a deeper pool beyond – ingenious. Guests may laze in the lovely gardens and listen to the caged love birds, but Conny is happy to help you plan visits in this fascinating area. An exceptionally fine, well-kept guest house.

Price	€175–€210. Apartments & cottage €1,350–€1,550 per week. (Cottage min. 2 weeks in July/Aug.)
Rooms	5 + 3. 3 doubles, 2 suites Cottage for 5, 2 apartments for 2.
Meals	Breakfast included. Dinner twice weekly, €45. Book ahead.
Closed	1–13 January; 17 February–3 March; 15–31 December.
Directions	D950 for Carpentras; at r'bout at Loriol du Comtat right on D107 for Monteux. 500m, small sign on right 'Talaud' marks road to Château.

Conny & Hein Deiters-Kommer
D107, 84870 Loriol du Comtat,
Vaucluse

Tel	+33 (0)4 90 65 71 00
Fax	+33 (0)4 90 65 77 93
Email	chateautalaud@infonie.fr
Web	www.chateautalaud.com

Hostellerie Château des Fines Roches

Only a marquis with a name like Falco de Baroncelli Javon could have come up with such an extravagant construction – turrets and towers, crenellations and arches – and build on a fine slope of a hill tumbling now in rows of vines. And the views! The soft rolling Alpilles, Mont Ventoux in its splendour and, on clear days, the Papal Palace in Avignon; an aperitif on the terrace at dusk is pure magic. The feeling is amazingly intimate inside: the little reception tucked under a cathedral-like arch, the stairs winding up the first floor. On the right are a stunning breakfast room and a library – parquet, panelling, books to the ceiling – where the Marquis met with literary personalities of the time; to the left is a dining room with tall windows. In summer, meals are usually served on the terrace. The décor is rustic Provençal, all greys and yellows, beds are mostly painted brass elegantly baldaquin'd, floors are tiled, some in white and blue, every bathroom sports robes and slippers, and the new young owners are planning a room with private access to tower's roof terrace. All this, and Avignon down the road.

Price	€129-€309.
Rooms	11: 10 doubles, 1 twin.
Meals	Breakfast €15-€20.
	Lunch €23-€60. Dinner €35-€80.
	November-April: restaurant closed
	Sun evening & Mon.
Closed	November.
Directions	From Avignon, N1 towards Sorgues;
	left on D17 towards Chateauneuf du
	Pape. Signed.

Monsieur & Madame Zennaro
Departementale 17 (Route de Sorgues),
84230 Châteauneuf du Pape, Vaucluse

Tel	+33 (0)4 90 83 70 23
Fax	+33 (0)4 90 83 78 42
Email	reservation@chateaufinesroches.com
Web	www.chateaufinesroches.com

Hotel

Le Mas des Grès

A jolly party atmosphere pervades in this meticulously restored hotel, where Nina looks after you and Thierry rustles up fine food from an open-plan kitchen; inspiration comes from his Italian grandmother, with a splash of Morocco thrown in. Join in with the preparation or simply saunter down and enjoy it – in the big beamed dining room with chunky terracotta floors. On warm evenings there's the pretty, vine-clad terrace with its twinkling lights and candles, and rustic tables and chairs. Bedrooms are plain and traditional with patchwork covers on firm beds and views over the fields; bathrooms are tiled top to toe and some have superb Italian showers. Nina knows everyone in the area and can whip up almost anything from expert wine tastings of Châteauneuf du Pape to bike trips through the Luberon, trout fishing with the kids and golf at one of the 15 courses in the area. A favourite is a guided nature hike to gather culinary plants and herbs; for collectors of antiques and brocante, L'Isle sur la Sorgue is up the road. Good value, family-friendly. *Cookery courses.*

Price	€85–€125. Suites €125–€145.
Rooms	14: 12 doubles, 2 suites for 4. Some rooms interconnect.
Meals	Breakfast €11. Picnic lunch €15. Buffet lunch €20 (July/August only).
Closed	11 November–15 March.
Directions	A7 Apt/Avignon Sud, D33 for 13km; cross Petit Palais on D24, at T-junc of D901, right to Apt. Hotel at 600m on right.

Nina & Thierry Crovara
Route d'Apt, Lagnes,
84800 Vaucluse

Tel	+33 (0)4 90 20 32 85
Fax	+33 (0)4 90 20 21 45
Email	info@masdesgres.com
Web	www.masdesgres.com

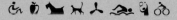

La Bastide de Voulonne

This bastide sits in splendid isolation in the lavender fields stretching beneath the ancient hilltop villages perched on the Luberon mountains. It matches our dream of the perfect Provençal farmhouse. As you swing into the circular driveway, there are ancient plane trees, a spattering of cyprus, tufts of lavender and blue shutters against golden ochre walls. The heart of this 18th-century farm is an inner courtyard where you can breakfast to the soothing sound of the fountain with staircases leading off each corner. The bedrooms (and beds) are huge, done in natural local colours, with tiled or parquet floors. The garden – more like a park – is vast, with a big pool not far from the house. New owners, Penny and Julien have refreshed the herb garden for the kitchen and menus centre round local food; cherries, apricots,pears, figs and raspberries come from their own orchards, After an aperitif with guests, dinner is served at separate tables – or at a communal one – in a big dining hall where the centrepiece is the carefully restored bread oven. A friendly place. *Two-day truffle courses in winter.*

Price	€122–€145. Family suites €175–€258. Family rooms for 3 €152–€168.
Rooms	13: 10 twins/doubles, 3 family suites for 3-5.
Meals	Breakfast €11. Dinner €30.
Closed	Mid-November–December; January/February: open by arrangement only.
Directions	From south exit A7 Cavaillon; at Coustellet, D2 to Gordes for 1km; right directly after white fence of Ets Kerry La Cigalette; 600m on left. Not in the village of Cabrières d'Avignon.

Penny & Julien Hemery
Cabrières d'Avignon,
84220 Gordes, Vaucluse
Tel   +33 (0)4 90 76 77 55
Fax   +33 (0)4 90 76 77 56
Email   contact@bastide-voulonne.com
Web   www.bastide-voulonne.com

Lumani

Minutes from the Pope's Palace and the mythical Pont d'Avignon, tucked into the medieval ramparts, is this handsome, blue-shuttered, 19th-century house. Walk off the street into a cool, lush garden with 100-year old plane trees, hammocks, striped chairs, sculptures, and shady spots for reading or contemplating; it is beautifully designed and blissfully peaceful (just the plashing of a fountain, the chirruping of birds). Inside are light-filled, minimalist rooms with abstract paintings on white or vibrant walls, tiled floors, clever lighting. Bedrooms are just as beautiful and truly restful; all look over the garden. Your hosts, Elisabeth (an artist) and Jean (an architect), encourage creative pursuits: they give you a sound-proofed music studio, provide tours and guidebooks on architecture and art, and offer classes in cookery. Allow them to look after you in the ochre red salon... or you may rent the whole house and do your own cooking. You are in the heart of Provence so explore the lavender fields, stride the hills and visit the delightful villages and their markets. Peaceful, creative, special.

Price	€90–€130. Suites €130–€160. Whole house available.
Rooms	5. 3 twins/doubles, 2 suites for 2-4.
Meals	Breakfast included. Restaurants 3-min walk.
Closed	Mid-November-mid-December; 6-8 January.
Directions	A7 exit north for town centre. Left at ramparts. Right at Café Lazare. Under door of St Lazare, immediately right onto Rempart St Lazare for 200m, signed.

Elisabeth & Jean Béraud-Hirschi
37 rue du Rempart Saint Lazare,
84000 Avignon, Vaucluse

Tel	+33 (0)4 90 82 94 11
Email	lux@avignon-lumani.com
Web	www.avignon-lumani.com

Bastide Le Mourre

Victorine fell in love with this old bastide years before it came on the market. Now she has her little piece of paradise, a blue-shuttered hamlet in the heart of the Luberon encircled by vines, olives, jasmine and roses. Attached to the house are the gîtes: the pigeonnier, the silkworm house, the wine stores, two barns and, at the top of the garden, blissfully secluded and shaded by an ancient oak, the little round Moulin for two. All have their own private entrance and terrace where breakfast is served, all are filled with light and colour, all will delight you. Imagine big sisal rugs on ancient terracotta floors, fine Provençal ceilings and painted wooden doors, open stone fireplaces and whitewashed stone walls, a piqué cotton cover on a baldaquin bed, a dove-grey dresser in a sweet, chic kitchen. Victorine was an interior designer and her love of texture, patina and modern art shines through. The pool is set discreetly on a lower level away from the house, the views will seduce you, the peace is a balm. *Minimum stay three nights.*

Price	€150-€210 (€880-€1,700 per week).
Rooms	6 houses, each with kitchen: 2 for 2, 3 for 4, 1 for 5-6.
Meals	Breakfast €12. Restaurants 5km.
Closed	Rarely.
Directions	Avignon to Apt to Coustellet to Oppède Le Vieux. On route to Oppède Le Vieux, first right Chemin du Mourre. Big house with blue shutters on left.

Victorine Canac
84580 Oppède,
Vaucluse

Tel	+33 (0)4 90 76 99 31
Fax	+33 (0)4 90 76 83 60
Email	lemourre@aol.com
Web	www.lemourre.com

Château La Roque

The first-known stronghold dominating the valley from this craggy lookout held back the Saracens in the eighth century; ceded to the Papal States in the 13th century, it was again an important strategic outpost. In 1741 it settled into peace as a private household. The peace remains blissful, the only interruption coming from the bees buzzing in the acacias; the views remain long and stretch over the floor of the valley. Jean, who knows his history, can tell you (in French) about the golden ratio used to build the castle. Bedrooms are huge, simple, bordering on spartan, but never cold. One has a big deep coral bed under high vaulted ceilings, and two antique chairs as bedside tables. Floors are terracotta, interspersed with polished ochre cement in some rooms. Bathrooms continue the theme: roomy, simple, each with big double basins – on old pedestals or perhaps set on tables. The evening's menu might be monkfish with a saffron sauce on a bed of green asparagus followed by a millefeuille with strawberries and marscarpone served on the vine dappled terrace or below in the garden. *Children over 11 welcome.*

Price	€100–€170. Suites €218–€240.
Rooms	5: 2 doubles, 3 suites.
Meals	Breakfast €15. Dinner €40 (except Sunday). Book ahead.
Closed	Rarely.
Directions	From Lyon, A7 exit Orange Sud for Carpentras; for Pernes les Fontaines; for St Didier; for La Roque 2km.

	Chantal & Jean Tomasino Chemin du Château, 84210 La Roque sur Pernes, Vaucluse
Tel	+33 (0)4 90 61 68 77
Fax	+33 (0)4 90 61 68 78
Email	chateaularoque@wanadoo.fr
Web	www.chateaularoque.com

Le Mas de Garrigon

Christiane, a writer and journalist, settled in the Lubcron after years in Africa, bought the plot of land and built the *mas* from scratch in 1979, using local materials and tailoring the house to the hill. The idea was to build a really special place to stay – each room has its own terrace looking out to the wild beauty of the hills. We don't generally recommend piped music… but the classical music Christiane plays does add to the atmosphere. In palest terracotta with lightest blue shutters, the house sits among cypress, olive and almond trees and is perfect in summer, when you can lounge by the pool, and perfect in winter too, when you can settle down by a crackling fire, maybe with a book from the well-stocked library. Inside is in complete and striking contrast to the muted, natural tones used outside: bedrooms are a joyful riot of reds, yellows and blues. Don't worry: Christiane's mix of bold and simple, traditional and daring is never garish, it all works perfectly. Great welcome, great food.

Price	€105–€145. Family room €145–€180. Half-board mandatory Easter-October, €260–€286.
Rooms	9: 6 doubles, 2 twins, 1 family room for 3.
Meals	Breakfast €16. Picnic lunch available. Lunch & dinner €45. Restaurant closed Mon & Tues, mid-Nov to Dec.
Closed	Rarely.
Directions	From Cavaillon on D2 between Gordes & St Saturnin d'Apt.

Christiane Rech-Druart
Route de St Saturnin d'Apt,
Roussillon en Provence, 84220 Gordes, Vaucluse

Tel	+33 (0)4 90 05 63 22
Fax	+33 (0)4 90 05 70 01
Email	mas.de.garrigon@wanadoo.fr
Web	www.masdegarrigon-provence.com

Le Mas des Romarins

Michel and Pierre bought this hotel – overlooking one of France's most beautiful villages – in May 2002. Forget the buildings on either side: the secluded pool and garden make you feel away from it all and you even have your own private path into town. The fabulous hilltop view of Gordes with its distant misty-blue mountains and surrounding plains encourages you to linger over a delicious buffet breakfast, usually taken on the terrace. Inside, the sitting room is comfortable without being over-lavish and the warmth of the open fire is welcome on days when the Mistral gets up. The bedrooms are done in ochres and smoky rusts to contrast with stone, oatmeal and cream of the two-tone walls. Parisian linens and soft furnishings are combined with traditional cotton prints, and the rooms are quite small but cool, comfortable and quiet; ask for one with a terrace. Four-course table d'hôtes are convivial; otherwise, let them book a restaurant for you and help you explore the local culinary delights (of which there are many) on your own. Easy living, great walking.

Price	€97–€160.
Rooms	13: 10 twins/doubles, 3 quadruples.
Meals	Breakfast €11.50. Dinner €28 (Mon, Wed, Fri & Sat). Restaurants 10-minute walk.
Closed	12 November–16 December; 2 January–11 March.
Directions	From Avignon, east on N7 then left onto N100 for Apt; left to Gordes. Route de Sénanque on left entering Gordes. Hotel 200m on right.

Michel Dimeux & Pierre Ticot
Route de Sénanque,
84220 Gordes, Vaucluse
Tel   +33 (0)4 90 72 12 13
Fax   +33 (0)4 90 72 13 13
Email info@hoteldesromarins.com
Web   www.hoteldesromarins.com

Entry 357 Map 16

Le Clos du Buis

The lovely village of Bonnieux has somehow avoided the crush of unchecked tourism. Le Clos sits up in its old heart, overlooking the town and the surrounding hills. Part of the structure used to be the town bakery; the owners have left the original store front as a reminder. Time and loving care have been given without restraint – Monsieur decided to return to his native village – and everything appears to have been here forever: Provençal country cupboards that reach up to the ceiling, old cement patterned tiles; one stone staircase with a good iron bannister leads up to clean, uncluttered bedrooms, the other down to the garden. One side of the house is 'in' town, the other is open to stunning views of endless hills. Provence is here on all sides, from the green and white checked cotton quilts on the beds to the excellent food served by your host in the yellow ochre dining room. If wine or weather keep you from the hills (good hikes abound), days can be spent browsing the book collection by the big stone hearth in the sitting room. Delightful.

Price	€84–€120.
Rooms	7: 2 doubles, 4 twins/doubles, 1 family room for 3.
Meals	Breakfast included. Dinner €25. Restaurants within walking distance.
Closed	Mid-November–mid-February. Open for Christmas & New Year.
Directions	From Avignon A7 to Aix exit 24; D973 to Cavaillon; left on D22 to Apt 30km; right on D36. In village centre.

Monsieur & Madame Maurin
Rue Victor Hugo,
84480 Bonnieux, Vaucluse

Tel	+33 (0)4 90 75 88 48
Fax	+33 (0)4 90 75 88 57
Email	le-clos-du-buis@wanadoo.fr
Web	www.leclosdubuis.com

Auberge du Presbytère

They say "when the wind blows at Saignon, tiles fly off in Avignon": the Mistral can blow fiercely down from the mountains to the Mediterranean. This fairytale 11th-century village of 100 inhabitants lies deep in the Lubéron hills and lavender fields; the auberge sits deep in Saignon, half hidden behind an ancient tree near the village's statue-topped fountain. Delicious meals are served under this tree, or in a pretty terraced garden, glassed in for the winter months. The bedrooms are simple but truly charming, colourwashed walls, country pieces, no TVs but Roger & Gallet soaps in lovely bathrooms with Italian stone block tiles. In Blue, a huge fireplace and a stone terrace looking out onto the hills... views from some of the rooms are breathless. A log fire burns on chilly days in the informal arched stone sitting area. Gérard, the new, young owner, will be faithful to the spirit of this hotel, and is in love with his new surroundings. A secret, splendid place from which to visit the hill towns. Or if you are fit, rent a bike and follow the cycling signs. Outstanding value.

Price	€58–€145.
Rooms	16: 14 twins/doubles, 2 with separate shower or bath. Some rooms connect.
Meals	Breakfast €9.50. Lunch & dinner €28–€38. Restaurant closed Wed.
Closed	Mid-January–mid-February.
Directions	From Apt N100 to Saignon village. At r'bout with 1 olive & 3 cypress trees to start of village, left lane marked 'riverains' to Place de la Fontaine.

Anne-Cécile & Gerhard Rose
Place de la Fontaine,
84400 Saignon, Vaucluse

Tel	+33 (0)4 90 74 11 50
Fax	+33 (0)4 90 04 68 51
Email	auberge.presbytere@wanadoo.fr
Web	www.auberge-presbytere.com

Auberge de Reillanne

The solid loveliness of this 18th-century house, so typical of the area, reassures you, invites you in. And you will not be disappointed: you'll feel good here, even if you can't quite define the source of the positive energy. Monique clearly has a connection to the spirit of the place and has used all her flair and good taste, making all the curtains and bedcovers herself, to transform the old inn into a very special place to stay. Bedrooms are large and airy, done in cool, restful colours with big cupboards and rattan furniture. There are beams, properly whitewashed walls and books. Bathrooms are big and simple too. Downstairs, the sitting and dining areas are decorated in warm, embracing colours with terracotta tiles, white tablecloths and flame-coloured curtains. This would be a place for a quiet holiday with long meditative walks in the hills, a place to come and write that novel or simply to get to know the gentle, delicate, smiling owner who loves nothing better than to receive people in her magical house. One of our favourites.

Price	€70–€75. Singles €55. Half-board €68 p.p.
Rooms	6: 3 doubles, 3 triples.
Meals	Breakfast €8.50. Dinner €23.
Closed	20 October–March.
Directions	N100 through Apt & Céreste. Approx. 8km after Céreste, left on D214 to Reillanne. Hotel on right.

Monique Balmand
04110 Reillanne,
Alpes-de-Haute-Provence

Tel	+33 (0)4 92 76 45 95
Fax	+33 (0)4 92 76 45 95
Email	monique.balmand@wanadoo.fr
Web	www.auberge-de-reillanne.com

Mas du Pont Roman

A land of treasures: Ligurian *bories* – igloo-like dry-stone huts – squat camouflaged in the landscape; Roman churches sit quietly as if time had not passed; a stunning 12th-century Roman bridge spans the river on the edge of this property, a recently renovated 18th-century mill at the end of tree-lined boulevard on the outskirts of a village. Marion graciously watches over your creature comforts while Christian, a most hospitable and jovial host, knows everybody and everything about the immediate area and the intriguing market town of Forcalquier. The sitting/drawing room, with a crackling fire on cool days, is an ideal spot to enjoy an aperitif before dinner; Christian will help you pick out your restaurant. An indoor swimming pool and two sauna rooms complement the spanking new bedrooms with their stone quarry tiles or parquet floors, pristine tiled bathrooms and soft coloured bedspreads. Beautiful grounds, stunning views, flowing water and an outdoor pool and terrace complete the picture. Organise your nightwatch for shooting star extravaganzas at the nearby St Michel Observatory.

Price	€75–€90.
Rooms	9: 3 doubles, 4 twins, 1 single, 1 family suite for 4.
Meals	Breakfast €8 (included out of season). Light meals available (summer only). Restaurants in village, 2km.
Closed	Rarely.
Directions	From Marseille A51 exit Forcalquier; N100 for Apt 3km. Enter village; left, on right at end of avenue of trees.

Christian & Marion Vial
Chemin de Châteauneuf, 04300 Mane en Provence,
Alpes-de-Haute-Provence

Tel	+33 (0)4 92 75 49 46
Fax	+33 (0)4 92 75 36 73
Email	info@pontroman.com
Web	www.pontroman.com

Villa Morelia

Villa Morelia has a fascinating history: far from isolating themselves in this village deep in the Alps, the inhabitants exported their textile skills first to Flanders, then to the Caribbean and in the 19th century to Mexico, where some 60,000 descendants still live. Many, however, returned and put their money and taste for things foreign to good use, building exotic villas in their valley. With its imposing height, asymmetric façades and coloured chimneys, the Villa Morelia, designed by a renowned Marseilles architect, Eugène Marx, stands out from the rest. Now Robert and Marie-Christine have opened it as a hotel and established an award-winning restaurant. This charming couple know quite a bit about cuisine, music, dogs and a relaxed style of living. You will love everything inside: high airy ceilings, walnut windows and doors, beautiful tiles and big bedrooms which manage the trick of looking both elegant and welcoming. On top of this, you can ski, go rafting or canyoning, the chef comes from the Eden Roc in Antibes and Robert will pick you up if you don't want to drive.

Price	€150–€190. Single €120. Family room €190–€225. Suite €280–€350.
Rooms	10: 4 doubles, 1 single, 2 family rooms for 3, 3 suites.
Meals	Breakfast €18. Picnic lunch available. Dinner €45–€75.
Closed	October–May.
Directions	7km from Barcelonnette on D900 Gap-Cuneo road. In centre of village.

Marie-Christine & Robert Boudard
04850 Jausiers,
Alpes-de-Haute-Provence

Tel	+33 (0)4 92 84 67 78
Fax	+33 (0)4 92 84 65 47
Email	info@villa-morelia.com
Web	www.villa-morelia.com

Entry 362 Map 16

La Bouscatière

If you ever had a dream of dramatic Provence, this must be it. The cliffs rise indomitably, the water tumbles down, the old village looks as if it grew here. This enchanting vertical house, firmly fixed to the rock since 1765, was originally a wood store then an oil mill. Its lowest level, in the village centre, houses the oil press; its highest, seventh level opens through the lush secluded garden with its tiny, ancient chapel (now a delicious bedroom with heavily carved Spanish bed and little terrace) to the top of the village and its perfect Romanesque church. Inside, all is country elegance and supreme comfort against a backdrop of exposed rock, white limewashed walls and original beams. This is a tiny preserved corner of old Provence; all rooms feel as though one is in some time honored and adored family house, with a vase of flowers here, an antique mirror there, and everywhere the scent of lavender and linen dried in the fresh air. The biggest bedroom is pretty grand, another has a tracery alcove, all are softly attractive. Guests are honored friends, to be cared for and spoiled. Perfect.

Price	€115–€190.
Rooms	5: 5 doubles.
Meals	Breakfast €5–€15. Dinner €30–€70, book ahead.
Closed	Rarely.
Directions	A8 from Nice exit 36 to N555 for Draguignan; D557 to Aups. D957 to Moustiers Ste-Marie. Follow road to highest point of village to parking area. Do not drive into village.

Geneviève & Joel Calas
04360 Moustiers Ste Mairie,
Alpes-de-Haute-Provence

Tel   +33 (0)4 92 74 67 67
Fax   +33 (0)4 92 74 65 72
Email   bonjour@labouscatiere.com
Web   www.labouscatiere.com

Le Moulin du Château

A sleepy place – come to doze. Your silence will be broken only by the call of the sparrow-hawk or the distant rumble of a car. This 17th-century olive mill once belonged to the château and stands at the foot of an ancient grove; the vast pressoir is now a reception area where modern art hangs on ancient walls. The Moulin is a long, low, stone building with lavender-blue shutters and the odd climbing vine, and stands in its own gardens surrounded by lavender and fruit trees. In the bedrooms light filters though voile curtains, shadows dance upon the walls. The feel is uncluttered, cool, breezy, with vibrant colours: turquoise, lilac, lime – luminous yet restful. This is an easy-going 'green' hotel where the emphasis is on the simple things of life. Edith and Nicolas use regional and organic food, boules is played under the cherry tree, poppies grow on an old crumbling stone staircase and views stretch across fields to village and château. There are bikes for gentle excursions into the countryside, and further afield are the Cistercian abbey of Le Thoronet, the Verdon Canyon and Digne Les Bains.

Price	€79–€102.
Rooms	10: 5 doubles, 2 twins, 1 quadruple, 1 triple, 1 suite.
Meals	Breakfast €9. Picnics €10. Dinner €32 (not Mon & Thurs). Restaurants nearby.
Closed	2 November–February.
Directions	From Gréoux les Bains D952 until Riez, then D11 for Quinson; head towards St Laurent du Verdon; take road after château. Signed.

Edith & Nicolas Stämpfli-Faoro
04500 Saint Laurent du Verdon,
Alpes-de-Haute-Provence

Tel	+33 (0)4 92 74 02 47
Fax	+33 (0)4 92 74 02 97
Email	info@moulin-du-chateau.com
Web	www.moulin-du-chateau.com

Château de Caféine

Ideal for couples. You and your beloved can simply drink in this unusual delight from architect extraordinaire Juan Valdez: you'll be mugging like mad as you kaffeeklatsch on the roof terrace with like-minded guests; rise early or latte and you'll find the breakfast table laid expressly for you. When it's time for tea you'll find the servings are lavish and you're swimming in hospitality. Some might argue that such establishments spread American-style culture just a little too far – the place appears modelled on the beverages available along those endless aimless US interstate highways – and yet sometimes, surely, each of us feels a need for speed. One quick visit to Château de Caféine will set you racing throughout the rest of your stay in the area with zest and zeal. While you're there, take a walk with the dogs, Cream and Sugar, or ask if you can borrow the horses, Spoon and Saucer. The owner – known simply as Cap – may seem a little jumpy at first, but don't worry. Cap's a good chap, and so's his wife, Ino.

Price	Free refills!
Rooms	None. Nobody sleeps here.
Meals	Plenty of beans to munch on.
Closed	Never.
Directions	From Lyon, exit 36 for Leverlecoude; at r'bout chateau is 300m after large spoon sculpture on left.

Cap & Ino Latte
Chemin de la Tasse,
04589 Leverlecoude,
Alpes-de-Haute-Provence

Email	doppio@latte.cup
Web	www.cuppa-at-home.cube.lait

Une Campagne en Provence

Water gushes and flows throughout the 170-acre estate; springs, streams and rivers abound… in the 12th century the Knights Templar created a myriad of irrigation channels. The stunning bastide keeps its massive fortress-like proportions and bags of character and charm. Martina and Claude love their Campagne and, thanks to their hospitality, it's a huge treat to stay. The main house is arranged around a central patio, with stairs leading up to the bedrooms. Simple Provençal furnishings are lit by huge windows, floors are *terre cuite*, there are cosy 'boutis' quilts and sumptuous towels and linen, and bathrooms are cleverly worked around original features. The well-stocked apartments have knockout views across vineyards or fields; with floors heated in low season, you'll never be chilly. Dinner has the accent on wonderful local produce and their own wine. Restive teenagers can relax in the media room, others may prefer the sauna, Turkish bath or outdoor pool. An isolated paradise for Templar enthusiasts, overseen by a charming young family, two geese and one very old dog.

Building and dry stone walling is carried out in the traditional manner; reclaimed materials - stone, wood, tiles - are used whenever possible; recycled water is directed to the gardens. Apart from achieving an architecturally and environmentally sympathetic restoration, Martina and Claude are to be applauded for their involvement with the organisation Forestavenir; every guest gets to plant a tree and 900 have been planted so far. They are deeply committed to the local sourcing of food and hold cookery courses; the hotel also hosts conferences and seminars on climate change.

Price	€85-€115. Apartments €570-€870 per week.
Rooms	4 + 4: 3 doubles, 1 studio for 2 (without kitchen). 3 apartments for 4, 1 studio for 2.
Meals	Breakfast included. Hosted dinner with wine, €26-€32.
Closed	Rarely.
Directions	A8 Aix-Nice exit St Maximin la Ste Baume; then D28 to Bras. After 9km, follow signs.

Monsieur & Madame Fussler
Domaine le Peyrourier, 83149 Bras, Var

Tel	+33 (0)4 98 05 10 20
Fax	+33 (0)4 98 05 10 21
Email	info@provence4u.com
Web	www.provence4u.com

SPECIAL
GREEN ENTRY
see page 12

Hôtel du Vieux Château

Once a hill fort on the Roman road linking Fréjus to Grenoble, Aiguines, overlooking the Lac de Ste Croix, has never stopped being a place of constant passage. The eye travels unhindered over the lavender-covered Plateau de Valensole towards the blue mountains in the distance. Frédéric, affable and smiley, was born in Aiguines and came home to roost after a busy and peripatetic youth. He is taking his time restoring the hotel, once part of the village's castle. "I want to get it right," he says. Getting it right means no fuss and frills, but a crisp refreshing simplicity. A good sense of colour marries yellow, blue and old rose with Provençal or tartan-patterned curtains, and bathrooms have rich hued Salernes tiles: deep turquoise, royal blue, salmon, grass-green. High rooms at the front have those views over the rooftops to the lake, others catch a glimpse of a castle. Bedrooms at the back, looking over a village street, are naturally quieter and may well be cooler in a searing summer. You are next to the bell tower; ear plugs are provided! A place with 'soul', intrinsically French.

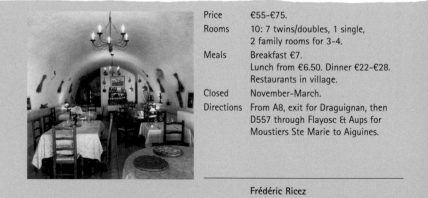

Price	€55–€75.
Rooms	10: 7 twins/doubles, 1 single, 2 family rooms for 3-4.
Meals	Breakfast €7. Lunch from €6.50. Dinner €22-€28. Restaurants in village.
Closed	November–March.
Directions	From A8, exit for Draguignan, then D557 through Flayosc & Aups for Moustiers Ste Marie to Aiguines.

Frédéric Ricez
Place de la Fontaine,
83630 Aiguines, Var

Tel	+33 (0)4 94 70 22 95
Fax	+33 (0)4 94 84 22 36
Email	contact@hotelvieuxchateau.fr
Web	www.hotelvieuxchateau.fr

Les Quatre Saisons

For those hooked on *The Da Vinci Code*, the Sainte Baume mountain range with its walks and legends revolving around Mary Magdalene is an easy drive. Or the hill villages of La Cadière d'Azur and Le Castellet with Templar connections may tempt; but you will rejoice upon your return to this lovingly run hideaway on a hill with its thick walls, warm yellow stone and cooling breezes. Didier and Patrice, with previous lives in the catering and hotel worlds, take superb care of you. Built 20 years ago, with careful recuperation of old doors, beams and stone, the main house and annexe cradle the pool mirroring a more southern architectural tradition. The main house, where winter guests can have pre-dinner drinks, has an impressive sunken circular area round a fireplace and a succession of spacious elegant rooms furnished with good Louis XVIII pieces. All rooms have their own private outdoor sitting area, be it a terrace or small sealed off patio beneath a vine-clad trellis. Care and thoughtfulness, heavenly food: it's a dream of a place. Thor, the French bulldog, welcomes other well-behaved dogs.

Price	€90–€110. Apartment €120–€130 (€700–€750 per week).
Rooms	7 + 1 apartment: 3 doubles, 2 twins, 2 suites for 2. Apartment for 2.
Meals	Breakfast included. Lunch €15–€25. Dinner €33–€35, book ahead.
Closed	15 days in January.
Directions	A50 exit 11 to Le Beausset. Left at big r'about onto D26 to Le Brûlat Castellet. Right after 1.5km, straight on small road until gate. Ring.

Patrice Darras & Didier Marchal
370 Montée des Oliviers,
83330 Le Castellet, Var

Tel	+33 (0)4 94 25 24 90
Email	reservation@lesquatresaisons.org
Web	www.lesquatresaisons.org

Hostellerie Bérard

"It was one of the best meals I have ever had in this region," said our inspector. René is Maître Cuisinier de France, Danièle is a qualified expert in the local wine and their son Jean-François now shines in their bistro, Le Petit Jardin. The emphasis is on Provençal food, using only organic, seasonal produce and herbs from their garden. Madame and Monsieur are true belongers: they grew up in this ancient village, opened in 1969 and have lovingly, respectfully restored this complex of highly evocative buildings: an 11th-century monastery; a blue-shuttered bastide; an old village *maison bourgeoise*; a painter's hideaway. The views from the dining room and the bedrooms are superb: framed visions of olive groves, of vines in their seried choreography and Templar strongholds on mountain tops in the distance. Each is a surprise: a delicate wrought-iron four-poster, with checked counterpane and toile de Jouy curtains is a favourite. Daughter Sandra, full of friendly enthusiasm, handles the day-to-day. A true family affair, bags of atmosphere, culinary delights; it doesn't get much better. *Cookery courses.*

Price	€90–€182. Suites €233–€276.
Rooms	40: 36 doubles, 4 suites for 4.
Meals	Breakfast €19. Lunch à la carte. Dinner €49–€140.
Closed	2 January–12 February.
Directions	A50 towards Toulon, exit 11. Follow signs to Cadière d'Azur. Hotel in centre of village.

Bérard Family
Rue Gabriel Péri,
83740 La Cadière d'Azur, Var

Tel	+33 (0)4 94 90 11 43
Fax	+33 (0)4 94 90 01 94
Email	berard@hotel-berard.com
Web	www.hotel-berard.com

Pastis

The tiny village in the south of France, serenaded by Colette in the 30s, glamorised by Brigitte Bardot in the 60s, has returned to international affection. Its tiny sparkling streets, its marzipan façades, its secret squares and pétanque-playing locals are still here; in summer, there's a party every night. Bliss, then, to find this peaceful oasis a brisk walk (eight minutes) from the fashionable centre. Step in off the street to find tall palms around a delicious pool, beautiful art on white walls and a lovely welcome from John and Pauline, delighted to have swapped design jobs in the UK for a small charming hotel (a wreck when they found it!). Now, beds are chic or antique, bed covers are embroidered white, and grey shutters open to balcony, patio or terrace. The décor is impeccable, the bathrooms superb (one with a copper bath) and there are a sprinkling of sea views. Play boules or piano, slip into the pool, be sociable by the bar or peaceful on your terrace, and enjoy breakfast whenever you like: this is the easiest, dreamiest place to unwind. *Secure parking.*

Price	€250–€600. Child €50.
Rooms	9. 9 doubles. (Possible triples or family room for 4.)
Meals	Breakfast €20–€30. Salads & snacks €20. Restaurants walking distance.
Closed	Never.
Directions	A8 exit 35 Le Luc towards La Garde Freinet, Grimaud & St Tropez. Hotel is on main road at entry to village on right, where N98 becomes Ave Général Leclerc.

John & Pauline Larkin
61 avenue du Général Leclerc,
83990 Saint Tropez, Var

Tel   +33 (0)4 98 12 56 50
Fax   +33 (0)4 94 96 99 82
Email reception@pastis-st-tropez.com
Web   www.pastis-st-tropez.com

La Maurette Roquebrune

Don't look for signs, there are none, Wolfgang doesn't want to "make it look like a hotel". La Maurette stands in splendid isolation, at the very top of a hill looking straight at a World Heritage site, the rock of Roquebrune, which in some way resembles Australia's Ayers Rock. Red earth, rock, Mediterranean vegetation, the place has an amazingly mysterious feeling about it. Built of the volcanic stone, La Maurette melds with its surrounding like some ancient settlement; it consists of a main house, several annexes and a castle-style gatehouse housing two rooms. Once past the entrance gate, visitors are greeted by a larger-than-life statue of a seated Rhodesian Ridgeback; the Blumbergs are among the world's best breeders. That and their hospitality activity are both undertaken with gusto and passionate commitment. Simple bedrooms all have quarry tiles and a Provençal style but are otherwise very different in size, colour and design; they also each have their own terrace and a bottle of wine waiting for their occupants. More a place for couples than for children.

Price	€85–€156.
Rooms	11 twins/doubles, 7 with kitchenettes.
Meals	Breakfast €11.
	Village restaurants 2km.
Closed	Mid-November–March.
Directions	A8 exit 37 for Fréjus & Roquebrune onto N7 then D7 at Le Pont du Prieur for Roquebrune sur Argens. Over Argens river, right, then left, left again, pass tree in middle of road. Well signed.

	Dr Christine & Wolfgang Blumberg
	83520 Roquebrune sur Argens, Var
Tel	+33 (0)4 98 11 43 53
Fax	+33 (0)4 98 11 43 52
Email	info@lamaurette.fr
Web	www.lamaurette.fr

Hotel de la Verrerie

No frills but so much to praise! La Verrerie may lack the patina of age but it has a matchless site. Glorious views stretch to the distant Alps from large well-proportioned windows and a lush garden that tumbles down to the river. Hardworking John and Debbie, lovely hosts, have swapped corporate travel for a densely wooded valley and a garden full of roses, palms, lavender and fruit… Join in with the pruning in autumn and you may get a free night! Bedrooms are large, peaceful, sunny, their chintzy furnishings being replaced by a fresh simplicity and excellent linen. One room, sky-lit, is beautifully cool in hot summer; practical, spotless bathrooms are en suite. A shared fridge in the kitchen keeps picnic foods fresh, the internet keeps you in touch and the baker delivers scrumptious croissants for breakfast. Just perfect for sightseers wanting a restorative base – on the edge of the ancient village of Les Adrets yet a few kilometres from the coastal road linking Provence and the Riviera. Bliss for inveterate walkers, and for families: a huge lake for swimming and watersports lies down the road.

Price	€50–€75.
Rooms	7: 5 doubles, 2 family rooms for 3-4.
Meals	Breakfast €8.
	Restaurants within walking distance.
Closed	Never.
Directions	A8 exit 39 to Les Adrets;
	right at roundabout; signed.

John & Debbie Orfila
Chemin de la Verrerie,
83600 Les Adrets de l'Esterel, Var
Tel   +33 (0)4 94 40 93 51
Email   reservations@laverrerie.com
Web   www.laverrerie.com

La Bastide du Pin

Such a glamorous drive from Nice, straight through the Massif des Maures; you'll need some white sunglasses and a soft-top motor. This gorgeous hideaway is reached through a wide gate and a drive bordered by ancient cypresses, and encircled by gardens of lavender, gravelled paths, sculptures and pool. It is blissfully peaceful. The shady patio – perfect for an aperitif before dinner – is more Tuscany than Provence; a delicious place to laze away a hot afternoon with only the tinkling fountain to disturb you. Bedrooms vary in their colours but they're French through and through, deeply swagged and chandeliered, comfortable and large; bathrooms have some ancient baths, one of which you can splash in while gazing on distant hills. Best of all: Claudie and Stéphane, whose unaffected charm – and crus classés in the cellar – make this so special. There is tea from Marriage Frères, coffee from Columbia, Stéphane's aperitif à la truffe and Claudie's homemade jams. The walking is demanding but full of unexpected medieval villages; the weekly market is a buzz.

Price	€80–€120. Cottages €500–€1,000 per week.
Rooms	7 + 3: 3 doubles, 1 family room, 3 suites. 2 cottages for 4-5, 1 cottage for 2-3.
Meals	Breakfast included. Pool lunch, summer only, €15. Dinner €28 (min. 6) twice weekly, May-Sept. Restaurants 2km.
Closed	Rarely.
Directions	From Nice A8 exit 36, N7 to Les Arcs, D10 to Lorgues. Signs to Salernes. Bastide 1km after Lorgues centre, 500m past fourth r'bout on left.

Claudie & Stéphane Dumont
83510 Lorgues, Var

Tel	+33 (0)4 94 73 90 38
Fax	+33 (0)4 94 73 63 01
Email	bastidedupin@wanadoo.fr
Web	www.bastidedupin.com

Hôtel des Deux Rocs

An enchanting hotel in a hilltop setting, led by a young and talented team. Julie and Nicolas share time spent in the company of the greats: Paul Bocuse, Michel Troigros, Michel Guérard. But what's special is that this is a refined yet intimate affair, bursting with personality and family friendliness. Expect polished antiques, portraits of noble heads along the stairway, a 17th-century sedan chair, exquisite fabrics on 18th-century chairs, a well-travelled suitcase here and there. New bathrooms are in ageless British style: white porcelain basins, reissued vintage fittings, roll top tubs... perfection; bedrooms are all generously different, all delightful. Hard to choose between the room with the red and white checked Pierre Frey fabric or the 'toy soldier' theme in bold red and blue. Some overlook the valley, others the wide spread of a splendid terrace with a cinematographic view. The plashing of the fountain accompanies fabulous food served under majestic plane trees, candlelit tables are set with small bouquets of rose, lilac and hortensia; breakfasts are a treat. *A real find.*

Price	€65–€135. Family rooms €125–€165.
Rooms	14: 11 doubles, 2 family rooms for 3, 1 family room for 4.
Meals	Breakfast €12. Lunch & dinner €28–€36. October-April: closed Sun eve, all day Mon; Tues lunch.
Closed	Rarely.
Directions	From A8 exit 39 Les Adrets; follow signs to Fayence, then Seillans. Hotel is at the top of village. From Marseille/Aix exit 36 Rémy–St. Tropez signs to Draguignan, then Fayence.

Julie & Nicolas Malzac–Heimermann
Place Font d'Amont,
83440 Seillans, Var

Tel	+33 (0)4 94 76 87 32
Fax	+33 (0)4 94 76 88 68
Email	hoteldeuxrocs@wanadoo.fr
Web	www.hoteldeuxrocs.com

Bastide Saint Mathieu

This is just where you want to be; near enough to the coast for a stroll along the Croisette and far enough from the vacationing hordes for serene surroundings and prime pampering. Wrought-iron gates open to a stunning 18th-century house of contemporary elegance. A massive stone edifice, the bastide overlooks fields and hills of olive and lemon trees. Grounds have been restocked with 3,500 plants: 60 new olive trees, grapefruit, figs, cherries, almonds. In one room, the huge canopied bed is placed right in front of the window to catch the early sun. In spite of the luxuries of CD player, internet connection, cashmere blankets and drinks tray, you feel you are staying with a friend – a very attentive one. Bathrooms are decadently gorgeous but never flashy. Fragrances and soaps may be from Molinard, Fragonard or Galimard: Saroya tries to be fair to all the old Grasse houses. Breakfast is as late as you like, watched over by an old painted angel by the fireplace. The pool is huge, or you can settle under an old plane tree with a coffee. A haven of delight, a civilised place.

Price	€270–€360.
Rooms	5: 2 twins/doubles, 1 double, 2 suites.
Meals	Breakfast included. Restaurants nearby.
Closed	Rarely.
Directions	A8 exit 42 Grasse Sud; cont. to r'bout (4 Chemins); 2nd exit before MacDonald's; left at r'bout; over next r'bout; cont. to Elephant Bleu car wash; exit r'bout for St Mathieu; under two bridges; left at T-junc.; right into Chemin de Blumenthal.

Soraya Colegrave
35 chemin de Blumenthal, 06130
Grasse, Alpes-Maritimes

Tel	+33 (0)4 97 01 10 00
Fax	+33 (0)4 97 01 10 09
Email	info@bastidestmathieu.com
Web	www.bastidestmathieu.com

Hôtel Le Cavendish

Some people have it and some don't. Madame Welter has more of it than most, and her talents show in every niche of this splendid rebirth of a Napoleon III edifice. Subtle are the modern comforts and splendid are the rooms, many with balconies or terraces. Sensuous, exuberant and almost edible is the choice of fabric and colour: crunchy raspberry taffeta, tasselled pistachio green, golden apricot silk, twilight mauve – yet never over the top. On the contrary, one feels as though one is a guest in the grand home of a *grand homme*, such as its namesake, Lord Cavendish. How convivial to have a complimentary open bar for guests in the evening, how attentive to offer leaf teas for breakfast, how sexy to dress the curvy Carrara marble staircase with candles at dusk, how elegant to slip between the lavender-scented sheets of a turned down bed at night. Freshly baked croissants, cakes and crumbles, homemade jams and a cheery staff make mornings easy, especially if you are attending one of the events at the Festival Hall, only ten minutes away. Superb. *Private beach nearby. Valet parking €20.*

Price	€130–€295.
Rooms	34 twins/doubles.
Meals	Breakfast €20.
	Complimentary bar 5pm–11pm
Closed	Never.
Directions	From Nice A8; left at roundabout on Boulevard Carnot; follow signs for Palais des Festivals. Signed.

Christine & Guy Welter
11 boulevard Carnot,
06400 Cannes, Alpes-Maritimes

Tel	+33 (0)4 97 06 26 00
Fax	+33 (0)4 97 06 26 01
Email	reservation@cavendish-cannes.com
Web	www.cavendish-cannes.com

Hôtel La Jabotte

Why is La Jabotte so special? Is it the courtyard scented with oranges or the bedrooms the colours of jewels? Or is it Claude and Yves, Belgians who came to the Cap one summer and fell for a small faded hotel. Today it is an exquisite jewellery box, an explosion of colour, beautifully clean and inviting. Yves is the artistic one, Claude oversees all, both are generous and kind. Tucked down a small side street, 60 metres from the beach, are polished stone floors and cherry-red walls, pots of roses and bright parakeets, a wagging white Westie, lavender and glasses of champagne. Pass the deep aubergine sofa, enter the gliding wall of glass and you find the enchanting pebbled courtyard off which bedrooms lie. Each has its table and chairs outside the door and pots of plants lovingly labelled; this feels more home than hotel. Bedrooms – Lavender, Citron, Papillon – are small but charming, shower rooms have L'Occitane lotions and fulsome towels. After fresh jams, oranges and croissants, saunter into Old Antibes – or drift down to the free sandy beach and your own parasol. *Limited parking, book ahead.*

Price	€70-€117. Suite €120-€157.
Rooms	10: 9 twins/doubles, 1 suite for 2-4.
Meals	Breakfast included.
Closed	Last 3 weeks of November; Christmas week.
Directions	Follow signs for Antibes Centre then Cap d'Antibes, Les Plages, La Salis. In small street 60m from Salis beach.

Yves April & Claude Mora
13 avenue Max Maurey,
06160 Cap d'Antibes, Alpes-Maritimes
Tel   +33 (0)4 93 61 45 89
Fax   +33 (0)4 93 61 07 04
Email   info@jabotte.com
Web   www.jabotte.com

Villa Val des Roses

You could drive here, park the car and not touch it until you leave: a sandy beach with a view to old Antibes is a minute away, the old town and market ten minutes and the shops five. Frederik and Filip are Flemish, in their twenties and found the Val des Roses a short while ago after searching for the 'perfect place'. Filip has all the necessary diplomas; both brothers are charming and sure to make this venture a happy one. They do everything themselves and put on an excellent breakfast, which you can have in your room, on the terrace or by the pool. They will also do light lunches to have by the pool. For dinner, they will recommend a place; phone ahead and make sure you get a good table. A definite find: not cheap, but well worth it. The gracious white house, with white shutters, is enclosed in its garden by high walls in a quiet little road. Inside, fabrics and walls are mostly white, cool and tranquil. Interestingly, the bedrooms are open plan, with a large oval bath giving a sybaritic touch. Many guests are return visitors. *Children over 14 welcome.*

Price	€150–€290.
Rooms	4: 3 suites for 2 3, 1 suite for 1.
Meals	Breakfast €16. Poolside snacks available.
Closed	Rarely.
Directions	From Antibes towards Cap d'Antibes, les plages, to Salis Plage. Keep shops on right. Immediately after Hotel Josse, at old stone archway, Chemin des Lauriers on right. Ring bell on gate.

Frederik & Filip Vanderhoeven
6 chemin des Lauriers,
06160 Cap d'Antibes, Alpes-Maritimes

Tel	+33 (0)6 85 06 06 29 (mobile)
Fax	+33 (0)4 92 93 97 24
Email	val_des_roses@yahoo.com
Web	www.val-des-roses.com

Hostellerie du Château

What do you do after a career as an international opera singer? You undertake a huge renovation of a château, of course (the foundations of which date from Roman times) and open a hotel and restaurant. Then you hunt out the perfect antique for each bedroom – each named after a composer – make sure fine linens dress top bedding, choose soft curtains to frame dreamy views and hang original art work on the walls. Love at first sight – that's how Véronique Von Hirsch describes her first visit to Le Bar sur Loup many years ago. You understand how her heart was captured when you meander around this authentic perched hill town, gaze over the ramparts to the long views over the valleys and watch village life while sitting at the hotel's terrace café. Peace reigns; the hordes on the coast are left miles behind. A talented chef whips up inventive meals in the glassed-in 'Bigaradier', named after the Seville orange so prevalent in the area. Oh, yes, Madame also founded an art school and is now artistic director of a vocal ensemble; evening concerts and weekend festivals are held here. A delight.

Price	€130-€180.
Rooms	6: 3 doubles, 2 twins, 1 suite.
Meals	Breakfast €12. Lunch €18-€30. Dinner €29-€63. Restaurant closed from Sun evening until Wed lunchtime and November-February.
Closed	Never.
Directions	From Grasse toward Nice on D2085; left on D2210 to Le Bar Sur Loup. On main square.

Madame Véronique Von Hirsch
Le Bigaradier, 6-8 place Francis Paulet,
06620 Le Bar Sur Loup, Alpes-Maritimes

Tel	+33 (0)4 93 42 41 10
Fax	+33 (0)4 93 42 69 32
Email	info@lhostellerieduchateau.com
Web	www.lhostellerieduchateau.com

Hôtel Restaurant le Grimaldi

You don't have to go to Haute Provence to find Provençal style: it's all here. The cobbled village of Haut de Cagnes – Brigitte Bardot had a house here in the 60s – oozes character, restaurants and artists' studios. With sweeping views, Hotel Grimaldi is high up on the main square, where locals play boules and meet for a chat, children bring bikes and tourists wander. On Friday evenings in summer, concerts draw people from miles around; there's quite a buzz. Rick was a New York banker who used to come here on holiday, then he decided to stay. Now he runs a jazz club in the basement too – but the hotel is so well-insulated you won't hear a thing. Bedrooms, in elegant shades of grey, off-white and cream, are uncluttered yet cosy, with russet floor tiles, reclaimed antique doors, Egyptian cotton, super beds. Snug bathrooms are white-tiled and stocked with fluffy towels. The beamed restaurant offers delicious food in chic, simple surroundings, spilling out to an enchanting terrace on the square. And there's a free navette to ferry you down to restaurants, markets and sea. *Parking €10 close by.*

Price	€115–€165.
Rooms	5: 4 doubles, 1 suite for 2.
Meals	Breakfast included.
	Lunch €12–€35. Dinner €26–€60.
	Restaurant closed January/February.
Closed	Never.
Directions	From Aix exit 47 Cagnes sur Mer, centre ville; then up the hill to Haut de Cagnes. Follow signs to Château Musée. Ask hotel about parking.

Rick Fernandez
6 place du Château, Haut de Cagnes,
06800 Cagnes sur Mer, Alpes-Maritimes

Tel	+33 (0)4 93 20 60 24
Fax	+33 (0)4 93 22 82 19
Email	contact@hotelgrimaldi.com
Web	www.hotelgrimaldi.com

Villa Saint Maxime

A modern gem, on a site facing St Paul de Vence – a retreat of vast white spaces. The house was built by a British architect during the first Gulf war. In an echo of the inner courtyard of eastern dwellings, the main atrium has a retractable roof allowing a cooling breeze to waft through in summer. Bold sweeping lines, marble and terracotta, a blue-parasoled pool and, in the central stairwell, a broken-glass garden that sparkles like Ali Baba's jewels. Each air conditioned room has a balcony or terrace to make the most of the view; bath and shower rooms are spectacular. Ann and John spent their early married life in this ancient, fortified village so beloved of Marc Chagall, and have deep emotional roots here. Ann collects modern art; there's a piece or two in your room, more in the famous Maeght Foundation down the road. Breakfast, with champagne if you wish, is any time at all, while a delicious homemade orange aperitif sets the mood for dinner. Immaculate restaurants and bars are a step away. *Children over 12 welcome. Unsupervised pool.*

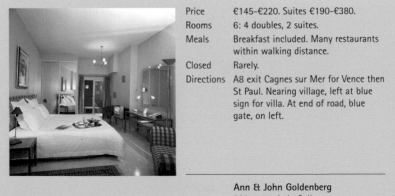

Price	€145–€220. Suites €190–€380.
Rooms	6: 4 doubles, 2 suites.
Meals	Breakfast included. Many restaurants within walking distance.
Closed	Rarely.
Directions	A8 exit Cagnes sur Mer for Vence then St Paul. Nearing village, left at blue sign for villa. At end of road, blue gate, on left.

Ann & John Goldenberg
390 route de la Colle,
06570 Saint Paul de Vence, Alpes-Maritimes

Tel	+33 (0)4 93 32 76 00
Fax	+33 (0)4 93 32 93 00
Email	riviera@villa-st-maxime.com
Web	www.villa-st-maxime.com

Hôtel Windsor

A 1930s Riviera hotel with a pool in a quiet palm grove and exotic birds in cages? All that… and much more. The Windsor has brought the Thirties into the 21st century by asking contemporary artists to decorate some of their rooms. The result: many gifts of wit, provocation, flights of fancy, minimalist sobriety, with Joan Mas's *Cage à Mouches* and cosmopolitan Ben's writing on the walls. The Antoine Beaudoin's superb frescoes of Venice, Egypt, India all our travel myths – and Tintin, everyone's all time favourite. Plain white beds have contrasting cushions or quilts; furniture is minimal and interesting; delightful little bathrooms, most of which have been redone, some directly off the room, are individually treated. All clear, bright colours, including the richly exotic public areas: the much-travelled owners chose an exquisitely elaborate Chinese mandarin's bed for the lobby; panelling and colourful plasterwork for the restaurant; a fine wire sculpture, stone and bamboo for the hall. Light filters through onto warmly smiling staff. Spoil yourself and opt for one of the superior or traditional rooms.

Price	€90–€175.
Rooms	57 twins/doubles.
Meals	Breakfast €12. Dinner à la carte, with wine, €29–€40. Restaurant closed Sundays.
Closed	Rarely.
Directions	In centre of Nice, 10-min walk from train station. A8 exit Promenade des Anglais. Left at museum on Rue Meyerbeer; right on Rue de France; 1st left Rue Dalpozzo.

Odile Redolfi-Payen & Bernard Redolfi-Strizzot
11 rue Dalpozzo, 06000 Nice,
Alpes-Maritimes

Tel	+33 (0)4 93 88 59 35
Fax	+33 (0)4 93 88 94 57
Email	contact@hotelwindsornice.com
Web	www.hotelwindsornice.com

Hôtel Les Deux Frères

Only the rich and famous have this view so go ahead, be brave, rise at the crack of dawn and wonder at the beauty of the light coming up over the ocean and along the coast. All terrace dining tables have views but you will be able to pick a favourite for hot coffee and croissants and linger even more. Willem, the Dutch owner who combines Provençal comfort with an exotic flavour – down to the seven languages he speaks and his restaurant's innovative dishes – is full of ideas. There is now a little snack bar next door for refreshments and he has added two refurbished apartments: you can either sleep in the old village store, with its bright yellow façade and the vintage set of scales in the window, or in the old bakery. And there are views of the coastline, mountainside or the old village square from every small, sparkling hotel room. Choose between an oriental blue and gold ceiling, a stylish lime green or a nautical blue. After parking in the village you will follow a short, fairly steep path. Ideal for the young and fleet of foot. Rooms may be small, but views are enormous.

Price	€100–€110. Singles €75.
Rooms	10 + 2: 10 doubles.
	2 apartments for 2 (microwave & fridge).
Meals	Breakfast €9. Lunch from €28. Dinner from €48. Restaurant closed Mon & Tues lunch in summer; Sun evenings; mid-Nov-mid-Dec; one week in March.
Closed	Never.
Directions	From Nice A8 exit 57 La Turbie then Roquebrune Cap Martin. Left at Roquebrune & Vieux Village. Stop at municipal car park & walk 50m.

Willem Bonestroo
Place des Deux Frères,
06190 Roquebrune Cap Martin, Alpes-Maritimes

Tel	+33 (0)4 93 28 99 00
Fax	+33 (0)4 93 28 99 10
Email	info@lesdeuxfreres.com
Web	www.lesdeuxfreres.com

Have you enjoyed this book? Why not try one of the others in the Special Places to Stay series and get 35% discount on the RRP *

British Bed & Breakfast (Ed 12)	RRP £14.99	Offer price £9.75
British Bed & Breakfast for Garden Lovers (Ed 4)	RRP £14.99	Offer price £9.75
British Hotels & Inns (Ed 9)	RRP £14.99	Offer price £9.75
Pubs & Inns of England & Wales (Ed 5)	RRP £14.99	Offer price £9.75
Devon & Cornwall (Ed 1)	RRP £11.99	Offer price £7.80
Ireland (Ed 6)	RRP £12.99	Offer price £8.45
French Bed & Breakfast (Ed 10)	RRP £15.99	Offer price £10.40
French Holiday Homes (Ed 4)	RRP £14.99	Offer price £9.75
French Hotels & Châteaux (Ed 5)	RRP £14.99	Offer price £9.75
Paris Hotels (Ed 6)	RRP £10.99	Offer price £7.15
Italy (Ed 5)	RRP £14.99	Offer price £9.75
Spain (Ed 7)	RRP £14.99	Offer price £9.75
Portugal (Ed 4)	RRP £11.99	Offer price £7.80
Croatia (Ed 1)	RRP £11.99	Offer price £7.80
Greece (Ed 1)	RRP £11.99	Offer price £7.80
Turkey (Ed 1)	RRP £11.99	Offer price £7.80
Morocco (Ed 2)	RRP £11.99	Offer price £7.80
India (Ed 2)	RRP £11.99	Offer price £7.80
Green Places to Stay (Ed 1)	RRP £13.99	Offer price £9.10
Go Slow England	RRP £20.00	Offer price £13.00

*postage and packing is added to each order

To order at the Reader's Discount price simply phone 01275 395431 and quote 'Reader Discount FH'.

Fragile Earth series

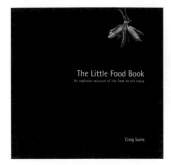

The Little Food Book   £6.99

"This is a really big little book. It is a good read and it will make your hair stand on end"
Jonathan Dimbleby

"…lifts the lid on the food industry to reveal some extraordinary goings-on"
John Humphrys

The Little Money Book   £6.99

"Anecdotal, humorous and enlightening, this book will have you sharing its gems with all your friends"
Permaculture Magazine

One Planet Living   £4.99

"Small but meaningful principles that will improve the quality of your life"
Country Living

"It is a pleasure to pick up and learn essential facts from"
Organic Life

To order any of the books in the Fragile Earth series call 01275 395431 or visit www.fragile-earth.com

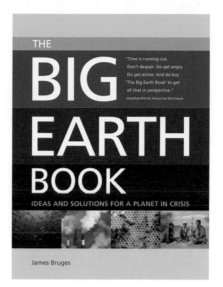

We all know the Earth is in crisis. We should know that it is big enough to sustain us if we can only mobilise politicians and economists to change course now. Expanding on the ideas developed in *The Little Earth Book,* this book explores environmental, economic and social ideas to save our planet. It helps us understand what is happening to the planet today, exposes the actions of corporations and the lack of action of governments, weighs up new technologies, and champions innovative and viable solutions. Tackling a huge range of subjects — it has the potential to become the seminal reference book on the state of the planet — it's the one and only environmental book you really need.

James Bruges's *The Little Earth Book* has sold over 40,000 copies and has been translated into eight languages.

Praise for *The Big Earth Book*:
"Time is running out. Don't despair. Do get angry. Do get active. And do buy *The Big Earth Book* to get all that in perspective." Jonathon Porritt, *Forum for the Future*

"This is a wonderful book — really informative but written in a very clear, easy-to-read way." Patrick Holden, *The Soil Association*

RRP £25.00 To order at the Reader's Discount price of £20 (plus p&p) call 01275 395431 and quote 'Reader Discount BEB FH'.

If you have any comments on entries in this guide, please tell us. If you have a favourite place or a new discovery, please let us know about it. You can return this form or visit www.sawdays.co.uk.

Existing entry

Property name: _____

Entry number: _____ Date of visit: _____

New recommendation

Property name: _____

Address: _____

_____

Tel/Email/Website: _____

Your comments

What did you like (or dislike) about this place? Were the people friendly? What was the location like? Did you enjoy the food?

_____

_____

_____

_____

_____

Your details

Name: _____

Address: _____

_____

_____ Postcode: _____

Tel: _____ Email: _____

Please send completed form to:
FH, Sawday's, The Old Farmyard, Yanley Lane, Long Ashton, Bristol BS41 9LR, UK

Wheelchair-accessible

At least one bedroom and bathroom accessible for wheelchair users. Please phone for details.

No car?

These places are within 10 miles of a bus/coach/train station and owner can arrange collection.

Quick reference indices

Quick reference indices

On a budget?

These places have a double room for €100 or under.

Secure parking

Parking area is locked and/or
has camera surveillance.

Quick reference indices

Photo: istock.com

② Hotel & Self-catering ⬛ **①** Provence – Alps – Riviera

③ Les Quatre Saisons

④ For those hooked on *The Da Vinci Code*, the Sainte Baume mountain range with its walks and legends revolving around Mary Magdalene is an easy drive. Or the hill villages of La Cadière d'Azur and Le Castellet with Templar connections may tempt; but you will rejoice upon your return to this lovingly run hideaway on a hill with its thick walls, warm yellow stone and cooling breezes. Didier and Patrice, with previous lives in the catering and hotel worlds, take superb care of you. Built 20 years ago, with careful recuperation of old doors, beams and stone, the main house and annexe cradle the pool mirroring a more southern architectural tradition. The main house, where winter guests can have pre-dinner drinks, has an impressive sunken circular area round a fireplace and a succession of spacious elegant rooms furnished with good Louis XVIII pieces. All rooms have their own private outdoor sitting area, be it a terrace or small sealed-off patio beneath a vine-clad trellis. Care and thoughtfulness, heavenly food: it's a dream of a place. Thor, the French bulldog, welcomes other well-behaved dogs.

⑤	Price	€90–€110. Apartment €120–€130 (€700–€750 per week).
⑥	Rooms	7 + 1 apartment: 3 doubles, 2 twins, 2 suites for 2. Apartment for 2.
⑦	Meals	Breakfast included. Lunch €15–€25. Dinner €33–€35, book ahead.
⑧	Closed	15 days in January.
⑨	Directions	A50 exit 11 to Le Beausset. Left at big r'about onto D26 to Le Brûlat Castellet. Right after 1.5km, straight on small road until gate. Ring.

Patrice Darras & Didier Marchal
370 Montée des Oliviers,
83330 Le Castellet, Var
Tel   +33 (0)4 94 25 24 90
Email   reservation@lesquatresaisons.org
Web   www.lesquatresaisons.org

⑩ 🚶 🚂 🐕 🛋 🏊 🚲   **⑪** Entry 368 Map 16